SOCIAL HOUSING IN THE MIDDLE EAST

SOCIAL HOUSING
IN THE
MIDDLE EAST

Architecture, Urban Development,
and Transnational Modernity

Edited by Kıvanç Kılınç and
Mohammad Gharipour

INDIANA UNIVERSITY PRESS

This book is a publication of

Indiana University Press
Office of Scholarly Publishing
Herman B Wells Library 350
1320 East 10th Street
Bloomington, Indiana 47405 USA

iupress.indiana.edu

Manufactured in the United States of America

Cataloging information is available from the Library of Congress.

ISBN 978-0-253-03984-2 (hardback)
ISBN 978-0-253-03985-9 (paperback)
ISBN 978-0-253-03988-0 (ebook)

1 2 3 4 5   24 23 22 21 20 19

CONTENTS

SOCIAL HOUSING IN THE MIDDLE EAST

1

INTRODUCTION

Global Modernity and Marginalized Histories of Social Housing in the Middle East

Kıvanç Kılınç and Mohammad Gharipour

THIS VOLUME BRINGS TOGETHER LESS WELL-KNOWN EXAMPLES OF social housing projects in the Middle East to explore transnational connections and their consequences that shaped low-cost dwelling practices in the region. The existing stock and heritage of social housing in the Middle East, as well as policies developed to deal with the housing shortage, are both varied and rich, but the study of these phenomena is scattered at best. Formed in response to this apparent vacuum in scholarship, this book pursues two separate but closely linked agendas.

First, it takes a snapshot of contemporary urbanscapes of the Middle East, where modernist social housing policies of the past century have been ineffective in competing with the neoliberal economic turn of the 1980s and the rampant urban transformation that followed, not to mention the destabilizing influence of ongoing wars, conflict, and political turmoil. Even in oil-rich countries of the Persian Gulf, a shortage of adequate and affordable housing remains an enduring yet largely unaddressed problem.[1] From Egypt to Iran, signature tall buildings, urban renewal projects, gentrified neighborhoods, coastal tourism infrastructure, massive shopping malls, and informal settlements are the main markers of Middle Eastern urbanism of the new century, while privatization increasingly takes hold of public spaces.[2] Issues of security, the growing number of refugee camps, and rural migration to cities are also entangled with the generalized lack of decent housing.

Second, this book contributes to recent, more inclusive architectural history writing traditions. By recounting the diverse practices of social housing in the region and looking beyond elite pursuits of architecture, the contributors respond to the following questions and attempt to write their critical histories: How did social housing contribute to the planning and development of Middle Eastern cities, or how did certain projects delve into contextual issues and the question of modernity in the region? Were solutions proffered that went beyond the much-acclaimed modernist mass housing typologies? What ties these settlements to the historical context, and what local and regional concepts have informed the design of new housing projects since the early twentieth century? How did traveling across diverse communities, cultures, and cities transform layouts? Finally, what is the role of spatial agency? In what ways did homeowners, tenants, and building contractors play a part in the production of the so-called modern vernacular,[3] along with architects, planners, and economic patronage of authorities?

In addressing these interlinked agendas exploring current urbanscapes and their various histories, stories gathered in this volume respond to a recent postcolonial turn in urban and architectural studies. In combination, they posit that all places that had their share in the making of what we call the experience of modernity are equal parts of a common human experience, although each also had its own way of dealing with it and, more pointedly, they demonstrate that globalization is *not* a new word.[4]

Social Housing as a Global Scene of Political Exchanges

Our understanding of social housing covers, very broadly, all types of subsidized housing built by public institutions, municipalities and national governments, or housing agencies for lower-income groups who are in need of accommodation and who, in existing market conditions, could not afford to purchase or rent without subsidies.[5] We contend that social housing, regardless of whether it is an integral part of an ideological project—such as the Siedlungen in Germany, the Workers' Communes in China, or the Superquadra in Brazil—*is* political. It is undoubtedly so, because "since the 19th-century outcry over the living conditions of the working class, housing has had a long and meaningful history as the sphere

in which progressive reform has been imagined, debated, and implemented."[6] Moreover, developing social housing programs always required
an active political imagining and agency, as public bodies seeking to build
or supply housing for those who cannot meet the expense on their own
do so primarily from a sense of a social contract committed to reforming
inequalities.

The first examples of workers' houses emerged as early as the nineteenth
century, when the effects of industrial and urban development became
widespread.[7] But it was in the early twentieth century when the scale and
scope of social housing went beyond scattered attempts to provide sufficient
habitable tenements to workers. The second CIAM (Congrès Internationaux d'Architecture Modern) meeting, which convened in 1929 in Frankfurt,
centered on the theme of *Die Wohnung für das Existenzminimum* (Housing
for minimal existence).[8] One concrete response to the search for a minimally designed, healthy, and affordable type of housing was Siedlungen,
experimental mass housing quarters built extensively in Germany both before and after World War I.[9] Earlier schemas of Siedlungen were shaped by
an implicit antiurbanism and consisted primarily of detached houses. The
terrible living conditions of late-nineteenth-century Mietskasernen (tenements) in Germany played a part in predominantly negative sentiments
against typically urban forms such as apartment blocks.[10] Beginning in
the early 1920s, mixed complex types, including multistory horizontal and
vertical apartment blocks, also appeared. The notion of including gardens,
which would enable inhabitants to live closer to nature so as to nurture
spiritual and physical health as well as support the household economy by
growing vegetables in their respective allotments, however, remained un-
changed.[11]

The short-term success of many housing programs for the lower-
income strata in Weimar Germany stemmed from the fact that progressive architects and planners such as Ernst May, Martin Wagner, Margarete
Schütte-Lihotzky, and Bruno Taut worked closely with social democratic
city governments and thus had the support of administrative bodies.[12] The
struggle there for workers' rights, socialist ideals, and unremitting arguments over the shape of the family merged with the growth of industrial
production and the new techniques applied to mass housing.[13] It is not surprising that, together with minimal housing units, Siedlungen were characterized by the collective activities they provided, and, on a larger scale, were
seen as a tool for social reform.

During the interwar and postwar periods, "modern idealism" was at the core of the urban reform and transformation agendas in major European countries.[14] As architectural historian Kenny Cupers has written in *The Social Project: Housing Postwar France*, the new housing settlements of postwar France embodied the "belief in modern architecture as a vehicle of social progress," in which social sciences were deployed in the service of urban planning and political management.[15] Many postcolonial regimes implemented modernist projects, echoing similar developmentalist agendas. Furthermore, the post–World War II world, dominated by tensions and competition between the two major camps of the Cold War, as well as the Third World movement of nonaligned nations, witnessed a growing US influence.[16] In addition to missionary and philanthropic activities of the Rockefeller and Ford Foundations, the Marshall Aid Programs signed with developing countries and small economies of Europe contributed significantly to the spread of this global influence.[17] US specialists toured the world as consultants, preparing reports for low-cost housing developments in urban and rural areas in India, Turkey, Guatemala, and the Philippines.[18]

On the other side of the Cold War aisle were the social housing experiments in Eastern Europe, Soviet Union, and the People's Republic of China. Because all housing in the former Soviet Russia and the Eastern Bloc was technically social housing and, at least in principle, equally distributed to all citizens, the term was never used to signify a specific type of dwelling.[19] After the collective housing experiments of the historical avant-gardes in the 1920s and early 1930s, wherein new typologies that went beyond a more conventional family unit were deployed, post-1950s efforts were largely characterized by huge mass housing programs that relied on prefabricated building technologies to reproduce variations of the *microraion* (microregion) layout.[20] During the same decade, Mao's China took over the zealous project of bringing "the end of the peasantry, its institutions, and its long-established way of life" with people's communes. As architectural historian Duanfang Lu vibrantly illustrated in her edited book *Third World Modernism*, in the communes life was both disciplined and collectivized; local residential units were replaced with modern housing, and "communal food, laundry and nurseries were provided to free women from traditional divisions of labour."[21]

Many differences in the economy of production, building types, and the scope of projects left aside, social housing endeavors were undertaken by socialist and capitalist regimes somewhat similarly until the neoliberal turn of the 1980s. In the decades that followed, states' professed agency in the production of social housing, and their direct involvement in both planning and construction, significantly diminished.

The Question of Spatial Agency:
New Challenges to Social Housing

In Mario Gandelzonas's words, the architectural profession has never been sufficient "to domesticate the wild economic and political forces that traverse the urban body to impose an order," even if it had enough desire.[22] Without a doubt, postcritical discourses signaled the end of any such desire. Beginning in the 1980s, architecture became increasingly submerged in neoliberal economic policies.[23] These years brought about the privatization of public services, cuts in the subsidization of social housing programs, and the rise of consumerist ideologies.[24] With the central governments' reduced role in market regulation, public-private partnerships emerged as a new model for producing lower-income housing, and the role of private contractors increased the cost of the projects.[25]

In the past few decades, a globally configured architectural community whose works are situated on the margins of the profession has countered this strong current. One such example is an exhibition, *Think Global, Build Social! Architectures for a Better World*, which brought together socially concerned housing projects, schools, health clinics, and slum-rehabilitation designs developed in the last ten years across the globe, including those by 2016 Pritzker Prize–winner Alejandro Aravena. Curated by Andres Lepik, it has been touring the world's cities since its inauguration to much acclaim in 2014.[26] The exhibition was first presented at the Deutsches Architekturmuseum and Architekturzentrum Wien, and its major European organizing institutions published a book on the selected works from the exhibition. The popularity of the event, and similar projects before it, such as *Small Scale, Big Change: Architectures of Social Engagement*, which opened to the public at the Museum of Modern Art (MoMA) in 2010, shows that architecture, after many decades of introversion and claims of professional autonomy, once again is veering toward championing a social mission and engaging with economic and social problems in the urban structures and lives of ordinary people. "Urban acupuncture," "small architectures," "urban agriculture," and "portable," "self-built," and "bottom-up" affordable housing built for the homeless or for lower-income constituents, have become much-visited themes by even large architecture firms around the globe.[27] Popular television documentaries such as *Rebel Architecture*, aired by Al Jazeera in 2014, covered a broad array of topics within the umbrella of social architecture, introducing architects from across the globe "who are using design as a form of activism and resistance to tackle the world's urban, environmental, and social crises."[28] Such endeavors have helped extend the limits of the profession to noncanonical practices beyond architecture with a capital A.[29]

Thus, increased enthusiasm in the global scene for spatial and social agency of architecture signals a shift in the tide.[30] As Aravena has eloquently pronounced, architecture once again "becomes a tool to fight poverty."[31] The good news about this comeback is that social housing now incorporates participatory design practices, and architects campaign in the form of civil society organizations rather than view themselves as part of top-down regulatory or policymaking mechanisms, or heroes capable of individually engineering a political revolution.[32] The bad news is that architects can no longer rely on the sweeping power of revolutionary regimes pouring resources into producing affordable housing, "emancipating" working women from housework, and cultivating solidarity between inhabitants by means of collective activities. To the contrary, while the desire may be back, the majority of the world's regimes are in favor of neoliberal economic models, which have put an end to many social housing projects in the first place. Architects and designers now have to operate within the little space left between a profit-driven global construction industry and the ever-growing flood of informal settlements.[33] Therefore, in Lepik's words, the tactics of a new generation of architects are "more pragmatic than programmatic in comparison to their historical predecessors."[34]

Mapping Spatial Agency in the Middle East

Think Global, Build Social! has recently shown in İzmir, Turkey's third-largest city.[35] Viewers visiting the exhibition, however, soon realized while a few of the examples showcased were selected from North Africa, the rest of the large map showed that the Middle East in its extended boundaries, including Turkey, remained completely blank. How should we explain the conspicuous absence of the Middle East from a global survey of architectural practices with strong social emphasis? Are designers reluctant to get actively involved in the betterment of their environments? Do governing bodies or public institutions in the region refrain from sponsoring or building such projects? Is there no demand to provide housing or education for the poor in Middle Eastern countries? Considering the history of social and sustainable design experiences in the region, why are we finding ourselves now awkwardly staring at an empty map?[36]

Sibel Bozdoğan argues in her commentary in the *International Journal of Islamic Architecture* that "there are surely practices in Egypt, Jordan or Lebanon among other places that engage in public advocacy and community design. . . . Nevertheless, these rarely make it out of the 'Humanitarian Design' category into the mainstream of architectural culture."[37] According to Bozdoğan, examples of "small architectures" involving spatial agency of the designers are scarce as a result of the political climate and prevalent architectural cultures in the region. This climate is dominated by grand projects and "big architectures," propagated by the undemocratic regimes and neoliberal policies continually pressing to incorporate the region into the machinery of a global economy. Indeed, exceptional, brief moments of emancipation in public art, not limited to the humanitarian design category, emerged in the region only recently together with the so-called Arab Spring. But more important, the very question of agency takes different forms in the Middle East, where continuous wars and displacement bar architects from venturing into design activism as much as they could in, say, Latin America or Central Europe; they are actively involved in humanitarian missions instead, which is an exigent matter of survival for the region.

The contents of this volume are informed by these discussions on the lack of contemporary projects in the Middle East "of an alternative, socially committed architecture," realized with "minimal financial expenditure but a great deal of initiative and creativity."[38] Yet they also aim to extend the meaning of spatial agency from the designers to the receiving end of the spectrum, and to the everyday activism of users who continue to actively inhabit their homes. The history of these dwellings is wrought with displacement as much as placement, and mobility much more than stability: How did people delve into the processes of modernization where temporary often assumed the meaning of permanent, and amid turmoil? What happened to the social housing units, for instance, when new users from the "peripheries" replaced the Europeans who previously inhabited them? What happened when the people stayed but their status was altered: "the principal user group of projects shifted from the 'colonial objects'—second class exploited individuals with few rights—to free 'subjects'"?[39] The following sections therefore lay the framework for the contributions in this book and for broader discussions of spatial agency by mapping out the history of modern social housing in the Middle East.

Resurgent Typologies: The Apartment Block and Informal Housing

As in many other places in the world, in Middle Eastern cities mass housing has been but one of the formulas drawn in response to the quest for finding the right form of "inhabiting on a large scale."[40] While "large scale" has not always been the most popular solution, it has often been deemed the most economically sound answer to the housing problem. In Turkey, for instance, *Siedlung*-inspired detached and semi-detached types dominated the urban scene until the end of the 1950s. In the first half of the twentieth century, the so-called "rental barracks" were likened to contemporary prisons, which were thought to have symbolized a transient and nomadic life.[41] Yet, beginning in the 1960s, these were gradually replaced by midrise and high-rise housing units,[42] the most repeated form of social housing in the region today. The ambiguous reception of the big concrete blocks in Turkey is by no means unique. Across the world, multistory-type social housing models mostly emerged because of financial constraints or the lack of available land.[43] For instance, in Iraq, multistory "public housing estates" that were built by various government agencies were mostly popular in the 1960s and 1970s.[44] These models differed from the "low-rise high-density urban blocks" that characterized the larger modernization and reconstruction programs laid out by the state in the 1950s and were seldom repeated.[45] In postrevolutionary Cairo, midrise modernist blocks were the widely adopted type in the 1950s and 1960s. This trend continued in the 1970s but gradually ceased in the 1980s, when regulation and planning gave way to the growth of informal settlements. Vast satellite cities built outside Cairo, once seen as a viable solution to stop mass migration to the capital city, ended up uninhabited or partially inhabited voids.[46] In many other countries in the region, "the tendency for most affordable housing projects to be located in peripheral and relatively remote locations . . . has resulted in problems of higher social and infrastructure costs."[47]

Nevertheless, in stark contrast to Egypt and Turkey, the history of rapid urbanization linked to oil economies in Kuwait, Saudi Arabia, and Bahrain meant that welfare housing translated into the single-family detached home, and the consideration of alternative types has been rare.[48] Similarly, in Iran, post-Revolutionary measures for centralization, such as the transition of ownership of urban wastelands to the government and regulation of the market, encouraged horizontal urban growth rather than high-rise developments. The second development plan of the Islamic Republic continued this policy by focusing on producing social housing under the campaign of "building small."[49] Contemporary developments, such as the ambitious but poorly received Mehr Project (2007), however, consisted predominantly of midrise apartment blocks.[50] In places where comprehensive government policies in social housing are yet to exist, such as the United Arab Emirates (UAE), private entrepreneurs who build affordable houses tend to reproduce existing high-rise models of luxury housing on a smaller scale and farther away from the city centers.[51]

While most countries chose to directly produce housing units, few of these attempts proved sufficient to meet rising needs. With increased migration to urban centers for prospects of better lives and jobs, as well as unending wars and conflict in the region, oceans of shantytowns began to emerge at the periphery of cities and towns. The unanticipated scale of informal housing in Jordan, Morocco, Turkey, and Yemen forced governments to look for more site-specific solutions, such as the sites-and-services approach, in which prospective users would be given cheap land and subsidies to build their own housing with affordable payment options, much below the market value.[52] Another strategy was applying aided self-help housing methods, especially when government (central and local administrations) means were limited.[53] When such attempts too fell short of providing sufficient housing supplies, primarily two things transpired: first, self-built vernacular housing typologies, including informal settlements in countries such as Egypt, Morocco, Tunisia, and Turkey, became customary urban forms in expanding cities. Second, small-scale contractors emerged as significant actors regulating the market in urban centers in competition with registered architects. In the second half of the twentieth century, cities in and around the Middle East were increasingly marked by "housing infill and densification" and self-help urban "apartment building extensions."[54]

Identity, Nation, and (Post)colonial
Social Housing Experiments

The contributors to this volume pointedly attend to various aspects of this transition in the Middle East, from grand, utopian modernist schemes to more moderate experiments in actual building practices. They address the decline of interest in planned urban development that engendered the growth of informal housing and the (re)emergence of anonymous builders. Yet, for much of the twentieth century, nationalist and developmentalist narratives still dominated the political agenda for many nation-states in the region. In both Iran and Turkey, for instance, the first half of the twentieth century was marked by social and cultural reforms along with aesthetic and architectural programs ambitiously pursued under the auspices of their pro-Western, powerful nationalist leaders, Reza Shah and Kemal Atatürk.[55] However limited the actual construction of social housing was in the interwar period, these leaders wholeheartedly embraced modernism's claim of universality, utopianism, and internationalism—of its refusal to be confined to any national borders or cultural traits—but were critical of the colonial and imperial mind-sets that had initially given birth to it.[56] These policies left their powerful imprint on contemporary Iranian and Turkish cities.

Whereas practices of European architects in the wider Middle East during the interwar years may be seen as a more likely form of "translation,"[57] the moment in which they were produced was nevertheless transitory. But what further complicates, if not significantly enriches, the history of social housing in the region is the colonial experiments that took place in the 1940s and early 1950s, as well as postcolonial practices that were built upon them or formulated in contestation with them. For that reason, authors in this book address how we might see the colonies beyond inert sites of Western experiments in (social) housing and critically revisit the cases where postcolonial architects dealt with the legacies of colonialism.

Colonial cities globally were typically characterized by a dual existence. Colonial planners developed neighborhoods for European settlers separate from the locals, often delineating the order between the two by means of a *cordon sanitaire*.[58] In *Urban Forms and Colonial Confrontations*, Zeynep Çelik wrote that "in terms of their architectural and urban design implications, policies regarding urban housing revolved around three issues: the choice between European and Algerian prototypes or a synthesis of the two, the physical separation of European and Algerian projects, and depiction of an appropriate style."[59] There the administration saw housing as a double-sided opportunity: it would address the "ever-deteriorating housing conditions and the growth of squatter settlements around Algiers"[60] at the same time it would make policing and military raids against protestors easier.[61]

It is not surprising that such colonialist precepts played a large part in determining the shape of housing programs and practices until the end of the colonial regime: *regroupement* policies of the 1950s, which produced modernist housing in the form of military camps built next to squatter settlements; designating "horizontal housing" more suitable for Algerian immigrants, referring to their rural roots;[62] and employing so-called vernacular architectural elements (such as the courtyard, as well as architectural forms that refer to a past Ottoman or Arab heritage)[63] in modernist schemas, to name a few.[64] Particularly in North Africa, the attempt by the French to categorize the colonial subject, not only in opposition to Europeans, but also by making distinctions within the native populations based on ethnic and religious identities, fashioned the housing types in the region.[65] In Morocco, for instance, GAMMA (Group of Modern Moroccan Architects), as part of their campaign for housing for the largest number, designed housing projects envisioned as "introverted units" of neighborhoods with courtyards, supposedly better fitting the locals, whereas highrise and midrise modern types were seen better suited to Europeans.[66] In "Depoliticizing Group Gamma," Aziza Chaouni writes that this approach to social housing was "strongly tinted by a colonial agenda and fell into generalizing racial clichés and over simplifications."[67] Ironically, however, the logic behind alluding to local architectural vocabulary also laid the desire to respond to the escalating anticolonial sentiments in the country: such cultural references would make new housing complexes look more familiar to the natives, matching well with their conventions, privacy concerns, and beliefs. This double-sided agenda, then, was related to the rising nationalist movements in the 1940s and 1950s; the metropole was now in search of reconciliation and sought softer ways to retain power. Toward the end of the colonial period in North Africa, works by French architects such as Fernand Pouillon and Roland Simounet showed great diversity, including temporary types of housing addressed to the poor living in *bidonvilles*—densely populated informal settlements composed of endless racks of tin-plate shelters, lined next to each other in the middle of the desert.[68] In Morocco, the "Carrières Centrales" housing developments in Casablanca (1951), built next to large slums there, included both low-rise and high-rise building types and were imagined as a utopian social housing experiment.[69] The source of inspiration for the architects was the *bidonvilles*.[70]

Postcolonial nation-states continued to be the sites where modernist undertakings, in localized interpretations as well as revivalist approaches, inspired by an imagined and idealized rural life, coexisted. For instance, in Beirut, Constantinos Doxiadis, upon an invitation by the Lebanese government and commissioned by the United States Operations Mission in Lebanon, worked on a plan for public housing that could be applied nationally. The idea was to develop different types of housing units befitting the Mediterranean climatic conditions as well as local topographical conditions.[71] In the case of Algeria, Karim Hadjri argues that during decolonization, many of the above-mentioned temporary social housing units built by the colonial administration for lower-income Algerians remained heavily inhabited, and "European" types of houses, although initially contested by many for being unsuited to local cultures and notions of privacy, continued to be seen as symbols of progress and social status.[72] Likewise, in newly independent Morocco, the courtyard was gradually freed from its colonial connotations and reintroduced within the architecture of contemporary housing. In the late 1940s, Hassan Fathy built his much-celebrated and equally contested rural homes in New Gourna using locally available materials and vernacular building methods.[73] The interest in the region in making use of sustainable technologies to provide shelter for the poor still continues. For instance, in 2010 the National Agency for the Development of Renewable Energy and Energy Efficiency in Morocco initiated a project in Marrakesh to build social housing units in villages using gabion baskets.[74]

Architecture in the Age of Turmoil: Extended Scope of Social Housing

Beyond (post)colonial legacies, which still inform the present in countless ways, two recent global and regional developments continue to shape contemporary social housing policies in the region: one is the larger neoliberal economic trends that hurl the Middle East into becoming a construction zone, with a reduced role for central authorities in housing production.

Growing inequality and privatization of services foster the expansion of self-help settlements around the region at the same time as the emergence of a transnational capitalist class as investors reconfigure the scene.[75] New cities are now being built from scratch in compressed timeframes with little or no concern for decent working conditions, such as Lusail City in Qatar, the host of the 2022 World Cup.[76] In Dubai's infamous labor camps, thousands of workers who are reported to be working long hours on giant construction sites are denied access not only to adequate housing, but also to freedom of movement, basic health care, and social security.[77] In Beirut, where mapping affordable housing, or any form of housing for that matter, has long been equated with "mapping security,"[78] the city's old neighborhoods are in continual transformation with the fast pace of high-rise and gated residential development. In the meantime, neoliberal economic policies in the region have not remained unchallenged. For instance, unequal urban development threatening to eat up the remaining bits of green spaces in Istanbul, coupled with rising cultural and religious conservatism, led to mass protests and unrest in 2013 with the Gezi movement in Turkey.

The second major development affecting social housing debates is the political conflicts and violence, tension, and wars in the region, which caused millions of people to take refuge in countries neighboring Syria and Iraq, such as Jordan, Lebanon, and Turkey. Some of the early camps, built for the hundreds of thousands of Palestinians who were forcibly displaced from their villages and towns in the occupied territories as Israel tactically used (and continues to use) housing needs as a tool for colonial expansion, eventually became permanent residential areas. While Palestinians have long been denied the right to return their homes and lands, in the words of a humanitarian aid expert, these camp cities may well be the "cities of tomorrow."[79] One such example is the camp established by the International Committee of the Red Cross near Zarqa for Palestinian refugees after the Arab-Israeli War in 1948. According to the United Nations Work and Relief Agency (UNRWA) website, the agency "replaced the original tents with concrete shelters and over the years the refugees have made improvements and added more rooms. The camp now resembles other urban quarters in Zarqa."[80] Social geographer Myriam Ababsa writes that the unprecedented scale of such developments, in addition to financial difficulties, made Jordan steer away from its more comprehensive social housing and slum-upgrading programs in the 1990s and focus instead on providing basic services and infrastructure.[81] The Nahr al-Bared camp in Lebanon has a similar story. In its old and newly built parts, one could see various permanent types of housing inhabited by diverse income groups. Almost completely destroyed during an armed conflict in 2007, the camp was rebuilt in 2011 by the UNRWA with the aim of reconstructing it "in a manner that preserves the social fabric through maintaining the camp's pre-destruction neighborhood layout."[82]

Beyond city centers, newly built refugee camps in the Middle East accommodate millions of people cramped in tiny shelters in a vast sea of desert—barren land blemished by scarce water and thus unsuited for agriculture.[83] Such crises drew the attention of not only humanitarian agencies, but also big manufacturers such as IKEA, to developing microdwellings, which go beyond either the container type or tent as a housing solution.[84] An exhibition at MoMA in October 2016, *Insecurities: Tracing Displacement and Shelter*, displayed "a range of objects, including the jointly-designed IKEA Foundation–UNHCR–Better Shelter modular emergency structure, along with works by Estudio Teddy Cruz, Henk Wildschut, and Tiffany Chung, among others."[85] Undoubtedly, the larger implications are becoming more devastating as homelessness and displacement in the region define a human tragedy of global dimensions. In the last six years, stories of these tragedies have been circulating in the news virtually every day: images of Syrian refugees sent back from European cities and borders to refugee camps, or the loss of life caused by desperate measures that families adopt to travel via land or sea to escape crises at home, to name a few. With these images and conditions in mind, is the time not ripe to rethink social housing as a category to include provincial refugee camps, as well as emergency dwellings, which, in practice, perform as permanent shelters?

Structure, Contents, and Methodologies of the Volume

In an attempt to respond to both the broad historical questions and urgent, contemporary crises raised in this introduction, the chapters in this book seek to give voice to hitherto sidelined histories of social housing and redefine recent debates on spatial agency in the wider Middle East from within a global perspective.[86] The essays show that the examples discussed at length here not only are part of the continually evolving vocabulary of modern architecture in the Middle East but also actively contribute to its making. On one hand, Middle Eastern modernisms have produced nuanced examples of social housing, ranging from localized and vernacular design solutions to postcolonial modernist experiments and so-called utopian schemas. On the other, the lower-income strata effectively mobilized locally available knowledge in building their environments, and social housing settlements were continually reappropriated by their inhabitants. As a result, working-class and lower-middle-class families extended the borders of the modernist paradigm in their quest for a modern life of their own. For that reason, this book extends the notion of modernity beyond large-scale projects and turns its attention to marginalized histories of less fashionable buildings, competing identity claims, and class aspirations.[87]

The volume thus consists of three main sections exploring the cultural and political context and the design, construction, and appropriation of social housing in the region. Within each section, chapters appear in chronological order. The first section includes chapters that discuss political, cultural, and economic contexts of social housing production in the Middle East from the 1950s to the present. In "Legitimizing the Jordanian State through Social Housing," Eliana Abu-Hamdi studies the use of housing in reshaping Jordan's cityscapes. In 1988, the Greater Amman Comprehensive Development Plan called for the construction of the new satellite city of Abu Nuseir. This bold planning action occurred in the midst of an era of modernization in which planning debates in Jordan, and elsewhere in the world, had shifted from debates about hygiene and the utopian ideals of the garden city to debates about the configuration of the modern city, public services, and the role of the state as an agent of social transformation. Abu-Hamdi argues that the newly established arm of the state in the Greater Amman Municipality designed and located the Abu Nuseir public housing project in such a way as to dismantle established forms of traditional communities and thereby create a more modern and thus more easily governable society.

In the next chapter, "Workers' and Popular Housing in Mid-Twentieth-Century Egypt," Mohamed Elshahed argues that during the 1950s, in the immediate aftermath of the 1952 coup d'état, the new regime in Egypt made serious attempts at confronting the housing issue, particularly with regard to low-income urban populations. These housing efforts were shaped in large part by the research, writing, and policy-driven approach of architect Mahmoud Riad. In a lecture delivered in 1947, Riad asserted the need for the state to immediately draft plans to provide housing for low-income workers as an essential step toward national modernization. Elshahed's analysis shows the shift in the geography of power in Egypt, from the architect to the small-scale contractor. A decade after Riad's pioneering lecture, the role of the architect as a respondent to urban Egypt's social demands faded and the state's ability to sustain such projects weakened, resulting in anonymous "modern" building typologies.

In the last chapter in the section, "Neoliberal Islamism and the Cultural Politics of Housing in Turkey," Bülent Batuman writes the history of state-subsidized mass housing, a major component of neoliberal urban policies in Turkey for the past two decades. Starting in the mid-1990s, housing provision increased in pace under the Islamic parties and assumed a role in the cultural politics of neoliberal Islamism. Batuman scrutinizes the utilization of housing for Islamic community building through two examples, which display spatial transformations of Islamist cultural politics and its internal conflicts over class relations, including the ambition to juxtapose slum upgrading with luxurious housing: a utopia where the rich would be rich and the poor would be poor yet they would live side by side with the shared identity of Islam. Through the comparative analysis of these two examples, the author discusses the architectural forms of Islamic community building and their political implications in Turkey.

The second section explores the identity politics of social housing in the modern and contemporary Middle East. The authors delve into colonial, national, and postcolonial formations of housing projects, as well as the development of housing as a (de)regulatory mechanism. In "Constructing Dignity: Primitivist Discourses and the Spatial Economies of Development in Postcolonial Tunisia," Nancy Demerdash explains how, after Tunisia's political independence from France in 1956, the country set out to actively commit to a new public program for social housing. What transpired in Tunisia was that those slum dwellers for whom social housing units were built could not afford the lifestyle and maintenance of even the most austere units. The chapter illuminates the complicities and ambivalence of the postcolonial nation-state and how the translations of utopian, state-sponsored rhetoric into programmatic aestheticization and demolition in Tunisia clashed with the ever-growing crises of habitation.

In the following essay, "Nation-Building in Israel: Negotiations over Housing as Grounds for the State-Citizen Contract, 1948–53," Yael Allweil examines the formation and consolidation of Israel's housing-based social contract and the continual negotiation between state and citizens over it. Calls for a renewal of the contract underlie the mass social unrest in the country during and since the summer of 2011. The chapter shows that its articulation in Israel included a housing regime aimed at transforming immigrants into proper citizens and excluding "improper" ones, with consequences for underpowered publics, especially Arab-Palestinian citizens. In doing so, Allweil explores how housing programs in Israel's history were planned and produced in direct response to continuing demands by citizens, deeply contesting the dominating scholarship of Israeli state housing, portraying regime and subjects as the opposing ends of modern governance.

In the third contribution to the section, "Social Housing in Colonial Cyprus: Contestations on Urbanity and Domesticity," Michalis Sioulas and Panayiota Pyla examine the phenomenon of social housing in Cyprus by analyzing the subsidized workers' housing in Omorphita, Famagusta, and Limassol. The essay ties these first appearances of social housing in Cyprus to post–World War II British reform policies on the island and to the general urbanization and industrialization processes at that time. Drawing on archival research in Cyprus, the authors highlight the broader British policies on housing in the colonies as well as the role of local politicians and architects in the formation of low-cost dwelling practices and an urban working class in Cyprus.

In the last chapter in the section, "Constructed Marginality: Women, Public Housing, and National Identity in Kuwait," Mae al-Ansari critically examines the cultural and gendered impacts of public housing in contemporary Kuwaiti society. In 2006, public discourse about the dilapidated condition of women's public housing in Sabah al-Salem, Kuwait, led many to call for the government's repossession of the property. Discussions of this process shed light on the plight of Kuwaiti female-headed households in public housing and the role of the built environment in the exacerbation of the conditions they lived under. Al-Ansari's research employs architectural narratives and stylistic dimensions to critically examine the role gender, power, and nationalism play in constructing a marginalized other. The underlying premise of the chapter is that the politics of identity are constructed by the politics of location.

The last section is on global exchanges and localized practices, which shaped the design and construction of social housing projects in the wider Middle East. The first contribution, Noam Shoked's "Rabbis, Architects, and the Design of Orthodox City Settlements," explores the complex dynamics of housing construction in contemporary Israel. Beginning in the late 1980s, Israel's attempts at annexing the West Bank through the construction of civilian settlements underwent a shift. Whereas previous settlements consisted of small and medium-sized suburban neighborhoods, now large-scale, state-led city settlements were built to house lower-income Orthodox Jews: "the Projects." Once they were inhabited, leaders of the Orthodox community took things into their own hands and adapted their cities to their needs. By elaborating on these negotiations and tracing a few of the architectural forms designed by state planners and then modified by the users, this contribution sheds light on the interrelations between governance and housing practices and complicates prevalent intellectual frameworks that prioritize top-down or, otherwise, more popular bottom-up design processes.

In the following chapter, "Notions of Class and Culture in Housing Projects in Tehran, 1945–60," Jaleh Jalili and Farshid Emami study the social housing projects constructed in Tehran in the 1940s and 1950s— Chaharsad-Dastgah, Narmak, and Aban. After the extensive modernization programs of the interwar period, Tehran had grown in size and population, and a new configuration of emerging social classes—a secular bourgeoisie, civil servants, and squatters—was rapidly changing the city's physical and social structure. These housing projects were conceived in a period of relative political freedom that followed the fall of the autocratic government of Reza Shah (reigned 1925–41). The authors resituate them not as self-contained entities located in the city's outskirts, but rather as components of a broader urban system subject to both top-down modernization and bottom-up actions of citizens.

In the final chapter, "Discrepant Spatial Practices: Contemporary Social Housing Projects in İzmir," Gülsüm Baydar, Kıvanç Kılınç, and Ahenk Yılmaz discuss the design, planning, and appropriation of two public housing settlements that were developed as part of larger urban renewal schemes. These projects reproduced a cramped version of a commonly repeated middle-class apartment typology in Turkey using low-quality materials and offered little space for sociability, which contributed to existing inequities and increased the discontent of their users. Spatial production in the Lefebvrian sense, however, did not cease to exist. The authors further argue that in their efforts to make a home out of the high-rise blocks, the dwellers continued to play a significant part in the material, social, and emotional (re)production of the built environment by setting their own modalities into given modernist housing schemes.

Reclaiming the Globality of Social
Housing in the Middle East

The chapters in this volume collectively share a scholarly zeal to expand the scope and content of existing literature on social housing so as to move beyond the temporal, geographical, and conceptual boundaries of the West.[88] In mainstream architectural history writing and discourse, modern architecture is defined as the invention and territory of the West, only later and partially adopted by "peripheral" countries in an attempt to catch up with the progress in the West.[89] It is not surprising that historians writing on the Middle East have limited their focus to select examples of modern architecture built for the elite social and cultural class and to the central government's role in shaping the built environment as part of its comprehensive modernization programs.[90] The story typically told in these studies is that at first the elites adopt Western and Central European modernism and these trends eventually trickle down to the middle and lower classes as well as to the "margins" of the nation-state. In the case of large cities, attention to urban forms in the region usually consists of a list of selected works of architecture and urbanism, either designed by foreign (star) architects commissioned by Western-oriented governments or built by Western-educated local professionals.

In response, the research presented in this volume reiterate contemporary scholarly debates over the globality of architectural modernism as a shared experience and the supposition that the experience of modernity is a multisited one.[91] The main task of the contributors is then to rescue modernism, in Jyoti Hosagrahar's words, from "the dominant discourse of a universal paradigm centered on an imagined 'West,'" "emphasize context and locality," and acknowledge "paradoxical features of modernities rooted in their particular conditions."[92] Indeed, this globality is made of multifarious exchanges of ideas, projects, layouts, construction materials, building styles, and expertise between different parts of the world and the Middle East in particular.[93] Our central goal in *Social Housing in the Middle East* is then to draw an unbiased, multilayered map to explore how social housing policies and projects both relate to and diverge from Western practices and, more important, to explore why such parallels and discrepancies matter in the first place. The volume seeks to attend to what ways, for instance, various visions, forms, and discourses of modernity have coexisted—not always peacefully—in the architectures of social housing built in the wider

Middle East. In this respect, this book is situated within the broad spectrum of critical postcolonial studies of architecture and urbanism.

Contributors also reveal that the impact of ordinary architectures in defining central discourses of modernism in the region goes far beyond what has been pictured in or excluded from mainstream architectural history texts. This effort concerns both the past and the present, if not the future, in its diverse projections. On the one hand, the traditions of what one might call "social housing of its time" have not yet been fully exhausted: for instance, there are strong collective "family house" experiences in the history of both Egypt and Turkey, like the *Rab'* and the *Cortejo*.[94] But were such practices ever transferred to modern housing typologies implemented in these countries, or elsewhere, during the twentieth century? On the other hand, the question of social housing is not a thing of the past but has come back in various new forms, including Aravena's more user-oriented designs, now opened to the public domain for free distribution,[95] and a new wave of refugee camps and shelters born out of emergency situations. Exchanges of trends, ideas, and projects significantly enhance the state of the globality of modernism, in spite of the fact that these stories rarely make it to the headlines in typical architectural histories. Given the current geopolitical stakes, doing new research to make sense of such lesser-known examples is a more urgent task than ever before.

Acknowledgment

The editors are thankful to all the contributors, to Heather Ferguson for reviewing earlier drafts of this introductory essay, to peer reviewers for providing very helpful comments on book chapters, to John Morris for copyediting this volume, to Meridith Murray for making the index, and to Jennika Baines and her colleagues at Indiana University Press for their hard work in the publication of this volume.

Notes

1. In the United Arab Emirates, for instance, "two distinct markets" operate, one "with subsidized housing for nationals" and another that provides "low cost market housing for expatriates." Craig Plumb, Hicham Hassouni, and Salah Sahyoun, *Why Affordable Housing Matters?*, Dubai: Jones Lang LaSalle, September 18, 2011, http://www.jll-mena.com/mena/en-gb/Research

/JLLMENA_Affordable%20Housing_2011.pdf. Also see Neha Bhatia, "Special Effort: Affordable Housing in the UAE," ConstructionWeekOnline.com, September 5, 2015, http://www .constructionweekonline.com/article-35251-special-report-affordable-housing-in-the-uae/5/.

2. Hasan-Uddin Khan, "A New Paradigm: Global Urbanism and Architecture of Rapidly Developing Countries," *International Journal of Islamic Architecture* 3, no. 1 (2014): 5–34.

3. For the concept of "vernacular modernism," see Anthony D. King, "Internationalism, Imperialism, Postcolonialism, Globalization: Frameworks for Vernacular Architecture," *Perspectives in Vernacular Architecture* 13, no. 2 (2006–7): 64–75.

4. Duanfang Lu, "Introduction: Architecture, Modernity and Identity in the Third World," in *Third World Modernism: Architecture, Development, and Identity*, ed. Duanfang Lu (London: Routledge, 2011), 1–28; Vikramaditya Prakash, "Epilogue: Third World Modernism, or Just Modernism: Towards a Cosmopolitan Reading of Modernism," in Lu, *Third World Modernism*, 255–76; Nezar Alsayyad, "From Modernism to Globalization: The Middle East in Context," in *Modernism and the Middle East: Architecture and Politics in the Twentieth Century*, ed. Sandy Isenstadt and Kishwar Rizvi (Seattle: University of Washington Press, 2008), 255–66; and Anthony D. King, *Spaces of Global Cultures: Architecture, Urbanism, Identity* (New York: Routledge, 2004). For an excellent source on the cultural aspects of globalism and modernity and the production of locality, please see Arjun Appadurai, *Modernity at Large: Cultural Dimensions of Globalization* (Minneapolis: University of Minnesota Press, 1996).

5. József Hegedüs, Martin Lux, and Nóra Teller, eds., *Social Housing in Transition Countries* (New York: Routledge, 2013). Mass housing is a relatively more fashionable topic among architectural historians around the world. This is not much of a surprise since "mass housing" is an umbrella term that refers to the mode of production rather than to the income groups that it services. See Florian Urban, *Tower and Slab: Histories of Global Mass Housing* (Abingdon, UK: Routledge, 2011).

6. The quotation is from Juliana Maxim and Can Bilsel's call for papers for The Housing Question: Nomad Seminar in Historiography, an international conference that took place at the University of San Diego on March 12–13, 2015, http://www.sandiego.edu/news/detail .php?_focus=49035.

7. See, for instance, Anne Power, *Hovels to High Rise: State Housing in Europe since 1950* (London: Routledge, 1993), 29–35.

8. Please see *CIAM II—Die Wohnung für das Existenzminimum: II. Internationale Kongresse für Neues Bauen und Städtisches Hochbauamt Frankfurt/Main* (Frankfurt: Englert und Schlosser, 1930); and Eric Paul Mumford, *The CIAM Discourse on Urbanism, 1928–1960* (Cambridge, MA: MIT Press, 2000), 27–44.

9. The design principles of this project followed the Garden City ideals, which emerged in England in the nineteenth century and then were transferred to major German cities in the early twentieth century. See Esra Akcan, *Architecture in Translation: Germany, Turkey, and the Modern House* (Durham, NC: Duke University Press, 2012), 30–38.

10. Power, *Hovels to High Rise*, 103; Esra Akcan, "The 'Siedlung' and the 'Mahalle': The Intertwined History of the Modern Residential Neighbourhood in Europe and Turkey," *Eurozine*, December 21, 2005, http://www.eurozine.com/articles/2005-12-21-akcan-en.html.

11. Hilde Heynen, *Architecture and Modernity: A Critique* (Cambridge, MA: MIT Press, 1999), 46–63; also see Susan R. Henderson, "Ernst May and the Campaign to Resettle the Countryside: Rural Housing in Silesia, 1919–1925," *Journal of the Society of Architectural Historians* 61, no. 2 (2002): 188–211; Winfried Brenne, ed., *Bruno Taut: Meister des farbigen*

Bauens in Berlin [Bruno Taut: master of colored construction in Berlin] (Salenstein, Switz.: Braun, 2005), 91, 164; Manfredo Tafuri, "The Attempts at Urban Reform in Europe between the Wars," in Manfredo Tafuri and Francesco Dal Co, *Modern Architecture 1* (London: Faber and Faber/Electa, 1986), 162.

12. Manfredo Tafuri, *Architecture and Utopia: Design and Capitalist Development*, trans. Barbara Luigia La Penta (Cambridge, MA: MIT Press, 1976), 112.

13. See Anton Kaes, Martin Jay, and Edward Dimendberg, eds., *The Weimar Republic Sourcebook* (Berkeley: University of California Press, 1995).

14. Andrea Dean, "Socially Motivated Architecture," in *Critical Architecture and Contemporary Culture*, ed. William J. Lillyman, Marilyn F. Moriarty, and David J. Neuman (New York: Oxford University Press, 1994), 126.

15. Kenny Cupers, *The Social Project: Housing Postwar France* (Minneapolis: University of Minnesota Press, 2014), xiiii, 95–182.

16. For the US influence on European architecture after World War II, see Jean-Louis Cohen, *Scenes of the World to Come: European Architecture and the American Challenge, 1893–1960* (Paris: Flammarion, 1995).

17. Burçak Keskin-Kozat, "Negotiating Modernization through US Foreign Assistance: Turkey's Marshall Plan (1948–1952) Re-interpreted" (PhD diss., University of Michigan, 2006).

18. See, for instance, Bernard Wagner, *Housing and Urban Development in the Philippines* (Manila: USAID, Housing and Urban Development Division, 1968); Bernard Wagner, *Housing in India*, 2 vols. (New Delhi: B. Wagner, 1964); Jeffry M. Diefendorf, Axel Frohn, and Hermann-Josef Rupieper, eds., *American Policy and the Reconstruction of West Germany, 1945–1955* (New York: Cambridge University Press, 1993).

19. Anneli Kahrik and Juri Kore, "Residualization of Social Housing and the New Programs," in *Social Housing in Transition Countries*, ed. József Hegedüs, Martin Lux, and Nóra Teller (New York: Routledge, 2013), 163; Irina Zapatrina, "The Ukraine: Waiting Lists without Housing," in Hegedüs, Lux, and Teller, *Social Housing in Transition Countries*, 294.

20. Daria Bocharnikova, "After Solving Housing Crisis in the USSR: NER Diagram for Future Settlements," paper presented at The Housing Question: Nomad Seminar in Historiography, University of San Diego, March 12–13, 2015; also see Daria Bocharnikova, "Inventing Socialist Modern: A History of the Architectural Profession in the USSR, 1954–1971" (PhD diss., European University Institute, 2014); for an overview of Soviet urban planning in the interwar and postwar periods, see Paul Stronski, *Tashkent: Forging a Soviet City 1930–1966* (Pittsburgh, PA: University of Pittsburgh Press, 2010). For a discussion on the *microraion* outside the Soviet Russian context, see Juliana Maxim, "Bucharest: The City Transfigured," in *Sanctioning Modernism: Architecture and the Making of Postwar Identities*, ed. Vladimir Kulić, Timothy Parker, and Monica Penick (Austin: University of Texas Press, 2014), 24–28.

21. Duanfang Lu, *Remaking Chinese Urban Form: Modernity, Scarcity, and Space, 1949–2005* (London: Routledge, 2006), 101–23, esp. 118.

22. Mario Gandelzonas, "The City as the Object of Architecture," *Assemblage* 37 (1998): 130.

23. Dean, "Socially Motivated," 125 and 129–30. According to the report written by the United Nations Economic Commission for Europe in 2014, "Over thirty years, the deregulation and privatization [sic] of social housing in Western Europe and the privatisation of housing in countries with transition economies have reduced the availability of affordable housing. Austerity measures, taken in response to the economic crisis, have reduced investments in social housing even further." See United Nations Economic Commission for Europe, "The Future of Social Housing: Environmental and Social Challenges and the

Way Forward," Workshop report, United Nations Economic Commission for Europe, February 4–5, 2015, Geneva, Switzerland, 5.

24. Roger Keil, "Third Way Urbanism: Opportunity or Dead End?," *Alternatives* 25, no. 2 (2000): 257.

25. Please see Brian Wheeler, "A History of Social Housing," *BBC NEWS*, April 14, 2015, http://www.bbc.com/news/uk-14380936. Also see Keil, "Third Way Urbanism," 248.

26. José Tomás Franco, "Alejandro Aravena Wins 2016 Pritzker Prize," *ArchDaily*, January 13, 2016, http://www.archdaily.com/780203/alejandro-aravena-wins-2016-pritzker-prize.

27. Nishat Awan, Tatjana Schneider, and Jeremy Till, *Spatial Agency: Other Ways of Doing Architecture* (London: Routledge, 2011); also see Jessica Mairs, "Richard Rogers' Prefabricated Housing for Homeless People Opens in South London," *dezeen magazine*, September 8, 2015, http://www.dezeen.com/2015/09/08/richard-rogers-prefabricated-housing-for-homeless-people-opens-in-south-london-mitcham-merton/; Amy Frearson, "Tatiana Bilbao Addresses 'Urgent Need' for Housing Mexico's Poorest Inhabitants," *dezeen magazine*, October 6, 2015, http://www.dezeen.com/2015/10/06/tatiana-bilbao-low-cost-social-housing-mexico-chicago-architecture-biennial-2015/; Owen Hatherley, "The Cult of Self-Build and Do-It-Yourself Won't Solve the Housing Crisis," *dezeen magazine*, January 29, 2016, http://www.dezeen.com/2016/01/29/opinion-owen-hatherley-social-mass-housing-versus-self-build-idealism-walter-segal/.

28. Al Jazeera, *Rebel Architecture*, http://www.aljazeera.com/programmes/rebel architecture/.

29. For excellent readings on the issue of spatial agency and new facets of social engagement in architecture, see Kenny Cupers, "Where Is the Social Project?," *Journal of Architectural Education* 68, no. 1 (2014): 6–8; Awan et al., *Spatial Agency*; Bryan Bell and Katie Wakeford, eds., *Expanding Architecture: Design as Activism* (New York: Metropolis, 2008).

30. It should be noted that we are by no means overlooking a long history of "participatory design" in the production of public housing. The emphasis here is on agency and activism, rather than involving the user in decision-making processes to a certain extent. See Kenny Cupers, "The Expertise of Participation: Mass Housing and Urban Planning in Post-war France," *Planning Perspectives* 26, no. 1 (2011): 29–53.

31. *PBS Newshour*, "Architecture Becomes a Tool to Fight Poverty through This Pritzker Winner," January 13, 2016, http://www.pbs.org/newshour/bb/architecture-becomes-a-tool-to-fight-poverty-through-this-pritzker-winner/.

32. The last three decades have witnessed the birth of affordable housing initiatives, campaigns, networks, and collaborative organizations both locally and globally. See, for instance, "Housing Europe" (The European Federation of Public, Cooperative and Social Housing), http://www.housingeurope.eu/section-37/about-us; and Baltimore Housing Roundtable's fair community development and affordable housing campaigns, https://www.baltimorehousin groundtable.org/.

33. Andres Lepik, "Think Global, Build Social! Contemporary Architects Are Actively Involved in Society," in *Think Global, Build Social! Architectures for a Better World* (Munich: Goethe Institut, 2013), 17.

34. Ibid., 19.

35. This exhibition was open to visitors between October 23 and November 13, 2015, at İzmir Architectural Center (İzmir Mimarlık Merkezi).

36. There are a few notable exceptions that deserve a mention, one of which is a cooperative housing program in Düzce, Turkey. This postearthquake reconstruction project, now

nearing completion, has been developed with participatory design practices. See Düzce Hope Homes, https://cohousingproject.wordpress.com/about/duzce-hope-homes/.

37. Sibel Bozdoğan, "A Case for Spatial Agency and Social Engagement in the Middle East," *International Journal of Islamic Architecture* 4, no. 1 (2015): 31–35. Also see İpek Türeli, "'Small' Architectures: Walking and Camping in Middle Eastern Cities," *International Journal of Islamic Architecture* 2, no. 1 (2013): 5–38.

38. "Think Global, Build Social! Architectures for a Better World," *Architekturzentrum Wien*, https://past.azw.at/page.php?node_id=3&page_id=836&lang_id=en.

39. Aziza Chaouni, "Depoliticizing Group Gamma: Contesting Modernism in Morocco," in Lu, *Third World Modernism*, 71.

40. See the call for papers for *The Housing Question*, http://www.sandiego.edu/news/detail.php?_focus=49035.

41. "TBMM Tutanak Dergisi," July 1, 1948, 555, quoted in Murat Balamir, "'Kira Evi'nden 'Kat Evleri'ne Apartmanlaşma: Bir Zihniyet Dönüşümü Tarihçesinden Kesitler" [Apartmentization from "rental houses" to "multistory houses": Snapshots from the history of a mind-set transformation], *Mimarlık* 260 (1998): 31, 32; Gönül Tankut, *Bir Başkentin İmarı, Ankara: 1929–1939* [The construction of a capital city, Ankara: 1929–1939] (Ankara: Middle East Technical University, 1990), 164.

42. İlhan Tekeli, "Türkiye Kentlerinde Apartmanlaşma Sürecinde İki Aşama" [Two phases in the 'apartmentization' process in Turkish cities], *Çevre* (July–August 1979): 79.

43. For instance, in Singapore, "the state espoused the large-scale development of modern high-rise apartment buildings, which proved effective in achieving comprehensive housing access in the land-scarce city-state." Lu, "Introduction," 10.

44. Republic of Iraq, Ministry of Construction and Housing, *Iraq Housing Market Study: Main Report*, prepared by Planning and Development Collaborative International in cooperation with Community Development Group Iraqi Central Office of Statistics and Information Technology, December 2006, ii, 30–31, http://www.humanitarianlibrary.org/sites/default/files/2013/05/4997_65700_IHMS_Main_Report.pdf.

45. Commissioned by the Greek firm Doxiadis Associates, this extensive development plan was conceived to include a slum-clearance program. See Lefteris Theodosis, "Victory over Chaos? Constantinos A. Doxiadis and Ekistics, 1945–1975," (PhD diss., Universitat Politècnica de Catalunya, 2015), 153, 165, 179; Lefteris Theodosis, "'Containing' Baghdad: Constantinos Doxiadis's Program for a Developing Nation," in *Ciudad del Espejismo: Bagdad, de Wright a Venturi* [City of mirage: Baghdad from Wright to Venturi], ed. Pedro Azara (Barcelona: Universitat Politècnica de Catalunya, 2008), 167–72.

46. Fawzy El-Gazaerly, Shahira Issa, and Dina K. Shehayeb, "Planning Cairo . . . ? A Chronology," in *Cairo Resilience: The City as Personal Practice*, ed. Dina Shehayeb and Shahira Issa, DI-WAN Series, ed. Philipp Misselwitz and Can Altay, published in collaboration with Prince Claus Fund for Culture and Development and the International Architecture Biennale Rotterdam, 2009, n.p.

47. Plumb, Hassouni, and Sahyoun, *Why Affordable Housing*, 3.

48. Sharifa AlShalfan, *The Right to Housing in Kuwait: An Urban Injustice in a Socially Just System*, research paper, LSE Kuwait Programme on Development, Governance and Globalisation in the Gulf States, May 2013. Also see Plumb, Hassouni, and Sahyoun, *Why Affordable Housing*, 14, 16.

49. "Housing in Iran," *Encyclopaedia Iranica*, http://www.iranicaonline.org/articles/housing-in-iran, last updated March 23, 2012.

50. *Guardian*, "Iran's Economy Struggles to Support Ahmadinejad's Ill-Conceived Housing Vision," January 30, 2014, http://www.theguardian.com/world/iran-blog/2014/jan/30 /irans-economy-struggles-to-support-ahmadinejads-ill-conceived-housing-vision.

51. Bhatia, "Special Effort." More recently, Dubai Municipality outlined a proposal "to introduce mandatory affordable housing quotas for all new residential developments." Please see Michael Fahy, "Affordable Housing Quotas in Dubai Are Long Overdue," March 12, 2015, *ConstructionWeekOnline.com*, http://www.constructionweekonline.com/article-32913 -affordable-housing-quotas-in-dubai-long-overdue/.

52. L. Yıldız Tokman, *Konut Politikaları Uygulamalarında Özel Bir Örnek: Yenimahalle* [A particular example in the housing policy applications: Yenimahalle] (Ankara: KentKoop Yayınları, 1985); Myriam Ababsa, "The Evolution of Upgrading Policies in Amman," paper prepared for the Second International Conference on Sustainable Architecture and Urban Development, Center for the Study of Architecture in the Arab Region, MPWH (Ministry of Public Works and Housing), University of Dundee, Amman, Jordan, July 2010; Ramdane Djebarni and Abdullah al-Abed, "Satisfaction Level with Neighbourhoods in Low-Income Public Housing in Yemen," *Property Management* 18, no. 4 (2000): 230–42.

53. For instance, see Cevat Geray, "Türkiye'de Kendi Evini Yapana Yardım Yöntemi Uygulaması" [The implementation of the aided self-help housing method in Turkey], *Amme İdaresi Dergisi* 5, no. 2 (1972): 42–73.

54. For examples from Morocco and Tunisia, please see Serge Santelli, "Self-Built Urban Housing, Rabat and Tunis," *Mimar* 17 (July–September 1985): 41–48; for Turkey, see Tahire Erman, "The Politics of Squatter (*Gecekondu*) Studies in Turkey: The Changing Representations of Rural Migrants in the Academic Discourse," *Urban Studies* 38, no. 7 (2001): 983–1002; for an extensive study on a number of Balkan and former Eastern European cities, see Stefan Bouzarovski, *Retrofitting the City: Residential Flexibility, Resilience, and the Built Environment* (London: I. B. Tauris, 2014), esp. 208–11.

55. Talinn Grigor, *Building Iran: Modernism, Architecture, and National Heritage under the Pahlavi Monarchs* (New York: Periscope/Prestel, 2009); Zeynep Kezer, *Building Modern Turkey: State, Space, and Ideology in the Early Republic* (Pittsburgh, PA: University of Pittsburgh Press, 2015); also see Touraj Atabaki, ed., *The State and the Subaltern: Authoritarian Modernisation in Turkey and Iran* (London: I. B. Tauris, 2007).

56. Isenstadt and Rizvi, *Modernism*; Prakash, "Epilogue."

57. For the critical use of the concept of "translation" in defining architectural exchanges between Turkish and German contexts, see Akcan, *Architecture in Translation*.

58. Zeynep Çelik, *Urban Forms and Colonial Confrontations: Algiers under French Rule* (Berkeley: University of California Press, 1997), 40. Also see Hugh Pouliot, "Between the Medina and the Metropole: Race and Urban Planning from Algiers to Paris (1930–75)" (PhD diss., Dalhousie University, 2011), esp. 15–21.

59. Çelik, *Urban Forms*, 115.

60. Ibid., 143.

61. Chaouni, "Depoliticizing," 64.

62. Çelik, *Urban Forms*, 161.

63. See Sheila Crane, "Architecture at the Ends of Empire: Urban Reflections between Algiers and Marseille," in *The Spaces of the Modern City*, ed. Gyan Prakash and Kevin M. Kruse (Princeton, NJ: Princeton University Press, 2008), 105–6.

64. Çelik, *Urban Forms*, 113, 114, and 131.

65. Zeynep Çelik writes that "Tony Socard, an architect who worked in collaboration with planners and built low-cost housing for Muslims, argued for three types of residences, on the premise of separating Muslims from European settlements. For the 'evolved' families that subscribed to the French lifestyle and values, European-type flats or villas were unquestionably the most suitable. Yet in some cities . . . 'artisan' classes had maintained a preference for the 'traditional courtyard house'; this type should be built, but not mixed with houses designed according to European formulas. The third category addressed the residents of the *bidonvilles* and approved a semi-rural pattern in specially designated quarters." Ibid., 116.

66. Chaouni, "Depoliticizing," 59, 62, 64.

67. Chaouni further argues that "Ecochard's housing for Moroccans was located on the city's outskirts, separated by a 'sanitary zone' free of construction. . . . Moreover, specific housing typologies were designed for each ethnic group: the Muslims, the Jews, and the Europeans, along an evolving spectrum of civilization. . . . Muslims were confined to introverted units with an enclosed courtyard, a multipurpose room, a faucet and a Turkish toilet." Ibid., 64.

68. Çelik, *Urban Forms*, 150; also see Karim Hadjri, "Vernacular Housing Forms in North Algeria," *Traditional Dwellings and Settlements Review* 5, no. 1 (1993): 65–67.

69. Marion von Osten, "Carrières Centrales," May 3, 2012, http://transculturalmodernism.org/article/131.

70. These architects were George Candillis, Alexis Josic, and Shadrach Woods (affiliated with GAMMA). See Cristiana Strava, "Adaptations of Vernacular Modernism in Casablanca," *Polis*, July 4, 2012, http://www.thepolisblog.org/2012/07/adaptations-of-vernacular-modernism.html.

71. Maria Lind, "Late-Modernist Housing," *ArtReview*, April 2014, http://artreview.com/opinion/april_2014_opinion_maria_lind_late-modernist_housing/. Please also see, Hashim Sarkis, *Circa 1958: Lebanon in the Pictures and Plans of Constantinos Doxiadis* (Beirut: Dar An-Nahar, 2003).

72. Hadjri, "Vernacular Housing," 66–67; also see Çelik, *Urban Forms*, 166.

73. See Hasan Fathy, *Architecture for the Poor: An Experiment in Rural Egypt* (Chicago: University Of Chicago Press, 1973).

74. Global Site Plans—the Grid, "Could This Catch On? Homes Made from Gabion Baskets That Are Sustainable, Affordable Housing," *Smart Cities Dive*, https://www.smartcitiesdive.com/ex/sustainablecitiescollective/marrakech-morocco-gabion-basket-homes-provide-sustainable-affordable-/1071546/.

75. Rami F. Daher, "The New Cities Landlords: The Transnational Capitalist Class," in *Amman: Neoliberal Urban Management*, ed. Rami Farouk Daher, DIWAN Series, ed. Philipp Misselwitz and Can Altay, published in collaboration with Prince Claus Fund for Culture and Development and the International Architecture Biennale Rotterdam, 2009, n.p.

76. Philippe Auclair, "Soccer Punch: How Qatar Came to Host the 2022 World Cup," *Newsweek* (Europe edition), June 12, 2013, http://www.newsweek.com/soccer-punch-how-qatar-came-host-2022-world-cup-224033.

77. See Human Rights Watch, "Building Towers, Cheating Workers: Exploitation of Migrant Construction Workers in the United Arab Emirates," vol. 18, no. 8(E) (2006), http://www.hrw.org/en/reports/2006/11/11/building-towers-cheating-workers; also see Human Rights Watch, "'The Island of Happiness': Exploitation of Migrant Workers on Saadiyat Island, Abu Dhabi," May 2009, https://www.hrw.org/report/2009/05/19/island-happiness/exploitation-migrant-workers-saadiyat-island-abu-dhabi.

78. Mona Fawaz, Ahmad Gharbieh, and Mona Harb, eds., *Beirut: Mapping Security*, DIWAN Series, ed. Philipp Misselwitz and Can Altay, published in collaboration with Prince Claus Fund for Culture and Development and the International Architecture Biennale Rotterdam, 2009, n.p.; also see Mona Fawaz, Mona Harb, and Ahmad Gharbieh, "Living Beirut's Security Zones: An Investigation of the Modalities and Practice of Urban Security," *City and Society* 24, no. 2 (2012): 173–95.

79. Talia Radford, "Refugee Camps Are the 'Cities of Tomorrow,' Says Humanitarian-Aid Expert," *dezeen magazine*, November 23, 2015, https://www.dezeen.com/2015/11/23/refugee-camps-cities-of-tomorrow-killian-kleinschmidt-interview-humanitarian-aid-expert/.

80. The United Nations Relief and Works Agency for Palestine Refugees (UNRWA), "Where We Work," https://www.unrwa.org/where-we-work/jordan/zarqa-camp.

81. These policies included creating "job opportunities" and "community involvement" as well as the betterment of physical conditions. See Ababsa, "The Evolution," 9–10; see also Myriam Ababsa, "Social Disparities between East and West Amman: GIS Diagnosis and Public Policies," in Daher, *Amman*, n.p.

82. Sultan Barakat, "Reconstruction of Nahr el-Bared Refugee Camp, Tripoli, Lebanon," 2013 onsite review report (Beirut: UNRWA), http://archnet.org/system/publications/contents/8744/original/DTP101243.pdf?1391602992.

83. For an exceptional documentary on the everyday life of a "temporary" refugee camp in northern Iraq, please see https://refugeerepublic.submarinechannel.com/.

84. "IKEA Unveils Solar-Powered Flat Pack Shelters for Easily Deployable Emergency Housing," *inhabitat*, http://inhabitat.com/ikeas-solar-powered-flat-pack-refugee-shelters-offer-easily-deployable-emergency-housing/.

85. "Insecurities: Tracing Displacement and Shelter," *MoMA Press*, May 4, 2016, http://press.moma.org/2016/05/insecurities-tracing-displacement-and-shelter/.

86. There are several, outstanding, collections bringing together various contemporary and historical social housing experiments and approaches beyond the typical focus in Western scholarship. *Housing and Social Change: East–West Perspectives*, edited by Ray Forrest and James Lee (Hove, UK: Psychology Press), delves into the global financial structures, local specificities, and transcultural contexts that shape social and affordable housing production in the Global South. A similar venture, *Social Housing in Transition Countries* (Abingdon-on-Thames, UK: Routledge), covers various types, models, and implementations of social housing in Eastern European countries developed in the postcommunist period. Edited by József Hegedüs, Martin Lux, and Nóra Teller, the book locates social housing practices with respect to their local, national, and regional production and in comparison with earlier forms of social housing in the region.

87. We should note that this book is not a survey and therefore does not claim to bring together all aspects of social housing production in the region. Our selection of each contribution is closely related to the structure of the book: chapters are strong representatives of relevant themes on the issue of social housing and spatial agency in the Middle East and seek to highlight the diversity of existing typologies across the region.

88. In mainstream architecture history books, mass housing in general and social housing as its subcategory are largely underrepresented. Please see Cupers, *Social Project*, xiv.

89. For Eurocentrism as discussed in postcolonial literature, please see James D. Sideway, "Postcolonial Geographies: An Exploratory Essay," *Progress in Human Geography* 24, no. 4 (2000): 591–612; Anthony D. King, "Cultures and Spaces of Postcolonial Knowledges,"

in *Handbook of Cultural Geography*, ed. Kay Anderson, Mona Domosh, Steve Pile, and Nigel Thrift (London: Sage, 2003), 381–97.

90. For the use of modernization theory, see Donald Quataert, "Ottoman History Writing and Changing Attitudes towards the Notion of 'Decline,'" *History Compass* 1 (August 2003): 2.

91. See similar discussions in Lu, *Third World Modernism*; Isenstadt and Rizvi, *Modernism*; King, *Spaces of Global Cultures*; and Abidin Kusno, *Behind the Postcolonial: Architecture, Urban Space and Political Cultures in Indonesia* (London: Routledge, 2000).

92. Jyoti Hosagrahar, *Indigenous Modernities: Negotiating Architecture, Urbanism, and Colonialism in Delhi* (Abingdon-on-Thames, UK: Routledge, 2005), 6, 7.

93. For a recent study on the less scrutinized dimensions of such global exchanges, see Łukasz Stanek, "Mobilities of Architecture in the Late Cold War: From Socialist Poland to Kuwait, and Back," *International Journal of Islamic Architecture* 4, no. 2 (2015): 365–98.

94. See André Raymond, "The Rabʿ: A Type of Collective Housing in Cairo during the Ottoman Period," in *Architecture as Symbol and Self-Identity*, ed. Jonathan G. Katz (Philadelphia: Aga Khan Award for Architecture, 1980), 55–62; Şebnem Yücel, "Minority Heterotopias: The Cortijos of İzmir," *Architectural Research Quarterly* 20, no. 3 (2016): 245–56.

95. Jenna McKnight, "Alejandro Aravena Makes Housing Designs Available to the Public for Free," *dezeen magazine*, April 6, 2016, http://www.dezeen.com/2016/04/06/alejandro -aravena-elemental-social-housing-designs-architecture-open-source-pritzker/.

Bibliography

Ababsa, Myriam. "The Evolution of Upgrading Policies in Amman." Paper presented at the Second International Conference on Sustainable Architecture and Urban Development, Center for the Study of Architecture in the Arab Region, MPWH (Ministry of Public Works and Housing), University of Dundee, Amman, Jordan, July 2010.

——. "Social Disparities between East and West Amman: GIS Diagnosis and Public Policies." In *Amman: Neoliberal Urban Management*, edited by Rahmi Daher, n.p. DIWAN Series, edited by Philipp Misselwitz and Can Altay, published in collaboration with Prince Claus Fund for Culture and Development and the International Architecture Biennale Rotterdam, 2009.

Akcan, Esra. *Architecture in Translation: Germany, Turkey, and the Modern House*. Durham, NC: Duke University Press, 2012.

——. "The 'Siedlung' and the 'Mahalle': The Intertwined History of the Modern Residential Neighbourhood in Europe and Turkey." *Eurozine*, December 21, 2005. http://www .eurozine.com/articles/2005-12-21-akcan-en.html.

Al Jazeera. *Rebel Architecture*. http://www.aljazeera.com/programmes/rebelarchitecture/.

AlShalfan, Sharifa. "The Right to Housing in Kuwait: An Urban Injustice in a Socially Just System." Research paper, LSE Kuwait Programme on Development, Governance and Globalisation in the Gulf States, May 2013.

Appadurai, Arjun. *Modernity at Large: Cultural Dimensions of Globalization*. Minneapolis: University of Minnesota Press, 1996.

Atabaki, Touraj, ed. *The State and the Subaltern: Authoritarian Modernisation in Turkey and Iran*. London: I. B. Tauris, 2007.

Auclair, Philippe. "Soccer Punch: How Qatar Came to Host the 2022 World Cup." *Newsweek* (Europe edition), June 12, 2013. http://www.newsweek.com/soccer-punch-how-qatar -came-host-2022-world-cup-224033.

Awan, Nishat, Tatjana Schneider, and Jeremy Till. *Spatial Agency: Other Ways of Doing Architecture.* London: Routledge, 2011.

Balamir, Murat. "'Kira Evi'nden 'Kat Evleri'ne Apartmanlaşma: Bir Zihniyet Dönüşümü Tarihçesinden Kesitler" [Apartmentization from "rental houses" to "multistory houses": Snapshots from the history of a mind-set transformation]. *Mimarlık* 260 (1994): 29–33.

Barakat, Sultan. "Reconstruction of Nahr el-Bared Refugee Camp, Tripoli, Lebanon." 2013 Onsite review report. Beirut: UNRWA. http://archnet.org/system/publications /contents/8744/original/DTP101243.pdf?1391602992.

Bell, Bryan, and Katie Wakeford, eds. *Expanding Architecture: Design as Activism.* New York: Metropolis, 2008.

Bhatia, Neha. "Special Effort: Affordable Housing in the UAE." ConstructionWeekOnline. com, September 5, 2015. http://www.constructionweekonline.com/article-35251-special -report-affordable-housing-in-the-uae/5/.

Bocharnikova, Daria. "After Solving Housing Crisis in the USSR: NER Diagram for Future Settlements." Paper presented at The Housing Question: Nomad Seminar in Historiography, University of San Diego, March 12–13, 2015.

———. "Inventing Socialist Modern: A History of the Architectural Profession in the USSR, 1954–1971." PhD diss., European University Institute, 2014.

Bozdoğan, Sibel. "A Case for Spatial Agency and Social Engagement in the Middle East." *International Journal of Islamic Architecture* 4, no. 1 (2015): 31–35.

———. *Modernism and Nation-Building: Turkish Architectural Culture in the Early Republic.* Seattle: University of Washington Press, 2001.

Brenne, Winfried, ed. *Bruno Taut: Meister des farbigen Bauens in Berlin.* Salenstein, Switz.: Verlagshaus Braun, 2005.

Bouzarovski, Stefan. *Retrofitting the City: Residential Flexibility, Resilience and the Built Environment.* London: I. B. Tauris, 2014.

Chaouni, Aziza. "Depoliticizing Group Gamma: Contesting Modernism in Morocco." In *Third World Modernism: Architecture, Development, and Identity*, edited by Duanfang Lu, 57–84. London: Routledge, 2011.

CIAM II—Die Wohnung für das Existenzminimum: II. Internationale Kongresse für Neues Bauen und Städtisches Hochbauamt Frankfurt/Main. Frankfurt: Englert und Schlosser, 1930.

Cohen, Jean-Louis. *Scenes of the World to Come: European Architecture and the American Challenge, 1893–1960.* Paris: Flammarion, 1995.

Crane, Sheila. "Architecture at the Ends of Empire: Urban Reflections between Algiers and Marseille." In *The Spaces of the Modern City*, edited by Gyan Prakash and Kevin M. Kruse, 99–143 (Princeton, NJ: Princeton University Press, 2008).

Cupers, Kenny. "The Expertise of Participation: Mass Housing and Urban Planning in Post-War France." *Planning Perspectives* 26, no. 1 (2011): 29–53.

———. *The Social Project: Housing in Postwar France.* Minneapolis: University of Minnesota Press, 2014.

———. "Where Is the Social Project?" *Journal of Architectural Education* 68, no. 1 (2014): 6–8.

Çelik, Zeynep. *Urban Forms and Colonial Confrontations: Algiers under French Rule.* Berkeley: University of California Press, 1997.

Daher, Rami Farouk, ed. *Amman: Neoliberal Urban Management.* DIWAN Series, edited by
Philipp Misselwitz and Can Altay, published in collaboration with Prince Claus Fund for
Culture and Development and the International Architecture Biennale Rotterdam, 2009.
———. "The New Cities Landlords: The Transnational Capitalist Class." In *Amman: Neolib-
eral Urban Management,* edited by Rami Farouk Daher, n.p. DIWAN Series, edited by
Philipp Misselwitz and Can Altay, published in collaboration with Prince Claus
Fund for Culture and Development and the International Architecture Biennale
Rotterdam, 2009.
Dean, Andrea. "Socially Motivated Architecture." In *Critical Architecture and Contemporary
Culture,* edited by William J. Lillyman, Marilyn F. Moriarty, and David J. Neuman,
125–32. New York: Oxford University Press, 1994.
Diefendorf, Jeffry M., Axel Frohn, and Hermann-Josef Rupieper, eds. *American Policy and the
Reconstruction of West Germany, 1945–1955.* New York: Cambridge University Press, 1993.
Djebarni, Ramdane, and Abdullah al-Abed. "Satisfaction Level with Neighbourhoods in Low-
Income Public Housing in Yemen." *Property Management* 18, no. 4 (2000): 230–42.
Erman, Tahire. "The Politics of Squatter (*Gecekondu*) Studies in Turkey: The Changing
Representations of Rural Migrants in the Academic Discourse." *Urban Studies* 38, no. 7
(2001): 983–1002.
Fahy, Michael. "Affordable Housing Quotas in Dubai Are Long Overdue." Construction-
WeekOnline.com, March 12, 2015. http://www.constructionweekonline.com/article
-32913-affordable-housing-quotas-in-dubai-long-overdue/.
Fathy, Hasan. *Architecture for the Poor: An Experiment in Rural Egypt* (Chicago: University of
Chicago Press, 1973.
Fawaz, Mona, Ahmad Gharbieh, and Mona Harb, eds. *Beirut: Mapping Security.* DIWAN
Series, edited by Philipp Misselwitz and Can Altay, published in collaboration with
Prince Claus Fund for Culture and Development and the International Architecture
Biennale Rotterdam, 2009.
———. "Living Beirut's Security Zones: An Investigation of the Modalities and Practice of
Urban Security." *City and Society* 24, no. 2 (2012): 173–95.
Forrest, Ray, and James Lee, eds. *Housing and Social Change: East-West Perspectives.* Hove,
UK: Psychology Press, 2003.
Franco, José Tomás. "Alejandro Aravena Wins 2016 Pritzker Prize." *ArchDaily,* January 13,
2016. http://www.archdaily.com/780203/alejandro-aravena-wins-2016-pritzker-prize.
Frearson, Amy. "Tatiana Bilbao Addresses 'Urgent Need' for Housing Mexico's Poorest
Inhabitants." *dezeen magazine,* October 6, 2015. http://www.dezeen.com/2015/10/06
/tatiana-bilbao-low-cost-social-housing-mexico-chicago-architecture-biennial-2015/.
Gandelzonas, Mario. "The City as the Object of Architecture." *Assemblage* 37 (1998): 128–44.
Geray, Cevat. "Türkiye'de Kendi Evini Yapana Yardım Yöntemi Uygulaması" [The imple-
mentation of the aided self-help housing method in Turkey]. *Amme İdaresi Dergisi* 5,
no. 2 (1972): 42–73.
Global Site Plans—the Grid. "Could This Catch On? Homes Made from Gabion Baskets That
Are Sustainable, Affordable Housing." *Smart Cities Dive.* https://www.smartcitiesdive
.com/ex/sustainablecitiescollective/marrakech-morocco-gabion-basket-homes-provide
-sustainable-affordable-/1071546/.
Goldstein, Amir. "The Kibbutz and the Ma'abara (Transit Camp): The Case of the Upper
Galilee Kibbutzim and Kiryat Shmona, 1949–1953." *Journal of Israeli History* 35, no. 1
(2016): 17–37.

Grigor, Talinn. *Building Iran: Modernism, Architecture, and National Heritage under the Pahlavi Monarchs.* New York: Periscope/Prestel, 2009.

Guardian. "Iran's Economy Struggles to Support Ahmadinejad's Ill-Conceived Housing Vision." January 30, 2014. http://www.theguardian.com/world/iran-blog/2014/jan/30/irans-economy-struggles-to-support-ahmadinejads-ill-conceived-housing-vision.

Hadjri, Karim. "Vernacular Housing Forms in North Algeria." *Traditional Dwellings and Settlements Review* 5, no. 1 (1993): 65–74.

Hatherly, Owen. "The Cult of Self-Build and Do-It-Yourself Won't Solve the Housing Crisis." *dezeen magazine,* January 29, 2016. http://www.dezeen.com/2016/01/29/opinion-owen-hatherley-social-mass-housing-versus-self-build-idealism-walter-segal/.

Hegedüs, József, Martin Lux, and Nóra Teller, eds. *Social Housing in Transition Countries.* Abingdon-on-Thames, UK: Routledge, 2013.

Henderson, Susan R. "Ernst May and the Campaign to Resettle the Countryside: Rural Housing in Silesia, 1919–1925." *Journal of the Society of Architectural Historians* 61, no. 2 (2002): 188–211.

Heynen, Hilde. *Architecture and Modernity: A Critique.* Cambridge, MA: MIT Press, 1999.

Hosagrahar, Jyoti. *Indigenous Modernities: Negotiating Architecture, Urbanism, and Colonialism in Delhi.* Abingdon-on-Thames, UK: Routledge, 2005.

Human Rights Watch. "Building Towers, Cheating Workers: Exploitation of Migrant Construction Workers in the United Arab Emirates." Vol. 18, no. 8(E) (November 2006). http://www.hrw.org/en/reports/2006/11/11/building-towers-cheating-workers.

Human Rights Watch. "'The Island of Happiness': Exploitation of Migrant Workers on Saadiyat Island, Abu Dhabi," May 2009. https://www.hrw.org/report/2009/05/19/island-happiness/exploitation-migrant-workers-saadiyat-island-abu-dhabi.

Kaes, Anton, Martin Jay, and Edward Dimendberg, eds. *The Weimar Republic Sourcebook.* Berkeley: University of California Press, 1995.

Kahrik, Anneli, and Juri Kore. "Residualization of Social Housing and the New Programs." In *Social Housing in Transition Countries,* edited by József Hegedüs, Martin Lux, and Nóra Teller, 163–79. New York: Routledge, 2013.

Keil, Roger. "Third Way Urbanism: Opportunity or Dead End?" *Alternatives* 25, no. 2 (2000): 247–67.

Keskin-Kozat, Burçak. "Negotiating Modernization through US Foreign Assistance: Turkey's Marshall Plan (1948–1952) Re-interpreted." PhD diss., University of Michigan, 2006.

Kezer, Zeynep. *Building Modern Turkey: State, Space, and Ideology in the Early Republic.* Pittsburgh, PA: University of Pittsburgh Press, 2015.

Khan, Hasan-Uddin. "A New Paradigm: Global Urbanism and Architecture of Rapidly Developing Countries," *International Journal of Islamic Architecture* 3, no. 1 (2014): 5–34.

King, Anthony D. "Cultures and Spaces of Postcolonial Knowledges." In *Handbook of Cultural Geography,* edited by Kay Anderson, Mona Domosh, Steve Pile, and Nigel Thrift, 381–97. London: Sage, 2003.

———. "Internationalism, Imperialism, Postcolonialism, Globalization: Frameworks for Vernacular Architecture." *Perspectives in Vernacular Architecture* 13, no. 2 (2006–7): 64–75.

———. *Spaces of Global Cultures: Architecture, Urbanism, Identity.* New York: Routledge, 2004.

Kozlovsky, Roy. "Temporal States of Architecture: Mass Immigration and Provisional Housing in Israel." In *Modernism and the Middle East: Architecture and Politics in the Twen-

tieth Century, edited by Sandy Isenstadt and Kishwar Rizvi, 139–60. Seattle: University of Washington Press, 2008.

Kusno, Abidin. *Behind the Postcolonial: Architecture, Urban Space and Political Cultures in Indonesia*. London: Routledge, 2000.

Lepik, Andres. "Think Global, Build Social! Contemporary Architects Are Actively Involved in Society." In *Think Global, Build Social! Architectures for a Better World*, 12–13. Munich: Goethe Institut, 2013.

Lind, Maria. "Late-Modernist Housing." *ArtReview*, April 2014. http://artreview.com/opinion /april_2014_opinion_maria_lind_late-modernist_housing/.

Lu, Duanfang, ed. *Remaking Chinese Urban Form: Modernity, Scarcity and Space, 1949–2005*. London: Routledge, 2006.

———. *Third World Modernism: Architecture, Development, and Identity*. London: Routledge, 2011.

Mairs, Jessica. "Richard Rogers' Prefabricated Housing for Homeless People Opens in South London." *dezeen magazine*, September 8, 2015. http://www.dezeen.com/2015/09/08 /richard-rogers-prefabricated-housing-for-homeless-people-opens-in-south-london -mitcham-merton/.

Maxim, Juliana. "Bucharest: The City Transfigured." In *Sanctioning Modernism: Architecture and the Making of Postwar Identities*, edited by Vladimir Kulić, Timothy Parker, and Monica Penick, 11–36. Austin: University of Texas Press, 2014.

McKnight, Jenna. "Alejandro Aravena Makes Housing Designs Available to the Public for Free." *dezeen magazine*, April 6, 2016. http://www.dezeen.com/2016/04/06/alejandro -aravena-elemental-social-housing-designs-architecture-open-source-pritzker/.

Mumford, Eric Paul. *The CIAM Discourse on Urbanism, 1928–1960*. Cambridge, MA: MIT Press, 2000.

Osten, Marion von. "Carrières Centrales." May 3, 2012. http://transculturalmodernism.org /article/131.

PBS Newshour. "Architecture Becomes a Tool to Fight Poverty through this Pritzker Winner," January 13, 2016. http://www.pbs.org/newshour/bb/architecture-becomes-a-tool-to -fight-poverty-through-this-pritzker-winner/.

Plumb, Craig, Hicham Hassouni, and Salah Sahyoun. *Why Affordable Housing Matters?* Dubai, UAE: Jones Lang LaSalle, September 18, 2011. http://www.jll-mena.com/mena /en-gb/Research/JLLMENA_Affordable%20Housing_2011.pdf.

Pouliot, Hugh. "Between the Medina and the Metropole: Race and Urban Planning from Algiers to Paris (1930–75)." PhD diss., Dalhousie University, 2011.

Power, Anne. *Hovels to High Rise: State Housing in Europe since 1950*. London: Routledge, 1993.

Prakash, Vikramaditya. "Epilogue: Third World Modernism, or Just Modernism; Towards a Cosmopolitan Reading of Modernism." In *Third World Modernism: Architecture, Development, and Identity*, edited by Duanfang Lu, 255–76. London: Routledge, 2011.

Quataert, Donald. "Ottoman History Writing and Changing Attitudes towards the Notion of 'Decline.'" *History Compass* 1 (August 2003): 1–10.

Radford, Talia. "Refugee Camps Are the 'Cities of Tomorrow,' Says Humanitarian-Aid Expert." *dezeen magazine*, November 23, 2015. https://www.dezeen.com/2015/11/23/refugee -camps-cities-of-tomorrow-killian-kleinschmidt-interview-humanitarian-aid-expert/.

Raymond, André. "The Rabʿ: A Type of Collective Housing in Cairo during the Ottoman Period." In *Architecture as Symbol and Self-Identity*, edited by Jonathan G. Katz, 55–62. Philadelphia: Aga Khan Award for Architecture, 1980.

Republic of Iraq, Ministry of Construction and Housing. "Iraq Housing Market Study: Main Report." Prepared by PADCO in cooperation with Community Development Group Iraqi Central Office of Statistics and Information Technology, December 2006. http://www.humanitarianlibrary.org/sites/default/files/2013/05/4997_65700_IHMS_Main_Report.pdf.

Santelli, Serge. "Self-Built Urban Housing, Rabat and Tunis." *Mimar* 17 (July–September 1985): 41–48.

Sarkis, Hashim. *Circa 1958: Lebanon in the Pictures and Plans of Constantinos Doxiadis.* Beirut: Dar An-Nahar, 2003.

Shehayeb, Dina, and Shahira Issa, eds. *Cairo Resilience: The City as Personal Practice.* DIWAN Series, edited by Philipp Misselwitz and Can Altay, published in collaboration with Prince Claus Fund for Culture and Development and the International Architecture Biennale Rotterdam, 2009.

Sideway, James D. "Postcolonial Geographies: An Exploratory Essay." *Progress in Human Geography* 24, no. 4 (2000): 591–612.

Stanek, Łukasz. "Mobilities of Architecture in the Late Cold War: From Socialist Poland to Kuwait, and Back." *International Journal of Islamic Architecture* 4, no. 2 (2015): 365–98.

Strava, Cristiana. "Adaptations of Vernacular Modernism in Casablanca." *Polis*, July 4, 2012. http://www.thepolisblog.org/2012/07/adaptations-of-vernacular-modernism.html.

Stronski, Paul. *Tashkent: Forging a Soviet City, 1930–1966.* Pittsburgh, PA: University of Pittsburgh Press, 2010.

Tafuri, Manfredo. *Architecture and Utopia: Design and Capitalist Development.* Translated by Barbara Luigia La Penta. Cambridge, MA: MIT Press, 1976.

Tafuri, Manfredo, and Francesco Dal Co. *Modern Architecture 1.* London: Faber and Faber/Electa, 1986.

Tankut, Gönül. *Bir Başkentin İmarı, Ankara: 1929–1939* [The construction of a capital city, Ankara: 1929–1939] Ankara: Middle East Technical University, 1990.

Tekeli, İlhan. "Türkiye Kentlerinde Apartmanlaşma Sürecinde İki Aşama" [Two phases in the "apartmentization" process in Turkish cities], *Çevre* (July–August 1979): 79.

Theodosis, Lefteris. "'Containing' Baghdad: Constantinos Doxiadis's Program for a Developing Nation." In *Ciudad del Espejismo: Bagdad, de Wright a Venturi* [City of mirage: Baghdad from Wright to Venturi], edited by Pedro Azara, 167–72. Barcelona: Universitat Politècnica de Catalunya, 2008.

———. "Victory over Chaos? Constantinos A. Doxiadis and Ekistics, 1945–1975." PhD diss., Universitat Politècnica de Catalunya, 2015.

Tokman, L. Yıldız. *Konut Politikaları Uygulamalarında Özel Bir Örnek: Yenimahalle* [A special example in the implementation of housing policies: Yenimahalle], Ankara: KentKoop Yayınları, 1985.

Türeli, İpek. "'Small' Architectures: Walking and Camping in Middle Eastern Cities." *International Journal of Islamic Architecture* 2, no. 1 (2013): 5–38.

United Nations Economic Commission for Europe. "The Future of Social Housing: Environmental and Social Challenges and the Way Forward." Workshop report, United Nations Economic Commission for Europe, February 4–5, 2015, Geneva, Switzerland, 1–72.

United Nations Relief and Works Agency for Palestine Refugees (UNRWA). "Where We Work." https://www.unrwa.org/where-we-work/jordan/zarqa-camp.

Urban, Florian. *Tower and Slab: Histories of Global Mass Housing.* Abingdon, UK: Routledge, 2011.

Wagner, Bernard. *Housing and Urban Development in the Philippines*. Manila: USAID (Housing and Urban Development Division), 1968.

———. *Housing in India*. 2 vols. New Delhi: B. Wagner, 1964,

Wheeler, Brian. "A History of Social Housing." *BBC NEWS*, April 14, 2015. http://www.bbc .com/news/uk-14380936.

Yücel, Şebnem. "Minority Heterotopias: The Cortijos of İzmir." *Architectural Research Quarterly* 20, no. 3 (2016): 245–56.

Zapatrina, Irina. "The Ukraine: Waiting Lists without Housing." In *Social Housing in Transition Countries*, edited by József Hegedüs, Martin Lux, and Nóra Teller, 292–303. New York: Routledge, 2013.

Zimmer, Lori. "IKEA Unveils Solar-Powered Flat Pack Shelters for Easily Deployable Emergency Housing." *Inhabitat*, November 11, 2013. http://inhabitat.com/ikeas-solar -powered-flat-pack-refugee-shelters-offer-easily-deployable-emergency-housing/.

KIVANÇ KILINÇ is Assistant Professor of architecture at Yaşar University in Turkey. He received his PhD (2010) in the History and Theory of Art and Architecture Graduate Program at SUNY Binghamton and his master's degree at the Middle East Technical University (2002). He also serves as managing editor of the *International Journal of Islamic Architecture*. Kılınç has published in such academic journals as *Architectural Histories, History and Memory, Digital Scholarship in the Humanities*, and *The Journal of Architecture*, as well as in edited books. His current research focuses on the transnational connections and their consequences that shaped social housing practices in contemporary Turkey and the Middle East.

MOHAMMAD GHARIPOUR is Professor at the School of Architecture and Planning at Morgan State University in Baltimore. He obtained his master's in architecture from the University of Tehran and his PhD in architecture and landscape history at Georgia Institute of Technology. He has received several grants and awards, including the Hamad Bin Khalifa Fellowship in Islamic Art, the Spiro Kostof Fellowship Award from the Society of Architectural Historians, the National Endowment in Humanities Faculty Award, and a publication award from the Foundation for Landscape Studies. Gharipour has published nine books, including *Bazaar in the Islamic City* (American University of Cairo Press, 2012), *Persian Gardens and Pavilions: Reflections in Poetry, Arts and History* (I. B. Tauris, 2013), *Historiography of Persian Architecture* (Taylor and Francis, 2015), *Contemporary Urban Landscapes of the Middle East* (Routledge, 2016), and *Synagogues of the Islamic World* (Edinburgh University Press, 2017). Gharipour is director and founding editor of the *International Journal of Islamic Architecture*.

PART I

SETTINGS OF SOCIAL HOUSING: POLITICS, AGENCY, AND SOCIAL REFORM

2

LEGITIMIZING THE JORDANIAN STATE THROUGH SOCIAL HOUSING

Eliana Abu-Hamdi

IN 1988, THE GREATER AMMAN COMPREHENSIVE DEVELOPMENT PLAN (the GACDP) called for the development of a new satellite city called Abu Nuseir. Constructed by the National Housing Corporation, the city consists of 3,667 dwelling units in apartment blocks separated by breezeways and single-family houses, all surrounding open spaces.[1] The design was chosen with measured intentions. It was meant to dismantle established forms of traditional communities and create a more modern and therefore more easily governable society to better ensure and maintain regime security, the autonomy of the state, and, by extension, the king. This bold planning occurred in the midst of an era of modernization in which planning debates in Jordan, and elsewhere in the world, shifted from issues of hygiene and the utopian ideals of the garden city to the nature of the modern city, public services, and the role of the state as an agent of social transformation.[2]

In Jordan, this transformation took on the tenor of nationalism and civic unity promoted through the provision of social housing and municipal growth. The construction of social housing was made possible by the consolidation of independent tribal village councils into one regulating body, the Greater Amman Municipality (GAM). Those responsible for the GACDP deemed the consolidation a necessary technical solution to a preexisting technical problem,[3] one that afforded the added benefit of destabilizing tribal control over development. According to the GACDP, the tribes had disproportionate control over the development of Amman, which was incommensurate with the state's expansion goals. The dissolution of these independent villages asserted the state's presence as a bureaucratic network and imposed regulations intended to disrupt the parochial and self-serving practices of the tribes. This move both solidified the state and redefined citizenship in terms of rights and privileges for pronationalists, or East Bank Jordanians, as opposed to Palestinian migrants.

To extend the reach of the state, the GACDP created the site plan and house design for new residential communities and went on to designate the ideal resident type, namely middle-income government employees.[4] The GACDP declared the benefit of the newly conceptualized public housing complex a state benefit and also made clear its bureaucratic responsibilities, or lack thereof, toward Palestinian refugee camps. The plan definitively resolved that the Jordanian government was not responsible for improvements to, or maintenance of, the refugee camps. This decisive position effectively exiled the camps, excluding them from the city and therefore from future municipal provisions.[5] Further, King Hussein's autocratic approach shone through in the way the state dispensed municipal benefits and financial subsidies. Areas of the city occupied by Palestinians received fewer subsidies. Those residing in the camps did not qualify for subsidies, as they are supported by United Nations Relief and Works Agency (UNRWA).[6] With government housing provided exclusively for the urban middle class, the Palestinian minority was, by default, situated as a provisionless low-income community.

Bureaucratic hostility toward the Palestinian community stemmed from growing hot spots of Palestinian nationalism that not only diluted the already tenuous sense of Jordanian identity but challenged the security of the regime directly through an attempted takeover of the Jordanian government that ultimately resulted in the 1970 civil war known as Black September. To temper the threats to his regime, Hussein launched a bureaucratic system that celebrated Jordanian identity and rewarded nationalism.[7] As much as public housing symbolized unity and nationalism for the East Bank Jordanian middle-class community, the lack thereof symbolized the state's political control over the large refugee camps in Amman and the remaining Palestinian communities throughout Jordan.

This chapter traces the discourse on public housing as a tool of social governance into the twenty-first century and presents evidence of the state's failure to exert social control through the provision of public housing. For all the city's and the monarchy's planning efforts, stark disparities and exclusions, socially and economically, persist in Amman, and the growing low-income class of East Bank Jordanians is as ill-housed as the Palestinians were decades prior. Further, this chapter will cite interviews conducted in 2013 with planning officials in the GAM to present the internal failings of the 1980s bureaucratization of Amman, arguing that despite decades of effort to dismantle traditional systems of social organization, tribalism remains a powerful force in urban planning in the city.

A Brief History of the Monarchy of Jordan

The Jordanian state was formalized in 1946 after its release from the British Mandate. First to govern the nation was King Abdullah I, as prince of Transjordan in 1924 and later as king of the Hashemite Kingdom of Jordan. After governing for only five years, Abdullah I was assassinated in Jerusalem on July 20, 1951, by a Palestinian gunman. Philip Robins, a political scientist at Oxford University, has argued that the assassination was an expression of Palestinian resentment and the desire to allocate blame for their dispossession.[8] This argument is supported by an account of growing Palestinian aggression against the monarchy, which, in 1970, culminated in the civil war. After Abdullah's assassination, despite open concern about his mental stability, Talal, his eldest son, was crowned king. His reign lasted for less than a year. Parliament, feeling great concern over Talal's erratic behavior (particularly his desire for political liberalization), declared him incapable of ruling.[9] King Hussein, Talal's son, began his reign in 1952 and continued for forty-seven years, until 1999. As noted by historian Mary Wilson, he came to be called the father of modern Jordan.[10]

King Hussein spent the early years of his reign in the 1950s and 1960s building a strong military. McGill University political scientist Rex Brynen has argued that this military force was "a primary vehicle of Jordanian state-building, bringing the Bedouin population of the East Bank under state control."[11] Now on the government payroll, a large number of East Bank Bedouins served as both agents of the state and a source of its support. In addition, throughout the 1970s and 1980s, the state continued to employ a substantial number of civil servants and dispensed large amounts of social welfare to its citizens. The state funded an ever-increasing standard of living and with it purchased obedience from its citizens. It was thus able to enjoy autonomy and become unaccountable to the public for any state decisions.

Only the parochial and communal practices of the city's various indigenous tribes, a hindrance to the modernization efforts and nationalist agenda of the state, threatened Hussein's autonomy. Linda Layne, in her study of tribes and nationalism in Jordan, observes that tribalism as a practice was "incompatible with full participation in a modern nation-state."[12] Tribe and nation in Jordan exist as a perpetual dialectic, one in which systems of traditionalism are in constant conflict with systems of modernization, and in this case, nation formation. Further, tribal land holdings and their decisions about private-interest development proved doubly problematic for the state and its attempts to take control of urban growth and transformation. The implementation of the GACDP countered tribal dominance, providing the state with a bureaucratic strategy to assert government controls, replacing tribal governance networks with a single, comprehensive governing body, the GAM.

Hussein struggled throughout his reign to establish GAM as the main governing body in Amman. Often planning decisions were infiltrated by parochialism, favoritism, and ultimately poorly written municipal rules and regulations that governed/regulated city planning and urbanization. These problems persisted into the reign of King Abdullah, Hussein's son and successor. Hussein attempted to develop a broad bureaucratic system to unravel the deep-rooted Bedouin practices, but, as a planner at GAM expressed in an interview, inequitable practices, discrimination, lack of awareness or concern for disparities, internal politicization of planning, and the persistent power of tribal and wealthy elites have continued to dominate planning logic in Amman, resulting in "short-sightedness, not being sensitive, comprehensive, not being bound to proper planning practice, [and] not having real democracy."[13] While Abdullah attempted to right a planning system gone wrong, deeply entrenched unregulated practices cannot be undone, as is evidenced by a public housing system in the twenty-first century that is as ill-conceived as it was in the 1980s. The only difference, however, is that low-income housing, once limited to the boundaries of the refugee camp, has become, under Abdullah's purview, a subsidy of the state.

The Expansion of the Bureaucratic Systems of the State

The development of the GACDP was made possible by a decade of great financial prosperity and a surprisingly sedate political climate. The financial growth of Jordan was fueled primarily by abundant foreign remittances and rentier capital grants from neighboring oil-rich nations. Saudi Arabia alone provided Jordan with $360 million per year between 1978 and 1988.[14] This enabled the state to provide substantial subsidies and welfare programs to its citizens that succeeded in accomplishing two important things for the state. As Brynen notes, the state purchased its autonomy through the dispensation of state benefits, in turn freeing itself from addressing domestic actors and their demands.[15] State-subsidized living enabled a system of "no taxation—no representation," which in turn provided the state with autonomy and freedom from accountability to its constituents.[16] Brynen further claims that "political legitimacy is, in a very real sense, 'purchased' through economic rewards. The distribution of state benefits (statutory or otherwise) thus overshadows both demands for redistribution and the importance of productive employment within society."[17] In exchange for the provision of social welfare, the state thus had relative autonomy in government decisions, including the conception and implementation of the GACDP.

The institutionalization of the state entailed a comprehensive review of state policies in all venues of planning and regulation.[18] The plan was written by a team of experts called the Joint Technical Team, composed of a private international consultant firm called Dar al-Handasah Consultants and personnel supplied by the municipality.[19] The GACDP presented a resolute, though agentless, set of recommendations for the improvement and modernization of Amman. The plan also recommended a variety of bureaucratic decrees and municipal regulations intended to moderate the impact of tribalism and Arab-Israeli political disputes, particularly as they manifest in hot spots of Palestinian nationalism in Jordan (fig. 2.1).

The primary and overarching goal of the 1988 GACDP was "to strengthen government control over all development."[20] In its final report, the GACDP presented findings on land ownership and existing development, concluding that the lack of state presence in the planning of Amman resulted from insufficiency in its land holdings.[21] The government owned only 28,580 *dunums* (approximately 285,000 square meters), or 5 percent of the total land within the municipal boundaries. The remaining 95 percent of land was privately owned and governed by the market-driven planning decisions of village councils. The central government was essentially powerless to direct development and urban growth in Amman.[22] By 1987, independent village councils had constructed twenty-four housing developments, while public housing developments numbered only eight.[23] The state was clearly not a significant actor in the development of Amman.

The GACDP presented a much-needed opportunity for the state to impose its control over developmental functions, thus embarking on a massive bureaucratization of the city, dovetailed with a campaign for Jordanian nationalism.

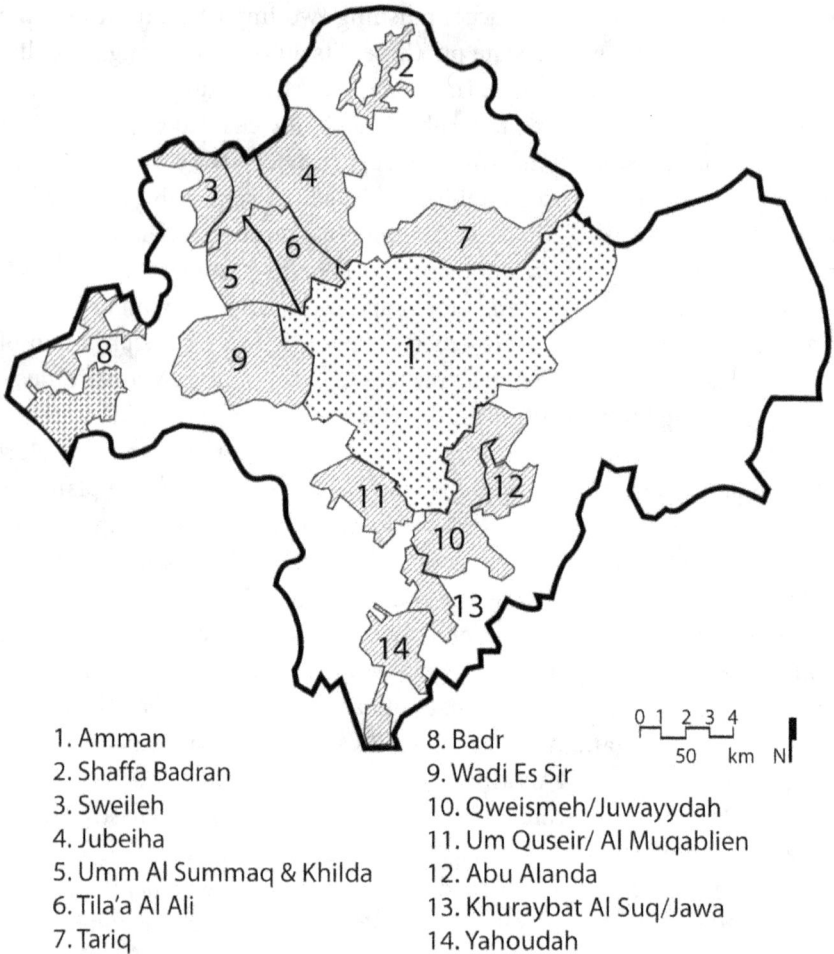

1. Amman
2. Shaffa Badran
3. Sweileh
4. Jubeiha
5. Umm Al Summaq & Khilda
6. Tila'a Al Ali
7. Tariq
8. Badr
9. Wadi Es Sir
10. Qweismeh/Juwayydah
11. Um Quseir/ Al Muqablien
12. Abu Alanda
13. Khuraybat Al Suq/Jawa
14. Yahoudah

Figure 2.1. Original municipalities. *Greater Amman Comprehensive Development Plan*, 2.4. Greater Amman Municipality, 1988.

During this era, nationalism came in the form of public, or subsidized, housing. Abu Nuseir targeted middle-income residents, serving several purposes. It extended the bureaucratic reach of the state by providing a highly sought after, and otherwise unattainable, commodity to the public: homeownership. In so doing, the state was able to exercise its bureaucratic control by providing a desirable public good. The architecture of this housing development embraced modern ideals of simple and uniform design. The site planning did not promote communal living, at least not in the traditional sense of the courtyard home, the otherwise dominant residential type. With the construction of Abu Nuseir, the state defined the architectural and political aesthetic of middle-income housing. Similarly, however, the state also defined its role in low-income housing, specifically in refugee camp housing for Palestinian residents. With the construction of Abu Nuseir, the state had accomplished the goal of, first, delineating classes, and second, delineating classes according to political allegiance. In other words, those who were Jordanian—or, at the least, allied to the state—tended to be middle-income and provided for. Those who were not, tended to be Palestinian, of low income, and residing in poor housing stock. It is thus not a coincidence that in the 1980s, and well into the twenty-first century, the majority of Palestinian refugee camps have been ill maintained and overpopulated. Bureaucratic actions enabled the impoverishment of Palestinian areas, as they did the growth of predominantly Jordanian areas.

Palestinian Refugee Camps of Amman

It was thus, by default, that low-income residents, those not benefiting from the state's generous welfare system, were the Palestinians in various refugee camps in Amman. Housing in these refugee camps was, for the most part, auto-constructed, supported by funding from UNRWA.[24,25] As in many other auto-constructed enclaves, housing units within the camp developed from the tents provided by UNRWA to more permanent structures, where rooms were hastily added when financially viable and necessary to accommodate a growing family. While the GACDP took particular care to provide public housing for citizens, the plan did not extend similar benefits to Palestinians. The GACDP frequently refers to the numerous refugee camps and squatter settlements in Amman, but only to note that the settlements are in need of maintenance and improvement.[26] The plan summarily declares that the camps are the responsibility not of the government, but of UNRWA.[27] Further, the GACDP five-year plan designated 951,964 Jordanian dinars,[28] or 35 percent of proposed regional investment, for development and improvement of three Transjordanian[29] governates—'Tafilah, Karak, and Ma'an—representing only 10 percent of the population.[30] In this way, the GACDP institutionalized the plainly disproportionate allocation of state funds in favor of East Bank Jordanians.

The level of discontent, perhaps even animosity, projected by the state toward its Palestinian population stems from the numerous Arab-Israeli conflicts, which directly affected the economic and political relationships between Jordan and other nations. Philip Robins argues that the economic, demographic, sociological, and, most important, political history of Jordan was transformed by the Palestinian conflicts (and subsequent refugee influxes) into the country during its formative years from 1946 to 1972.[31] He argues further that each of these instances, ranging from an overnight influx of more than three hundred thousand refugees in 1948 to the loss of the West Bank in 1967—the country's most lucrative area for natural resources—scripted Jordan's political position and defined its capacities for domestic production and international trade.[32] The war of 1967 traumatized Jordan and made clear three things to King Hussein. First, diplomacy was indispensable. Jordan could not stand or sustain itself alone. Second, it certainly could not take on a conflict with Israel's unbeatable military. And finally, Hussein realized that Jordan was in fact a weak state and would have very little political influence on the region, so he focused his energy on strategizing to prevent war and any further conflict through diplomacy.[33] In other words, Jordan was politically traumatized by the many Arab-Israeli conflicts over the years, placing it in a condition of dependence for political guidance and support.

In 2010, UNRWA reported 1,983,733 refugees still living in the thirteen Palestinian refugee camps in Amman.[34] University of Louisville anthropologist Julie Peteet noted that the camps had become a commemorative space of deterritorialization and dispossession, marked with a sense of "dependency and humiliation," in that refugees felt labeled as victims in need of charity.[35] The camps also "symbolized colossal loss and defeat, but they also became a potent political field in which to organize and express national identity and sentiment."[36] The fear of invisibility fueled the Palestinian longing for home, the reacquisition of territories, and political rights. As a result, social and political practice manifested in an intangible way within in the camp, not necessarily connected to the *place* they occupied. Rochelle Davis, a cultural anthropologist at Georgetown University, noted that Palestinians, upon exile, sought foremost to recreate social hierarchies and relationships as a way to define their position in society. Once exiled to a camp, a Bedouin may be next to a rural peasant and also next to an urban resident. Such was the architecture of the camp, wherein social identities that existed in Palestine were now broken. Camp occupants therefore looked at their new social surrounding and sought to place themselves within the hierarchy. Without homes or possessions, identity could not be informed by housing commodity, as it was within Jordanian communities. Rather, family name and social standing informed identity. In this way, much of camp tradition relied on a memory of a past and the affective re-creation, or perhaps reimagination, of a Palestinian place and identity. As Davis explains, "Palestinian national identification is framed in terms of geographic origin and sentiment toward Palestine, and hence the name Palestinian. Palestinian nationalism has been and continues to be a land-based identity, rooted in discourse about an integral relationship between people and the land, unlike other identification practices in which people think of themselves in categorical ways that bind them to other people, such as shared ethnicity, religious affiliations, common language, or national origin."[37]

Refugee camp politics, for the most part, revolved around the propagation and maintenance of a shared Palestinian identity, passed on to future generations. Village histories document this lost past, abundant with maps and charts that call out names and residences, laying a claim to territories through this insider knowledge of the *place*. These village histories continue to be written and published in the twenty-first century, commemorating the past and documenting social histories through time, providing a compass for Palestinian national identity in the face of larger global trends.[38] But tribalism, kinship, and communalism were not as severe a threat to the state as they were within the East Bank Jordanian population. In other words, Palestinian political and social activism was confined to the camps after the civil war and was not in competition with the state's nationalist agenda.

It was clear that Palestinian nationalism was transcendent and unshakable in its attachment to the *place* it originated from. In their work on the Baqa'a refugee camp, the largest of the thirteen in Amman, Jamal Alnsour and Julia Meaton—professors at the German Jordanian University and the University of Huddersfield, respectively—suggest that in fact there is little attachment between the Palestinian refugees and the camp they reside in, specifically the dwelling within it.[39] Furthermore, they draw a correlation between the livability and maintenance of the home and the emotional attachment of the residents to it. But, as Davis suggests, identity is not connected to the dwelling, but rather to larger nationalist structures that trespass on the boundaries of the home, camp, and host nation. Subsequently, houses in refugee camps are ill maintained and in a constant state of deterioration. Limitations on its funds prevent UNRWA from providing sufficient support to amend the deterioration, and, as previously stated, the Jordanian government is unwilling to participate in maintaining the camps.

The physical conditions of these dwellings are consequently subpar, and the camps are little more than overpopulated shantytowns. Density in the various camps ranges from 29,000 to 115,000 persons per square kilometer (78,000 to 310,000 per square mile), above the average 30,000 inhabitants per square kilometer in other overcrowded places, such as the cities of Kolkata and Mumbai.[40] The majority of dwellings were auto-constructed and did not adhere to any building code or planning regulation. Neither UNRWA nor the Jordanian municipality took steps to manage construction types or techniques, as to do so was considered a mark of permanency and a violation of the Palestinian community's belief in *al awda*, or the right to return to Palestine. Houses therefore vary in shape, size, design, and color. The regularity of the three-bay villa and courtyard home, most dominant in East Amman, is absent from the refugee camps. The low-income residents of the camps rather use found materials to amend and expand their dwellings when possible in irregular and inconsistent ways.[41] Alnsour and Meaton conducted a survey of seven hundred representative dwellings in Al Baqa'a camp and found the majority to be in violation of building codes and poorly ventilated, insulated, and constructed, rendering the structures unstable, particularly in the case of hasty additions. Finally, for infrastructure, the camp relied on sewerage, electricity, and water connections provided by the Jordanian government in the 1970s that were never maintained afterward. As a result, the majority of houses in Alnsour and Meaton's study group reported these services to be inadequate; most have running water in their dwellings only two days a week and electricity three days a week.[42] As a result of a prolonged state of perceived impermanency, a lack of attachment to the dwelling within the camp, and the disinvestment of the Jordanian government, the refugee camps in Amman remain the largest low-income housing sectors of the city.

The *Bayt*

In contrast, the *bayt*, a graduated iteration of the traditional Circassian hut of the late nineteenth and early twentieth centuries, was the dominant middle-income housing type in the city.[43] The Circassians, expelled from Russia, where they were in fear of religious persecution, first migrated to Jordan in 1878.[44] Upon arriving in the area today known as downtown Amman, they had few building materials available to construct houses. Living among remaining Roman ruins, they borrowed stones from these monuments as building material for their settler huts. To grow Amman into a modern city, the settlers systematically dismantled the classical city, which University of Durham geographer Jane Hacker called "one of the handsomest cities of Imperial Rome outside of Italy."[45] The resulting hut architecture was a simple orthogonal form with a thatch roof that could be easily and quickly constructed.

As Amman's population continued to grow, more villas were constructed in this aesthetic, dominating the urban landscape.[46] Located in an area called Jabal Amman, near the downtown, is a very typical example, today used as a primary school, called the Arwa Bint al-Hareth School, originally commissioned by Rustom Rasheed Hashem (fig. 2.2). The basic architectural principles of the *bayt* (plural: *buyut*), or three-bay villa, consists of a simple cubic form with window bays along the front elevation and a series of interior rooms surrounding a central hall,[47] which was, as University of Nevada historian Marwan Daoud Hanania notes, the most often used room in the house to host family gatherings and visitors.[48] The use of the various spaces was dictated by what Rensselaer Polytechnic Institute anthropologist Linda Layne calls "Arab architectonics," or the manners and postures of tribal communities and their practices within the home, which represent larger political structures and define social and tribal identities.[49]

In her analysis, Samantha Laine, now the Digital Media Producer at the Christian Science Monitor, notes the growing sophistication of the architecture and importance of the home in the 1970s and 1980s is a mark of an imminent integration into a capitalist mode of production.[50] In other words, while tribal traditions showed exceptional resiliency in the face of ever-growing state structures, the capitalist nature of competition infiltrated, in this case taking shape in the evolving design and aesthetic of the traditional home, influenced by surrounding areas of the Levant. For example, though the Circassian house can be considered a humble expression of modern simplicity, the *bayt* represented the growth of the region, as these houses were able to express both traditional elements and Western influences, integrated into traditional designs by the expertise of architects primarily from Palestine, Syria, and Lebanon, who had studied in Europe, Turkey, Egypt, and the United States.[51] Traditional elements and locally characteristic stone building blocks for exterior walls continued to be used widely, in addition to the installation of decorative tiles from Palestine that impressed visitors and conveyed the status of the owner. Within these communities, a *mukhtar* (village leader) would preside over and represent smaller units, such as a tribe, neighborhood, or group.[52] In deference to

Rainbow Street

Front Yard

Central Hall

Rear Yard

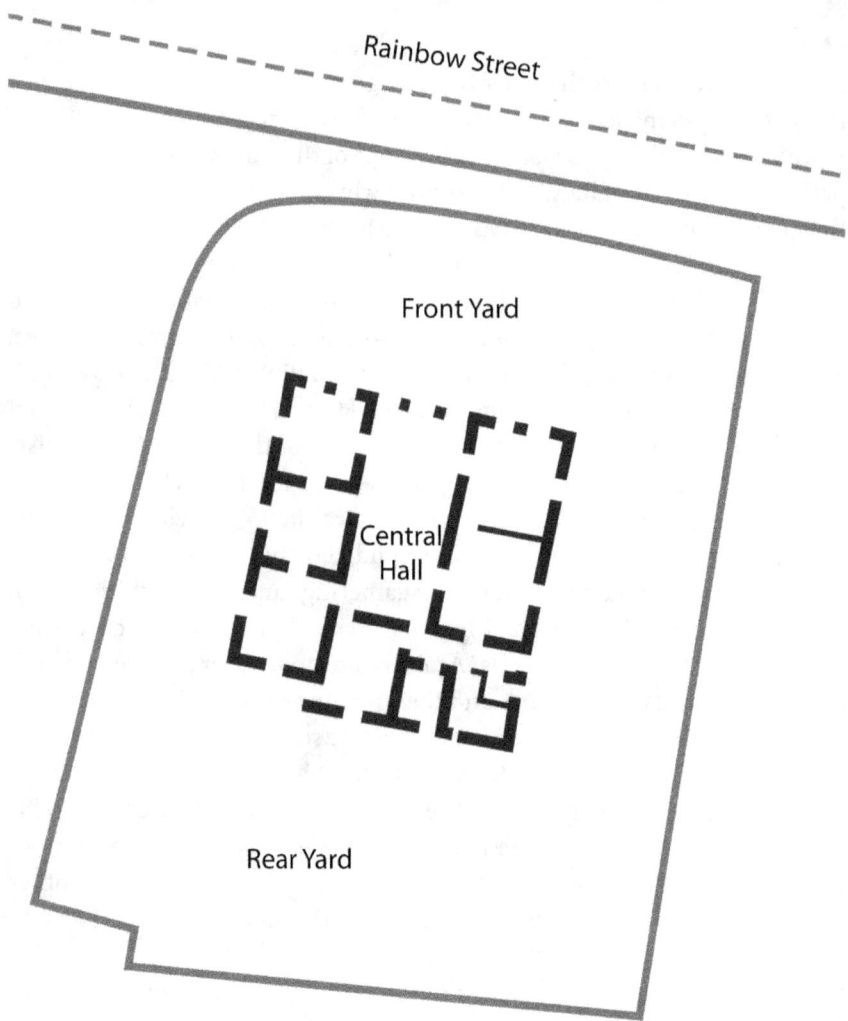

Figure 2.2. Hashem House. Photograph by Eliana Abu-Hamdi.

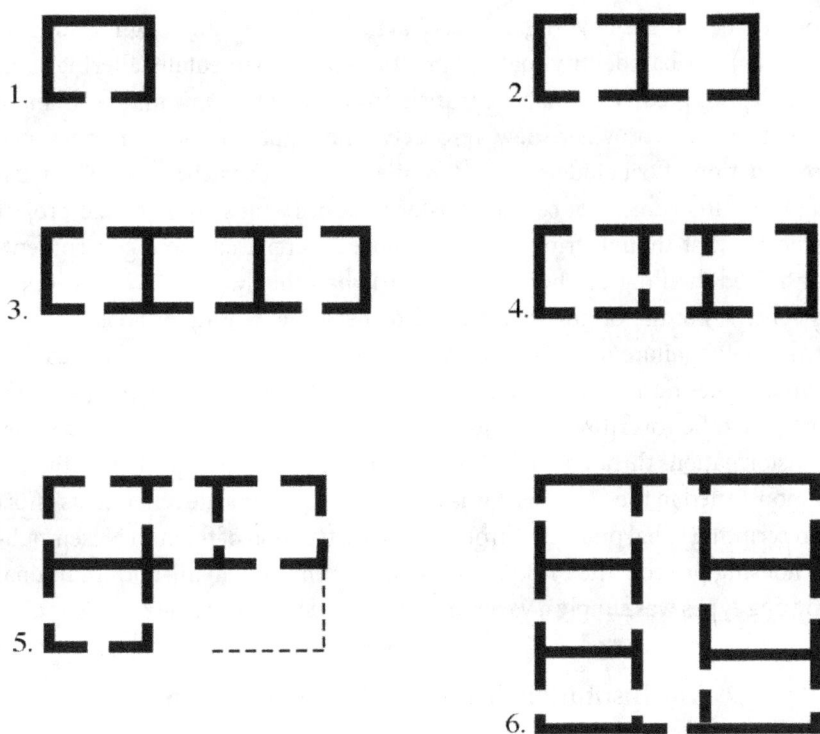

Figure 2.3. Vernacular architecture, Amman. Diagram by Eliana Abu-Hamdi.

the social hierarchy within these communities, the *mukhtar* always had the largest house, for to build one that was grander than his was a mark of disrespect. This is not to say that community-centric architecture and housing layout did not become increasingly sophisticated as rooms were added to the back of dwellings to accommodate a growing family. But as the rear of the dwelling expanded, the size and grandeur of the façade remained the same, always slightly less prestigious than that of the *mukhtar*'s home.

The population of Amman continued to grow as a result of the state's active promotion of rural to urban migration and the sedentarization of the various tribes. The state constructed a public housing project in the Jordan Valley, an agricultural corridor, in an effort to increasingly integrate Bedouin communities into an ever-growing bureaucratic system of provisions and welfare.[53] As migrant communities, Bedouin tribes traditionally constructed and transported tents as their domestic space. As the populations became more sedentary, however, the tents transitioned to mud huts, then stone houses, such as the *bayt* (fig. 2.3). As Layne notes, the state sought to under-mine some tribal identity-making practices by fundamentally altering their lifestyle, not predicting that the transition from tent to *bayt* and permanent residence "also provided new resources and opportunities for the social construction of tribal identities."[54] While the state constructed public hous-ing as an instrument of social transformation, Layne's study of the project indicates that though tribe members indeed purchased these government-subsidized dwellings, in her account nearly half the dwellings were occupied by renters, not the originally intended owners. The renting of houses hinted at the state's failure to maintain residency of Bedouin tribes of the area and demonstrates rather the persistent tradition of Bedouin mobility.[55] This is not to say that the government considered their attempt to promote desired social transformations through public housing a failure not to be repeated. Rather, as demonstrated in the GACDP, it was not long before the state renewed its effort at rescripting tribal practices through the construction of the Abu Nuseir pub-lic housing project. The 1988 plan to revise community living and traditional housing types was simply a variation on a decades-long theme.

The Institutionalization of Housing in Amman

The 1988 GACDP was the product of the "Jordanization" of the state, wherein "every state agency underwent a comprehensive review of its poli-cies in order to conform with the new concept of Jordan, changing regula-tions on everything from drivers licenses to marriage regulations."[56] The premise of this reform was to fundamentally reconfigure the state and fo-cus more on the production of a domestic identity and nationalist unity. To further promote Jordanian unity, the state inserted itself into public life, making itself indispensable to its citizens through the distribution of wel-fare benefits, particularly government-subsidized housing. In this era, pub-lic housing became a real, tangible vessel that projected the state's messages of nationalism and visions of a Jordanian, rather than tribal, identity. Abu Nuseir in particular represented a modern future, an alternative to tribal living, and, above all, a way to fulfill dreams of homeownership.

The Joint Team proposed the construction of satellite housing, such as Abu Nuseir, by designating resident communities on the basis of norma-tive socioeconomic data, including criteria such as economic compatibility and an area's need for an industrial workforce. The team ignored established social factors such as kinship or communalism as criteria for community grouping. As University of California anthropologist Paul Rabinow has argued, planners—the techno-experts in the modern era—viewed the city less as a sociopolitical space and more as a sociotechnical environment they could regulate.[57] Thus, the Joint Team intentionally designed the seven districts and associated housing projects according to criteria that better managed or "normalized" society.[58] The design of the new communities relied on what Rabinow calls a "middling modernism,"[59] concerned more with efficiency than with the social implications of the district "communities." Essentially, these districts, while communal, were strategically organized with no other binding feature, such as kinship or tribal affiliation, in mind.[60] Abu Nuseir provided a sense of community through proximate locations of dwellings and the provision of open spaces, but specifically not along the lines of kinship,[61] as the *buyut* of the previous generation could. Rather, Abu Nuseir presented a new homogeneous social composition with new social habits and new familial constructs. Conversely, the social structure of the *buyut* of the twentieth century is based upon the extended family and the traditional family structure, in which the married son often lives with his parents, or, at the very least, close to them.[62] The social complexity of the *bayt* is therefore dismantled within a homogenized housing system such as Abu Nuseir.

The Politics and Aesthetics of Abu Nuseir

Abu Nuseir was constructed by the National Housing Corporation and consists of 3,667 dwelling units arranged within a combination of apartment blocks and single-family houses. The purpose of the new city was to provide housing for middle-income government employees and to incentivize homeownership. The satellite city is located on the periphery of the municipal boundary, and its context and design served as a prototype for a modern way of life outside the network of tribal communalism. The Joint Team meticulously crafted the technocratic design of the complex. Fuad Malkawi—a planner and researcher and urban development specialist at the World Bank—conducted a series of interviews ten years after the city's completion. He notes several instances when Joint Team planners dismissed public needs and opinions because "people of the street do not know what is good for them"—in contrast to the team's technical expertise.[63]

Regardless, by 1999, twenty-two thousand people lived in the residential development, with an average household of six people.[64] Upon completion, nuclear families occupied most of the houses, the vast majority of which

Figure 2.4. Abu Nuseir public housing project, https://archnet.org/system/media_contents/contents/16341/original/IAA7318.JPG?.

had both a male and a female head of household, while a smaller number, less than 10 percent, had only a female head of household.[65] The overall demographics of Abu Nuseir were nearly uniform. For example, the overwhelming majority of residents were married, had finished high school, were full-time employees, and owned their home.[66] Most had moved to Abu Nuseir upon its completion, and none stated any plans to move away. The desire to stay, however, had less to do with overall satisfaction with a dwelling than with its affordability. Owning a dwelling in an urban area of Amman outside this development was simply infeasible. The affordability of the government-subsidized units at Abu Nuseir incentivized residents to separate from their previous communities for the opportunity to own a home.

Abu Nuseir is composed of a series of residential buildings whose design is inarguably modern in that it invokes Taylorist ideals of minimalist design, rationalization, and standardization of building components reminiscent of the International Congresses of Modern Architecture's (CIAM) ideals (see fig. 2.4).[67] The minimalist design did not consider individual or familial needs. Rather, CIAM design's sanitized and standardized

Figure 2.5. Panorama of Abu Nuseir public housing project. Architect: Schindler and Schindler, Amman, Jordan. Photograph by Saad Khrais, 2016.

appearance represents an architecture and planning that draw on a set of socialist ideals, and it is constructed, as UC Berkeley anthropologist Jim Holston explains, to serve as a template for *social transformation*: "modern architecture and planning are the means to create new forms of collective association, personal habit, and daily life."[68] Therefore, in creating a satellite city based on the principles of modern design, GAM created a new social norm of planning, one that was not based on communalism, kinship, or a traditional household. Further, Abu Nuseir's design correlates little with the GACDP's mandate that any proposed housing project use local materials and emulate indigenous architectural styles. Malkawi conducted an interview with an urban designer from the Joint Team, Samir Subhi, about the proposed organization of space and community in Abu Nuseir. Subhi openly acknowledged the unconventional design of the city but stated, "people will learn to adopt it. . . . [T]hey will learn about the use of the various amenities and the importance of open spaces by using them."[69] In other words, the technical experts in the field declared this new housing format the most appropriate, even if unfamiliar (fig. 2.5).

GAM in the Twenty-First Century

Critics and current planners often overlook the impact of the GACDP, regarding the program as yet another failed planning effort with few projects realized. It is not the projects or tangible results that are most relevant, however, but the social and cultural norms that the GACDP attempted to reinvent. This era, whether viewed as the Jordanization of the state, the modernization of Jordan, or the triumph of transnational rentierism, represents an aggressive attempt to define a nation and a people. The state could not actively disrupt cultural practices or redirect political allegiances, and so it disrupted the places where cultural practices took place: the home and, by extension, the community. The GACDP and its related regulations were the culmination of decades of struggle to moderate the impact of tribalism on state policies and the formation of a unified Jordanian identity.

GAM launched two campaigns, one in 2002 and a second in 2009, in a concerted effort to develop a branded identity for Amman. In addition, King Abdullah II, Hussein's son and successor, tried to encourage unity through a heavy-handed set of royal initiatives, the Jordan First Initiative, which was perhaps most aggressive in its focus on promoting systems of allegiance and nationalism. The initiative adduces notions of nationalism and unity, specifically suggesting that the public's desire for progress should conform to a vision heavily inflected by state interests. King Abdullah launched the initiative as a mechanism for molding a particular type of citizen, created by, as the initiative states, "a unified social fibre that promotes their sense of loyalty to their homeland, and pride in their Jordanian, Arab and Islamic identity."[70] The notion of unity implicit in the initiative was intended to transcend tribal identities that had long fractured the nation. The initiative worked to "reformulate the state-individual relationship. . . . In summary, Jordan First is a philosophy of governance. It is based on the premise of placing Jordan's national interest at the forefront of all considerations of civil society."[71] In other words, the Jordan First Initiative attempted to limit the reach of the tribal elites in the planning of Amman by making it their civic responsibility to comply with state interests.

Despite the efforts put forth by the GACDP, political, ethnic, and tribal divisions persist, and they continue to hinder the state's efforts to unify identity and promote a sense of nationalism. An interview with a GAM planner revealed that projects and proposals are often approved and constructed to satisfy a request made by the wealthy elite. Therefore, despite Hussein's attempt to Jordanize the state, and Abdullah's various national slogans to promote a collective interest, GAM bureaucrats continue to fulfill the unsuitable planning requests of the wealthy elite out of a sense of either political or social obligation. This causes planning departments at GAM, as a planner explained, to move forward with various projects haphazardly, each division working according to its own agenda, under pressure, and without foresight. Planning in Amman is thus a circular, even regressive, process. Without collaboration between departments or the administrative ability to refuse inappropriate proposals, planners at GAM continue to work under the thumb of tribalism and elite demands.[72]

Low-Income Housing in the Twenty-First Century outside the Refugee Camp

As part of his nationalist agenda, Abdullah II tried in earnest to address the unfulfilled promises in the GACDP, particularly those related to public housing. Upon his ascension, Abdullah repeatedly declared his top concerns to be the wavering economy and his public's welfare. To that end, nine years into his reign, on February 26, 2008, Abdullah launched the Decent Housing for Decent Living Initiative. The initiative proposed a five-year plan to construct one hundred thousand units of public housing, beginning with twenty-five hundred units for low- to middle-income residents. The initiative further declared that this housing would be constructed specifically for "public-sector employees, armed forces, security services, and retired military personnel and civilians."[73] Here again, the units were intended for occupants of the historically Jordanian-dominated public sector. This gesture, while declared under the banner of nationalism, again exacerbated existing divisions.

The only public housing project developed by this royal housing initiative was the King Abdullah bin Abed al Aziz City in Zarqa, called Sakan Kareem, or Decent Living (fig. 2.6). The project provides approximately 229,260 square meters of residential space in 2,052 individual units ranging in size from 90 to 130 square meters (approximately 970 to 1,400 square feet). The project had three phases. Phase one delivered 696 apartments, and phase two promised 700 apartments by 2010. Phase three was to consist of 656 apartments and was slated for completion in early 2011. To date, phases one and two have been completed; phase three has been split into phase 3A and 3B, with 3A 69 percent complete and 3B 58 percent complete.[74] The project stalled in 2011 because of an impending investigation of corruption allegations against project developers. Additional municipal and administrative mishaps caused all parties involved in the project to redirect blame to one another for its failure.[75] The majority of project managers, however, pointed to the Ministry of Public Works and Housing as the largest culprit in causing the project's failure. In February 2014, the Lower House Finance

Figure 2.6. Government housing project (Sakan Kareem), http://abdoeng.com/Portals/0/EasyGalleryImages/3/6/sstb1prn.jpg.

Committee agreed, stating that the ministry had selected improper locations for the housing initiative projects. The majority of project sites were located in areas with almost no access to public services or facilities such as health centers, schools, or bus service.[76] As a result, only 37 percent of the completed units, far below the predicted outcome, have been sold.[77]

Rami Daher, a scholar of contemporary architecture, suggests that such public housing initiatives were proposed only to make way for new, neoliberal developments in central Amman. He cites three specific low-income neighborhoods that were pushed out of the city core, displaced to the periphery into low-income housing developments, perpetuating an economically divided city.[78] Despite Abdullah's efforts to brand a unified city and people, the sociopolitical practices related to planning are little changed. The bureaucratic reach of the neoliberal state exhibits little difference from that of the welfare state in its inability to moderate the influence of independent tribal interests (see fig. 2.7).

Conclusion

After the collapse of the welfare system, there was no measure of bureaucracy or nationalist agenda that could provide GAM with the autonomy necessary to temper the reach of wealthy elites and tribal interests. Curiously, however, the neoliberal shift has provided the state with a certain

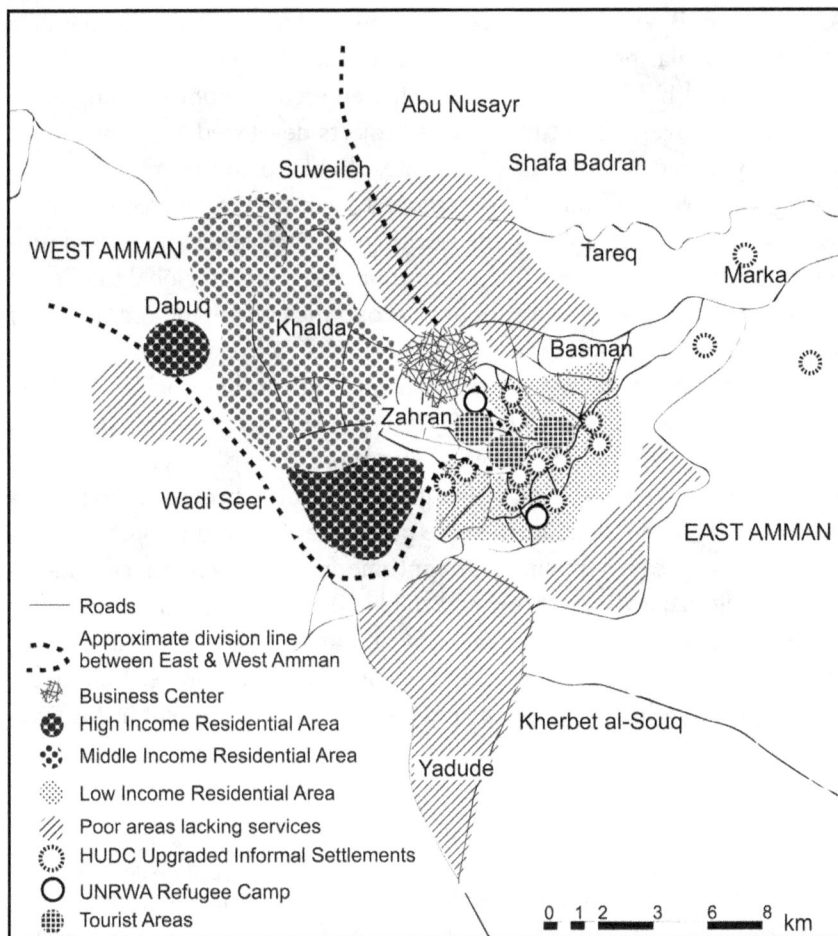

Figure 2.7. Social disparities. From *Atlas of Jordan: History, Territories and Society.* Beirut: Presses de l'Ifpo, 2013. https://books.openedition.org/ifpo/5045, 400.

measure of freedom to find a new foothold for itself in an otherwise historically ungovernable system of planning. Though the role of the state is believed to be diminished, as University of British Columbia geographer Jamie Peck argued, the *"ideological shape* of the state has not changed as much as neoliberal reformers would have us believe."[79] The state, rather, enjoys a certain elasticity, as well as the ability, under the premise of reform, to reinvent its role and responsibility in the project of development and the political economy of urbanism in Amman. Much as in the fellow

Arab states of Egypt and Morocco, the neoliberal moment allowed the state to shift particular projects to the private sector, setting itself up with a new source of wealth. In this way, the state has entered a tenuous collaboration with private investors to fund private projects developed by its own public agency, called MAWARED. The state, unable to control planning, has instead inserted itself into the persistent system of unregulated planning, making itself indispensable to the workings of the market and related processes of development, showing "exceptional resistance to global trends," as Laura Guazzone and Daniela Pioppi—economic consultant and professor of Middle Eastern studies, respectively—argue.[80] The elasticity afforded to the state in this contemporary era of neoliberalism has enabled Jordan's neo-authoritarian regime to thrive off its network of personal patronage, though at the cost of becoming entangled more deeply in its ever-evolving and ever-growing web of elites. Though a financially successful model, this system exists to the detriment of the public welfare, and projects such as public housing developments will continue to be market-driven endeavors, causing disparities to grow and the low-income community to be ill-housed. Abdullah may espouse the ethic of unity in his national campaigns, but to no avail, as market-driven logics continue to dominate, making inevitable the growing system of inequity in housing ever present in Amman.

Notes

1. Tawfiq M. Abu-Ghazzeh, "Housing Layout, Social Interaction, and the Place of Contact in Abu-Nuseir, Jordan," *Journal of Environmental Psychology* 19, no. 1 (1999): 47.

2. Paul Rabinow, *French Modern: Norms and Forms of the Social Environment* (Chicago: University of Chicago Press, 1989), 332.

3. Fuad K. Malkawi, "Hidden Structures: An Ethnographic Account of the Planning of Greater Amman" (PhD diss., University of Pennsylvania, 1996), 73.

4. Ibid., 158.

5. Greater Amman Municipality and Dar al-Handasah Consultants, *Greater Amman Comprehensive Development Plan*, Report Five: Final Report, 6.15. Amman: Greater Amman Municipality, 1988.

6. Rex Brynen, "Economic Crisis and Post-Rentier Democratization in the Arab World: The Case of Jordan," *Canadian Journal of Political Science* 25 (1992): 82.

7. See Marc Lynch, *State Interests and Public Spheres: The International Politics of Jordan's Identity* (New York: Columbia University Press, 1999); and Curtis Ryan, *Jordan in Transition: From Hussein to Abdullah* (Boulder, CO: Lynne Rienner, 2002).

8. Philip Robins, *A History of Jordan* (New York: Cambridge University Press, 2004), 74.

9. Mary Wilson, *King Abdullah, Britain and the Making of Jordan* (Cambridge: Cambridge University Press, 1987), 215.

10. Robins, *History of Jordan*, 35.

11. Brynen, "Economic Crisis," 82.

12. Linda Layne, *Home and Homeland: The Dialogics of Tribal and National Identities in Jordan* (Princeton, NJ: Princeton University Press), 98.

13. Ayman Smadi, lead transportation planner at the Greater Amman Municipality, interview, Amman, Jordan, June 1, 2013.

14. Karla Cunningham, "Regime and Society in Jordan: An Analysis of Jordanian Liberalization" (PhD diss., University of New York at Buffalo, 1997), 119.

15. Brynen, "Economic Crisis," 74.

16. Cunningham, "Regime and Society in Jordan," 119.

17. Brynen, "Economic Crisis," 74.

18. Lynch, *State Interests and Public Spheres*, 115.

19. Raed al Tal, "Structures of Authority: A Sociopolitical Account of Architectural and Urban Programs in Amman, Jordan" (PhD diss., Binghamton State University of New York, 1986), 169.

20. Robert A. Beauregard and Andrea Marpillero-Colomina, "Amman 2025: From Master Plan to Strategic Initiative, Amman Institute," 9, http://www.slideshare.net/Amman Institute/amman-2025-from-master-plan-to-strategic-initiative-amman-institute, accessed November 17, 2013.

21. Greater Amman Municipality and Dar al-Handasah Consultants, *Greater Amman Comprehensive Development Plan*, Report Five: Final Report, 9.4.

22. Ibid.

23. Ibid., 6.14.

24. Ibid., 6.15.

25. As defined by Teresa Caldeira, auto-construction is the practice in which dwellings are largely constructed by their residents, who build not only their own houses but also their neighborhoods.

26. Ibid., 13.44.

27. Ibid., 6.15.

28. In 1988, 951,964 Jordanian dinars was equal to approximately US$1.4 million.

29. East Bank nationalists are those of Bedouin origin who consider Jordan their nation, while the Palestinian residents had no claim to Jordan, political or otherwise.

30. Brynen, "Economic Crisis," 82.

31. Robins, *History of Jordan*, 82.

32. Ibid., 126–27.

33. Ibid.

34. Jamal Alnsour and Julia Meaton, "Housing Conditions in Palestinian Refugee Camps, Jordan," *Cities* 36 (2014): 65.

35. Julie Marie Peteet, *Landscape of Hope and Despair: Palestinian Refugee Camps* (Philadelphia: University of Pennsylvania Press, 2005), 94.

36. Ibid., 94.

37. Rochelle Davis, *Palestinian Village Histories: Geographies of the Displaced* (Stanford, CA: Stanford University Press, 2011), 221.

38. Ibid., 231.

39. Alnsour and Meaton, "Housing Conditions," 68.

40. Ibid., 66.

41. Ibid., 69.

42. Ibid., 71.

43. Marwan Daoud Hanania, "From Colony to Capital: A Socio-economic and Political History of Amman, 1878–1958" (PhD diss., Stanford University, 2010), 258.

44. Jane Hacker, *Modern 'Amman: A Social Study* (Durham, UK: Durham Colleges in the University of Durham, 1960), 7.

45. Ibid., 18.

46. Hanania, "Colony to Capital," 326.

47. Ibid., 257.

48. Ibid., 178.

49. Layne, *Home and Homeland*, 55.

50. Samantha Laine, "Amman's Real Estate Market Booms with Iraqis Who Have Fled Their Homeland for Good," *Northeastern University Journalism Abroad*, August 2, 2012, http://northeasternuniversityjournalism2012.wordpress.com/2012/08/02/.

51. Hanania, "Colony to Capital," 260.

52. Ibid., 106.

53. Layne, *Home and Homeland*, 53.

54. Ibid.

55. Ibid., 64.

56. Lynch, *State Interests*, 115.

57. Rabinow, *French Modern*, 320.

58. Ibid., 10.

59. A term borrowed from Paul Rabinow's *French Modern*. In middling modernism, both the norms and the forms of social technology become autonomous. This approach, which accelerated after World War I, entailed the transformation of the object to be worked on from a historico-natural milieu into a sociotechnical one.

60. Malkawi, "Hidden Structures," 158.

61. Ibid.

62. Ibid.

63. Ibid., 155.

64. Abu-Ghazzeh, "Housing Layout," 47.

65. Ibid.

66. Ibid., 54.

67. Eric Mumford, *Defining Urban Design: CIAM Architects and the Formation of a Discipline, 1937–1969* (New Haven, CT: Yale University Press, 2009), 3.

68. Jim Holston, *The Modernist City: An Anthropological Critique of Brasilia* (Chicago: University of Chicago Press, 1989), 31.

69. Malkawi, "Hidden Structures," 159.

70. "'Jordan First' Will Be Working Plan to Promote Loyalty," *Jordan Times*, October 31, 2002.

71. "Jordan First," *Guide to Jordanian Politics Life*, http://www.jordanpolitics.org/en/documents-view/62/jordan-first/41, accessed October 18, 2013.

72. Ayman Smadi, lead transportation planner at the Greater Amman Municipality, interview, Amman, Jordan, June 1, 2013.

73. "King Abdullah," http://kingabdullah.jo/index.php/en_US/initiatives/view/id/105.html, accessed February 26, 2008.

74. "The Royal Housing Initiative," *Madaen al Nour*, http://www.madaenalnour.com/index.php?option=com_content&view=article&id=89&Itemid=71&lang=en, accessed February 18, 2016.

75. In 2013, an interview with lead transportation planner at GAM, Ayman Smadi, extended to a discussion of the Sakan Kareem housing project. The planner admitted that the project was so inaccessible—approximately two hours away from Amman by car—that it exacerbated existing issues of disparity and exclusion in Amman. The transportation planner explained that the site was chosen primarily for its affordability, while little consideration was given to its inconvenient location "in the middle of nowhere!" Soon after project completion and occupation, the planner began to receive letters from social services, welfare ministries, and Sakan Kareem residents. All the letters appealed for a bus or a transit hub that would connect the site to Amman, where many residents worked. The planner stated that he could not comply; he could not justify supplying a bus for such a small development. Interview, June 1, 2013.

76. Khaled Neimat, "MPs Blame Gov't for 'Failure' of Housing Initiative," *Jordan Times*, February 24, 2014, http://www.jordantimes.com/news/local/mps-blame-gov%E2%80%99t-failure%E2%80%99-housing-initiative#sthash.7XzxA8hI.dpuf.

77. Ibid.

78. Rami Farouk Daher. "Neoliberal Urban Transformations in the Arab City: Meta-narratives, Urban Disparities and the Emergence of Consumerist Utopias and Geographies of Inequalities in Amman," *Urban Environment* 7 (2013): 105.

79. Jamie Peck, "Geography and Public Policy: Constructions of Neoliberalism," *Progress in Human Geography* 28, no. 3 (2004): 397 (emphasis in original).

80. Laura Guazzone and Daniela Pioppi, eds., *The Arab State and Neo-Liberal Globalization: The Restructuring of State Power in the Middle East* (Reading, UK: Ithaca Press, 2009), 6.

Bibliography

Abu-Ghazzeh, Tawfiq M. "Housing Layout, Social Interaction, and the Place of Contact in Abu-Nuseir, Jordan." *Journal of Environmental Science* 19, no. 1 (1999): 41–73.

Alnsour, Jamal, and Julia Meaton. "Housing Conditions in Palestinian Refugee Camps, Jordan." *Cities* 36 (2014): 65–73.

Al Tal, Raed. "Structures of Authority: A Sociopolitical Account of Architectural and Urban Programs in Amman, Jordan." PhD diss., Binghamton State University of New York, 1986.

Beauregard, Robert A., and Andrea Marpillero-Colomina. "Amman 2025: From Master Plan to Strategic Initiative, Amman Institute." http://www.slideshare.net/AmmanInstitute/amman-2025-from-master-plan-to-strategic-initiative-amman-institute. Accessed November 17, 2013.

Brynen, Rex. "Economic Crisis and Post-Rentier Democratization in the Arab World: The Case of Jordan." *Canadian Journal of Political Science* 25 (1992): 69–97.

Cunningham, Karla. "Regime and Society in Jordan: An Analysis of Jordanian Liberalization." PhD diss., University of New York at Buffalo, 1997.

Daher, Rami Farouk. "Neoliberal Urban Transformations in the Arab City: Meta-narratives, Urban Disparities, and the Emergence of Consumerist Utopias and Geographies of Inequalities in Amman." *Urban Environment* 7 (2013): 99–115.

Davis, Rochelle. *Palestinian Village Histories: Geographies of the Displaced.* Stanford, CA: Stanford University Press, 2011.

Greater Amman Municipality and Dar al-Handasah Consultants. *Greater Amman Comprehensive Development Plan*, Report Five: Final Report. Greater Amman Municipality, 1988.

Guazzone, Laura, and Daniela Pioppi, eds. *The Arab State and Neo-Liberal Globalization: The Restructuring of State Power in the Middle East*. Reading, UK: Ithaca Press, 2009.

Hacker, Jane. *Modern 'Amman: A Social Study*. Durham, UK: Durham Colleges in the University of Durham, 1960.

Hanania, Marwan. "From Colony to Capital: A Socio-Economic and Political History of Amman, 1878–1928." PhD diss., Stanford University, 2010.

Holston, Jim. *The Modernist City: An Anthropological Critique of Brasilia*. Chicago: University of Chicago Press, 1989.

"'Jordan First.' *Guide to Jordanian Politics Life*. http://www.jordanpolitics.org/en/documents-view/62/jordan-first/41. Accessed October 18, 2013.

Jordan Times, "'Jordan First' Will Be Working Plan to Promote Loyalty." October 31, 2002.

Laine, Samantha. "Amman's Real Estate Market Booms with Iraqis Who Have Fled Their Homeland for Good." *Northeastern University Journalism Abroad*, August 2, 2012. http://northeasternuniversityjournalism2012.wordpress.com/2012/08/02/.

Layne, Linda. *Home and Homeland: The Dialogics of Tribal and National Identities in Jordan*. Princeton, NJ: Princeton University Press, 1994.

Lynch, Marc. *State Interests and Public Spheres: The International Politics of Jordan's Identity*. New York: Columbia University Press, 1999.

Madaen al Nour, "The Royal Housing Initiative." http://www.madaenalnour.com/index.php?option=com_content&view=article&id=89&Itemid=71&lang=en. Accessed February 18, 2016.

Malkawi, Fuad K. "Hidden Structures: An Ethnographic Account of the Planning of Greater Amman." PhD diss., University of Pennsylvania, 1996.

Mumford, Eric. *Defining Urban Design: CIAM Architects and the Formation of a Discipline, 1937–69*. New Haven, CT: Yale University Press, 2009.

Neimat, Khaled. "MPs Blame Gov't for 'Failure' of Housing Initiative." *Jordan Times*, February 24, 2014. http://www.jordantimes.com/news/local/mps-blame-gov%E2%80%99t-failure%E2%80%99-housing-initiative#sthash.7XzxA8hI.dpuf.

Peck, Jamie. "Geography and Public Policy: Constructions of Neoliberalism." *Progress in Human Geography* 28, no. 3 (2004): 392–405.

Peteet, Julie Marie. *Landscape of Hope and Despair: Palestinian Refugee Camps*. Philadelphia: University of Pennsylvania, 2005.

Rabinow, Paul. *French Modern: Norms and Forms of the Social Environment*. Chicago: University of Chicago Press, 1989.

Robins, Philip. *A History of Jordan*. New York: Cambridge University Press, 2004.

Ryan, Curtis. *Jordan in Transition: From Hussein to Abdullah*. Boulder, CO: Lynne Rienner, 2002.

Wilson, Mary. *King Abdullah, Britain and the Making of Jordan*, Cambridge: Cambridge University Press, 1987.

ELIANA ABU-HAMDI is Project Manager of the Global Architectural History Teaching Collaborative at the Massachusetts Institute of Technology. She is also Adjunct Assistant Professor at Hunter College in Manhattan. She earned a PhD in Architecture from UC Berkeley with a designated emphasis in global metropolitan studies. Her research on architecture and development in Jordan contributes to debates on the political economy of urbanism in developing cities and establishes connections between the geopolitical histories of these cities and their urban present. She is also an experienced architectural practitioner and educator and has taught design, history, theory, and urban studies courses. Her future research focuses on processes of urban ruination and abandoned projects in the United States and abroad.

3

WORKERS' AND POPULAR HOUSING IN MID-TWENTIETH-CENTURY EGYPT

Mohamed Elshahed

IN 1947, THE THIRD ARAB ENGINEERING CONFERENCE WAS held in Damascus, hosted by the Syrian president.[1] The conference was the largest of such professional gatherings and included a wider range of panels than the previous two, held in Cairo and Alexandria in 1945 and 1946, respectively. These momentous meetings of Arab engineering professionals took place during a critical moment in the region's urban history. Urban populations were on the rise, rural-to-urban migration was increasing, and the demand for affordable housing was high. The end of World War II signaled the start of a new era in which Arab engineers and architects sought to play a major role in national development projects and to realize their modernist visions. During the war years, construction activities across the region nearly came to a halt because of the rising costs of building materials, and the housing situation worsened drastically.

One of the key panels during the 1947 conference was on the topic of housing. On the basis of the presented papers, the panel made ten recommendations encouraging governments to invest in planning new residential quarters and provide incentives for businesses and industries to build housing for their workers.[2] It also advised drafting laws that would encourage individuals to become members of housing cooperatives that would enjoy no or low taxes, in addition to having access to affordable land for development and to public transport and facilities. The profits of construction companies would have to be limited to a certain percentage, and the governments of the region should closely monitor the prices of building materials and their production and distribution to guarantee the equal rights of producers and consumers of materials essential to the building trade.

This chapter focuses on the housing question in Egypt between the years 1947 and 1962, when the phrase *azmat al-iskan* (the housing crisis) saturated the press (fig. 3.1). The chapter begins with a close reading and analysis of a published 1947 lecture by Mahmoud Riad on workers' housing that shaped government approaches and experimentations during the following decade. This previously unstudied lecture and its subsequent publication shed new light on the policy-driven methods and approaches of Egypt's most prominent architect and civil servant as he engaged with the housing question during a critical time in Egypt's urban development and population shift to cities. The chapter moves between discursive analysis of Riad's lecture and exploring built projects and cites journalistic coverage of the housing crisis. What were the proposals and efforts to build housing for the masses in Egypt, and how did architects respond to the pressing demand for affordable housing? How did the state, in light of the major political changes in Egypt during the period covered in this chapter, affect architects' attempts to respond to the housing question? This chapter responds to these questions and argues that despite the rich history of local architects seeking to find solutions for affordable and social housing, the lack of government policies and shortsighted politics stifled the evolution of long-lasting solutions to Egypt's pressing housing problems, which persist to this day.

Early Experiments in Housing Workers

During the 1920s, the profession of architecture was increasingly Egyptianized after decades of dominance by European practitioners. A prominent example of this indigenization process was architect, planner, and civil servant Mahmoud Riad. He studied architecture at Cairo University in the late 1920s before completing his architectural education in Liverpool. Between 1953 and 1960, Riad was the head of the Cairo Municipality.[3] From the late 1940s, he made discursive and architectural contributions to the development of housing in Egypt, which contrasted with earlier practices by Egyptian architects. For much of the 1930s and 1940s, the architectural profession in Egypt was preoccupied with designing private dwellings, villas,

أزمة الإسكان

بقلم:
زينب محمد حسين

Figure 3.1. "Housing Crisis!" *Al-Idha'a* magazine (Cairo, 1966), 11. Coverage of the issue permeated all media. This example is from a magazine dedicated to radio and entertainment.

and luxury apartments that catered to a small segment of society. Nevertheless, there were some early experiments in providing affordable housing during this time. The state, represented by the Public Works Ministry, cooperated with private landowners and construction companies, such as the Heliopolis Oasis Company, in order to build what was dubbed economic housing. One such project was a housing development of 180 units at 'Abbasiyya, completed in 1920.[4] Other housing projects were commissioned by the railway company, such as the company housing projects it implemented in Sayeda Zeynab in Cairo and Abu Za'bal north of the city. Large industries also commissioned and built housing such as the company town built in Mahalla for textile workers in 1941.[5] Some architects and planners saw workers' housing, as well as low-income housing and village reform plans, as necessary for national progress.[6]

One of the outcomes of the growth in industrialization after Egypt's 1919 Revolution and the establishment of new industries owned by the country's first national bank, Banque Misr, was the demand for workers' housing projects.[7] Architects proposed several affordable housing and workers' housing projects, such as "City for 100 inhabitants in Alexandria" (published 1921), a housing scheme for the district of Sayeda Zaynab (1928), and another workers' housing scheme for the same district proposed in 1929.[8] The most notable industrial complex and worker housing settlement were in Mahalla al-Kubra for the Misr Company for Spinning and Weaving. Architect Ali Labib Gabr designed many of the company's buildings, including the worker housing.[9] These apartment buildings consisted of four levels raised off the ground by columns in Corbusian fashion. Each floor consisted of two apartments, and each apartment consisted of two bedrooms, a reception/living room, a dining room, a kitchen, a bathroom, and a servants' room. The elevations of these buildings were minimalist and understated, and the overall massing was cubic. Windows, balconies, and horizontal articulations created lines of shadow on the white rectangular structure. The apartment plans offered generous spaces for the family along with a separate staircase for servants with direct access to the kitchen. These apartments, while commissioned by industrial companies with thousands of workers, served only a fraction of the workforce, the administrators. Other housing typologies within this scheme included attached housing units sharing a small garden. The spaces of these workers' units were less generous, but the communal services offered by the housing complex compensated for what they lacked in square footage: "cantinas and cafeterias, hospitals, markets and coffee shops, an open-air cinema, welfare centers, sporting fields, bathhouses, and automated laundry facilities."[10] This model was too costly for smaller companies to replicate.

The majority of Egypt's workers, particularly those working for small factories and workshops, were left with few affordable options. By the end of World War II, the problem of how to provide affordable modern dwellings for the poor and working majority became a topic of debate. In 1949, the Ministry of Social Affairs (*Wizarat al-shu'un al-igtima'iyya*) published a study on low-income housing written by Mahmoud Riad along with social reformer Ahmad Hussein.[11] The study, which shaped social housing policy for the following decade, built on a 1947 study by Riad. In a 1947 lecture, Riad cited census data to argue in favor of immediate intervention by the state and private companies in providing affordable housing. According to the 1937 census, the mortality figures for Egypt were 27.2 per thousand per annum. In Mexico, they were 24.6 people per thousand, in England, 12.4, and in the Netherlands, 8.8.[12] For Riad, these relatively high mortality figures in Egypt were directly connected to poor living conditions, particularly the lack of hygienic and well-planned domestic spaces. Riad argued that solving Egypt's housing problem was a necessary step toward national development and progress. The high mortality rate, he wrote, was due to the spread of disease in unhealthy dwellings, fires spreading quickly between ramshackle houses, lack of clean water, absence of sufficient sewage networks, and limited access to direct sunlight and fresh air. In 1937, Cairo's population stood at 1,312,096. By 1944, that number had reached 1,455,400: a 2 percent annual increase. According to Riad, thirty thousand new housing units should have been built in that span of time.[13]

During World War II, the construction industry nearly came to a halt in Egypt. By the end of the war, the country's population had increased by four hundred thousand inhabitants, which should have been matched by at least eighty thousand new housing units.[14] The construction of housing was further delayed by the postwar political turmoil and the high cost of building materials. In an attempt to respond to the housing shortage, in 1949 the government initiated a housing program that "barely benefited one thousand families across the country."[15] Workers carried the brunt of the shortage in affordable housing. Low incomes and high building costs spelled a catastrophic future for Egyptian cities and for the quality of life for the country's urban majority. One observer of Egyptian affairs at the time noted, "The workers' primary desire, after food, is for decent housing. And because they form the productive force in Egypt's new industrial complex, a sincere effort must be made to satisfy their demand."[16] In this context, Riad's lecture was a comprehensive urgent attempt to confront the problem of workers' housing.

Mahmoud Riad's *Masakin al-'ummal*

Riad delivered his lecture, simply titled "Workers' Housing" (*Masakin al-'ummal*), on March 20, 1947, before an audience of fellow architects, businessmen, and politicians at the Egyptian Royal Society of Engineers. It was published by Misr Press later that year. "Housing is one of our national problems and we must confront it," he declared. Relying on statistical information and census data and—presenting case studies of collective housing in locations as varied as Vienna, the Bronx, Cleveland, and Berlin—Riad argued for the necessity of housing implemented by the Egyptian state. He concluded his lecture by showcasing a development that he had designed for the workers of a textile factory in Kafr al-Dawwar, north of Cairo (fig. 3.2). Riad made a compelling case for government intervention and the need for subsidized housing:

> The average Egyptian family is composed of five persons; they need a domestic space that includes a sitting room, two bedrooms, a kitchen, and a bathroom. Such units were built before the war at a cost of one hundred Egyptian pounds. If we consider this as the basic unit for our calculations and that twenty such units can be built in an acre of land which costs one hundred Egyptian pounds in normal market conditions, and if we consider the costs for preparing agricultural land for construction and supplying this land with services at a cost of nine hundred pounds, then the average cost per housing unit will become one hundred and fifty Egyptian pounds in addition to 8 percent for maintenance and taxes. This means that the rental cost for each unit will be one Egyptian pound per month. At this rate, workers must earn a minimum of six pounds per month, which is far greater than the average income for unskilled and even skilled workers despite the rise in their wages in the past few years.[17]

Riad's engagement with the question of housing and industrialization stems from his careful study of the contemporary conditions of Egyptian cities along with detailed statistical and census data. For example, Riad noted that the number of industrial workers in Cairo had increased from 65,037 in 1927 to 84,718 in 1937 and that most industrial workshops on average consisted of only three workers. This, he argued, meant that while small factories and workshops were the primary employers of Cairo's workers,

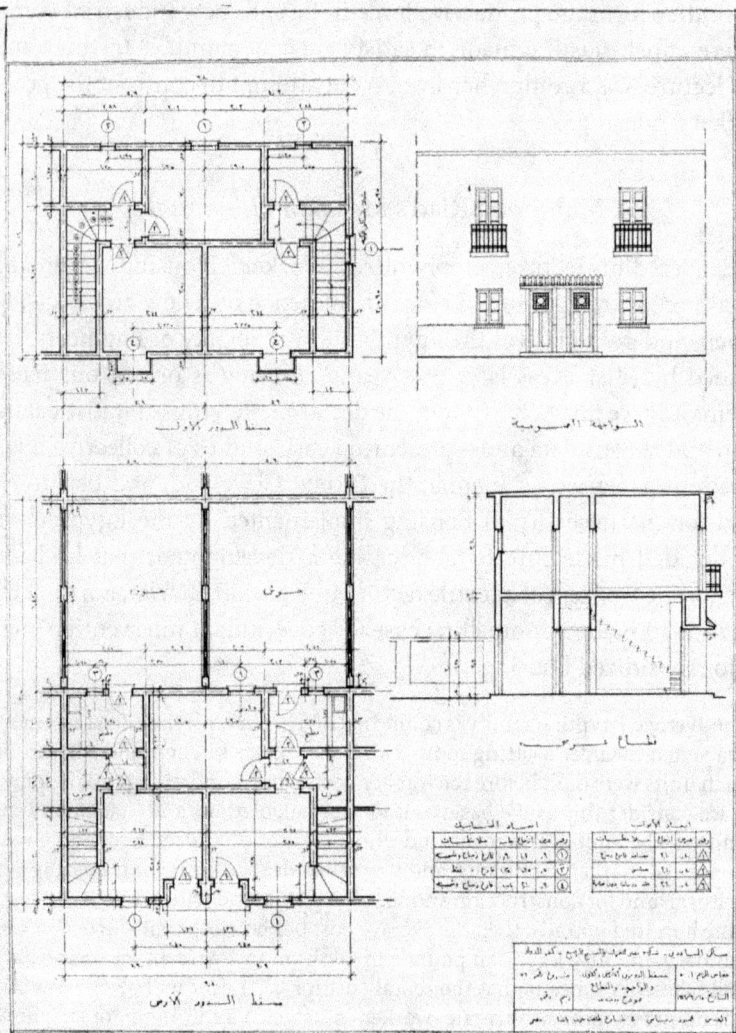

(رسم ١٦)

نموذج لمساكن العمال بشركة مصر للغزل والنسيج الرفيع من القطن المصرى بكفر الدوار

على شكل وحدات كل وحدة لسكنين ويحوى السكن غرفة جلوس وغرفتين نوم ومطبخ ودورة

مياه وحوش ويمكن ضم إحدى غرف النوم للسكن المجاور ليتوفر السكن للعائلات الكبيرة والصغيرة

Figure 3.2. Sample family duplex unit in the Kafr al-Dawwar textiles factory workers' housing designed by Mahmoud Riad (1943–44). From Mahmoud Riad, *Workers' Housing* (Cairo: Misr Press, 1947), 38.

the owners of these small workshops were unable to offer adequate housing to their employees. In these cases, he concluded, the state must intervene to accommodate the housing needs of this working class.

Two forces drove Riad's discourse: modernism as a design approach and national development in the provision of efficient hygienic housing as an essential step for national progress. He explicitly warned that failing to provide healthy housing for workers and those with limited incomes would have devastating effects on national modernization efforts.[18] Riad located the origins of the housing crisis at the intersection of several developments in Egyptian society: the limited social mobility of the poor, the increase in population, and the lack of industrial development. To support his argument, Riad referred to a study that argued that in the previous fifty years Egypt's population had doubled while the country's agricultural land increased by only 10 percent. Riad then went on to prescribe a remedy: an increase in industrialization coupled with workers' housing developments would provide jobs, stimulate the economy, and absorb the growing population into modern housing estates.[19]

In his approach, Riad subordinated architecture to social, political, and economic factors. In contrast to his Turkish peers, for example, Riad, did not speak of the modern dwelling as a civilizing apparatus for crafting modern subjects.[20] Rather than discussing the aesthetic or stylistic attributes of the modern house or apartment designed for workers, Riad spent much of his lecture describing in detail the practical needs for housing Egypt's working class. The discrepancy between the average worker's income and the cost of workers' housing had led many companies to abandon workers' housing projects altogether.[21] Riad identified seven studies that would need to be conducted before designing and implementing a housing development plan. The first study would determine the needed number of units by considering the number of overcrowded units, the number of unsanitary and unsafe units, the annual population growth, and the number of condemned buildings. The second study would analyze finances and track inflation, the country's political and economic conditions, currency stability, and stock market trends and interest rates. From these factors, the costs of construction could be determined along with average rents and the required state policy to stabilize or subsidize rents. The third study would outline the current legal framework controlling construction and make suggestions to improve such laws. The third study would identify the stakeholders responsible for housing construction based on number of employees, worker salaries, and access to affordable housing. The stakeholders could be municipalities, local councils, cooperative societies, nongovernmental organizations, individuals assisted by the state, insurance companies, or banks. The fourth study would identify financial assistance in the form of loans to companies to undertake housing construction. The fifth study would focus on building materials, costs, and labor. The sixth study would determine population density and the size of housing units according to number of family members. The seventh study would determine rents in correlation to living costs and income.[22]

In his lecture, Riad pointed to England for a detailed case study of how the state intervened in housing construction before and after World War II (fig. 3.3). He argued that measured state intervention in the construction sector, particularly housing, could lead to an increase in construction companies and greater participation by community associations and cooperatives, which would eventually relieve the state from direct intervention. In addition, Riad stressed the significant role of municipalities and local communities in directly participating in responding to housing needs. He also stressed that in England homeownership, rather than rental, was a significant factor in the relative success of its postwar reconstruction. Riad presented the example of an interwar English house that cost 480 Egyptian pounds to build but under the existing Egyptian rental law would have brought in a monthly rent of just over 3 Egyptian pounds, expensive by the standards of the time. The equivalent amount of this monthly rent in England would allow the tenant to own their unit after twenty years. Riad stressed that this was possible in England because of the strong presence of cooperatives and resident associations, as well as state subsidies and financial assistance to residents. In Riad's view, successful dwellings for workers and low-income residents result from carefully envisioned and implemented policies that confront the complex economics of housing.[23]

Riad went on to showcase nine models of cooperative housing from the interwar period, from various locations, from different political and economic structures, and utilizing different urban and architectural typologies.[24] Each one was presented on a slide consisting of a photograph, data pertaining to date of construction and architect, a section drawing, a parti/site diagram, a typical unit plan, and a view of the urban condition that was replaced by the project. The examples were mostly from the early 1930s and came from a variety of social, political, and geographical settings. What tied the projects together was the involvement of municipal government and state funds in providing quality housing that was affordable to a large

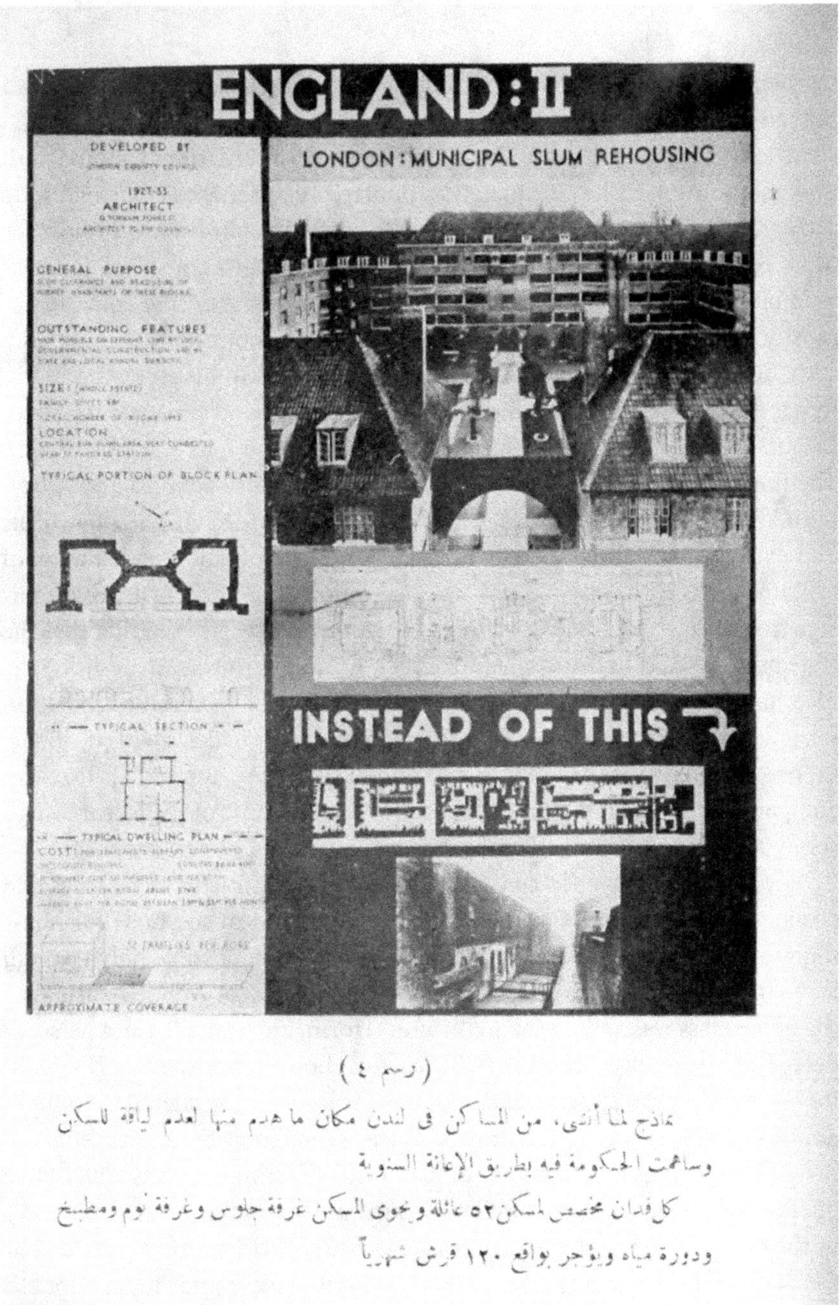

Figure 3.3. Sample slide from Mahmoud Riad's worker housing lecture as published in 1947. The slide shows a slum-rehousing project near Pancras Station in central London, built in 1927–33 and designed by G. Topham Forrest, architect at the London County Council. From Mahmoud Riad, *Workers' Housing* (Cairo: Misr Press, 1947), 8.

segment of the population, including workers. Such projects had not been implemented in Egypt on the same scale.

Riad's research-based multidisciplinary and international approach to understanding housing ultimately supported his proposed housing estate project, which was already under construction in 1947. Riad's project for Misr Textiles and Weaving Company was designed to house 366 families on a plot of twelve acres (thirty families per acre). The design consisted of mostly freestanding units, each made up of three rooms, a bathroom, and a kitchen in addition to a small outdoor space. True to his style, Riad went into great detail about the building materials, costs, and construction specifications of his project to ensure minimum cost and maximum efficiency. The townhouse design proposed by Riad for the Misr Textiles and Weaving Company housing is simple, utilizing a cubic design with flat roofs and plain façades. This design was the result of a meticulous calculation of building costs rather than a stylistic adaptation of a modernist worker village from elsewhere. Riad concluded his lecture by recommending that the state provide land in Cairo to realize such housing projects. In addition, he recommended that the state should control building-material distribution for housing projects to reduce middlemen, provide workers with no-interest or low-interest loans to build and purchase homes, and reduce taxes on companies investing in workers' housing. The outcome of the lecture was a series of policy recommendations rather than a fixed design proposal.

As mentioned above, a central argument made in Riad's lecture was that economic progress in Egypt relied on finding practical solutions for housing workers and low-income residents. This would be possible only through cooperation between architects, capitalists, and the state. While housing for the upper class was an issue of architectural form, individuality, and personal taste, Riad introduced a new set of issues on housing for the working class for Egyptian architects, investors, and state officials to consider. For example, although hygiene (modern bathrooms) was a prerequisite in bourgeois domestic space (presented by architects and manufacturers as a product to be purchased as a key aspect of modern living that also signified social mobility), in the case of workers' housing it was a necessity that had to be provided by the state and industrialists in order to prevent disease and improve public health. In 1948, Riad drew plans for Masakin al-'Ummal, a housing complex in Cairo's Imbaba district, implementing ideas expressed in his lecture during the previous year. Under a new law for social housing, law 206 of 1951, the state began to complete the project, perhaps the fullest realization of his ideas.[25]

A New Era for Social Housing

During the 1950s, social housing was referred to in Egypt as *al-iskan al-sha'bi* (popular housing). It emerged as a priority for the state for both political and practical reasons.[26] Providing housing and access to services for all Egyptians across the country's vast territory was politically wise because of the urgency of the situation. Popular housing schemes were envisioned for families earning less than twenty-five Egyptian pounds monthly.[27] This meant that the state gave itself the responsibility for housing a rather large percentage of the urban population. A key aspect of Riad's vision for financing such housing relied on the partnership between the state and industrialists. After nationalization and sequestering of properties and capital belonging to the pre-1952 financial elite, however, the state emerged as the sole financial power able to undertake housing projects without the support of the private sector. Financing such an endeavor proved difficult from the start. To undertake the enormous task, the new regime formed a committee called al-Majlis al-'Ali li-l-Ta'mir (the Supreme Council for Construction), which was responsible for researching available options and models and drafting plans, policies, budgets, and proposals. Some of the earliest recommendations made by the council included the requirement that commercial and industrial enterprises provide housing to their workers (inspired by Mahmoud Riad's recommendations from 1947). The council also recommended that the state hold the right to forcibly evict residents of "unhealthy districts" and to redevelop the land.[28] A state policy for mass housing was beginning to be formulated for state-sponsored reorganization of cities to absorb and house the majority.

The Popular Housing and Development Company (PHDC) was a public company established in 1954 and commissioned by the government to implement projects for workers' housing as well as slum-clearance projects.[29] This task was enormous because "since the government's limited resources available for housing projects must be directed toward satisfying the industrial workers and the civil servants, it seems doubtful that the regime can also engage in large-scale slum clearance."[30] The PHDC was part of a publicly funded consortium of companies responsible for housing and development in various parts of Cairo and the country. The building types the company built followed standardized designs of freestanding four-story apartment blocks built in clusters. Earlier published designs included balconies for the modestly sized apartments, a feature that later disappeared.

Figure 3.4. Renderings of popular housing (no location specified). From *al-Musawwar* maga-zine (Cairo, 1957), 67.

A compact entryway and stairwell was at the center of each building block, and each floor included two apartments, each composed of two bedrooms and a small living space in addition to a compact kitchen and bathroom (fig. 3.4).

In March 1954, construction of popular housing commenced in three peripheral areas of Cairo: Imbaba, Hilmiyyat al-Zaytun, and Helwan. "Twenty thousand poor families join the elite!" a headline in *al-Musawwar* proclaimed. The popular housing program, as reported in *al-Musawwar*, aimed to construct 20,000 units in eight months, making homeowner-ship possible to twenty thousand underprivileged households.[31] By 1962, however, only 4,066 units were built in those areas, according to official reports.[32] Later, PHDC initiated housing for workers across the country, starting with a pilot project for the railway company workers at Abu Za'bal in Cairo that cost two million Egyptian pounds for building twenty-eight hundred housing units.[33] A prototypical project based on the Abu Za'bal experiment, costing seven hundred thousand Egyptian pounds, was adapted for several state-owned companies in various locations: an oil re-finery company in the city of Suez (fig. 3.5), a fertilizer company in Aswan, a steel company in Aswan and Helwan.[34] These projects mainly consisted of two-story building blocks with compact duplex apartments built in close proximity to public services such as schools. The PHDC also built mid-dle-income apartments for police officers at 'Abbasiyya in Cairo. By 1959, the company spearheaded a national program to house municipal workers whose monthly wages were below thirty pounds (the average monthly wage

Figure 3.5. Housing project for the managers and administrators block at the Egyptian Company for Fertilizers and Chemicals in Suez. Designed by Sayed Karim, ca. 1959. Postcard, Mohamed Elshahed personal collection.

was 37.1 pounds in 1952–53 and 59.3 in 1962–63).[35] The program built about one hundred units for municipalities across the country (fig. 3.6). In total, the collective effort of the PHDC, the housing cooperatives, and municipalities, among other government entities, built around twenty thousand units between 1952 and 1958, with another eight thousand units completed later.[36]

In the immediate aftermath of the 1952 coup d'état, the new regime in Egypt attempted to confront the growing housing crisis, particularly among low-income urban populations. While Riad's ideas formed the intellectual foundation for Egypt's housing policies, in his capacity as head of the Cairo Municipality he did not have direct control of the various housing efforts across the country. Affordable housing programs, paired with slum-clearance projects, were fertile ground for the new regime to make visible its ability to confront one of the country's most pressing demands, the need for social housing for the masses. Affordable housing was implemented across the country with little regard to specific conditions, however, and without taking into account the careful recommendations in Riad's study. Instead, a reductive formalistic design, rooted in Riad's emphasis on economic considerations, was replicated and built across the country. The task of providing housing on a mass scale was enormous, and while there were major advances in expanding the infrastructure network and the implementation of key housing projects, ultimately the demand was too great,

Figure 3.6. Housing developments by state-owned companies in Fayoum (left) and Qalyoubiya (right). From *al-Musawwar* magazine (Cairo, 1964), 54.

leading to an increase in the frequency of the word *crisis* in connection with housing. A decade after his pioneering lecture, the role of the architect as a respondent to urban Egypt's social demands faded and the state's ability to sustain such projects weakened.

Confronting the Housing Crisis

By the end of the 1950s, the Egyptian government was providing housing to workers, the poor, and the middle class in addition to implementing slum-clearance projects. As one commentator noted, "Since the government's limited resources available for housing projects must be directed toward satisfying the industrial workers and the civil servants, it seems doubtful that the regime can also engage in large-scale slum clearance."[37] Yet there was at least one notable slum-clearance project. In a 1959 report designed to showcase urban improvements, the state, through its mouthpiece magazine *Bina'al-Watan*, published pictures of the Zinhum district before and after it was rebuilt. The Zinhum slum on the edge of historic Cairo was transformed as part of a slum-clearance program, and new housing blocks were constructed in its place. In the published image, the white, rectangular four-story blocks stretch into the distance, with the citadel and historic Cairo looming behind. The slum clearance of Zinhum provided residents with modern housing units and services. The message of the published report is clear: modern housing signified progress.[38] But such overly optimistic portrayals of the state's housing efforts were overshadowed by reports of the deepening housing crisis.

While Zinhum and other housing projects were significant steps toward confronting the housing crisis, they were hastily constructed and failed to conform to Riad's suggested seven studies or the Supreme Council for Construction's recommendations. The need to quickly construct new housing units was increasingly overshadowed by political opportunism rather than a genuine interest in solving the housing crisis in an economically sustainable way. There were cracks in the propagated image of state-led large-scale housing construction. Articles and interviews focusing on the lack of housing proliferated in the press despite government promises to alleviate the problem. "One hundred five million pounds spent and 153,000 units built yet the housing problem hasn't been solved!" reads a headline in *al-Idha'a*, an entertainment magazine.[39] The housing crisis in the 1960s was escalating, with no sign of relief.[40] The state struggled to properly respond to the continuing need for affordable housing through designs or policies. The topic pervaded popular discourse so much that it was covered in popular entertainment magazines typically concerned with theater, radio, and cinema. Interiors of popular housing units were published by Al-Ahram in 1965 (fig. 3.7). A year later, *al-Idha'a* published a report that included interviews with the housing minister as well as architects and housing specialists. The following lines sum up the situation:

> Finding an apartment is *the* topic of conversation among the people. Couples delay their marriages for years until they find an apartment. In the street, a woman complains to her friend about the down payment she made for an apartment. In a village, a college student studying in Cairo tells his fellow villagers about the brokers in the city who took advantage of him. In coffee shops, people discuss the distribution of new government flats. One asks, why the preference to those who pay more? Is that the socialism they speak of? Another says he fears that distributed government apartments will become the focus of competitive black market. A third man confirms the black market is already thriving. "There must be a solution to this problem" shouts yet another man.[41]

Such a gloomy outlook on the question of housing was not unusual in the press. This kind of report contrasted with the ways in which government companies building housing wished to present themselves in the very same magazines. From the late 1950s and throughout the 1960s, nearly every

Figure 3.7. Interiors of popular housing units. From *al-Ahram* magazine (Cairo, 1965), 38.

popular magazine periodically published reports and images of the government's housing constructions. The message from the state was clear: "We're working on it." The press portrayed housing minister Ezzat Salama in 1966 as a hardworking man who spent his days touring the dozens of construction sites around the country and meeting with architects, housing committees, and state officials in an attempt to find solutions to the housing question. Housing dominated the national conversation and became a reflection of the undeveloped and incomplete socialist vision propagated by President Gamal Abdel Nasser and state officials.[42]

The housing crisis in Egypt proved that the state alone could not build enough affordable housing to absorb demand. A 1958 study by the Ministry of Municipal and Rural Affairs concluded that Egypt needed to build seventy-two thousand housing units annually in order to keep up with population growth and replace existing inadequate housing.[43] This housing crisis challenged the relevance of architects and their practices, which had long catered to individual clients. The need for housing built in large quantities resulted in the rise of a new type of professional: the housing contractor. A 1956 profile of Hassan Abulfottuh in *al-Musawwar* celebrates the young contractor as a "great builder" who helps relieve the housing crisis: "In the last five years alone he built 1,406 popular housing units in [the northern suburb of] Hilmiyyet al-Zaitoun, sixty-six villas for a housing cooperative in [the Giza suburb of] Haram, eighty-seven villas for the teachers union at Cairo University, and forty-six apartment buildings, including

1,100 apartments in the Zinhum slum-clearance project."[44] Abulfottuh accomplished this with the help of two architects, Mustafa Tharwat and Ibrahim Alfar, as well as one thousand builders. Their contracts were valued at 1.5 million Egyptian pounds in projects, as well as 3 million pounds in contracts for construction projects in Saudi Arabia, facilitated by the Egyptian government. The state-owned Popular Housing and Development Company awarded these lucrative contracts. The 1963 article "A Building Revolution" included a photo of the building contractor Henry Madi with Marsa Matruh's, provincial representative of the housing minister. The caption announced, "Contractor Henry Madi Urbanizes the Western Desert."[45] Less than a decade earlier, architects such as Mahmoud Riad were pictured with state officials as the builders of the future. Economic realities and the demand for housing replaced the architect with a new kind of local actor, the development contractor. In the face of *azmat al-iskan* (housing crisis), the relevance of architects in Egypt diminished. Rather than approach housing with Riad's meticulous calculations, contractors simplified and repeated a housing typology with minimal costs to yield maximum profit, a step toward the consequent liberalization of the Egyptian economy that took off in the 1970s after the total collapse of the Nasser regime and the dominance of the state in all matters, including housing construction.

Legislative and Infrastructural Measures

Much of the housing construction carried out by the state focused on expanding utilities and infrastructure with water, electricity, and sewage projects across the country in both urban and rural areas. Between 1952 and 1963, the number of residents in urban areas with access to clean drinking water in cities outside Cairo, Alexandria, and the cities around the Suez Canal doubled from 2.2 million to 4.5 million.[46] Cairo alone added two million new users to the sewage system. "Eight additional cities witnessed sewage infrastructure investment at a 300 percent increase from the total investment of the previous thirty years, bringing two million new users in those cities."[47] Roads and bridges also witnessed sizable increases in state funds across the country, improving the overall quality of urban life and creating a better urban environment for the creation of new housing.

Another considerable step taken by the state as part of its efforts to respond to the housing crisis was a series of legislative interventions targeting rents and property laws. In the first decade after the 1952 coup, at least five new laws were introduced that affected housing and property rights, creating an unfavorable environment for private housing investment. In 1952, law 199 lowered apartment rents across the board, appeasing tenants but angering property owners. Law 55 in 1958 and laws 168 and 169 in 1961 lowered property taxes for landlords who offered lower rents. In 1962, law 46 based rents on set criteria designed to lower rents by an average of 35 percent. Every apartment had to be checked by an official committee in order to determine a suitable rent from set criteria. This process proved difficult to control.[48] In 1965, housing minister Mohamed Abu Nussair reported that the committee received fifty thousand requests for rent adjustment, half of which came from Cairo alone. The task of evaluating rent in individual cases was nearly impossible, which led to the rent-reduction law of 1965, which was applied universally. The new rent-reduction law also affected public housing. It limited the maximum rents of two-bedroom apartments to under three Egyptian pounds per month.[49] The state also required landlords to fill vacant apartments within two months or the state would do so without their approval. These legal interventions applied to all buildings built after 1944. Still, the housing crisis continued unabated, and attempts such as Riad's to use locally produced knowledge and expertise to confront the problem with architecture generated through research and economic considerations became a forgotten episode in history.

"Housing the Masses" in Egypt

Egypt's brief experimentation with social housing in the aftermath of World War II was part of a regional and global experience. Regionally, architects and engineers across the Middle East recognized the need to act quickly to provide solutions to the mounting housing problem. The housing panel at the 1947 Arab Engineering Conference is a testament to the regional dynamic of the housing question. Globally, housing the masses emerged as a core concern for the architectural profession as well as governments. From the center of Belgrade to the suburbs of Paris, balancing local politics and economics with global architectural trends produced new forms of social housing.[50] During this critical time, architect Mahmoud Riad attempted to provide an approach to housing that was grounded in both the local and the global. By referring to detailed statistical information and meticulously analyzing the economics of housing (from the costs of building materials to financing options and low-income wages), Riad proposed methods for approaching housing policy in Egypt. Not only did his study display aware-ness of local politics and economies, but it was international in its scope, analyzing case studies from around the world.

Why did Riad's findings and recommendations fail to produce a sus-tainable housing policy suitable for Egypt's needs? To answer that question, it is possible to speculate on the impact of political opportunism on the success of housing policies. In addition to economic pressures, architects such as Riad faced the challenge of maintaining professional autonomy. The new regime needed to hastily showcase, or fabricate, success stories to circulate in the media through which it could gain legitimacy. Images of modern housing blocks built around the country were politically necessary. Short-term political gains overrode long-term planning. Thus, the globally prevalent housing question, already complex, was compounded by local po-litical dynamics, namely Egypt's coup d'état. In this context, not only did the country fail to produce lasting housing policies built on the work of ar-chitects such as Riad, but the profession of architecture suffered while new realities pushed architects to the side as other actors such as contractors emerged and as the urban majority's exclusion from the piecemeal housing policies resulted in the emergence of unplanned urban areas around the country.

Notes

1. Tawfiq Ahmad 'Abd al-Gawwad, "The Third Arab Engineering Congress," *Al Emara* 7, nos. 5–6 (1947): 4.

2. For a comprehensive history of Egypt's workers' movement, class struggle, and trade unions, see Joel Beinin and Zachary Lockman, *Workers on the Nile: Nationalism, Commu-nism, Islam, and the Egyptian Working Class, 1882–1954* (Cairo: American University in Cairo Press, 1998).

3. Mercedes Volait, *Architectes et architectures de l'Egypte moderne, 1830–1950* (Paris: Maisonneuve et Larose, 2005), 416.

4. Ibid., 309–11.

5. Ibid., 336.

6. The link between national development and housing reform in general and housing workers in particular has been made in other national contexts linked directly to increases in industrialization. See, for example, Nicholas Bullock and James Read, *The Movement for Housing Reform in Germany and France, 1840–1914* (Cambridge: Cambridge University Press, 1985).

7. Eric Davis, *Challenging Colonialism: Bank Misr and Egyptian Industrialization, 1920–1941* (Princeton, NJ: Princeton University Press, 1983).

8. Volait, *Architectes et architectures,* 309–12.

9. Ibid., 336–37.

10. Mercedes Volait, "Egypt 1914–1954: Global Architecture before Globalization," in *Fundamentalists and Other Arab Modernisms,* ed. George Arbid (Beirut: Arab Center for Architecture, 2014).

11. Ahmad Hussain and Mahmoud Riad, *Machru' li-tawfir al-sakan lil-tabaqa al-mahduda al-dakhl fi misr* [Project for providing low-income housing in Egypt] (Cairo: Ministry of Social Affairs, 1949).

12. Mahmoud Riad, *Workers' Housing* (Cairo: Misr Press, 1947), 3. The lecture was also published in November 1947 in the professional engineers' journal *Majallat al-Muhandesin.*

13. Ibid., 8.

14. Samir Fikry, "Popular Housing in Egypt," *Al Emara* 13, no. 1 (1957): 17–18.

15. *Progress since the Revolution* (Cairo: Ministry of Social Affairs, n.d.), 31 (my translation).

16. Keith Wheelock, *Nasser's New Egypt: A Critical Analysis* (New York: Frederick A. Praeger, 1960), 127.

17. Riad, *Workers' Housing,* 6.

18. Riad's argument for workers' housing in Egypt is embedded in a global history of worker housing and company towns. Since Riad's lecture is concerned more with workers in small workshops than those in large factories, however, he does not favor or specify the housing of workers in new towns built adjacent to companies or factories. Nonetheless, it is useful to think of his efforts in relation to company towns, which appear to have been part of his research on the topic of housing workers. The literature on company towns is vast. Relevant examples include Josep Padro Margo and Lluis Casals, *Colonia Guell: Industria, Arquitectura y Sociedad* (Manresa, Spain: Angle, 2002); Martin Doughty, *Building the Industrial City* (Leicester, UK: Leicester University Press, 1986); Alison Hoagland, *Mine Towns: Buildings for Workers in Michigan's Copper Country* (Minneapolis: University of Minnesota Press, 2010); John Garner, *The Company Town: Architecture and Society in the Early Industrial Age* (New York: Oxford University Press, 2002).

19. Riad's proposed solution to Egypt's housing crisis, increasing industrialization to employ and house vast numbers of poor Egyptians, builds on the concept of the functional city, where workers can enjoy the comforts of modern life.

20. Sibel Bozdoğan, *Modernism and Nation Building: Turkish Architectural Culture in the Early Republic* (Seattle: University of Washington Press, 2001), 211.

21. In January 1944, the average income was 98 piasters for fifty hours of work. In July of that same year, the average had increased to 115 piasters for fifty-one hours of work. At the same time, housing for workers built by companies such as Misr Textiles and Weaving was costing the exorbitant sum of four hundred pounds per unit. Riad, *Workers' Housing,* 6.

22. Ibid., 9.

23. Ibid., 11–18.

24. The nine examples are Welwyn Garden City in England (Louis de Soissons and Arthur Kenyon, 1931); a municipal slum rehousing project commissioned by the London County Council (G. Topham Forrest, 1927–33); the Hillside Housing Development in the Bronx (Clarence Stein, 1932); the "Reconstruction of Blighted District" in Cleveland (Walter McCormack, 1932); Berlin Municipal and Cooperative Housing (Gropius, Scharoun, and Haring, 1930); the Zurich Cooperative Community (seven members of Swiss Werkbund, 1931); Rotterdam Municipal and Cooperative Housing (J. J. P. Oud, 1930); Nizhni Novgorod

Workers' City in Russia (Giprogor State Town Planning Agency, 1930–33); and the Vienna Municipal Apartment Block–Karl Marx Hof (Karl Ehn and Josef Bittner, 1926–30).

25. Volait, *Architectes et architectures*, 338–41.

26. After World War II, "with the creation of new industrial centers and the swelling of already overcrowded cities, there has been an extreme shortage of adequate, low-cost living accommodations. While buildings, especially after Agrarian Law 178/1952, have been a preferred investment for private citizens, none of this capital has gone into the construction of housing within reach of the laboring classes. Instead, numerous luxury apartments, priced far above the average Egyptian's income in order to yield an annual return of 8 to 10 per cent, have been built." Wheelock, *Nasser's New Egypt*, 122.

27. Ibid., 125.

28. Ibid.

29. Tawfiq 'Abd al-Gawwad, *Misr Al-'imara fi al-Qarn al-'ishrin* [Egyptian architecture in the twentieth century] (Cairo: Anglo-Egyptian Publishers, 1989), 27.

30. Wheelock, *Nasser's New Egypt*, 127.

31. "Twenty Thousand Poor Join the Elite" [in Arabic], *al-Musawwar*, May 28, 1954 (my translation).

32. *United Arab Republic: The Year Book 1963* (Cairo: Information Department, 1963), 149.

33. Ibid., 150.

34. Wheelock, *Nasser's New Egypt*, 124–25.

35. For the average per capita income shown, see *United Arab Republic: The Year Book 1963*, 72.

36. Wheelock, *Nasser's New Egypt*, 124–25.

37. Ibid., 127.

38. *Bina' al-Watan*, July 1959.

39. *Al-Idha'a*, March 1966. Published numbers of built housing fluctuate in the press. A 1965 special edition of *Bina' al-Watan* on housing claimed that since 1952 there had been over 170,000 housing units built, including 79,000 affordable housing units (*masaken iqtisadiyya*), 44,700 urban units, and 48,114 rural units.

40. Some additional published numbers on the state's efforts to meet the housing demand: by 1962, there had been 5,000 units built at the Islamic Missions City in the Azhar District, 7,972 units built by the Cairo Municipality in various districts, and 1,097 units built by the Ministry of Awqaf (total units for Cairo 14,069). In addition, the Alexandria Municipality had built 880 units. Data from *United Arab Republic: The Year Book 1963*, 150.

41. *Al-Idha'a*, March 1966, 12 (my translation).

42. Zayneb Hussein, "The Housing Minister Speaks to the Magazine about the Housing Crisis," *Al-Idha'a*, March 5, 1966.

43. This annual demand for housing construction would cost 36 million pounds (if each housing unit cost five hundred pounds). (This annual cost for housing was double what the government had spent on housing between 1952 and 1958.) Wheelock, *Nasser's New Egypt*, 126.

44. Anonymous, "The Housing Crisis on Its Way to End," *al-Musawwar*, July 1956, 43.

45. Anonymous, "A Building Revolution," *Bina' al-Watan*, August 1963, 155 (my translation).

46. *Bina' al-Watan*, housing special issue, 1965, 8.

47. Ibid.

48. Mohamed Abu Nasir, "An Explanatory Note of the Rent Reduction Law by the Housing Minister," *Bina' al-Watan*, housing special issue, 1965, 2–3.

49. This affected nearly two hundred thousand families: thirty-five thousand of them in Cairo and the rest in other cities. Ibid., 5.

50. For Belgrade, see Brigitte Le Normand, *Designing Tito's Capital: Urban Planning, Modernism, and Socialism in Belgrade* (Pittsburgh, PA: University of Pittsburgh Press, 2014); for Paris, see Kenny Cupers, *The Social Project: Housing Postwar France* (Minneapolis: University of Minnesota Press, 2014).

Bibliography

'Abd al-Gawwad, Tawfiq. *Misr Al-'imara fi al-Qarn al-'ishrin* [Egyptian architecture in the twentieth century]. Cairo: Anglo-Egyptian Publishers, 1989.

———. "The Third Arab Engineering Congress." *Al Emara* 7, nos. 5–6 (1947).

Beinin, Joel, and Zachary Lockman. *Workers on the Nile: Nationalism, Communism, Islam, and the Egyptian Working Class, 1882–1954*. Princeton, NJ: Princeton University Press, 1987.

Bozdoğan, Sibel. *Modernism and Nation Building: Turkish Architectural Culture in the Early Republic*. Seattle: University of Washington Press, 2001.

Bullock, Nicholas, and James Read. *The Movement for Housing Reform in Germany and France, 1840–1914*. Cambridge: Cambridge University Press, 1985.

Cupers, Kenny. *The Social Project: Housing Postwar France*. Minneapolis: University of Minnesota Press, 2014.

Davis, Eric. *Challenging Colonialism: Bank Misr and Egyptian Industrialization, 1920–1941*. Princeton, NJ: Princeton University Press, 1983.

Doughty, Martin. *Building the Industrial City*. Leicester, UK: Leicester University Press, 1986.

Fikry, Samir. "Popular Housing in Egypt." *Al Emara* 13, no. 1 (1957): 17–18.

Garner, John. *The Company Town: Architecture and Society in the Early Industrial Age*. New York: Oxford University Press, 2002.

Hoagland, Alison. *Mine Towns: Buildings for Workers in Michigan's Copper Country*. Minneapolis: University of Minnesota Press, 2010.

Hussain, Ahmad, and Mahmoud Riad. *Machru' li-tawfir al-sakan lil-tabaqa al-mahduda al-dakhl fi misr* [Project for providing low-income housing in Egypt]. Cairo: Ministry of Social Affairs, 1949.

Margo, Josep Padro, and Lluis Casals. *Colonia Guell: Industria, Arquitectura y Sociedad*. Manresa, Spain: Angle, 2002.

Normand, Brigitte Le. *Designing Tito's Capital: Urban Planning, Modernism, and Socialism in Belgrade*. Pittsburgh, PA: University of Pittsburgh Press, 2014.

Riad, Mahmoud. *Workers' Housing*. Cairo: Misr Press, 1947.

Volait, Mercedes. *Architectes et architectures de l'Egypte moderne (1830–1950): Genèse et essor d'une expertise locale*. Paris: Maisonneuve et Larose, 2005.

———. "Egypt 1914–1954: Global Architecture before Globalization." In *Fundamentalists and Other Arab Modernisms*, ed. George Arbid. Beirut: Arab Center for Architecture, 2014.

Wheelock, Keith. *Nasser's New Egypt: A Critical Analysis*. New York: Frederick A. Praeger, 1960.

MOHAMED ELSHAHED is British Museum curator for Modern Egypt. He teaches at the Department of Architecture at the American University in Cairo. He is the founding editor of Cairobserver.com, a web and print platform for architecture and urban culture with a focus on Cairo. Elshahed obtained his PhD from the Middle East Studies Department at New York University. His doctoral dissertation, *Revolutionary Modernism? Architecture and the Politics of Transition in Egypt, 1936–1967,* addressed architecture and urban planning in Egypt before and after the 1952 coup d'état. Elshahed also holds a MS in architectural studies from MIT and a BA from the New Jersey Institute of Technology.

4

NEOLIBERAL ISLAMISM AND THE CULTURAL POLITICS OF HOUSING IN TURKEY

Bülent Batuman

HOUSING HAS BEEN A MAJOR COMPONENT OF NEOLIBERAL urban policy for the past two decades. In brief terms, neoliberalism represents the contemporary phase of the capitalist mode of production, making particular use of urban space through processes of commodification and gentrification for the sake of capital accumulation. Within this context, housing has been an important field in the utilization of urban space as a means of capital accumulation. This has also been the case in Turkey, with certain characteristics shared by numerous nations in the Middle East and North Africa region. After the Cold War, Islam began to assume a global identity as a populist response to neoliberalism across the Third World. As I will discuss here, with the dismantling of welfare mechanisms, Islamic networks of solidarity, successfully deployed by the Ikhwanul Muslimin (Muslim Brotherhood) in the Middle East, began to be more influential than ever. Especially where authoritarian regimes were marked by corruption and failure to maintain popular consent, political Islam rose as the major positional power. A similar process took place in Turkey; throughout the 1990s, Islamists organized in successive parties increased their influence, which resulted in the rise of the Justice and Development Party (AKP) to power in 2002. Since then, the AKP has expanded its hegemonic control through a constant struggle with the secular establishment, represented by the military and the state bureaucracy. The AKP has strengthened its position through

the zealous fulfillment of neoliberal market demands and a populist welfare system utilizing bottom-up Islamic social networks and municipalities.
Throughout this chapter, the particular strand of pro-Islamic politics of the
AKP will be called neoliberal Islamism, as the party did not seek to transform the state structure into a theocratic one but rather aimed to reorganize
civil society in Islamic terms to the extent that economic relations allowed.

Since the mid-1990s, housing provision gained increasing pace under the
successive Islamist parties, initially via the local governments, and assumed
a role in the cultural politics of neoliberal Islamism. This chapter scrutinizes the utilization of housing for Islamic community building through
two examples. One of these is Başakşehir, which began as social housing in
an industrial zone in Istanbul in 1994. While the rise of Başakşehir was far
from a preconceived scheme, it has nevertheless been characterized as an
Islamist settlement and embodies all aspects of the Islamist enterprise in
shaping everyday life as well as its deficiencies. Constructed in four phases,
Başakşehir displays spatial transformations of Islamist cultural politics and
its internal conflicts over class relations. While the first phase was built as
social housing and later occupied by pious middle-class families, the fourth
phase (built in 2002) is a typical example of an upper-class gated community with an Islamic brand. The second example is an urban regeneration
project in Ankara along the road tying the city to the international airport.
The main idea here was to juxtapose slum upgrading with luxurious housing: a utopia where the rich would be rich and the poor would be poor yet
they would live side by side, sharing an Islamic identity. Shared practices
(and spaces) of Islamic faith were expected to serve as the ideological apparatus to build a new urban realm, an alternative to the capital city of
republican modernism. What is lacking in the story of Başakşehir is the
urban poor; and the most significant aspect of the North Ankara City Entrance project was the objective of transforming the existing squatter settlement and the relocation of squatters into modern high-rise blocks. Through
the comparative analysis of continuities and differences between these two
examples, this chapter will discuss the built forms of Islamic community
building and their political functions.

Urbanization and Islamist Mobilization in Turkey

The postwar period in Turkey, as in other developing regions of the world,
witnessed a rapid phase of urbanization that powerfully affected the

social and political environment. Squatters created spontaneous urban settlements in and around existing cities (especially the major ones with already large populations). Self-built *gecekondus* emerged as the primary form of working-class housing, significantly reducing the cost of living for the squatters, thus providing cheap labor for industry.[1] After the 1980s, with the help of new legislation, early squatters were given permission to replace their single-story *gecekondus* with four- to five-story apartment buildings. The commodification of the *gecekondu* areas turned the squatters into landlords benefiting from the comprehensive redevelopment of these areas in the form of apartment buildings. Where it was not feasible for contractors, it was the *gecekondu* owners themselves who acted as developers. They directly employed workers for construction and built their apartment buildings without any professional expertise or the required construction permits.[2] Soon a new term—*varoş*—was coined to represent the post-*gecekondu* quarters, characterized by densely built, low-quality apartment buildings. This new term was far from being neutral; it implied a threat to the urban order with an imagined tendency to (criminal or political) violence. The transformation of the single-story *gecekondus* into multistory apartments led to the emergence of new class positions within the post-*gecekondu* neighborhoods.[3] While the early squatters transformed into a new type of petty bourgeoisie, the latecomers constituted a new urban proletariat chained to the landlords, with whom they shared the same habitat as tenants.

Islamist mobilization almost always speaks to the urban poor with emphasis on moral, ethical, and religious sensibilities. Yet, as sociologist Asef Bayat has shown, Islamism as a political movement, rather than being a social movement of the urban poor, mainly has a middle-class character.[4] The urban poor have often supported Islamists as a strategic choice for social survival.[5] In a similar fashion, the Islamist movement in Turkey was spearheaded by provincial middle-class entrepreneurs in the 1970s yet gained an urban character after the 1980s. The post-*gecekondu* petty bourgeoisie sought upward mobility and a way out of the socioeconomic space of the *varoş*; therefore, they became the major group finding a voice in the RP, the predecessor of the AKP, which was active in the 1990s.[6] For the post-*gecekondu* petty bourgeoisie, the Islamist discourse emphasizing morality and ethics supported economic and political empowerment. In their quest for upward mobility, they presented the Islamists with the chance to be influential within the social space of the *varoş*. While mainstream political parties remained impervious to urban poverty, the Islamist cadres actively worked within the *varoş* and established a network of aid and solidarity in the early 1990s. This strategy allowed them to gain control of local administrations in the major cities, and they utilized this power to further improve their aid network as an original "welfare system." After the AKP came to power in 2002, this welfare system was formalized and integrated within the state functions. Thus, the urban politics of Islamism in Turkey relied on a particular form of populism: not a top-down version imagining a homogeneous mass whose interests are identified with those of the state, but one that affirms (class) differences while referring to faith and morality as the common denominators.[7] This particular form of populism linked the two segments sharing the habitat of *varoş*—the postsquatter petty bourgeoisie and the new generation of immigrants—with the existing squatter quarters.

Building an Islamic Suburb: Başakşehir

The takeover of Istanbul in 1994 was a victory conceived by the Islamists as the second Muslim conquest after 1453.[8] This was the first step not only for the Islamists in their gradual rise to power, but also for the newly elected Mayor Erdoğan in his long march to the presidency.[9] One of the first actions of the Islamist administration under Erdoğan was the reorganization of the municipal establishment KİPTAŞ (Residence and Development Plan Industry and Trade), which was initially founded to produce metropolitan-scale urban plans. It was remodeled as a construction company to undertake housing production, and one of its initial projects was Başakşehir, at the western fringes of the city. The name referred to a wheat sheaf, which was a symbol in the RP's emblem.

The location of Başakşehir had been envisaged as suitable for social housing as early as the 1980s because of its proximity to İkitelli Organized Industrial Zone, the largest industrial park in Turkey (fig. 4.1). The initial project displayed social housing features with low-cost/low-quality materials and smaller floor areas. The most important problem was the lack of resources, since the RP municipalities were denied government funds and advertisements were met with skepticism. Hence, fundraising quickly turned into an issue of Islamic solidarity, which coincided with the postsquatters' desire to move out of the *varoş*. Therefore, it was mostly the post-*gecekondu* petty bourgeoisie who invested in the project. Their main motive

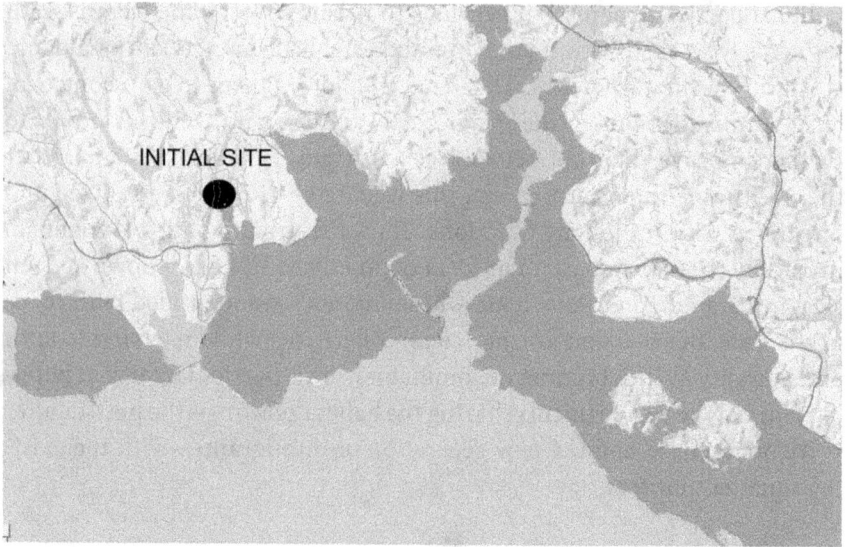

Figure 4.1. The location of Başakşehir development at the fringes of Istanbul's urban area in the mid-1990s. OpenStreetMap image reworked by the author.

to leave the *varoş* behind turned into strategic support for the RP, which promised them (social) relocation. Başakşehir, in this respect, represented a move out of the *varoş* not only physically but also representationally: it was not only the poverty and insecurity that the postsquatters were leaving behind, but also the stigma.[10] As a result, all the apartments were sold before construction began.

After this, Başakşehir rapidly developed in stages. The first stage (hereafter Başakşehir I) had 3,004 units in 79 apartment blocks of various height (six, eight, and ten floors). The second phase contained 2,304 units in 62 blocks with various heights of six, eight, nine, and ten floors. Başakşehir I was not envisaged as an enclosed complex but as the first step of an open-ended settlement. By the end of 1998, there were already twenty-five thousand residents in Başakşehir I and II (fig. 4.2). The major motivation for moving to Başakşehir was (and still is) being together with people who share similar moral values and the coherent sense of community created by the relative homogeneity of the population.[11] The residents feel that they are sharing their lifestyle with devout neighbors and "God-fearing" (honest) shopkeepers (fig. 4.3).[12] They believe that religion makes Başakşehir safe: women are not afraid to go out at night.

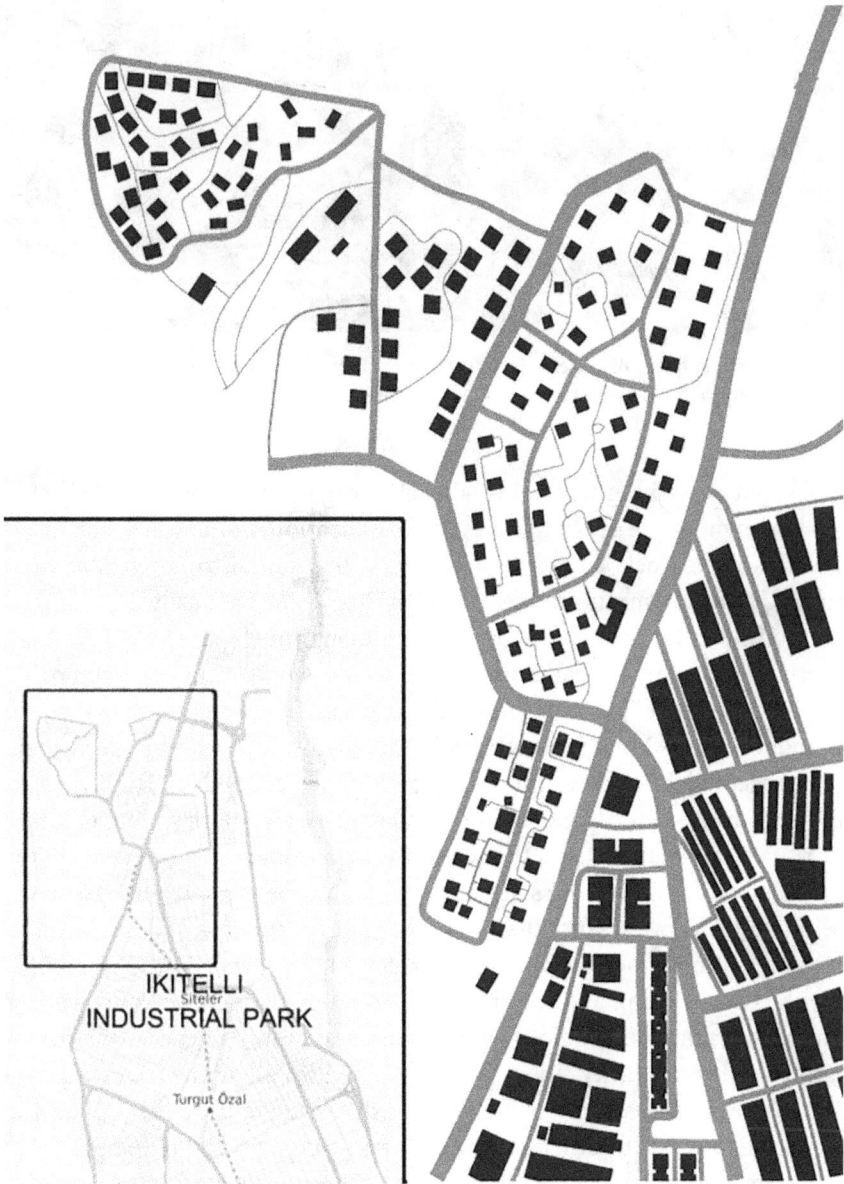

Figure 4.2. The location of the initial project in its relation to the İkitelli Industrial Park and the site plan showing Başakşehir I (left) and II (right). Drawing by Gülse Eraydın.

Figure 4.3. Street life in Başakşehir I and II. Note the billboards with religious advertisements. Photographs by Bülent Batuman, August 2015.

What is striking in the initial spatial organization of the Başakşehir development is the lack of spaces for socialization and cultural activities. But this initial lack should be understood in relation to the gender politics of Islamic community life, since Başakşehir, as primarily a residential environment, is used mostly by women during the daytime. A typical activity in the Islamic neighborhoods is *sohbet* (conversation), juxtaposing daily chat with religious teaching. These informal religious gatherings are found in various Muslim societies with different emphases on religious performance.[13] While these informal meetings are conducted as all-men or all-women sessions, the *sohbets* of men are generally more formal in terms of rituals and content, and the socialization accompanying religious rituals mostly involves business networking. The women's gatherings assume a semipublic character since these activities present them with their only medium for interacting with public life, albeit in a controlled way. The *sohbet* involves the reading and interpretation of religious texts by pious women and discussions on religious performances as well as general themes of family and community. These gendered activities allow the Islamist activists to utilize neighborhood relations to disseminate their views, and the religious activity, in return, legitimizes and facilitates the development of extrafamilial sociability for the women.[14] The meetings allow for new Islamic subjectivities, new ways of reclaiming Islamic knowledge, and new ways of integrating spirituality with female gender roles as mothers and wives.[15] Thus, the lack of spaces for socialization in Başakşehir I and II was almost a natural feature in that the housing estate is understood as a feminine space where the men are absent during the day. This would later change in tandem with the consolidation of AKP's political hegemony in the country, which will be discussed later in this chapter.

If we look at the context within which Başakşehir was developing, while the district was growing, political tension was escalating across the country. In February 1997, the military published a memorandum obliging the government to take anti-Islamist measures. The success of Başakşehir in its housing production and its recognition as an Islamist ghetto were not unnoticed by the military and the secularist establishment. A site facing Başakşehir I was already allocated for émigrés from Bulgaria who arrived in Turkey after the fall of the socialist regime there. Construction of a migrant compound was begun in Başakşehir in 1996. The land planned to become Başakşehir III was forced to be developed in the form of smaller cooperatives by independent contractors. In addition, after the devastating earthquake in 1999, new housing blocks were begun in the area as well (they would be finished in two phases in 2001 and 2002). Finally, the military planned a housing compound for its officers and acquired land in the district in 1997. In other words, the two-stage Başakşehir development was rapidly surrounded by various housing developments, with an attempt to confine this Islamist niche and diversify the growing settlement (fig. 4.4). Although the future of Başakşehir was envisaged as an integral neighborhood, with the rise of different housing estates, Başakşehir I and II were enclosed as separate compounds with fences and secured gates. In spite of these, Erdoğan's KİPTAŞ was already attempting to take the Islamist housing enterprise to a new level.

By the second half of the 1990s, the Islamist housing enterprise found an emerging demand for luxurious housing among the rising pious bourgeoisie.[16] Hence, Başakşehir IV was planned to contain social housing apartments as well as luxury villas. The project met with an unanticipated level of demand for the houses, especially the villas.[17] Although it was not intended as such, the project was perceived as a gated community for the pious bourgeoisie, who were under threat from the military. The location of Başakşehir IV also reflected the political pressure on the Islamists. It was to be built in a narrow strip at the edge of the municipal border and adjacent to a vast military compound. Hence, Başakşehir IV was literally a marginal settlement: it was away from the earlier stages as well as major transportation routes and was located on a site bordered by the barren valley to the west and the military zone to the east.

Nevertheless, with the AKP coming to power in 2002, Başakşehir IV gradually became the focal point of the district together with the fifth stage

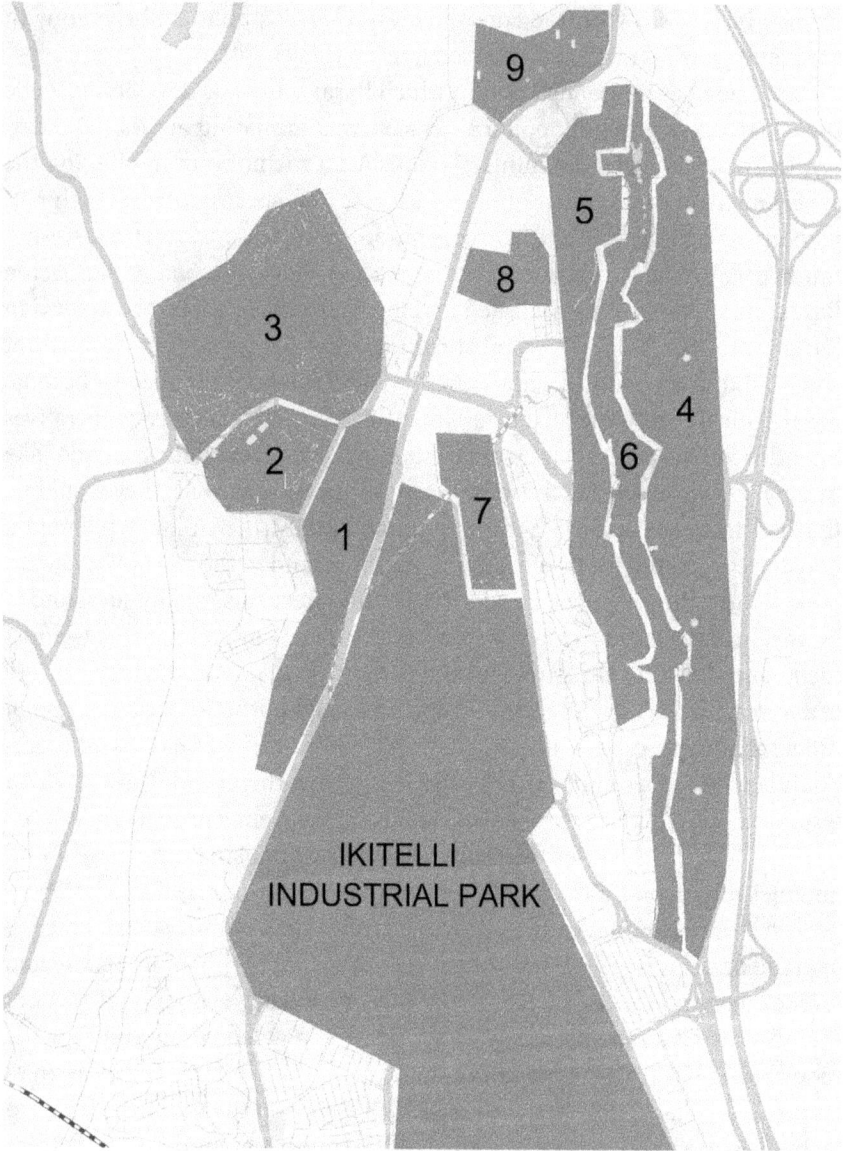

Figure 4.4. Başakşehir development with later stages: 1. Başakşehir I (1995–96); 2. Başakşehir II (1996–98); 3. Onurkent (envisaged as Başakşehir III—1998–2000s); 4. Başakşehir IV (1998–2002); 5. Başakşehir V (2005–7); 6. recreational valley (2008); 7. migrant compound (1996); 8. housing for earthquake victims (1999–2002); 9. housing compound for military officers (1998–2008). Map created by the author using OpenStreetMap image.

located across the valley.[18] The two stages surrounding the five-kilometer-long valley were to be an integral settlement for a population of sixty-six thousand, with the valley as a unifying recreational space. This integral settlement was now envisaged as a microcosm of an imaginary Istanbul. This conservative image of the city rejected its heterogeneity, which it viewed as morally threatening, and referred to its Ottoman past through nostalgic references. The individual compounds of Başakşehir V were named after Istanbul's historic neighborhoods, such as Salacak, Ortaköy, and Aşiyan. Here, nostalgia not only concerns an ideological reference to Ottoman history but—more importantly—refers to the harmonious everyday life within the traditional neighborhood—a construct of the conservative imaginary. Nostalgia is a symptomatic response to social change that triggers longing for an idealized past.[19] That is, nostalgia is a matter of the present more than it is a matter of the past: the past that is longed for is a constructed situation primarily addressing the present condition. Hence, the nostalgic reference to a harmonious Ottoman city is a symptom of the unresolved tensions within the district.

As will be discussed, with the addition of the latest stages, Başakşehir illustrates the AKP's social vision and the tensions inherent in this vision. The AKP's neoliberal Islamism pragmatically supports the rise of the Islamic bourgeoisie and overlooks conspicuous consumption, which would normally be intolerable in Islamic terms. Yet a major component of this project is the transformation of the urban poor. Although Başakşehir did not contain a poor population, it was the laboratory for experiments with new regimes of control in residential areas. These experiments would become the source for later implementations of the Housing Development Administration (TOKİ), which the following section discusses. After the discussion of the second example, which is a renewal project for a squatter district, a joint evaluation of the two examples will assess the social tensions inherent to Islamic community building.

North Ankara City Entrance Project

In 2003, TOKİ was granted new powers in urban regeneration, which now allowed the establishment of companies, the launching of projects to create new funds, and the use public land without charge. With a series of regulations, institutions and administrations responsible for housing and land development (such as the Undersecretariat of Housing and the Land

Office) were closed down and their assets were handed over to TOKİ. In 2004, the administration was granted planning authority in the areas that would be redeveloped. Moreover, with the same legislation, it gained the power to determine the value of expropriation in squatter areas. In 2007, the duties of the Ministry of Public Works regarding *gecekondu* prevention and slum clearance would also be transferred to TOKİ. With these regulations, the administration became exempt from almost all the bureaucratic mechanisms and could freely expropriate, plan, and redevelop areas. It turned into the major actor in housing production and the main facilitator of public-private partnerships. As a result, the number of houses built by TOKİ between 2003 and 2010 reached five hundred thousand, a figure that was merely forty-three thousand in the period 1984–2003.[20]

Concurrent with the restructuring of TOKİ, a law was passed specifically for Ankara, which defined an urban regeneration project for the squatter areas along the road connecting the airport to the city center in 2004 (fig. 4.5). The North Ankara City Entrance Project was the prime example of urban regeneration endeavors of the neoliberal Islamists and set the guidelines for future examples. Since the road from the airport was a gate to the capital city, the project was presented as a national undertaking. It was argued that the façades of this prestigious urban axis display "the nation" to the "foreign visitors," hence it had to be cleared of the squatter houses. The law authorized the Ankara Greater Municipality and TOKİ to redevelop the area through the joint company TOBAŞ. The area contained ten thousand five hundred squatter homes and, since the squatters were promised they would move into their new homes in late 2007, the evacuation process was rather peaceful. As it turned out, residents settled in temporary locations had to wait until 2013.[21]

The project is a significant attempt to develop a model for space production compatible with the ideological choices of neoliberal Islamism. After the Başakşehir experience in Istanbul, the power of the central government was for the first time added to the capabilities of the Islamist municipal administrations in the project. In this regard, the project can be compared to the construction of a new district to shelter the new government buildings of the young republic and villas for the state elite in the 1920s.[22] Yenişehir, literally the "new city" of Ankara, was built on the expropriated land across the railroad, which until then had served as the southern border of the town. This new city rising on a tabula rasa was seen as the site for the creation of the symbolic locus of the republic. In the following decades, the

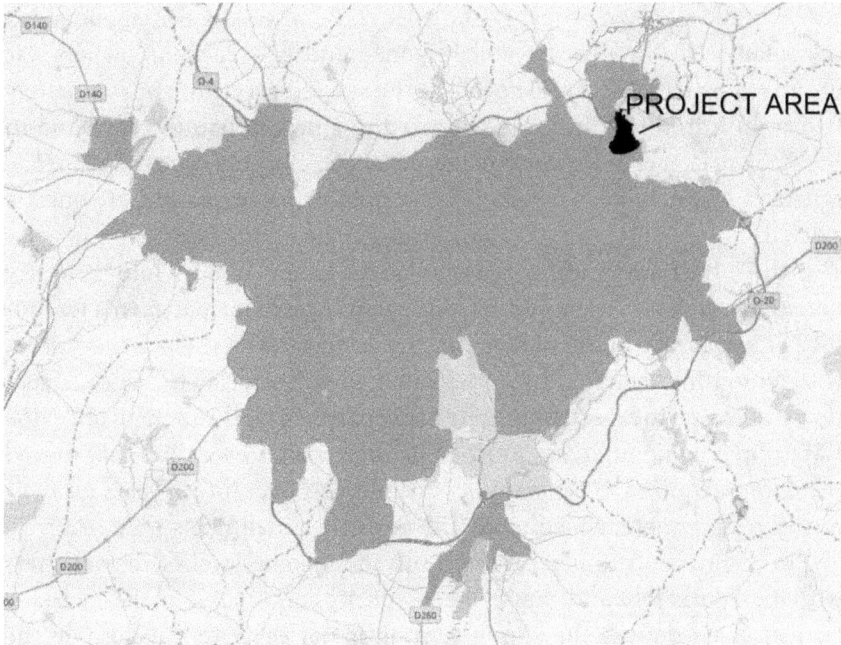

Figure 4.5. Location of North Ankara project site within Ankara's urban area. OpenStreetMap image reworked by the author.

railroad continued to act as the demarcation line separating the poor north and the wealthy south.

Within this context, it is not surprising to see the Islamists attempting to build a symbolic alternative to southern Ankara, which represented not only wealth but also republican ideology, with the presidential palace located on the southern hills overlooking the city. Back in the 1990s, the northern district of Keçiören, which has its own administrative body, was treated by the Islamists as the alternative to republican Ankara, with Islamic representations of space and conservative daily practices.[23] While the newly built town hall was decorated with symbols recalling Ottoman and Islamic symbolism, the municipality enforced an alcohol ban and introduced gender segregation in urban space.

Within the organization of the North Ankara project, the inhabitants were placed in four categories according to their legal status defined by their history in the area: those who owned title deeds (or equivalent documents) resulting from earlier amnesties, those who built their homes before

2000 but did not own proper documents, those who settled after 2000, and the tenants. The first group of eighty-one hundred *gecekondu* owners was promised apartments in the project; the second group of approximately fifteen hundred families was relocated to a new housing compound in Karacaören, farther to the north of the actual site. The final two groups, the late squatters and tenants, were denied any right to the area and were quickly evicted.[24]

While they were waiting to return to the area and move into their new homes, the squatters were either temporarily located in apartments for municipal employees or encouraged to live as tenants in different locations, with a monthly rent aid of approximately $150. The delay in the construction process led to an extended state of dependence on the municipality. The Karacaören compound was finished in 2008, and the families that moved there were required to pay monthly installments over fifteen years for their ninety-square-meter apartments. The monthly installments were relatively low in comparison to market rates, but the income level of the squatters without regular jobs and employment security continues to make it a heavy burden. Even though the administration is not eager to foreclose on the apartments in cases of failure to pay installments, squatters without regular jobs often give up and choose to sell their share to TOKİ.[25] This model has been used in cases where the squatters were either very poor or marginalized because of their ethnic identities (Roma in Sulukule and Kurds in Ayazma, both in Istanbul) or simply because the rent gap in the area encouraged swift gentrification. In such cases, the squatters have been forced to move to a new TOKİ compound far away from their living environment, with monthly payments way beyond their income level.[26] The distance from these compounds to the city centers, the lack of social facilities in the compounds, and the level of poverty result in rapid deterioration, decrease in apartment prices, and social problems such as drug use and crime.[27]

If we turn to the renewal area, the project site is morphologically a valley; both the slopes and the bottom were filled with *gecekondus,* and the road was located on the eastern side. While the existing urban fabric of low-income Keçiören surrounded the project site on the west, the empty terrain on the east is actually a continuous hill overlooking a lake to the east. Therefore, most of the high-rises built for the *gecekondu* owners were located on the western side, and the road was also relocated to this slope (which also required the construction of a bridge with heat to prevent icing). In this way, the road acted as a border between the low-income housing on

Figure 4.6. Slum clearance in the project site: 2004 versus 2015. From Google Earth.

the western slope and the vast valley containing seven hundred thousand square meters of recreational area (fig. 4.6). The eastern part of the site has views of the lake on the east and the valley on the west. The valley is virtually an extension of the high-income section, which contains ten thousand units in luxury high-rises as well as terrace houses and detached villas.

Housing Subjects of Neoliberal Islamism

It is necessary now to discuss these two examples in terms of the social production of space with respect to economy, governance, and culture. All three of these domains are interconnected and display mechanisms producing new subjectivities with reference to neoliberal restructuring and Islamization. What is crucial here is the neoliberal character of AKP's Islamism, which finds its reflection in the privatization of services and the making of a new type of governmentality. The making of a neoliberal civility is a crucial dimension of Islamic community building in Turkey. Neoliberal civility includes the disciplining of inhabitants, particularly the transformation of the postsquatters into middle classes. The biopolitics of middle-classness is pursued through the agency of the companies (KİPTAŞ in Başakşehir and TOBAŞ in the North Ankara project), which emerge as neoliberal dispositives par excellence. The making of a neoliberal civility is coupled with the Islamization of public life, which is realized with the involvement of faith-based organizations, yet controlled by the municipalities.

Here, the political economy of housing concerns the resident, who, within the new urban regeneration mechanism, is cut off from the traditional solidarity networks inherent in the squatter neighborhood. As public land is developed with the collaboration of TOKİ and the respective municipalities, expropriation of squatter areas is pursued on terms defined by these agents, and the surplus rent is redistributed to private investors undertaking construction. Therefore, squatters are left with the choice either to move out or to use the expropriation money as a down payment and take TOKİ loans to own a new apartment in the same area. The major aspect of this strategy is the immense powers vested in TOKİ and the municipalities, which results in two striking consequences: the maximization of profit and the lack of public participation in decision-making processes. This mechanism turns the *gecekondu* owner into an entrepreneurial subject seeking profit maximization through urban renewal.[28] The invention of resident categories with respect to their legal status thwarts group mobilization against renewal.[29]

The disciplinary role of indebtedness within the neoliberal economy has been a topic of scrutiny in recent years.[30] Indebtedness also plays its role in the domain of housing: the squatter moving into her new home does not own the house and has to pay her mortgage regularly for a longer time in comparison to a direct purchase.[31] Meanwhile the ownership of the apartment remains with TOKİ. These conditions produce political consent in two ways: while the indebted resident refrains from showing support to opposition parties so as not to face obstacles in her interactions with the municipal authority, she also feels the urge to support the AKP for the sake of economic stability.[32] For instance, although the residents of Karacaören frequently voice their dissatisfaction with the compound, the election results display overwhelming support (89 percent) for the AKP.[33]

Privatization also plays an important part in this new model of urban development, within which the companies (KİPTAŞ and TOBAŞ) assume major functions. As establishments created and authorized by the municipalities, the companies represent the transfer of certain powers of public authority to the market. And so, while a citizen, especially under the early Islamist rule of the RP, could visit the mayor and make requests for municipal services, the transfer of the control of housing to the companies makes it impossible to find an interlocutor for the mortgage payer. It is not even the company itself that collects the installments, but private banks. Moreover, the managerial authority is further privatized through the establishment of new companies. Istanbul Metropolitan Municipality established Boğaziçi Management, the first company specialized in housing management, in 1997. This was later followed by TOKİ's Emlak Management in 2009. Today, the housing compounds produced by KİPTAŞ and TOKİ are run by one of these two companies. Normally, the power to manage a multiunit building belongs to the residents, who establish an executive board. In the case of TOBAŞ, however, all the titles are in the hands of TOKİ, and in Başakşehir KİPTAŞ continuously postpones the necessary paperwork for the residents to be given title deeds. As a result, control of the social environment is always in the hands of the management companies. This situation not only strips the residents of their right to their environment but also forces them to accept disciplining through the rules, regulations, and staff of the company. The failure to pay maintenance fees results in threatening notices, which are highly uncommon in regular apartment buildings in Turkey. In sum, the companies serve as alienated mechanisms of discipline.

Another control mechanism emerging from economic organization is the partition of the housing complex into smaller divisions. Dividing the housing development serves a number of functions. It is first of all an efficient method of increasing the speed of housing production. The smaller clusters make it possible to assign to smaller subcontractors. This limits the need for higher skills and know-how, which in return expands the network of clientelist relations centered on KİPTAŞ and TOBAŞ horizontally and vertically. Subcontracting also reduces the companies' liabilities. But the definition of clusters does not only serve in the physical production of the district. It also plays a significant role in the social (re)production of space. The random definition of the scale of the cluster defines a unit which is *not* self-sufficient. The unit is merely a cluster of apartment buildings and is dependent on the spatial configuration of the overall settlement. Since the social use of space does not produce scales (such as street or neighborhood), the managerial scales are dictated to the social life in the settlement. Thus, the spatial organization of the housing estate is strictly tied to its managerial organization, which introduces scales of control over both the political economy of construction and the regulation of everyday life.

While both KİPTAŞ and Boğaziçi Management are municipality establishments, they are profit-seeking companies, distancing the municipality from the residents in their relation to the municipality. That is, the companies as mediators depoliticize the demands of the residents. Ironically, the staff members of the companies are determined at every level through partisan relationships, which leads to a decrease in the quality of service.[34] The relocated squatters are subject to rules and regulations rearranging the rhythms of their everyday practices. In the new housing complexes, they are introduced to written rules prohibiting the "misuse" of the environment, such as the expansion of indoor activities (cooking, hosting guests, growing vegetables, etc.) to the outside and the violation of a clear-cut differentiation of public and private spaces. These rules conflict with the former patterns of everyday life for the squatters and result in squatters being frequently warned by the security staff.[35]

Everyday life in the new housing compounds is regulated by these companies; and it is not only the houses that are controlled in this way. As mentioned earlier, the earlier compounds such as Başakşehir lacked social facilities. After AKP's coming to power in 2002, the housing projects began to include open spaces, which were not only recreational areas but also venues for Islamic mass practices such as fast-breaking. In addition, the municipalities under the AKP began to establish cultural centers for various events. In the two examples discussed, there are large valleys transformed into central public spaces for residents from different social backgrounds to share social space (fig. 4.7). In Başakşehir, the postsquatters meet with Islamic bourgeoisie; in North Ankara, the squatters have limited access to the valley. The valley in Başakşehir contains cafés, restaurants, and sports facilities as well as open and closed spaces for different functions, such as a twelve-hundred-person amphitheater and a thousand-person wedding venue. The valley within the North Ankara project site contains more than seventy buildings that house municipal functions, an amphitheater for five thousand people, a five-star hotel, shopping centers, cafés, restaurants, exhibition halls, wedding venues, specific centers for the youth, the elderly, and women, sports grounds, playgrounds, and so on. Both the valleys have mosques in strategic locations, making them visible. In Ankara, the largest *külliye* (complex centered on a mosque) is being built, with a fifteen-thousand-person mosque overlooking the valley (fig. 4.8).

Figure 4.7. The appropriation of the parking lot by postsquatters: women airing cotton and picnicking in the shade of the retaining wall on the right. Photograph by Bülent Batuman.

Within these public spaces of gathering, the class positions reflect themselves in distinct spatial practices. Typical actions transgressing "normal" behaviors in a park (such as stepping on the grass and eating sunflower seeds) are commonly seen in the compounds built for the squatters. The residents are expected to sit on the benches and not the grass. Yet they prefer to bring their rugs to lie on the grass together with their tea

Figure 4.8. North Ankara project site: (left to right) the (colored) high-rise blocks for *gecekondu* owners (the large *külliye* under construction is visible in the distance), the relocated road to the airport, the recreational valley, the luxury residences under construction. Photograph by Bülent Batuman.

mugs to picnic. These habits are also seen in Başakşehir, performed by the residents of the earlier stages in the valley. One interesting development is that the wealthier residents of Başakşehir have transformed some of the villas closer to the park into "women's cafeterias."[36] They serve food and even provide service for events organized in these spaces as well as their clients' homes. These are gendered spaces exclusive to women and used for upper-class *sohbet* meetings. The retreat of the wealthy female residents of Başakşehir IV to the indoor space illustrates class distinction and the reluctance of the Islamic bourgeoisie to mingle with their post-*gecekondu* neighbors. In all the parks, the municipalities hire security companies; their main function, rather than actually providing safety, is disciplining the lower classes.

Finally, on the cultural level, what is at stake is the Islamization of public life, which is also directed by the municipality and realized with the involvement of faith-based organizations. The Islamic communities (*cemaat*) have always been important in Islamist politics and social life in Turkey.[37] The *cemaat*s are established around a charismatic leader, and some *cemaat*s are affiliated with hierarchically organized orders (*tarikat*). Such religious groups have always been influential, but their visibility increased after 2002. The informal communities began to formalize their organizations with the establishment of associations, NGOs, foundations, and even companies. The links between the religious communities and the affiliated formal organizations are almost never openly acknowledged. Yet the formalization of the organizations makes them recognizable institutions, vulnerable to state control. The government, or the municipality for that matter, creates opportunities for the activities of these religious communities toward Islamization of everyday lives of citizens, provided that the community is operating through traceable and registered organizations such as associations, foundations, or companies. They are provided with lots or buildings that belong to the municipality, to be used as student housing, schools, and private tutoring centers. The venues of the municipalities, which increased in number after 2002, are allocated to these organizations for cultural and educational activities as well as charity work. In both Başakşehir and North Ankara, all the social and cultural facilities belong to the municipality, and they are used almost exclusively for events with Islamic content. Nonreligious residents complain that there is no cultural activity not associated with Islam.[38]

Conclusion

While themes such as urban renewal and gentrification have often been discussed within the context of the Middle East as local cases of global trends, the relationship between Islamic religiosity and the production of urban space has received little attention.[39] Similarly, the housing enterprise of the Islamist government in Turkey has often been discussed in terms of its political economy. What is noteworthy in AKP's housing policy is not only the sheer quantity of housing production but also the attempts at Islamic community building through these projects. While squatter populations are disciplined in housing compounds of TOKİ, Islamic gated communities have emerged first as retreats for the growing pious bourgeoisie and later as manifestations of a new lifestyle. The AKP's neoliberal Islamism envisages religion as the unifying component of social life. The most important aspect of this vision is the attempt to maintain social cohesion without any concern for closing the gap between the rich and the poor. Referring to faith and morality as the source of a harmonious social formation, the AKP consistently aimed at controlling poverty rather than reducing it. Two decades of practice, initially in the local governments and then through the total control of central government, first generated ad hoc housing environments and later gave way to large-scale projects. Başakşehir was the prime example of the early experiments in housing development, which transformed significantly throughout the two decades. TOKİ's North Ankara project, on the other hand, was the most ambitious attempt at building an Islamist utopia.

As this chapter discussed, although the neoliberal Islamist utopia promised the cohabitation of different classes, it did not offer the reduction of the income gap between them. Instead, this utopia was founded on the belief that shared faith and practices of religiosity would facilitate peaceful cohabitation. The indifference to class distinctions expresses itself in plan types of housing units. Typical floor plans are proposed for postsquatter families and for middle-class ones, differing only in size and quality of construction materials. In this respect, the Islamist utopia of religious community building in Turkey ended up creating conservative middle-class subjectivity, forcing various class positions to fit into this ideal image. This, in return, led to class conflicts within the housing environments. In Başakşehir, the postsquatter residents of Başakşehir I and II are marginalized with the rise of Başakşehir IV. The residents of Başakşehir I–II and Başakşehir IV despise each other's everyday lives. For the former, the latter represent the "nouveau riche," while the latter view the former with reference to the *varoş*.[40] In the cases of slum upgrading—as illustrated by the example of North Ankara—the government categorizes the squatters as those given a chance to live side by side with the rich, albeit at the price of heavy mortgage payments. This option does not guarantee homeownership, requires strict obedience to the mechanisms of community building, and dictates class hierarchy. Since continuation of squatter life is not an option, the poorer squatters are also forced into TOKİ compounds, where they are subject to rules and regulations alien to their lifestyles.

Acknowledgments

The discussion presented in this chapter is part of a larger study; see, Bülent Batuman, *New Islamist Architecture and Urbanism: Negotiating Nation and Islam through Built Environment in Turkey* (Abingdon and New York: Routledge, 2018).

Notes

1. İlhan Tekeli, *Türkiye'de Yaşamda ve Yazında Konut Sorununun Gelişimi* [The development of the housing question in social life and in literature in Turkey] (Ankara: TOKİ, 1996);

Çağlar Keyder, "The Housing Market from Informal to Global," in *Istanbul: Between the Global and the Local*, ed. Ç. Keyder (Lanham, MD: Rowman and Littlefield, 1999), 143–60.

2. Tansı Şenyapılı and Ali Türel, *Ankara'da Gecekondu Oluşum Süreci ve Ruhsatlı Konut Sunumu* [Gecekondu building process and housing provision in Ankara] (Ankara: Batıbirlik, 1996).

3. Utku Balaban, "Conveyor Belt of Flesh: Urban Space and Proliferation of the Industrial Labor Practices" (PhD diss., SUNY Binghamton, 2011).

4. Asef Bayat, *Street Politics: Poor People's Movements in Iran* (New York: Columbia University Press, 1997); Asef Bayat, *Life as Politics: How Ordinary People Change the Middle East* (Stanford, CA: Stanford University Press, 2013), 172–73.

5. Peter Mandaville, *Global Political Islam* (London: Routledge, 2007), 98–101.

6. Although Turkish Islamism has a longer history in the republican era, the major Islamist party that was active in the late 1980s was the Welfare Party (RP). Most of the major Turkish cities were taken over by the RP in the 1990s, and the political influence of Islam gradually increased, primarily through the municipal policies of the RP. Nevertheless, the Islamist movement went through a significant transformation in the second half of the decade. This has been a result of, on the one hand, the military intervention in 1997 and, on the other, their experience in local and central governments leading them to reconciliation with the market if not with the state. After the outlawing of the RP in 1998 and its successor the Virtue Party (FP) in 2001, the Islamists split into two factions. While the older generation maintained the radical Islamist discourse of the 1990s, the younger generation, led by Recep Tayyip Erdoğan, established the AKP. The AKP broke away from anticapitalist, anti-Western discourse and embraced an agenda of democratization in the face of constant threat from the military.

7. Cihan Tuğal, *Passive Revolution: Absorbing the Islamic Challenge to Capitalism* (Stanford, CA: Stanford University Press, 2009).

8. Tanıl Bora, "Istanbul of the Conqueror: The 'Alternative Global City' Dreams of Political Islam," in Keyder, *Istanbul*, 47–75.

9. Erdoğan was sentenced to imprisonment in tandem with the closing of the RP in 1998 and was banned from politics. The ban was later lifted, and he became the prime minister in 2003. After serving in this post for eleven years, he was elected president in 2014.

10. Ayşe Çavdar, "Loss of Modesty: The Adventure of Muslim Family from *Mahalle* to Gated Community" (PhD diss., Europa-Universitat Viadrina Frankfurt, 2013).

11. Selin Gürgün, "A Visual Ethnographic Approach to Islamic Lifestyles: The Case of Başakşehir" (master's thesis, Bilkent University, 2014).

12. Ibid., 45.

13. For instance, see Ahmad Fauzi Abdul Hamid, "Transnational Islam in Malaysia," in *Transnational Islam in South and Southeast Asia: Movements, Networks, and Conflict Dynamics*, ed. Peter Mandaville, Farish A. Noor, Alexander Horstmann, Dietrich Reetz, Ali Riaz, Animesh Roul, Noorhaidi Hasan, Ahmad Fauzi Abdul Hamid, Rommel C. Banlaoi and Joseph Chinyong Liow (Seattle: National Bureau of Asian Research, 2009), 145; and Asef Bayat, *Making Islam Democratic: Social Movements and the Post-Islamist Turn* (Stanford, CA: Stanford University Press, 2007), 49, for Egypt; Pieternella van Doorn-Harder, *Women Shaping Islam: Reading the Qur'an in Indonesia* (Urbana: University of Illinois Press, 2006), 95–97, for Indonesia; and Helen Falconer, "Gathering for the Sake of Allah: An Ethnographic Account of a Women's Halaqa Group in Cardiff, UK" (master's thesis, Cardiff University, 2010), for migrant communities in Europe.

14. Amélie Le Renard, *A Society of Young Women: Opportunities of Place, Power, and Reform in Saudi Arabia* (Stanford, CA: Stanford University Press, 2014), 92.

15. Smita Tewari Jassal, "The *Sohbet*: Talking Islam in Turkey," *Sociology of Islam* 1, nos. 3–4 (2014): 188–208.

16. Ayşe Buğra and Osman Savaşkan, *New Capitalism in Turkey: The Relationship between Politics, Religion, and Business* (Northampton, UK: Edward Elgar, 2014)

17. "İkitelli Konutları Kapışıldı" [İkitelli residences were snatched up], *Milliyet*, August 26, 1998, 27.

18. Nurullah Gündüz, "Uydu Kentin Mekansal Üretimi: Başakşehir 4. ve 5. Etaplar" [Spatial Production of Satellite City: Başakşehir 4. and 5. Phases] (PhD diss., Istanbul University, 2015).

19. Sallie Westwood and John Williams, "Imagining Cities," in *Imagining Cities: Scripts, Signs, Memories*, ed. Sallie Westwood and John Williams (London: Routledge, 1997), 1–16; Svetlana Boym, *The Future of Nostalgia* (New York: Basic Books, 2001).

20. TOKİ, *Building Turkey of the Future: Corporate Profile, 2010/2011* (Ankara: TOKİ, 2011).

21. Bülent Batuman, "Minarets without Mosques: Limits to the Urban Politics of Neoliberal Islamism," *Urban Studies* 50 (2013): 1095–11.

22. Bülent Batuman, *The Politics of Public Space: Domination and Appropriation in and of Kızılay Square* (Saarbrücken, Ger.: VDM, 2009).

23. Güven Arif Sargın, "Displaced Memories, or the Architecture of Forgetting and Remembrance," *Environment and Planning D: Society and Space* 22 (2004): 659–80.

24. TOKİ, *Gecekondu Dönüşüm Kentsel Yenileme Projeleri* [*Gecekondu* upgrading urban renewal projects] (Ankara: TOKİ, 2011), 84–95.

25. Tahire Erman, "Kentsel Dönüşüm Projeleri ve Yeniden Yerleşme Deneyimleri: Karşılaştırmalı ve Zaman Boyutlu bir Yaklaşım" [Urban transformation projects and resettlement cases: a comparative and time-sensitive approach] TÜBİTAK Project No. 109K360 (Ankara: TÜBİTAK, 2014).

26. Gülçin Erdi Lelandais, "Space and Identity in Resistance against Neoliberal Urban Planning in Turkey," *International Journal of Urban and Regional Research* 38 (2014): 1785–806; Binnur Oktem Unsal, "State-Led Urban Regeneration in Istanbul: Power Struggles between Interest Groups and Poor Communities," *Housing Studies* 30, no. 8 (2015): 1299–1316.

27. Erman, "Kentsel Dönüşüm Projeleri."

28. Ozan Karaman, "Resisting Urban Renewal in Istanbul," *Urban Geography* 35, no. 2 (2014): 290–310.

29. Tuna Kuyucu, "Law, Property, and Ambiguity: The Uses and Abuses of Legal Ambiguity in Remaking Istanbul's Informal Settlements," *International Journal of Urban and Regional Research* 38 (2014): 609–27. For a process in which Hezbollah's urban renewal projects in the poor suburbs of Beirut utilized a similar strategy of various levels of compensation to diminish opposition to renewal projects, see Hiba Bou Akar, "Displacement, Politics, and Governance: Access to Low-Income Housing in a Beirut Suburb" (master's thesis, MIT, 2005), and Ananya Roy, "Civic Governmentality: The Politics of Inclusion in Beirut and Mumbai," *Antipode* 41, no. 1 (2009): 159–79.

30. David Graeber, *Debt: The First 5,000 Years* (New York: Melville House, 2011); Maurizio Lazzarato, *The Making of the Indebted Man: An Essay on the Neo-liberal Condition* (Amsterdam: Semiotext(e), 2012).

31. Başak Ergüder, "2000'li Yıllarda Türkiye'de Hanehalkı Borçlanması: Konut Kredileri ve Toplumsal Refah" [Household indebtedness in Turkey in the 2000s: housing loans and social welfare], *Praksis* 38 (2015): 99–128.

32. Ayşe Buğra and Çağlar Keyder, *New Poverty and the Changing Welfare Regime of Turkey* (Ankara: UNDP, 2003); Elife Kart, "Yoksulluğun Mekanlarında Borçluluğun ve "Borçlu'nun Üretilişi" [The production of indebtedness and the "indebted" within the spaces of poverty], *Praksis* 38 (2015): 155–78.

33. Erman, "Kentsel Dönüşüm Projeleri."

34. For narratives on the partisan relations shaping the interactions between municipalities, companies, and residents, see Tahire Erman, *"Mış Gibi Site": Ankara'da Bir TOKİ-Gecekondu Dönüşüm Sitesi* ["As if housing": A TOKI-*Gecekondu* transformation compound in Ankara] (Istanbul: İletişim, 2016), 139–70.

35. Erman, "Kentsel Dönüşüm Projeleri." For similar frustrating experiences of former squatters in Bezirganbahçe, Istanbul, see Cihan Uzunçarşılı Baysal, "Ayazma'dan Bezirganbahçe'ye: Yeniden İskanın Yarattığı Kültürel Mağduriyetler ve Yeni Kimlik İnşası" [From Ayazma to Bezirganbahçe: Cultural victimization created by resettlement and new identity formation], *Dosya* 16 (2009): 35–41.

36. Rumeysa Çavuş, "Bir Kent Planlamak: Siyasi İktidarın Yüzü Olarak Peyzaj" [Planning a city: landscape as the face of political power], *Sosyal Bilimler: MSGSÜ Sosyal Bilimler Enstitüsü Dergisi* 7 (2013): 21–33.

37. Şerif Mardin, *Religion and Social Change in Modern Turkey: The Case of Bediüzzaman Said Nursi* (Albany: SUNY Press, 1989).

38. Gürgün, "Visual Ethnographic Approach," 65–67.

39. Nezar AlSayyad, "Medina—the 'Islamic,' 'Arab,' 'Middle Eastern,' City: Reflections on an Urban Concept," in *Urban Design in the Arab World: Reconceptualizing Boundaries*, ed. Robert Saliba (Farnham, UK: Ashgate, 2015), 17–25.

40. Gürgün, "Visual Ethnographic Approach," 94.

Bibliography

Abdul Hamid, Ahmad Fauzi. "Transnational Islam in Malaysia." In *Transnational Islam in South and Southeast Asia: Movements, Networks, and Conflict Dynamics*, edited by Peter Mandaville, Farish A. Noor, Alexander Horstmann, Dietrich Reetz, Ali Riaz, Animesh Roul, Noorhaidi Hasan, Ahmad Fauzi Abdul Hamid, Rommel C. Banlaoi and Joseph Chinyong Liow, 141–66. Seattle: National Bureau of Asian Research, 2009.

AlSayyad, Nezar. "Medina—the 'Islamic,' 'Arab,' 'Middle Eastern,' City: Reflections on an Urban Concept." In *Urban Design in the Arab World: Reconceptualizing Boundaries*, edited by Robert Saliba, 17–25. Farnham, UK: Ashgate, 2015.

Balaban, Utku. "Conveyor Belt of Flesh: Urban Space and Proliferation of the Industrial Labor Practices." PhD diss., SUNY Binghamton, 2011.

Batuman, Bülent, *New Islamist Architecture and Urbanism: Negotiating Nation and Islam through Built Environment in Turkey*. Abingdon and New York: Routledge, 2018.

———. *The Politics of Public Space: Domination and Appropriation in and of Kızılay Square*. Saarbrücken, Ger.: VDM, 2009.

Bayat, Asef. *Life as Politics: How Ordinary People Change the Middle East*. Stanford, CA: Stanford University Press, 2013.

———. *Making Islam Democratic: Social Movements and the Post-Islamist Turn*. Stanford, CA: Stanford University Press, 2007.

———. *Street Politics: Poor People's Movements in Iran*. New York: Columbia University Press, 1997.

Bora, Tanıl. "Istanbul of the Conqueror: The 'Alternative Global City' Dreams of Political Islam." In *Istanbul: Between the Global and the Local*, edited by Çağlar Keyder, 47–75. Lanham, MD: Rowman and Littlefield, 1999.

Bou Akar, Hiba. "Displacement, Politics, and Governance: Access to Low-Income Housing in a Beirut Suburb." Master's thesis, MIT, 2005.

Boym, Svetlana. *The Future of Nostalgia*. New York: Basic Books, 2001.

Buğra, Ayşe, and Çağlar Keyder. *New Poverty and the Changing Welfare Regime of Turkey*. Ankara: UNDP, 2003.

Buğra, Ayşe, and Osman Savaşkan. *New Capitalism in Turkey: The Relationship between Politics, Religion and Business*. Northampton, UK: Edward Elgar, 2014.

Çavdar, Ayşe. "Loss of Modesty: The Adventure of Muslim Family from *Mahalle* to Gated Community." PhD diss., Europa-Universitat Viadrina Frankfurt, 2013.

Çavuş, Rumeysa. "Bir Kent Planlamak: Siyasi İktidarın Yüzü Olarak Peyzaj" [Planning a city: Landscape as the face of political power]. *Sosyal Bilimler: MSGSÜ Sosyal Bilimler Enstitüsü Dergisi* 7 (2013): 21–33.

Ergüder, Başak. "2000'li Yıllarda Türkiye'de Hanehalkı Borçlanması: Konut Kredileri ve Toplumsal Refah" [Household debt in Turkey in the 2000s: housing loans and social welfare]. *Praksis* 38 (2015): 99–128.

Erman, Tahire. "Kentsel Dönüşüm Projeleri ve Yeniden Yerleşme Deneyimleri: Karşılaştırmalı ve Zaman Boyutlu bir Yaklaşım" [Urban regeneration projects and re-settlement experiences: a comparative and time-sensitive approach]. TÜBİTAK Project No. 109K360, 2014.

———. *"Mış Gibi Site": Ankara'da Bir TOKİ-Gecekondu Dönüşüm Sitesi* ["As if housing": A TOKI-*Gecekondu* transformation compound in Ankara]. Istanbul: İletişim, 2016.

Falconer, Helen. "Gathering for the Sake of Allah: An Ethnographic Account of a Women's Halaqa Group in Cardiff, UK." Master's thesis, Cardiff University, 2010.

Graeber, David. *Debt: The First 5,000 Years*. New York: Melville House, 2011.

Gündüz, Nurullah. "Uydu Kentin Mekansal Üretimi: Başakşehir 4. ve 5. Etaplar" [Spatial Production of Satellite City: Başakşehir 4th ve 5th Phases]. PhD diss., Istanbul University, 2015.

Gürgün, Selin. "A Visual Ethnographic Approach to Islamic Lifestyles: The Case of Başakşehir." Master's thesis, Bilkent University, 2014.

Jassal, Smita Tewari. "The *Sohbet*: Talking Islam in Turkey." *Sociology of Islam* 1, nos. 3–4 (2014): 188–208.

Karaman, Ozan. "Resisting Urban Renewal in Istanbul." *Urban Geography* 35, no. 2 (2014): 290–310.

Kart, Elife. "Yoksulluğun Mekanlarında Borçluluğun ve "Borçlu"nun Üretilişi" [The production of indebtedness and the "indebted" within the spaces of poverty]. *Praksis* 38 (2015): 155–78.

Keyder, Çağlar. "The Housing Market from Informal to Global." In *Istanbul: Between the Global and the Local*, edited by Çağlar Keyder, 143–60. Lanham, MD: Rowman and Littlefield, 1999.

Kuyucu, Tuna. "Law, Property, and Ambiguity: The Uses and Abuses of Legal Ambiguity in Remaking Istanbul's Informal Settlements." *International Journal of Urban and Regional Research* 38 (2014): 609–27.

Lelandais, Gülçin Erdi. "Space and Identity in Resistance against Neoliberal Urban Planning in Turkey." *International Journal of Urban and Regional Research* 38 (2014): 1785–1806.

Lazzarato, Maurizio. *The Making of the Indebted Man: An Essay on the Neo-liberal Condition.* Amsterdam: Semiotext(e), 2012.

Le Renard, Amélie. *A Society of Young Women: Opportunities of Place, Power and Reform in Saudi Arabia.* Stanford, CA: Stanford University Press, 2014.

Mandaville, Peter. *Global Political Islam.* London: Routledge, 2007.

Mardin, Şerif. *Religion and Social Change in Modern Turkey: The Case of Bediüzzaman Said Nursi.* Albany: SUNY Press, 1989.

Milliyet. "İkitelli Konutları Kapışıldı" [İkitelli residences were snatched up]. August 26, 1998.

Roy, Ananya. "Civic Governmentality: The Politics of Inclusion in Beirut and Mumbai." *Antipode* 41, no. 1 (2009): 159–79.

Sargın, Güven Arif. "Displaced Memories, or the Architecture of Forgetting and Remembrance." *Environment and Planning D: Society and Space* 22 (2004): 659–80.

Şenyapılı, Tansı, and Ali Türel. *Ankara'da Gecekondu Oluşum Süreci ve Ruhsatlı Konut Sunumu* [*Gecekondu* building process and housing provision in Ankara]. Ankara: Batıbirlik Yayınları, 1996.

Tekeli, İlhan. *Türkiye'de Yaşamda ve Yazında Konut Sorununun Gelişimi* [The development of the housing question in social life and in literature in Turkey]. Ankara: TOKİ, 1996.

TOKİ. *Building Turkey of the Future: Corporate Profile, 2010/2011.* Ankara: TOKİ, 2011.

———. *Gecekondu Dönüşüm Kentsel Yenileme Projeleri* [Gecekondu transformation urban renewal projects]. Ankara: TOKİ, 2011.

Tuğal, Cihan. *Passive Revolution: Absorbing the Islamic Challenge to Capitalism.* Stanford, CA: Stanford University Press, 2009.

Unsal, Binnur Oktem. "State-Led Urban Regeneration in Istanbul: Power Struggles between Interest Groups and Poor Communities." *Housing Studies* 30, no. 8 (2015): 1299–316.

Uzunçarşılı Baysal, Cihan. "Ayazma'dan Bezirganbahçe'ye: Yeniden İskanın Yarattığı Kültürel Mağduriyetler ve Yeni Kimlik İnşası" [From Ayazma to Bezirganbahçe: Cultural victimization caused by resettlement and new identity formation]. *Dosya* 16 (2009): 35–41.

Van Doorn-Harder, Pieternella. *Women Shaping Islam: Reading the Qur'an in Indonesia.* Urbana: University of Illinois Press, 2006.

Westwood, Sallie, and John Williams. "Imagining Cities." In *Imagining Cities: Scripts, Signs, Memories,* edited by Sallie Westwood and John Williams, 1–16. London: Routledge, 1997.

BÜLENT BATUMAN studied architecture at the Middle East Technical University (Ankara, Turkey). He received his PhD in history and theory of art and architecture from SUNY Binghamton in 2006. He currently teaches urban design and politics of modern urbanism in the Department of Urban Design and Landscape Architecture at Bilkent University, where he is Department Chair. His current research focuses on the spatial politics of Islamism. His articles have been published in various journals, including *Journal of Architecture, Journal of Architectural Education, Journal of Urban History, Urban Studies, Urban Design International, Cities, Political Geography,* and *METU Journal of the Faculty of Architecture.* He is author of *New Islamist Architecture and Urbanism: Negotiating Nation and Islam through Built Environment in Turkey* (Routledge, 2018).

PART II

HISTORIES OF SOCIAL HOUSING: IDENTITY, NATION, AND BEYOND

5

CONSTRUCTING DIGNITY: PRIMITIVIST DISCOURSES AND THE SPATIAL ECONOMIES OF DEVELOPMENT IN POSTCOLONIAL TUNISIA

Nancy Demerdash

Inciting his readers' empathy and pity in a 1953 newspaper editorial on "Habitat: Universalism and Regionalism" in the *Zürcher Zeitung*, Sigfried Giedion (1888–1968), a Swiss art and architectural historian and secretary-general for the Congrès Internationaux d'Architecture Moderne (CIAM), called attention to the question of how architecture can generate dignity while conforming to the environmental and cultural norms of a region.[1] Addressing the dire living conditions of both rural and urban areas scattered across the Maghreb, his title spoke to the urgency of the broader global problem of habitat. That also happened to be the theme of CIAM's Ninth International Congress, which convened at the École des Arts et Métiers in Aix-en-Provence, France, from July 19 to 21, 1953. From the Atlas Mountains in Morocco to other so-called remote and far-off villages nestled in the Sahara, stretching between Algiers and Tunis, people make do with the realities and material constraints of their environment. Singling out the *bidonville*, or "tin can," towns, constructed mostly from metal refuse, Giedion underscored the grim quality of life prevalent throughout the entirety of postwar North Africa, but he also cited the work of architect Pierre-André Emery (1903–1982)[2] and his team, consisting of Jean de Maisonseul, Louis Miquel, Jean-Pierre Faure, and Roland Simounet. CIAM-Alger, the Algerian branch of CIAM, collectively sought, through the prevalent form of the *bidonville,* to understand "the problem [of human habitation] . . . in its total reality: its forms, its multiple expressions, and its life."[3] Giedion admired CIAM-Alger's anthropological study of what the group perceives to be vernacular[4] by use of the *grille* (grid);[5] this methodology was thought to be the means by which one could derive notions on how to restore dignity in rapidly urbanizing, but not yet fully industrialized, countries. His remark that a "hut in Cameroon has more aesthetic dignity than most prefabricated houses" not only captures an important dialectic in postwar modernist construction between materiality and dignity, but it also reflects a historical moment marked by a pivotal shift in attitudes away from the prominence of the machine aesthetic and toward so-called primitive building modes and typologies.[6] What this suggests too is a self-reflexive moment for modernism, looking inward onto itself, finding that its modular frames, standardized iron posts, and cold, characterless cement are, in fact, devoid of dignity.

The lingering question that persists here is, how can such dignity be restored if it is presumed to be lost? For Le Corbusier and his ilk, the standardization of building and methods of prefabrication was a revolution in and of itself, but he boldly forewarned of the palpable prospects of upheaval and sociopolitical revolution if architecture served only the few and not the many.[7] For other staunch modernists, quelling the ubiquitous *crise du logement* (housing crisis) was the means and the ends of staving off revolutionary fervor[8] and transform society through the built environment.

In this manner, the politics of labor and class were equally bound up with colonial spatial divisions based on constructions of racial and ethnic difference. In Tunisia, as the prominent Tunisian historian Paul Sebag argues, the insufficient housing for laborers in countryside farms or mining villages actively contributed to the overcrowding and slum proliferation in the Tunis medina.[9] It is the myth of the primitive that not only stands in to connect these places but actually forwards the evolution-driven and racializing threads in regionalist discourses on "habitat" and "habitation" as well. During the 1930s, the discourses of the *bidonville* in particular became synonymous with the areas known as *village nègre,* and the manner in which these self-built settlements were understood was in terms of racial difference and blackness.[10] With anticolonial movements gaining popular momentum in these urban nodes across the Maghreb, and the specter of decolonization becoming ever more real, the restoration of dignified dwelling for the masses posed tremendous consequences for the political mobilization of rapidly urbanizing but increasingly discontented North African peoples.

This essay examines how the discourses of primitivism that persisted in the architectural and governmental ideologies of the Tunisian Protectorate (1912–56) continued in those of the postcolonial Tunisian nation-state. Decolonization as it occurred in Tunisia repeated much of this cycle of economic dependence in spite of statehood and national autonomy, just as the Jewish-Italian, Tunisia-born critic Albert Memmi describes,[11] with the intention of maintaining external assistance to promote national development[12] through investment in the private sector.[13] Employing Colombian anthropologist Arturo Escobar's multipart definition,[14] one must see development both as an experience and as a form of sociocultural and economic production and as a discursive means of representing the so-called Third World. This essay will explore the ways in which the discourses of development and modernization worked together. Paying particular attention to the ways that cultural and urban policy economically positioned the nation-state toward the West, the essay also highlights how the goals of urban development coincided with the project of developing the average Tunisian. The primitivization of an urbanized peasantry—a transitional and racialized class of people—remained in the modernization projects of the so-called postcolony. These modernizing aims were advanced to the detriment of the local populations. And out of these economic continuities that resulted from the enterprise of development looms not only the widening global and local gap between rich and poor, but ultimately the fashioning of politico-economic and foreign policies that imposed dire spatial effects on Tunisian cities.

"A Healthy Home": *Gourbis, Bourguibisme,* and the Postcolonial Primitive

In a campaign speech delivered on November 1, 1959, at Metlaoui, a phosphate-mining village in southwestern Tunisia, President Habib Bourguiba addressed local workers, calling upon them to put trust in the newly formed nation-state government to improve their lot while deploring their living conditions in *gourbis*, or hollow earthen structures covered by a thatched roof or tent canvas (fig. 5.1):

> Individual prosperity is dependent on collective prosperity. Individual leisure cannot be surrounded by collective misery. An enterprise cannot be successful

Figure 5.1. a. "Sousse, *Gourbis et Bédouins*"; b. "Tunisie, *Gourbi*." Postcards, no date. Nancy Demerdash, private collection.

unless its workers are satisfied with their lot. . . . [W]hen an employer exploits his workers and destroys the results of their labour, the State is responsible for establishing order. . . . I have told you of these governmental policies so that you might realize that the State upholds the interests of the working class. Its attention is given to the poor and to the weak. It gives them work, a just salary, a more noble life. But this noble life needs a healthy home too. It is unbeliev- able that a labourer works all his life hoping to build a tiny home or that an employer accepts the services of a man for ten or twenty years without helping him to live elsewhere than a *gourbi*. We have decided upon a project: homes will be built and the cost will be shared by the beneficiary, the employer and the State. The working man will have a healthy home.[15]

Bourguiba's political platform was clearly rooted in paternalistic prom- ises to provide "a more noble life" and a "healthy home" for these Tuni- sian workers and villagers; such promises bolstered his claim to continue governing this fledgling nation-state (declared independent from France just three years prior, in 1956). Between 1956 and 1970, these insalubrious *gourbivilles* were systematically destroyed.[16] A national census of popula- tion and housing conducted in May 1966 attributed the spread of informal settlements to migration flows.[17] For Bourguiba, the squalor of Tunisian workers' compounds went hand in hand with fiscal exploitation of former colonial industries (e.g., mining companies, farms). Efforts to modernize all aspects of the new nation-state (including housing and urban develop- ment) entailed a simultaneous process of cleansing and eradicating poverty and its urban imprint.

Portrayals of *gourbivilles* and *bidonvilles* as both vernacular and primi- tive resulted in a troubling conflation of voluntary nomadism (pasto- ral or not) and those mass migrations that are brought about by famine, drought, and the general economic struggles and agricultural hardships of the countryside. Pejorative mythologies of rural and pastoral peoples (which emerged as the postwar academic discourse of "peasant studies")[18] living in the Maghrebi hinterland conveniently fit into an equally absurd and perverse myth of modernization. Across the rhetoric of progress and modernization programs of both the imperial apparatus and nation-state we see primitivizing discourses about housing the masses prevail. This chapter examines how such oppositions were constructed in modernist architectural and urban experimentation. As historian Timothy Mitchell reminds us, the making of the self—in this case, the nation aspiring toward modernization—always accompanies the making of Otherness,[19] or, as it was embodied in Tunisia, in the depreciatory representation of rural life as chaotic, primitive, and potentially transgressive. Systematic demolition of the present, through the demonization of the urban peasant, also allowed for the creation of myths of the past and of the future as well.[20]

Yet *dégourbification*, advertised as the enabler of an incontestable progress, was actually a practice that continued from the Protectorate.[21] Urban migrants formed communities within these peripheral *gourbivilles* from the early twentieth century onward, and the postcolonial state, in keeping with the precedents of the Protectorate, sought to aestheticize urban spaces. Elevating the status of the farmer and worker alike, for this new national project, essentially appropriated the colonial myth, transforming the common Tunisian man from *fellah* to *évolué*.[22] Though very different from his contemporaries, such as President Gamal Abdel-Nasser of Egypt and President Léopold Sédar Senghor of Senegal, Bourguiba, like them, deemed this peasantry to be the dispossessed proletariat.[23]

In its conception, modernity also necessitated economic self-reliance and conviction in political autonomy. But in the historical moment just following independence, what was the archetypal "healthy home" of a Tunisian worker supposed to look like, and how was it to be achieved architecturally? What exactly constituted this vision of Tunisian architectural modernity,[24] and how did architects of the era attempt to execute this vision? And perhaps most important, was the "working class" always the key patron in mind, or were other interests upheld in spite of the working class's dire lodging needs? In a case not dissimilar to the Carrières Centrales of Casablanca, revenue from the housing projects constructed for these displaced *gourbiville* dwellers in many instances was insufficient for maintaining this newly coerced living standard and supporting the kind of lifestyle stipulated from above by the government.

What has been little debated in the scholarship is the slippage between the vernacular and the primitive in modernism, and how this essentializing discourse of the "primitive" permeates the descriptions of both types of living and building conditions. Across the rhetoric of progress and modernization programs of both the imperial apparatus and the nation-state, we see primitivizing discourses prevail on the subject of housing the masses. Do any formal linkages actually exist between the construction traditions of vernacular rural dwellings, on the one hand, and urban *bidonville* settlements on the other?

Ethnographers and anthropologists might argue that certain cultural habits or patterns contribute to the parallels between these conditions of building. Indeed, a wide scholarly vocabulary has sought to label traditional settlements and dwellings, including such terms as *indigenous, tribal, primitive, folkloric,* and *popular,* among others.[25] Yet as the Cold War produced the very discourse of development, it arose as a legitimation point intrinsic to nations' plans for material advancement. But in the process, as Escobar illustrates, development became nothing more than the "top-down, ethnocentric, and technocratic approach, which treated people and cultures as abstract concepts, statistical figures to be moved up and down in the charts of progress."[26] But knowing where to situate the informal settlements of the *bidonville*—architecturally, politically, and historiographically—has always been the sore spot abraded by modernism's colonial baggage. Throughout the Maghreb in this critical juncture of tremendous transition, the spatial politics of habitation in the urban nodes were inextricably linked to impasses and problems of housing development in rural areas.[27]

Opérations Gourbis

Two types of "self-built" habitat projects can be identified in the protectorate period—the *gourbiville*[28] and the "periurban self-built habitat."[29] With the rapid influx of rural-urban migrants[30] (fleeing poverty caused in part by infertile crops) as well as European manual laborers (mostly Italians, Maltese, and Spaniards), a "self-built habitat" policy was enforced in the early 1930s to allay the housing shortage. In that the official housing market was an unviable option for lower-income families, the community of urban poor was essentially forced to build for themselves. In contrast to other ethnic groups in colonial Tunisia, French settlers (mostly) had access to the units of the *Habitations à bon marché* (low-cost housing).[31] The urban/ rural divide was exacerbated by class politics; Tunisian urbanites (in Arabic, *baldiyya,* denoting the middle class or bourgeoisie) referred to those from desert villages as *afaqi* (those from beyond the horizon).[32]

The *gourbiville* districts came into being spontaneously in the 1930s and 1940s, in the immediate vicinity of Tunis; they generally arose on state-owned land or on land of unclear legal status, and they were occupied by rural migrants who built earthen, clay, or brick structures.[33] All in all, these settlements emerged from the city's physical and spatial lack of sufficient infrastructure to accommodate a burgeoning influx of rural migrants.[34]

Formally enacted in a decree on March 16, 1957, state-sponsored efforts at razing the *gourbis* (*dégourbification*)—which were effectively part of a strategy for collectively forgetting or erasing the imprint of impoverished modes of living—went hand in hand with methods of "beautification."[35] Planning operations entailed both selective preservation of certain districts and treatment of problems that contributed to urban decay, such as *mal-logés* (poorly housed populations), *îlots insalubres* (unsanitary neighborhoods), and *bidonvilles* (shanty or "tin can" towns). But the stigmatization (and primitivization) of the *gourbi* dwelling type and *gourbivilles* preceded nationalization.[36] Low-cost housing initiatives had existed in Tunisia even under the Protectorate, though they were somewhat poorly funded. The *habitations à bon marché* societies were established in Tunisia in 1919.[37] For Tunisian workers mining in the southern region of the valley of Medjer, for example, a housing program was undertaken in 1937 intended to rehouse approximately 244 people, though World War II had interrupted construction plans. Hygiene, and the path to modern living, with all its amenities, lay at the center of these concerns:

> We had to be content with reconstructing, on a rational plan and with the best methods, houses less uncomfortable than *gourbis*. . . . The goal was to offer the worker, on leaving the *gourbi*, a house that was more spacious and easier to keep clean, without unduly transforming habits and a way of life that had a long and sustained tradition. The plan that was adopted was made up of two principal pieces, permitting the separation of the parents' and the children's rooms. A small kitchen forms a right angle at the end of the building. A second shed is reserved for goats, which previously shared the *gourbi* with their owners.[38]

Gourbis, as *toûb* mud-brick dwellings, were deemed primitive habitations: by introducing modern living, not just in terms of infrastructure (e.g., running water, electricity) but in terms of modern interiors, replete with furniture and other trappings of Western living spaces, it was thought that these fixtures might in turn bring about a lifestyle change and, with it, a societal evolution.

From 1954 onward, *opérations gourbis* was a Protectorate campaign opposing the growth of *gourbivilles*. In the 1950s, the Service d'Architecture et d'Urbanisme was integrated with the activities of the Commissariat à l'Urbanisme, l'Habitat et Tourisme.[39] Gérard Blachère, the official commissioner for reconstruction and housing in the early 1950s, described the lack of sturdiness of these *gourbi* homes:

> The poorest part of the population has the habit, since they have given up their nomadic life, of providing cob walls or walls of unmortared stone in their dwellings, the roof being made of boughs, covered with a layer of clay

whitewashed with lime. If these buildings are rain-proof and fairly cool in summer and warm in winter, they have, on the contrary, many disadvantages, apart from the considerable risk of fire; it should be remembered that these buildings have a single room, scantily separated by blankets, that the floor of beaten earth does not allow the interior of the house to be properly cleaned, and that the building is at the mercy of floods and even of a fairly strong stream. The builders customarily plant their buildings without regard to their surroundings, so that the agglomerations so constituted cannot be properly repaired nor improved; frequently, it is impossible to lay out roads, streets, sewer pipes, etc.[40]

The criticisms of *gourbivilles'* unplanned nature carry echoes of Orientalists' attacks on the medinas of North Africa as being anarchical, disorganized, and crowded.

Dégourbification *for the Development of the Tunisian* Évolué

Bourguiba's ideological rhetoric of progress,[41] which dominated his writings well into the 1960s, has to be seen within the larger framework of reorienting Tunisian ways of life. Bourguiba's modernization program fundamentally entailed repositioning Tunisian attitudes toward Islam; this runs completely counter to nineteenth-century Orientalist understandings of *patrie*, which bear fundamental links to Islamic ways of life.[42] Bourguiba's strong dislike for Nasser's brand of pan-Arabism meant that Tunisian political progress would be defined along different lines, ones that did not fit under any Arab heading; Tunisia joined the Arab League somewhat belatedly, in 1958.[43] Fearing the negative economic impact of nationalization, Bourguiba steered the country away from complete isolationism, counter to what occurred in Nasserite Egypt.[44] The ideology of *Bourguibisme*[45] promoted the notion that forward progress, on the one hand, and clinging to Muslim values and religious practices on the other, were not only mutually exclusive but also antithetical to the end goal of modernization (e.g., the August 1956 decree abolishing polygamy; the January 1960 decree calling for the abrogation of work abstinence during the holy month of Ramadan).[46]

Indeed, this "openness" touted by Bourguiba—not dissimilar to the economic liberalization policies of *infitah* promoted by Egypt's president Anwar Sadat—might bring about the "reorientation of Tunisia toward the West[, which] would represent progress and prosperity, the very objectives that an independent Tunisia aspired to."[47] At the heart of Bourguibism lay a project of "cultural synthesis" (*synthèse culturelle*), or a complete cultural renewal, which entailed a rewriting of history.[48] Bourguiba's desire to uphold and promulgate the nation's ancient heritage of Mediterranean civilization, dating back to the Phoenicians and Romans, went hand in hand with his economic interest in orienting the country toward Western markets and capital flows. Replacing France's former role, the United States provided ample aid to Tunisia ($239.2 million from 1956 to 1961 alone), on the condition that the young nation pursue a path of liberal economic development.[49] Nevertheless, France maintained its economic imprint on Tunisia despite diplomatic ruptures, through the permission of none other than President Habib Bourguiba himself.[50] Aid not only perpetuated debt but also tended to seep into the pockets of the national bourgeoisie, as theorist Frantz Fanon would famously write.[51] The Western slant in Bourguiba's economic policies and identitarianism—revealed through actions such as abolishing religious charitable endowment *habous* lands or denouncing the fast during Ramadan—coincided with the onslaught of an authoritarianism that molded Tunisian national identity by abandoning cultures and traditions deemed counter to the cause of modernization. As a nation that outwardly positioned itself as being politically aligned with Western economic development,[52] contrary to nonaligned nations like Egypt,[53] for instance, Bourguiba sought to distance Tunisia from socialist ideological leanings and marginalize Islamic tradition.

Even so, the cultural program of Bourguiba's administration ranked relatively low in the list of priorities for the new nation-state, with other concerns such as public health and education reform taking precedence. But matters of public health and hygiene directly coincided with the underlying aim of rural and urban purification within the broader *dégourbification* program. On housing needs, Bourguiba proclaimed, "Substantial progress has been made in sanitation and housing construction, particularly for lower and middle-income families. . . . The fact that the government is working to build a modern, progressive nation explains why its prestige has remained intact in spite of the heavy responsibilities it has had to shoulder. Tunisia's progress in every area during the last ten years . . . is visible to the naked eye; every Tunisian senses it and sees it all around him."[54] Dubbed a sign of progress, the national project of *dégourbification*—the demolition of the old *ghorfas* and *gourbis* constructed by this disenfranchised and otherwise homeless class—contributed to the much grander task of modernization, stalling the specter of so-called underdevelopment. *Dégourbification* had ramifications for the transformation, and merging, of the countryside as well as the urban centers.

Thus, discourses on habitation and cleanliness can be seen as a part of a much larger continuation of the colonial-era *mission civilisatrice*, exercised to its fullest. We can see how, by expunging any residual traces of earthen building materials and by introducing the "needs" of the household, the imposition of contrived domesticity and superficial amenities is supposed to fuel the desire for some illusory progress.[55] The thought, roughly, is this: if one can transform and reconstruct the homes of the Tunisian workers, one can thereby control and contain their desires, needs, and habits; the goal here is to transform the Tunisian into an *évolué*, an individual who has "evolved" from his or her natural state. This purification of the home and the individual alike parallels what the literary theorist Kristin Ross has labeled the "ideologeme of hygiene" and the metaphorical cleansing of the nation in postwar France.[56] At the height of these systematic *gourbiville* demolitions, many homeless inhabitants, originating in the Sahelian steppes and other regions of the hinterland, often fled to the center of the medina in Tunis, as opposed to the usual formation of a perimeter around the city.[57] As the prominent Tunisian historian Paul Sebag writes, internal demographic shifts occurred within Tunis; for example, part of the native Muslim Tunisian population deserted the city center for the prestige of the suburbs, seeking an "apartment or a villa with electricity, plumbing, or running water, abandoning the bare and open floor plan of their fathers."[58]

Nevertheless, these grandiose visions belie the grim physical realities of displacement and dislocation. The disciplinary repression of spontaneous settlements was written into new planning codes; the law of February 4, 1976, for instance, declared the construction or installation of barracks a punishable crime.[59] To make matters worse, the housing demand far outpaced construction timetables. In 1956, nearly one hundred thousand people who had migrated from rural regions to the outskirts of Tunis lived in these spontaneously constructed *gourbivilles*,[60] often built illegally on land of the *habous* or indigenous religious foundation.[61] From 1960 to 1965, five such *gourbivilles* were demolished in Tunis, to be replaced by a new housing scheme, under which the construction of one hundred eighty thousand new buildings was proposed. Only one hundred four thousand of these were actually realized (about 80 percent allocated as private housing and only 20 percent as popular housing).[62] Ahmed Kassab has analyzed the mostly unsuccessful state attempts to control irregular and illegal *gourbivilles*.[63] First off, demolition was a costly endeavor. For example, the *gourbivilles* of Mellassine and Djebel Lahmar (Red Mountain) outside Tunis were left untouched for lack of funds. Even when *gourbis* were razed, the urban poor residing in squatter settlements similar to the *gourbivilles* were openly resistant to externally imposed transferal schemes; these new outposts usually become sequestered ghettos.[64] These dislocations of Tunisians continued well into the 1970s.[65] Social housing developments, it was assumed, would inhibit the growth of spontaneous settlements.[66] In 1975, the Ministry of Housing attempted to remove inhabitants from Djebel Lahmar, not far from the University of Tunis. A new residential neighborhood called Cité Ibn Khaldun (fig. 5.2) was constructed, but it was built with little regard for the sociological needs of families, particularly the need for privacy.[67] By the 1980s, birthrates had surged, but in the late colonial and early independent years, increased population densities in cities were due to migration patterns.[68]

The selection of which *gourbivilles* to leave alone and which to demolish points to the unsettling discriminatory class and racialized politics at play in the postcolonial state. Bourguiba used the language of insurgency to characterize the threat posed by the "slums and grottoes" to the state authority, calling upon the extraction of "shady elements, which at night, out of the holes of slums and grottoes of the hill of Sidi-Raïs-Ali, operate in the capital, transgress the laws, disturb public order, and sustain a climate of insecurity."[69] For Bourguiba, not only would the construct of modernity place dignified living within reach of these so-called delinquent or unscrupulous people, but these ideologies would form the very basis of his housing policy. Yet as these newly urbanized ruralites, Bedouins, and nomads[70] settled in the city or along its peripheries, their perceived failure to successfully integrate into society was demonized and criminalized by a state that for its part failed to provide adequately for a shiftingly dynamic but sedentarizing population.

Policy implications of the seemingly innocuous term *habitat* abound in the shifting postwar milieu, on both sides of the Mediterranean. In Tunisia, the dialectical processes of *gourbi* construction and *dégourbification* continued well into the 1980s. From 1975 to 1984 alone, the average annual growth rate of informal settlements remained steady at 3 percent, which over time resulted in about 1.3 million rudimentary dwellings by the mid-1980s.[71] The Caisse Nationale d'Épargne Logement, created in 1973,

Figure 5.2. Cité Ibn Khaldun, Tunis (1974). Architect: Société Centrale pour l'Équipement.
© Courtesy of architect. Source: Aga Khan Award for Architecture.

and the Société Nationale Immobilière, created in 1974, were jointly tasked with allocating finances for new social housing complexes. And although educational reform was a cornerstone of Bourguiba's political agenda, the qualifications and vocational training required on the part of laborers and workers to execute the projects remained minimal.[72] Nevertheless, the ideological rhetoric of evolution and rationality seeped into nearly every sector of life, suggesting that Tunisians had yet to "evolve" in a manner appropriate for a postcolonial modernity; even in architectural training programs in the early nation-state, students were encouraged to understand the problems of the environment in a rational manner. Paired with an aerial view of the Tunis medina, a 1960 brochure from the École Nationale Supérieure d'Architecture in Tunis highlights the professionalization of architects through model-making and methodologies that very much parallel CIAM functionalist principles, suggesting that the progressive evolution of the architect must parallel that of the nation.

Conclusion: Inhabiting Contradiction

The primitivizing discourses that undergirded the extermination of informal settlements point to the threat that mobile or nomadic populations posed to the nation-state. The discourses on habitat and habitation in general attempt to reckon with the changing relationship not only between countryside and town, but between humanity, living, and labor. As Abdellah Hammoudi reflects on Pierre Bourdieu's *Travail et travailleurs en Algérie* (1963), it is the forced encounter with colonial capitalism that burdens the Algerian peasant.[73] Redesigning the urbanized peasantry's habitus—or manner by which an individual interacts with his environment—through land ownership, consumption, and values of capitalist living means that control and domination over this precarious demographic can then be exercised. The rhetoric of decolonization ensured the uprooting of the vestigial colonial presence—including excising the capitalist mechanisms of extraction and exploitation that wrought havoc on colonies. In policy and practice, however, the Tunisian nation-state apparatus quietly let many of these insidious forms continue. To this day, *bidonvilles* remain a hot point in Maghrebi politics; the "Ville sans bidonville programme" instituted by the Moroccan government with the support of the World Bank[74] seeks to eliminate *bidonvilles* in Morocco completely.

This notion of the vernacular intersects with the subtexts of primitivism, and, by extension, racial divisions endemic to colonial and imperial
rule[75] are embedded in the postwar architectural discourses on habitation.
Many CIAM delegations sought to understand the *bidonville* as a vernacular architectural typology (all the while failing to address the colonial beginnings of such informal settlements). But this globally engaged impulse in
the 1950s reflected an introspective moment of crisis for the Euro-American
architectural avant-garde. Inasmuch as the grid sought to provide a prefabricated identity for an urbanized dweller, it was a tool that also served
to expand the role of the architect as orchestrator and enforcer of order
against the backdrop of tidal waves of global political change. Much of this
discourse on habitation attempts to reconfigure what it is to be a consuming
human in a capitalist apparatus. But gridding, or rationalizing, the *gourbiville,* it would seem, remains as mythical an endeavor as the encroaching
threat of the *gourbi.*

Acknowledgments

My research in Tunisia and archives in Switzerland and France would not
have been possible without the support of a Donald and Mary Hyde Fellowship from Princeton University. I wish to thank Esther da Costa Meyer and
M'hamed Oualdi for their rigorous engagement with and investment in this
project since its beginning. When I presented a version of this paper at the
Sterling and Francine Clark Art Institute, for the colloquium "Aesthetics
of the *Bidonville*," Katarzyna Pieprzak, Sheila Crane, and Gretchen Head
enriched my own perspectives on this material with new insights. Most of
all, I thank the editors of this volume, Mohammad Gharipour and Kıvanç
Kılınç, for their attention to detail and input, and for their coordination of
the panel "Global Exchanges of Social Housing in the Middle East" at the
Society of Architectural Historians meeting in April 2016.

Notes

1. Sigfried Giedion, "Habitat: Universalität und Regionalismus," *Neue Zürcher Zeitung,*
September 8, 1953. "Die bescheidene Haltung, die durch instinktives Einfühlen in die Bedürfn-
isse entlegener Völker und Kulturen spürbar wird, kommt ebenso in Le Corbusiers Kapitol
der neu gegründeten Stadt Chandigarh in Indien, wie in den 'grilles' eines 'Bidonville'

inmitten von Algier zum Ausdruck. 'Bidonvilles' nennt man jene aus Benzinkanistern und Abfällen regellos entstandenen Eingebornenviertel. Ein solches 'Bidonville' wurde von P. A. Emery und seinen Freunden untersucht, um zu erfahren, was aus diesen regellos hingestreuten, selbstgebauten Blech- und Bretterhütten zu lernen sei. Es zeigte sich dabei, daß die Bewohner, die aus der Sahara, vom Atlas, aus Marokko und Tunis um des Broterwerbes willen nach Algier strömen, auch in diesen 'slums' es verstanden haben, mit einfachsten Mitteln ihre Umgebung, ihren Lebensgewohnheiten entsprechend, zu gestalten. Auch die seit der Urzeit gewohnten Fresken fehlen nicht an den Wänden. . . . Eine Hütte in Kamerun hat mehr ästhetische Würde als die meisten vorfabrizierten Häuser. So beobachten wir im kulturellen Leben des Westens ein deutliches Nachlassen der rein rationalistischen Haltung, auf der anderen Seite aber das Verlangen der primitiven Völker, unsere Produktionsmethoden sich anzueignen." GTA Archives, Eidgenössische Technische Hochschule (ETH)-Zürich, CIAM IX folder.

2. "Modern Architects Hold First Postwar Congress," *Architectural Forum* 87 (November 1947): 65.

3. Zeynep Çelik, "Learning from the *Bidonville*: CIAM Looks at Algiers," *Harvard Design Magazine*, no. 18 (2003): 70–74.

4. I take the vernacular to stand for structural forms and plans—e.g., arcades, cupolas, domes, caravanserais, courtyard homes—that can be found in Tunisian architecture prior to French colonization.

5. The grilles or grids were initially developed by Le Corbusier in 1946 and then later refined by the ASCORAL group in 1947 for CIAM's Seventh Congress in Bergamo in 1949. See Tom Avermaete, *Another Modern: The Postwar Architecture and Urbanism of Candilis-Josic-Woods* (Rotterdam, Neth.: Nai, 2005). See also Sigfried Giedion, *A Decade of Contemporary Architecture* (Zurich: Girsberger, 1954), 32, 35. See also Annie Pedret, "CIAM and the Emergence of Team 10 Thinking, 1945–1959" (PhD diss., MIT, 2001), 72.

6. Jonathan Hale, "Edited Out of Contemporary Theoretical Discourse Yet Central to the Way We Think about Architecture: Primitive," *Architecture Review Quarterly Report* 8, no. 1 (2004): 9–10. "[S]o-called 'primitive architecture' has often been referred to as providing a kind of prelapsarian, purified form of life, free of the supposedly contaminating influences of contemporary society. The fact that the architecture of a mythical past is often illustrated by examples taken from a less-than-mythical present-day elsewhere—a south-sea island, African village or French fisherman's shack—only highlights the problematic nature of these attempts to find support for contemporary radicalism within a conservative tradition."

7. Le Corbusier, *Towards a New Architecture* (1927; repr., New York: Dover, 1986), "Architecture or Revolution."

8. F. Salhi, "Marché du travail, crise du logement et grande entreprise. Le cas de la sidérurgie à Annaba-El Hadjar (Algérie)" (thèse de 3e cycle, Université de Paris XII, Institut d'Urbanisme de Paris, 1983), 72. "[L]a crise du logement crée un climat social qualifié de pré-révolutionnaire."

9. Jean-Marie Miossec, "La politique d'habitat en Tunisie depuis l'Indépendance," in *Habitat, état et société au Maghreb*, ed. Pierre Robert Baduel (Paris: Centre de Recherches et d'Études sur les Sociétés Méditerranéennes, 1986), 17. Originally cited from Paul Sebag, *La Tunisie: Essai de monographie* (Paris: Éditions Sociales, 1951).

10. Here I cite the recent work of Sheila Crane and her paper "Mapping the History of the Bidonville: Aesthetics of Containment and Mobility," presented at the Sterling and Francine Clark Art Institute colloquium "Aesthetics and the Bidonville" in May 2016.

11. Albert Memmi, *Decolonization and the Decolonized*, trans. Robert Bononno (Minneapolis: University of Minnesota Press, 2006), 1913 (cited to Kindle e-book edition). "'Debt elimination,' though generous in appearance, merely delays the problem. What prevents the poor from borrowing again, and continuing their cycle of dependence on rich countries? . . . On the contrary, it simply perpetuates inequality. Waiting for salvation from a colonial power, not a former colonial power is . . . illusory."

12. Carol Mae Barker, "The Politics of Decolonization in Tunisia: The Foreign Policy of a New State" (PhD diss., Columbia University, 1971), 3.

13. Michael Christopher Alexander, "Between Accommodation and Confrontation: State, Labor, and Development in Algeria and Tunisia" (PhD diss., Duke University, 1996), 9.

14. Arturo Escobar, *Encountering Development: The Making and Unmaking of the Third World* (Princeton, NJ: Princeton University Press, 1995), 10–11. Escobar treats development as a "historically singular experience, the creation of a domain of thought and action." The goal of his text is to "examine the establishment and consolidation of this discourse and apparatus from the early post–World War II period to the present; analyze the construction of a nation of underdevelopment in post–World War II economic development theories; and demonstrate the way in which the apparatus functions through the systematic production of knowledge and power."

15. Habib Bourguiba, *Electoral Campaign Speeches, October 26–November 5, 1959* (Tunis: Secretary of State for Information Publications, 1959), 64–68.

16. Morched Chabbi, "Politiques urbaines et régulations en Tunisie: Le cas du grand Tunis (1960–2007)," in *Habitat social au Maghreb et au Sénégal: Gouvernance urbaine et participation en questions*, ed. Julien Le Tellier and Aziz Iraki (Paris: Harmattan, 2009), 133.

17. Béchir Chebab Tekari, "Habitat et dépassement du droit en Tunisie: Les constructions spontanées," in Baduel, *Habitat*, 165–66.

18. Timothy Mitchell, *Rule of Experts: Egypt, Techno-Politics, Modernity* (Berkeley: University of California Press, 2002), 123. Citing Richard Critchfield's anthropological descriptive realism account of an Egyptian peasant named Shahhat, Mitchell makes note of George Foster's foreword, which traces the transition of the descriptor "folk" to "peasant" after World War II.

19. Ibid., 14.

20. Memmi, *Decolonization and the Decolonized*, 657.

21. Miossec, "Politique," 20–21. "Le renforcement des classes transitionnelles, moyennes et aisées, principalement en ville a eu pour conséquence une forte poussée de villas et plus du tiers des logements citadins est constitué de logements de type moderne (villas et appartements). Les opérations de dégourbification, de réhabilitation visant à la résorption de l'habitat insalubre et rudimentaire ont été efficaces puisque ce type d'habitations 'chute.' . . . Progrès incontestable mais ce type de logement (qui recouvre une grande diversité de formes: gourbi, maamera et autre abri en pisé; kib et autre abri en branchage; tent; baraque; ghorfa de type Matmata; logements dans un local non destiné à l'habitation) 'abrite' encore aujourd'hui plus de 100,000 ménages soit près d'un Tunisien sur dix."

22. M. Pierre Berthault (ingénieur agricole, Commissaire du Crédit Foncier de France près le Crédit Foncier d'Algérie et de Tunisie), *La propriété rurale en Afrique du Nord*, Conférence donnée le 4 mars 1936 à l'Institut National Agronomique (Alençon, Fr.: Imprimerie Alençonnaise, 1936), 22. "Almost everywhere the colonist is for the native the guide, the initiator of new methods. European property, although forming only a minority, thus has a special social role, a role of social elite, moral framework, but a social role that does not make

easy rapid progress for the native, because Islam remains a formidable barrier that separates the two psychologies, the two mentalities, the two civilizations. Islam, with the attendant concerns and status of the family, makes the needs of the native person different from ours. He directs his culture with conceptions other than those of the European. His house remains primitive. . . . His agricultural equipment remains rustic and inexpensive. . . . It is not desirable, neither socially nor to the view of national standing, that the Frenchman who colonizes North Africa is given the ideal of the primitive and harsh life of the fellah" (my translation).

23. Bill Freund, "Labor and Labor History in Africa: A Review of Literature," *African Studies Review* 27, no. 2 (1984): 9. See also Jean Lacouture, *The Demigods: Charismatic Leadership in the Third World*, trans. Patricia Wolf (New York: Knopf, 1970); Charles-André Julien, *L'Afrique du nord en marche* (Paris: Julliard, 1952).

24. Gaston Lionel Franco, ed., *La Tunisie devant son avenir* [Tunisia faces the future] (Paris: Le Monde économique, 1956), 5. "All this has had a profound effect on the Tunisian conscience, torn between Oriental and Western tendencies—terms which until now have reflected the opposition between medieval traditionalism and the modern world. A new concept has entered the picture which, highlighted by the rivalries displayed at Bandung, adds to the complexity of North African questions."

25. Jean-Paul Bourdier and Nezar AlSayyad, Prologue to *Dwellings, Settlements, and Tradition: Cross-Cultural Perspectives*, ed. Jean-Paul Bourdier and Nezar AlSayyad (New York: University Press of America, 1989), 5.

26. Escobar, *Encountering Development*, 44.

27. "Urbanisation et habitat du grande nombre: L'approche marocaine," in *Villes et sociétés au Maghreb: Études sur l'urbanisation*, ed. R. Duchac (Paris: CNRS, 1974), 115–16.

28. Nnamdi Elleh, *African Architecture: Evolution and Transformation* (New York: McGraw-Hill, 1997), sec. 5.2.

29. Paolo Colarossi, "Measures for Urban Rehabilitation in Tunis," *Environmental Design: Journal of the Islamic Environmental Design Research Centre* 1 (1985): 44; Morched Chabbi, *L'urbain en Tunisie: Processus et projets* (Tunis: Nirvana, 2012). According to Chabbi, this type of habitat—the *habitat spontané périurbain*—included the vast majority (around 74 percent) of the population in the *gourbivilles* and outskirts of Tunis.

30. Freund, "Labor and Labor History," 4. Labor migrations posed both political and social problems for the urban planner.

31. "Direction des domaines et de la colonisation," in *La colonisation en Tunisie* (Bourg, Fr.: Victor Berthod, 1931), 68–69.

32. L. Carl Brown, "Bourguiba and Bourguibism Revisited: Reflections and Interpretation," *Middle East Journal* 55, no. 1 (2001): 43–57.

33. Serge Santelli, *Medinas: Traditional Architecture of Tunisia* (Tunis: Dar Ashraf, 1992), 151–52. See also Serge Santelli and Bernard Tournet, "Évolution et ambiguïté de la maison arabe contemporaine au Maghreb: Étude de cas à Rabat et Tunis," in *Espace centré: Figures de l'architecture domestique dans l'Orient méditerranéen*, ed. Catherine Bruant (Marseille: Parenthèses), 49. "[À] Tunis les quartiers de Saïda Manoubia et Melassine se sont réalisés progressivement le long des rives inondables du lac Sedjoumi au début des années quarante. Dans les deux villes, la population d'origine rurale a évidemment reproduit un habitat de type rural (en Tunisie: le *gourbi*, d'où le mot gourbiville donné à ces quartiers spontanés) utilisant des matériaux précaires: toub pour le *gourbi* en Tunisie. . . . Le *gourbi* est composé d'une pièce rectangulaire à laquelle on accède par une porte basse s'ouvrant sur le milieu de la pièce. De chaque côté de la porte, se trouvent, un espace de repos constitué par une banquette

maçonnée sur laquelle on déroule des nattes pour dormir, et un espace de rangement qui fait face au précédent, pouvant servir de cuisine."

34. Michel Deloge, "Les perspectives de l'urbanisme de Tunis," *L'Architecture d'Aujourd'hui* (1955): 86.

35. Çelik notes that the first French law on *urbanisme*, from March 14, 1919, called for state regulation of growth and investment in "beautification." See Zeynep Çelik, *Urban Forms and Colonial Confrontations: Algiers under French Rule* (Berkeley: University of California Press, 1997), chap. 2. She also highlights the fact that this French discourse on squatter settlements traces back to the 1930s, in reference to the *bidonvilles* of Algeria (especially El-Kattar, one of the first *bidonvilles* to emerge outside Algiers).

36. Edmond Doutté and Augustin Bernard, "L'habitation rurale des indigènes de l'Algérie," *Annales de Géographie* 26, no. 141 (1917): 219.

37. Deloge, "Perspectives," 86.

38. "Experiences rurales: Essais d'habitation ouvrières," *Revue de l'Institut des Belles Lettres Arabes*, no. 32 (4th trimester, 1945): 439–40 (my translation).

39. Deloge, "Perspectives," 86.

40. Gérard Blachère, "Reconstruction and Housing," in *Tunisia 54: 72 Years of Franco-Tunisian Collaboration* (Paris: Encyclopédie mensuelle d'Outre-mer, 1954), 168.

41. "Discours de Habib Bourguiba," *L'Action*, December 17, 1956. "Tunisia, whose tradition is essentially Arab-Muslim intends not to live in a vacuum and become a closed society, a prospect incompatible with our deep desire to live in close communion with modern life. Our path in this area is to have windows open to other cultures, especially to Western culture, in order to take hold of reality. Thus our country, while remaining faithful to its cultural past, will have forged the instruments of its future. French culture is one of the largest and richest in the modern world and the tribute we pay to the academics here present bears witness to what we owe to thinkers such as Descartes, Voltaire, Diderot, Rousseau, and many others."

42. André Demersemann, "Formulation de l'idée de patrie en Tunisie de 1837 à 1872," *Revue de l'Institut des Belles Lettres Arabes*, no. 114 (1966), 134.

43. Kenneth Perkins, *A History of Modern Tunisia* (Cambridge: Cambridge University Press, 2004), 142.

44. Michael Clark, "Bourguiba Bars Nationalization: Tunisian Chief Says Foreign Capital Has Nothing to Fear—Praise for Nasser Faint," *New York Times*, August 20, 1956.

45. Hichem Djaït, "Le métier d'historien en Tunisie," in *Être historien aujourd'hui*, ed. René Rémond (Paris: UNESCO; Toulouse, Fr.: Erès, 1988), 86. Tunisian historian Hichem Djaït explains how these discourses worked to mobilize Bourguiba's following.

46. Lorna Hahn, "Tunisia: Pragmatism and Progress," *Middle East Journal* 16 (Winter 1962): 18–28.

47. Mohamed Bergaoui, *Tourisme et voyages en Tunisie: Le temps des pionniers, 1956–1973* (Tunis: Mohamed Bergaoui, 2003), 53.

48. Driss Abbassi, *Entre Bourguiba et Hannibal: Identité tunisienne et histoire depuis l'indépendance* (Aix-en-Provence, Fr.: IREMAM; Paris: Karthala, 2005), 18.

49. Christopher Alexander, *Tunisia: Stability and Reform in the Modern Maghreb* (London: Routledge, 2010), 70.

50. Ibid., 91. Bourguiba apparently vetoed an idea proposed by the Arab League to pursue an economic boycott of France. He is also purported to have proclaimed to an angry crowd that he would cooperate with the French to defeat underdevelopment, at the height of the 1961

Bizerte crisis (when France sought to extend a runway at an airbase in Bizerte, leading to a bloody fight over this residual marker of its colonial power)

51. Frantz Fanon, *The Wretched of the Earth* (New York: Grove, 1963), 100–101. "At the core of the national bourgeoisie of the colonial countries a hedonistic mentality prevails—because on a psychological level it identifies with the Western bourgeoisie from which it has slurped every lesson. It mimics the Western bourgeoisie in its negative and decadent aspects without having accomplished the initial phases of exploration and invention that are the assets of this Western bourgeoisie whatever the circumstances.

52. Jacob Abadi, *Tunisia since the Arab Conquest: The Saga of a Westernized Muslim State* (Reading, UK: Ithaca, 2013), 468. "On his visit to Washington in the spring of 1961, Bourguiba obtained a grant of $800 million and $20 million in technical aid. In addition, Kennedy agreed to send a CIA delegation to Tunisia to examine development projects, for which the Tunisians were asking an additional $20 million, and food surpluses valued at $10 million."

53. Alexander, *Tunisia*, 33. "He saw Nasser as a self-aggrandizing egomaniac who manipulated pan-Arab rhetoric and other political leaders to bolster Egypt's interests and his own stature."

54. Habib Bourguiba, "The Tunisian Way," *Foreign Affairs* 44, no. 3 (1966): 485.

55. "Experiences rurales: Essais d'habitation ouvrières," *Revue de l'Institut des Belles Lettres Arabes*, no. 32 (4th trimester, 1945): 447. "Dans l'ensemble, les améliorations ont été appréciées, et, en faisant mesurer dans les faits l'intérêt d'un progrès, font désirer les maisonnettes décrites plus haut: désir général et très vif chez les jeunes."

56. Kristin Ross, "Starting Afresh: Hygiene and Modernization in Postwar France," *October* 67 (Winter 1994): 27–28.

57. Hédi Eckert and Jalal El-Kefi, "L'espace traditionnel de la ville de Tunis. La médina et les deux R'bat: faubourg ou gourbiville?," in *Les influences occidentales dans les villes Maghrébines à l'époque contemporaine. L'urbanisation au Maghreb: Systèmes culturels et systèmes urbains*, Actes du Colloque d'Aix-en-Provence, Mai 1970 (Aix-en-Provence, Fr.: Éditions de l'Université de Provence, 1974), 230. "Djebel Lahmar, Ras Tabia and Somrane-Khaznadar to the northwest, Najâh, Mellassine and Sayyeda Mannoubîya to the west, Zitoun el-Djerbi and Bordj 'Ali Râïs to the south and Bïr el-Bey and Ech-Chouk to the east, they concentrate their 160,000 inhabitants in the urban perimenter, of which they comprise thirty-four percent of the communal population. . . . our recent solvency survey, which also covered five gourbivilles, revealed fundamental similarities between the populations of the central medina and those living in the gourbivilles, both of which are predominantly rural migrants" (my translation).

58. Paul Sebag, "La décolonisation et la transformation des quartiers traditionnels de Tunis," in *Influences occidentales*, 253.

59. Béchir Chebab Tekari, "Habitat et dépassement du droit en Tunisie: Les constructions spontanées," in Baduel, *Habitat*, 166–67. "Aussi, la dégourbification doit-elle se faire par l'assainissement. L'assainissement se heurte cependant à des difficultés multiples, notamment sur le double plan foncier et financier. Dans les bidonvilles, la plupart des ménages n'ont pas la propriété du sol sur lequel ils se sont implantés, ou ils ont dans les meilleurs cas une propriété contestée."

60. Eckert and El-Kefi, "Espace traditionnel," 224.

61. Serge Santelli, *Tunis: Le creuset méditerranéen* (Paris: CNRS, 1995), 105.

62. Morched Chabbi, "Politiques urbaines et régulations en Tunisie: Le cas du grand Tunis (1960–2007)," in *Habitat social au Maghreb et au Sénégal: Gouvernance urbaine et participation en questions*, ed. Julien Le Tellier and Aziz Iraki (Paris: Harmattan, 2009), 133.

63. Ahmed Kassab, "Trois types de quartiers populaires à Béjà," *Revue tunisienne des sciences sociales* 8 (1971): 91–119. See also Naima Karoui, "Famille et travail: Les ouvrières de Menzel Bourguiba," *Revue tunisienne des sciences sociales* 13 (1976): 75–98.

64. Charles Correa, "Urban Housing in the Third World: The Role of the Architect," in *Architecture and Community: Building in the Islamic World Today*, ed. Renata Holod (New York: Aperture, 1983). See also Franco, *Tunisie devant son avenir*, 95; "Cité Ibn Khaldun," Aga Khan Trust for Culture, https://archnet.org/sites/98, accessed February 14, 2013. "The Ibn Khaldun settlement was conceived as a pilot project for the relocation of the population of two squatter settlements in the outskirts of Tunis. The first phase, consisting of the construction of 1,500 units (out of 5,100 projected units) for low-to-middle income residents, was completed in 1974. The chosen site was next to the squatter settlements. Three types of dwelling units were developed ranging from a two-room house on one level to a five-room house organized on two levels and set around a courtyard. The units were assembled in a variety of ways to form articulated linear blocks with an average density of 40 units/ha. The basic structure is load-bearing brick walls and reinforced concrete frame. All exterior surfaces are covered with cement and plaster."

65. David Seddon, "Winter of Discontent: Economic Crisis in Tunisia and Morocco," MERIP Reports, no. 127, *Insurrection in North Africa* (Richmond, VA: Middle East Research and Information Project, September–October 1984), 13. The author describes the urban and economic conditions of the poor that led to the January bread riots of 1984. Ettadhamen, to the west of Tunis, grew the most rapidly (more so than the northern *habitat spontané périurbain* of Borj Louzir and Aïn Zaghouan); in 1970 there were five hundred houses, which mushroomed to forty-five hundred houses by 1975. See Diana Wylie, "The Importance of Being at-Home: A Defense of Historic Preservation in Algeria," *Change over Time* 2, no. 2 (2012): 172–87. See also Nabila Oulebsir, *Les usages du patrimoine, monuments, musées et politique coloniale en Algérie (1830–1930)* (Paris: Éditions de la Maison des Sciences de l'Homme, 2004).

66. Sebag, "Décolonisation," 250.

67. Fredj Stambouli, "Social Aspiration in Tunisian Architecture," in *Toward an Architecture in the Spirit of Islam*, ed. Renata Holod (Philadelphia: Aga Khan Award for Architecture, 1978), 95.

68. H. R. T. Davies, "Regional Planning in Tunisia," *Geography* 74, no. 3 (1989): 255. "The 1980 survey records much higher figures than the national average (1.0) for households living in shanties (gourbis) in Tunis (2.6), Sousse (2.1), Sfax (2.6) and Monastir (2.3), emphasizing the economic attractiveness of these *Gourvernorat* to many Tunisians. Yet the increasing urbanisation has not in many areas led to a decline in rural population."

69. Santelli, *Tunis*, 109. Author's translation.

70. Fredj Stambouli, "Tradition et modernité à travers les processus d'urbanisation en Tunisie," in *Influences occidentales*, 266.

71. Sid Boubekeur, *Économie de la construction à Tunis* (Paris: Harmattan, 1987), 10–16. "Thus, it seems that the degourbification campaign was much more marked by the evolution of one type of housing to another than by the resorption and replacement of the existing gourbis."

72. Boubekeur, *Économie de la Construction à Tunis*, 89.

73. Abdellah Hammoudi, "Phenomenology and Ethnography: On Kabyle Habitus in the Work of Pierre Bourdieu," in *Bourdieu in Algeria: Colonial Politics, Ethnographic Practices, Theoretical Developments*, ed. Jane E. Goodman and Paul A. Silverstein (Lincoln: University of Nebraska Press, 2009), 206–7.

74. "Leçons du programme 'Villes sans bidonvilles' au Maroc," presented by Mr. Najib Lahlou, Expert du Développement urbain au Maroc, the World Bank. See http://einstitute .worldbank.org/ei/lessons-program-morocco-french, accessed June 7, 2015. Here I am indebted to a presentation by Katarzyna Pieprzak on literary representations of the *bidonville*, delivered in the "Before the Contemporary" symposium at Northwestern University in May 2015.

75. Marion von Osten, "Architecture without Architects—Another Anarchist Approach," *E-Flux Journal*, no. 6 (May 2009).

Bibliography

Abadi, Jacob. *Tunisia since the Arab Conquest: The Saga of a Westernized Muslim State.* Reading, UK: Ithacas, 2013.

Abbassi, Driss. *Entre Bourguiba et Hannibal: Identité tunisienne et histoire depuis l'indépendance.* Aix-en-Provence, Fr.: IREMAM; Paris: Karthala, 2005.

Alexander, Christopher. *Tunisia: Stability and Reform in the Modern Maghreb.* London: Routledge, 2010.

Alexander, Michael Christopher. "Between Accommodation and Confrontation: State, Labor, and Development in Algeria and Tunisia." PhD diss., Duke University, 1996.

Avermaete, Tom. *Another Modern: The Postwar Architecture and Urbanism of Candilis-Josic-Woods.* Rotterdam, Neth.: Nai, 2005.

Baduel, Pierre Robert, ed. *Habitat, état et société au maghreb.* Paris: Centre de Recherches et d'Études sur les Sociétés Méditerranéennes, 1986.

Barker, Carol Mae. "The Politics of Decolonization in Tunisia: The Foreign Policy of a New State." PhD diss., Columbia University, 1971.

Berthault, Pierre. *La Propriété rurale en Afrique du Nord (Conférence donnée le 4 mars 1936 à l'Institut National Agronomique).* Alençon, Fr.: Imprimerie Alençonnaise, 1936.

Blachère, Gérard. "Reconstruction and Housing." In *Tunisia 54: 72 Years of Franco-Tunisian Collaboration Encyclopédie Mensuelle d'Outre-Mer.* Paris: Encyclopédie mensuelle d'Outre-mer, 1954.

Boubekeur, Sid. *Économie de la construction à Tunis.* Paris: L'Harmattan, 1987.

Bourdier, Jean-Paul, and Nezar AlSayyad, eds. *Dwellings, Settlements, and Tradition: Cross-Cultural Perspectives.* New York: University Press of America, 1989.

Bourguiba, Habib. *Electoral Campaign Speeches, October 26–November 5, 1959.* Tunis: Secretariate of State for Information Publications, 1959.

———. "The Tunisian Way." *Foreign Affairs* 44, no. 3 (1966): 480–88.

Brown, L. Carl. "Bourguiba and Bourguibism Revisited: Reflections and Interpretation." *Middle East Journal* 55, no. 1 (2001): 43–57.

Çelik, Zeynep. "Learning from the *Bidonville*: CIAM Looks at Algiers." *Harvard Design Magazine*, no. 18 (2003): 70–74.

———. *Urban Forms and Colonial Confrontations: Algiers under French Rule.* Berkeley: University of California Press, 1997.

Chabbi, Morched. "Politiques urbaines et régulations en Tunisie: Le cas du grand Tunis (1960–2007)," in *Habitat social au Maghreb et au Sénégal: Gouvernance urbaine et participation en questions*, edited by Julien Le Tellier and Aziz Iraki, 131–48. Paris: L'Harmattan, 2009.

———. *L'Urbain en Tunisie: Processus et projets*. Tunis: Nirvana, 2012.

Clark, Michael. "Bourguiba Bars Nationalization: Tunisian Chief Says Foreign Capital Has Nothing to Fear—Praise for Nasser Faint." *New York Times*, August 20, 1956.

Colarossi, Paolo. "Measures for Urban Rehabilitation in Tunis." *Environmental Design: Journal of the Islamic Environmental Design Research Centre* 1 (1985): 44–53.

La Colonisation en Tunisie. Bourg: Victor Berthod, 1931.

Le Corbusier. *Towards a New Architecture*. 1927. New York: Dover, 1986.

Correa, Charles. "Urban Housing in the Third World: The Role of the Architect." In *Architecture and Community: Building in the Islamic World Today*, edited by Renata Holod, 45–49. New York: Aperture, 1983.

Crane, Sheila. "Mapping the History of the Bidonville: Aesthetics of Containment and Mobility." Paper presented at the Sterling and Francine Clark Art Institute colloquium "Aesthetics and the Bidonville," May 2016.

Davies, H. R. T. "Regional Planning in Tunisia," *Geography* 74, no. 3 (1989): 255–59.

Deloge, Michel. "Les Perspectives de L'urbanisme de Tunis." *L'Architecture d'Aujourd'hui* (1955): 86.

Demersemann, André. "Formulation de l'idée de patrie en Tunisie de 1837 à 1872." *Revue de l'Institut des Belles Lettres Arabes*, no. 114 (1966).

Djaït, Hichem. "Le métier d'historien en Tunisie." In *Être historien aujourd'hui*, edited by René Rémond, 83–93. Paris: UNESCO; Toulouse, Fr.: Erès, 1988.

Doutté, Edmond, and Augustin Bernard. "L'habitation rurale des indigènes de l'Algérie." *Annales de Géographie* 26, no. 141 (1917): 219–28.

Duchac, R., ed. *Villes et sociétés au Maghreb: Études sur l'urbanisation*. Paris: CNRS, 1974.

Eckert, Hédi, and Jalal El-Kefi. "L'espace traditionnel de la ville de Tunis la médina et les deux Rbat faubourg ou gourbiville?" In *Les influences occidentales dans les villes Maghrébines à l'époque contemporaine: L'urbanisation au Maghreb: Systèmes culturels et systèmes urbains, Actes du Colloque d'Aix-en-Provence, Mai 1970*. Aix-en-Provence, Fr.: Éditions de l'Université de Provence, 1974.

Elleh, Nnamdi. *African Architecture: Evolution and Transformation*. New York: McGraw-Hill, 1997.

Escobar, Arturo. *Encountering Development: The Making and Unmaking of the Third World*. Princeton, NJ: Princeton University Press, 1995.

"Experiences rurales: Essais d'habitation ouvrières." *Revue de l'Institut des Belles Lettres Arabes*, no. 32 (4th trimester, 1945): 439–48.

Fanon, Frantz. *The Wretched of the Earth*. New York: Grove, 1963.

Franco, Gaston Lionel, ed. *La Tunisie devant son avenir* [Tunisia faces the future]. Paris: Le Monde économique, 1956.

Freund, Bill. "Labor and Labor History in Africa: A Review of Literature." *African Studies Review* 27, no. 2 (1984): 1–58.

Giedion, Sigfried. *A Decade of Contemporary Architecture*. Zurich: Editions Girsberger, 1954.

———. "Habitat: Universalität und Regionalismus." *Neue Zürcher Zeitung*, September 8, 1953.

Goodman, Jane E., and Paul A. Silverstein, eds. *Bourdieu in Algeria: Colonial Politics, Ethnographic Practices, Theoretical Developments*. Lincoln: University of Nebraska Press, 2009.

Hammoudi, Abdellah. "Phenomenology and Ethnography: On Kabyle Habitus in the Work of Pierre Bourdieu." In *Bourdieu in Algeria: Colonial Politics, Ethnographic Practices, Theoretical Developments,* edited by Jane E. Goodman and Paul A. Silverstein, 199–54. Lincoln: University of Nebraska Press, 2009.

Hahn, Lorna. "Tunisia: Pragmatism and Progress." *Middle East Journal* 16 (Winter 1962): 18–28.

Hale, Jonathan. "Edited Out of Contemporary Theoretical Discourse yet Central to the Way We Think about Architecture: Primitive." *Architecture Review Quarterly Report* 8, no. 1 (2004): 9–12.

Holod, Renata, ed. *Architecture and Community: Building in the Islamic World Today.* New York: Aperture, 1983.

Kassab, Ahmed. "Trois types de quartiers populaires à Béjà." *Revue tunisienne des sciences sociales* 8 (1971): 91–119.

Le Tellier, Julien, and Aziz Iraki, eds. *Habitat social au Maghreb et au Sénégal: Gouvernance urbaine et participation en questions.* Paris: L'Harmattan, 2009.

Memmi, Albert. *Decolonization and the Decolonized.* Translated by Robert Bononno. Minneapolis: University of Minnesota Press, 2006.

Miossec, Jean-Marie. "La politique d'habitat en Tunisie depuis l'Indépendance." In *Habitat, État et Société au Maghreb,* edited by Pierre Robert Baduel, 17–35. Paris: Centre de Recherches et d'Études sur les Sociétés Méditerranéennes, 1986.

Mitchell, Timothy. *Rule of Experts: Egypt, Techno-Politics, Modernity.* Berkeley: University of California Press, 2002.

"Modern Architects Hold First Postwar Congress." *Architectural Forum* 87 (November 1947): 65.

Mons, Jean. "Les Problèmes de reconstruction en Tunisie." *L'Architecture d'Aujourd'hui,* no. 20 (October 1948): 2.

Osten, Marion von. "Architecture without Architects—Another Anarchist Approach." *E-Flux Journal,* no. 6 (May 2009).

Oulebsir, Nabila. *Les usages du patrimoine, monuments, musées et politique coloniale en Algérie (1830–1930).* Paris: Éditions de la Maison des Sciences de l'Homme, 2004.

Pedret, Annie. "CIAM and the Emergence of Team 10 Thinking, 1945–1959." PhD diss., MIT, 2001.

Perkins, Kenneth. *A History of Modern Tunisia.* Cambridge: Cambridge University Press, 2004.

Rémond, René, ed. *Êntre historien aujourd'hui.* Paris: UNESCO; Toulouse, Fr.: Erès, 1988.

Ross, Kristin. "Starting Afresh: Hygiene and Modernization in Postwar France." *October* 67 (Winter 1994): 22–57.

Salhi, F. "Marché du travail, crise du logement et grande entreprise. Le cas de la sidérurgie à Annaba-El Hadjar (Algérie)." Thèse de 3e cycle, Université de Paris XII, Institut d'Urbanisme de Paris, 1983.

Santelli, Serge. *Medinass: Traditional Architecture of Tunisia.* Tunis: Dar Ashraf Editions, 1992.

———. *Tunis: Le creuset méditerranéen.* Paris: CNRS, 1995.

Santelli, Serge, and Bernard Tournet. "Évolution et ambiguïté de la maison arabe contemporaine au Maghreb: Étude de cas à Rabat et Tunis." In *Espace centré: Figures de l'architecture domestique dans l'Orient méditerranéen,* ed. Catherine Bruant. Marseille: Parenthèses, 1987.

Sebag, Paul. "La décolonisation et la transformation des quartiers traditionnels de Tunis." In *Les influences occidentales dans les villes Maghrébines à l'époque contemporaine: L'urbanisation au Maghreb systèmes culturels et systèmes urbains, Actes du Colloque d'Aix-en-Provence, Mai 1970.* Aix-en-Provences, Fr.: Éditions de l'Université de Provence, 1974.

———. *La Tunisie: Essai de monographie.* Paris: Éditions Sociales, 1951.

Seddon, David. "Winter of Discontent: Economic Crisis in Tunisia and Morocco." *MERIP Reports*, no. 127, Insurrection in North Africa. Richmond, VA: Middle East Research and Information Project, September–October 1984, 7–16.

Stambouli, Fredj. "Social Aspiration in Tunisian Architecture." In *Toward an Architecture in the Spirit of Islam*, edited by Renata Holod, 95. Philadelphia: Aga Khan Award for Architecture, 1978.

———. "Tradition et modernité à travers les processus d'urbanisation en Tunisie." In *Les Influences occidentales dans les villes Maghrébines à l'époque contemporaine: L'Urbanisation au Maghreb systèmes culturels et systèmes urbains, Actes du Colloque d'Aix-en-Provence, Mai 1970.* Aix-en-Provence, Fr.: Editions de l'Université de Provence, 1974.

Wylie, Diana. "The Importance of Being at-Home: A Defense of Historic Preservation in Algeria." *Change over Time* 2, no. 2 (2012): 172–87.

NANCY DEMERDASH is Assistant Professor of Art History in the Department of Art and Art History at Albion College. Her research interests focus on architecture and visual cultures of the Maghreb. She holds an MA and PhD in art and archaeology from Princeton University and an MS in architecture studies from MIT. Her previous publications have appeared in the *International Journal of Islamic Architecture, New Middle Eastern Studies, Journal of North African Studies, Perspective: actualité en histoire de l'art,* and the *Journal of Arabian Studies.* Currently, she is preparing her manuscript for publication and serves as assistant editor for the *International Journal of Islamic Architecture.*

6

NATION-BUILDING IN ISRAEL: NEGOTIATIONS OVER HOUSING AS GROUNDS FOR THE STATE-CITIZEN CONTRACT, 1948–53

Yael Allweil

THE ERUPTION OF MASS SOCIAL PROTEST IN ISRAEL in 2011, the largest protest movement since the 1970s, focused on popular demands for dwelling as a basic right of citizenship. Protesters formed a polity based on dwelling, enacted via a dwelling act: the creation of dozens of tent camps all over the country. The movement demanded that the state renew its housing commitment to the citizens, framing housing as the central element of Israel's social contract and a basic term underlying Israeli citizenship.[1] This study investigates the formation of Israel's housing-based social contract, asking why the relationship between state and citizens in Israel is framed by housing, and how housing has become the central and decisive component of Israel's state-citizen contract.

During its first five years (1948–53), Israel's fragile sovereignty encountered what it perceived as three pressing challenges, addressed in three separate housing programs—an exceptional number of planning schemes in such a short period. The first threat was perceived to be Israel's "enemy" citizenry, Arab-Palestinians who had not been "swept away" during the 1948 War. Israel's first housing policy enacted to counter this threat included settling immigrants in vacated Arab-Palestinian houses and lands in primarily agricultural border areas. The second perceived threat was posed by the Jewish Agency (JA) and the Jewish National Fund (JNF), whose continued involvement in postindependence settlement threatened to create a state within a state and subject Israel to the sovereignty of world Jewry. The threats were addressed through the *ma'abara* housing policy, which removed immigrants from JA-controlled reception camps and settled them in temporary single-family dwellings, with the goal of cementing their allegiance to state and country. The third perceived threat was the immigrants themselves, primarily Mizrahim arriving from Arab and Muslim countries, who refused to accept the state's definition of proper housing and proper citizenship, rejecting the regime and threatening the very legitimacy of the state. This threat was eventually addressed by a plan to disperse the masses across the country while accepting immigrants' understanding of proper housing as permanent, good-quality dwellings for all. These policies attest to the extent of the governmental crisis and to the perceived value of housing as a means of addressing the crisis.

Much has been written about Israel's mass housing and planning efforts of the "long 1950s" focusing on the planning and construction of immigrant towns and on the social consequences for immigrants and society, especially for Mizrahim, as an explicit tool for marginalization of this new citizenry that was used to preserve Ashkenazi dominance of state apparatus and resources.[2] Surprisingly little attention, however, has been given to the first five years, consisting primarily of temporary and ad hoc architecture and planning, which became a laboratory for future definitions of the housing-based social contract. This study portrays a much more nuanced relationship between state and citizens and questions the assumption that immigrants were docile in the face of the strong state apparatus by introducing overlooked data on citizens' active negotiations of national dwellings.

Why Housing? Conceptual Framework and Object of Inquiry

The term *housing* has been framed in the Euro-American context of the post–World War II period within the discipline of urban planning and defined as the social problem of ensuring that all members of society have access to a dwelling. Defined as such, *housing* engages key social issues such as who counts as a member of society and who is to ensure housing provision. Studies on the issue look at the mechanisms that produce and distribute housing solutions for different publics. In a key text about the relationship between nation-state and citizens, Peter Marcuse discusses what he defines as "the myth of the benevolent state," exposing the mechanisms by which postwar nation-states used the basic terms of the social contract—such as housing—in order to dominate (rather than care for) their citizens.[3] The postwar ideological struggle between East and West was waged, to a great extent, on citizens' concrete dwelling environments, introducing many to homeownership and good-quality dwellings.[4]

In contrast with institutional building types representing the nation, such as capital complexes or exhibition complexes, housing is far more than just a representation or symbol of the nation, but rather it is a tool with which subjects are formed, values are inscribed, and class struggle, in the broadest sense, is waged.[5] In addition, housing embodies the nation-state's idea of what it means to "be at home" as a member of the imagined community of the nation.[6] More than any other constructed form, then, housing can serve as a tool for questioning the modern nation-state as a cultural-political institution. Housing's significance lies in being simultaneously private and public, carrying the burden of what it communicates to others about one's identity and membership. Housing serves as a system of inclusion and exclusion from political membership, national identity, and political community.

Yet, as an institution, housing is not solely the domain of the state: rather, housing is one way to institutionalize the relationship between two significant actors—state and citizens—rather than a relationship between actor and passive recipient. A number of architectural studies have identified the private-domestic space of housing as the site for continuous struggle over the identity of the nation and political body of citizens. Notable are works by John Archer on the roots of American-dream suburban housing; Becky Nicolaides on blue-collar suburbs; Diane Harris on the construction of race in American postwar housing; Li Zhang on Chinese urban migrants' housing solutions in the city; Teresa Caldeira on the construction of social class in Brazilian gated condominiums; Heynen and Baydar on modern domesticity as structuring a gendered social order based on the redefinition of spaces and gender roles; Andrew Shanken on architecture as a site for proposing alternative visions for the nation; and Margaret Crawford on alternative forms of housing created by the 1960s generation.[7]

As the scope of housing studies has extended our understanding of dwellings beyond form and function to include issues of urbanization and development, gender, class, race, and globalization,[8] the framework proposed here maintains housing studies' focus on the social issues and power mechanisms that produce and distribute housing while reintroducing to this discussion the architectural lens of data collection and inquiry.

Israeli Housing as Nation-Building

Planning historians Kallus and Law-Yone have shown that housing has served Israel's nation-building project in its mission of connecting subjects and homeland in order to form a sovereign political entity legitimated by the people. This task has been addressed by associating national home and individual housing and also by the state assuming a mediating role in the relationship between citizens and homeland.[9]

Sovereignty brought dramatic changes to the Zionist nation-building enterprise, including access to land, citizenry, and planning. Land, a major obstacle for pre-state Zionism, was made available to the Israeli public as a form of collective landownership by means of membership in the state as landowner. Moreover, when the UN partition compromise of 1947 fell apart, leading to the 1948 war, Israel enlarged its territory at the expense of areas designated for the Arab-Palestinian state and nationalized them as parts of the Jewish homeland.[10] Access to land, a paralyzing issue for pre-state Zionism, was thus removed as a problem for the new state of Israel.

The second major consequence of statehood was control over legal citizens and the ability to take in immigrants and grant them citizenship without international restrictions.[11] Large numbers of Jewish immigrants flocked to the country after independence, doubling Israel's population in three years (1948–51).[12] Israeli leaders, especially the first prime minister, David Ben-Gurion, identified the new immigrants as both a legitimating factor for Israel as a Jewish homeland and as a source of manpower for nation-building.[13] Facing the burden of caring for so many homeless new citizens, some called for restrictions on immigration. Early national leaders insisted, however, that Israel should admit every Jew willing to immigrate, since housing the Jewish people was the state's raison d'être.[14] Israel's Declaration of Independence thus tied political independence to immigration and housing. The connection was subsequently inscribed in a formal law, the Law of Return, enacted in July 1950, which acknowledged the right of every Jew to immigrate and become an Israeli citizen.[15] Yet as Yaacobi, Zvi Efrat, and others have shown, state leadership regarded the immigrants, Holocaust survivors and Jews of Arab and Muslim countries, as "victims" and "primitives," unfit "human material" for the heroic pioneer enterprise of state-building. Planning served state leadership as a key tool for the education and molding of immigrants into good Zionist subjects.[16] At the same time, the state tried to evade its responsibility for its Arab-Palestinian citizenry, who were legally granted equal citizenship with statehood, and subjected them to military rule as "enemy citizens" to be governed outside the civilian state mechanism.[17]

Third, statehood introduced comprehensive planning to Zionist nation-building, which contrasted with piecemeal pre-state planning by the JA and JNF. Pre-state efforts had not included a national or even regional component and were limited to the realm of the settlement.[18] According to Kallus and Law-Yone, "While Zionism aspired to produce a new space fit for a new society—a new environment for the 'new Jew'—the shape of this environment or the model by which it would be designed were never given any thought."[19] Within the new Israeli state, the Governmental Planning Administration, under the Ministry of Labor, aimed to do just that. Formed in March 1949, it was put in charge of master planning, general planning, and housing.[20] Architect Arieh Sharon, a kibbutz member, Bauhaus graduate, and designer of David Ben-Gurion's house in Tel Aviv, was appointed head of the department. The very idea of planning at the time meant facing the challenges posed by mass immigration and control of state lands. It needed to house incoming citizens while staking a claim to the land and securing national borders. These goals changed rapidly, however, as perceptions of the most pressing perceived threats to national sovereignty changed.

Works examining Israel's first acts of national planning generally describe the state's mass-housing project as directed primarily at the immigrants in an attempt to make them proper citizen-subjects while excluding them from loci of power, in a process similar to what political scientist James Scott described as "seeing like a state."[21] Planning is seen to have given rise to the social categories that still characterize Israeli society.[22] Scholars of planning Yacobi, Shadar, and Yiftachel show how intense planning was used to associate the social and geographical periphery with Jews of Mizrahi origin and cement them as an underclass.[23] Specifically, the literature universally condemns immigrant housing in Israel in the 1950s and 1960s as bad quality housing. Both temporary *ma'abara* tent towns and permanent *shikun* mass-housing blocks built in the 1960s are cited as material evidence of discrimination against the mostly Mizrahi immigrants.[24] Scholarly accounts and popular discourse consider immigrant housing to have been a violent act toward the new citizens, intended to keep them outside good-subject circles and centers of power. Among these, Ella Shohat's essay is particularly notable for invoking Edward Said's *j'accuse* of Zionism (written a decade earlier) to analyze Mizrahi immigrant absorption as a colonial enterprise.[25] Thus, it ties together state treatment of Mizrahim and Palestinians. Meanwhile, scholars of political geography and planning Jabareen, Khamaisi, and Yiftachel examine the exclusion of Arab-Palestinian citizenry from planning as directly related to their alienation, racialization, and political marginalization outside the sphere of "proper" citizenship in Israel as a Jewish homeland.[26]

Literature on the Israeli housing-as-nation-building project generally accepts the premise of the state apparatus as a strong governing mechanism capable of enforcing itself on its subjects. This literature focuses on the policy and economics involved in planning processes and on state leaders and bureaucrats as actors framing and conducting housing-as-governance. Discussion of citizens' roles in shaping housing environments locates their influence in small-scale alterations to housing blocks in bottom-up attempts to personify anonymous housing blocks, as Yacobi discusses, following Holston's study of Brasilia as the epitome of the modernist city.[27] These studies relegate the study of architecture to small-scale alterations in resistance to planning (rather than the study of architecture in and for itself) and maintain the top-down, bottom-up assumption of the power relations between state and citizens embedded in housing as a category of scholarly inquiry.

First State-Citizen Contract: Pioneer Citizenship in Agricultural Border Settlement

During and immediately after the 1948 War, the main threat to Israeli sovereignty was perceived to be the same as before statehood—namely, Palestinian claims to the same homeland. Therefore, Israel's first planning policy employed the same tactics and strategies as pre-state agencies had, posited on staking claim to the land through rural settlement and agricultural cultivation. This policy required citizens willing to assume the role of pioneer land cultivators in border settlements, like the pioneers who participated in the early years of Zionist settlement. The new state expected postindependence immigrants to settle along the borders and contribute to this goal, in a state-citizen contract requiring immigrants to perform the pioneer role in dwelling and settlement.[28] Pioneer border settlements were the only physical, economic, and cultural planning for the absorption of immigrants during and after the war, offering housing and resettlement in exchange for securing the nation's borders.[29] This social contract reflected an ethos of rooting oneself in the homeland via toil on the land and maintained the Zionist tradition of using settlements to establish political borders.[30]

Pioneer border settlement involved not only international borders, consolidated after the war, but also internal borders within the country, between the state's Jewish citizenry and its Arab-Palestinian enemy citizenry, those Palestinians who had remained within Israel's borders as potentially hostile citizens. As a result of the war, some four hundred Arab-Palestinian agricultural villages were emptied of their inhabitants, as were numerous Arab-Palestinian houses in the country's main cities; some hundred and sixty thousand, however, managed to remain.[31] Most of Israel's Jewish population was located in the center of the country, while most of its Arab-Palestinian population lived in its postwar periphery. This postwar condition was enforced by a military regime that restricted movement of the remaining Arab-Palestinian population.[32] Settlement in the country's periphery, among the enemy Arab-Palestinian population, was defined, therefore, as part of the pioneer enterprise.

The border district of Ramla was central to this policy, as it included the significant external border with the Jordanian-held West Bank and two main internal border areas around the enemy cities of Ramla and Lod. These were two main Arab-Palestinian population hubs until 1948 that had been designated by the UN partition plan to be part of the Palestinian state.[33] The Ramla district, being at the center of the country, was allocated a significant number of pioneer settlements in three frameworks: vacated housing within the cities of Ramla and Lydda, urban subsistence farms surrounding these cities, and border *moshav* agricultural settlements along the Jordanian border. These three options were all premised on the principle of self-help housing, namely the provision of very basic state support to be employed by immigrants-cum-pioneers, including access to "deserted" housing, construction materials, and core housing.

Most scholarly work on the mass housing of immigrants has focused on the northern and southern districts of the country.[34] But data presented by Haim Darin-Drabkin in 1955 indicated that the population growth in the Ramla area by 1955 exceeded that in all other areas of Israel. Indeed, it amounted to 2,143.5 percent, a result of its target as a site of immigrant settlement. In comparison, the population of the extensively studied Beersheba district grew by 1,779 percent, the Jezreel district grew by 181 percent, and the Tel Aviv–Jaffa district grew by 87.2 percent.[35] Therefore, the Ramla district can be identified as the most significant area of immigrant settlement under the first housing policy.[36] The dearth of scholarly attention to the Ramla district, in comparison with its relative and absolute role, arguably results from its settlement dynamics of self-help housing by the immigrants themselves as the driving force, while scholarly attention is directed primarily at state-driven forced resettlement by way of new towns and mass housing (fig. 6.1).

Some six hundred thousand Palestinians were displaced from homes and settlements during the war, and the vacated properties became a significant component of the postwar housing stock, with some hundred and twenty-four thousand immigrants moving into these properties between May 1948 and December 1949.[37] Use of vacated housing was unplanned, as can be seen from the initial demolition of properties by the authorities to prevent Arab-Palestinians from returning to them.[38] The takeover of vacated housing came as a result of actions by homeless immigrants, who did not receive services from the state in the first year of independence, before any planning institutions were established. As the state did not provide immigrants any housing solutions at the time, it accepted the immigrants' use of vacated units. State involvement in immigrant housing in vacated properties was limited to determining their legal status; they were declared state property by the Deserted Areas Order of May 16, 1948. The Amidar governmental company was formed to manage these properties and charge rent to the immigrants who settled in them. Since vacated housing was essentially up for grabs, immigrants who arrived in the first few months after independence found better-quality, or at least intact, properties to occupy. Immigrants arriving shortly thereafter found houses of lesser quality or ones that had been partially destroyed during the war. Moreover, the pace of immigration and extent of housing needs soon led to the subdividing of houses to serve several families, each occupying a room (fig. 6.2).[39] An immigrant from Bulgaria recounts, "We arrived in the port of Haifa on October 28, 1949. . . . Buses took us to the immigrant reception camps in Hadera where we received a warm meal, blankets, iron beds and canvas tents. . . . My father started looking for a house and soon found one. It was a house in early stages of construction, with no windows or paving, but it served us as

RAMLA — SUB-DISTRICT.

POPULATION INCREASE from 1948 to 1955 — 2143.5%

1948 — 2,981 persons — 0.4% of total

1955 — 66,878 persons — 4.2% of total

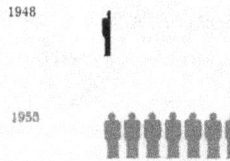

1948

1955

SUMMARY OF BUILDING 1948—1955

TYPE OF BUILDING	DWELLING UNITS	% *	BUILT IN SETTLEMENTS	
			founded before 1948	founded after 1948
Housing for immigrants in urban and semi-urban areas	2,016	2.6	3	1
Housing in agricultural settlements **	4,344	10.3	6	50
TOTAL	6,360	5.4	9	51

*) *Percentage of total built in the country.*

**) *For immigrants and old settlers.*

Figure 6.1. Population growth, number, and type of new settlements in the Ramla district, 1948–1955. Darin-Drabkin, *Housing in Israel*, p. 242-44.

Figure 6.2. Jewish immigrants in war-damaged structures in Azur, 1949. Photograph by Zoltan Kluger. Israel National Photo Collection, Jerusalem.

a roof over our heads."[40] Another immigrant recounts, "We were assigned a room in a house on the central Yefet Street [in Jaffa]. It was a beautiful house with painted ceilings which belonged, we were told, to a rich pharmacist who had fled the country. Ours was a two-room wooden section outside the main house, with an attached bathroom and kitchen. . . . Each section of the house was occupied by a different family."[41]

Deserted housing served the Arab-Palestinian citizenry as well, appropriated by internal refugees who were trapped outside their home villages at the close of the war and restricted by the military regime from returning and thus were forced to find housing for themselves in vacated dwellings in other villages. Cohen and others give accounts of bitter conflicts among internally displaced villagers, revolving around the issue of accepting absentee homes and lands vacated by refugees as compensation for land in their original villages.[42] Architect Hana Farah recounts his family's displacement from Birem to nearby Jish: "Grandma, grandpa and their cousins 'selected' a vacated house . . . what will [they] do? They were living in a vacated home and their own home probably housed people who came by boats. . . . One day an older woman came back from Lebanon, sneaked through the border. . . . She pushed open the gate . . . a large key in her hand. . . . [H]er husband and son remained in Lebanon and she alone returned and made do—had to make do—with the single room to which she held a key."[43]

By May 1949, the number of immigrants exceeded the vacated housing stock, and this option was no longer available. The enemy Arab city was to be contained by several new Jewish neighborhoods that were planned to surround and encircle it. The first of these was the Amidar Shacks neighborhood, erected right outside the Arab city of Ramla in early 1950. It combined urban housing and land cultivation in the form of self-help subsistence agriculture. The neighborhood included some fifty wooden shacks, each serving two families. Each family was allocated a living space of 8 by 4.2 meters (34 square meters) and a plot of land 18 by 40 meters (700 square meters or 0.07 hectares). The half-shack included two rooms and a water tap. Toilets were located at the far side of the plot in a small shack placed on a septic tank.

The ratio between shack size and plot area of approximately 700 square meters indicates that the shack was self-help core housing within a plot that was understood to be the family home. The land—the long-aspired-to Zionist dream—served immigrant families for growing produce, as unemployment was a major problem and many families relied on rations alone. Neighborhood families found several apricot and almond trees on their plots, part of an orchard that had previously existed along the main road, and used their plots to grow vegetables and fruit and to keep chickens and goats. The small plots of land facing the enemy provided each immigrant family a source of livelihood during the decade-long austerity period established by the Israeli government from 1949 to 1959.[44] Since shacks were extremely small, families used them primarily for sleep and considered the entire plot their homes, spending most of their time outside in vine-covered sheds and working in vegetable gardens. This approach continued the early kibbutz, where the member's room served primarily for sleep and most of the member's time was spent in communal areas (fig. 6.3).

Soon families began to expand their living spaces by doing their own building, adding structures to accommodate additional family members, married children, and small production workshops. Disassembled wooden barrels found in the area, flattened and hammered to a wooden frame, served as building material. These wooden walls were then covered with tar paper to prevent water leakage. Next, stone ovens were built in the yards surrounded by additional self-constructed shacks made of scrap wood and

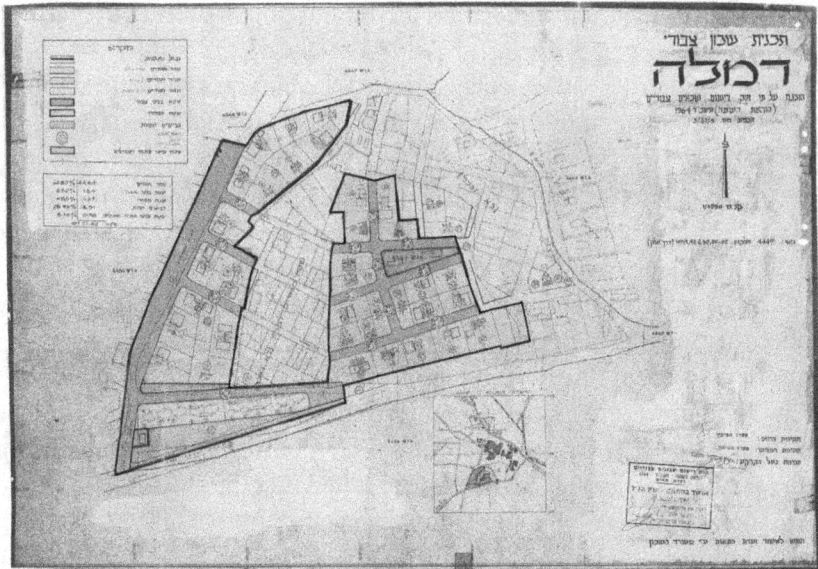

Figure 6.3. Ramla Shack neighborhood in the Ramla public housing plan, prepared per the law of Public Housing Registration, 1964, which regulated the existing condition. Neighborhood location outside the Arab city is marked in bottom diagram. Note ratio between half-shack and plot size. Israel Land Administration Archive, Jerusalem. Plan 3/57/3 file.

disassembled barrels.[45] Core housing and access to land offered new citizens the prospect of becoming pioneer "good subjects." In exchange, they were required to contribute to the national goal of border defense against the internal enemy.

Despite the state definition of its Arab-Palestinian citizens as enemy citizenry, the social reality forming in and around Ramla and Lod (as well as in Jaffa and Haifa) after the settlement of Jewish immigrants inside and immediately surrounding enemy neighborhoods produced constructed environments that blurred the definition of proper and enemy citizens. The consequence of this housing policy, driven by the immigrants themselves, was the transformation of the enemy population hubs to mixed cities. Unlike the regime's intended goal of containing and marginalizing the enemy citizenry, surprising cooperation formed in most formerly Arab cities. Moreover, settling Jews in vacated housing disrupted the spatial separation between Jews and Arabs that was embedded in the military regime mechanism, which could not be enforced in mixed areas, thus questioning the very definition of the Arab-Palestinian population and space as the enemy.[46]

External border settlements employed the pioneer agricultural model of pre-state settlement to gain a stake of national land. In February 1949, a special meeting of the *moshav* movement was convened in Ramla to propose the absorption of immigrants in *moshav* settlements under the slogan "From the camps to the village." Later known as the Ramla Convention, the meeting included leaders David Ben-Gurion and Levi Eshkol, who enthusiastically "accepted the call."[47] The *moshav* framework was a cooperative model of family-based agricultural farms, which seemed more appropriate than the kibbutz model for immigrants who were Zionists but not necessarily communists.[48] Ramla was chosen to host the convention because the district was designated as an area for immigrant settlement. The subsequent Plan for Rural Settlement of March 1949 stated that the government would act to direct immigration to *moshav* settlements.[49]

In July 1949, Prime Minister Ben-Gurion outlined the government's course of action toward agricultural settlement for the four upcoming years. The planning guidelines included settling one hundred fifty thousand immigrants in five hundred new settlements, forming a belt of border settlements that would play a key role in border defense and help safeguard state sovereignty over territory. The guidelines also specified that the settlements would engage in intensive agricultural production to supply food to a growing population living on food rations.[50]

The housing type designated for immigrant *moshavim* was the "blockon," named after its construction method of hollow concrete blocks, the first model for permanent housing that was proposed by the Planning Department of the Ministry of Labor and Construction. The model was a single-story structure of two dwelling units of twenty-four square meters each, built of concrete blocks on a cast concrete floor.

The first blockon, "an experimental standard house," was built on the grounds of the government headquarters in Tel Aviv (Hakirya) in the course of one day in June 1949, to be examined and approved by all ministries and relevant professionals.[51] Initially, each dwelling unit included a single room and a water tap. The "dry" toilets (not connected to a sewage system) were located in a small shack outside the house. Later versions of the blockon included an internal ceiling and a plywood partition separating parents from children.[52] The blockon was to serve as a self-help unit for a "growing house," much like the shacks discussed above.[53]

In May 1949, preparations were already made for constructing three thousand blockon units across the country.[54] Seventy-eight hundred units of the basic blockon were constructed, some of them by the dwellers themselves.[55] The housing department did not regard the blockon as permanent housing, but rather as core self-help housing.[56] State planners and architects never proclaimed its small size and limited amenities good enough for the immigrants, but rather accepted it as a first step toward self-sufficiency, connection to the land, and better living conditions.[57] The blockon was, therefore, proper pioneer housing in the Israeli historical framework, a continuation of the pioneer tradition, which, by definition, embedded self-help as practice and principle.

One such *moshav* was Tirat Yehuda, founded in 1949 on nationalized land of the former Palestinian village of al-Tira by the Jordanian border. In order to ensure that Arab-Palestinian refugees would not be able to return and claim the village, the state sold the land (along with other land) to the JNF, whose founding edicts determined that all lands under its control be used for Jewish settlement.[58] Tirat Yehuda's plan, prepared by the Settlement Department of the JA, included thirty-five agricultural farms and twenty-two subsistence farms following the design principles formulated for the JA by architect Richard Kauffman for agricultural kibbutz and *moshav* settlements in the 1920s.

A core of public services (school, clinic, meeting hall) was surrounded by houses and farms. Behind each member family's house lay its agricultural fields, with the plots and houses in the inner core designated for professionals living in the *moshav,* such as the doctor, the teacher, and the agronomist. Tirat Yehuda plan was submitted in 1951 and approved in 1954, after all its houses had already been built and its fields cultivated, making statutory registration a mere formality.[59]

The immigrant settlers of Tirat Yehuda, Jews from Hungary, Yemen, and Libya, initially occupied the vacated stone and earth houses of al-Tira. They were employed by the JA in road construction until new houses and fields were laid out. Then, in 1950, the JA supplied them with concrete blocks so they could build blockon housing for themselves. The border location of Tirat Yehuda meant an everyday reality of attacks by infiltrators coming across the Jordanian border. These attacks generally amounted to sabotage and the theft of crops. The most lethal attack, in June 1953, included shooting and throwing a grenade into one of the houses, resulting in the death of one resident (figs. 6.4 and 6.5).[60]

Figure 6.4. Immigrant building a house for his large family of ten members now living in one room, 1949. Photographer unknown. Israel National Photo Collection, Jerusalem.

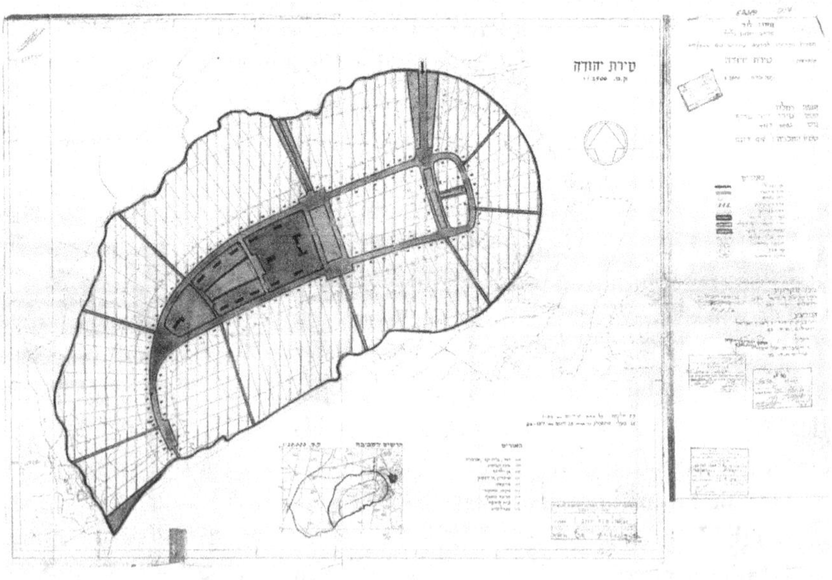

Figure 6.5. Tirat Yehuda plan, 1951–54. Remains of the village of al-Tira at the top right-hand corner of area scheme. Israel Land Administration Archive, Jerusalem. Plan 415/חגפ file.

From the perspective of the state, the activities of the Tirat Yehuda immigrants—building their own homes, securing the border, and cultivating the homeland—marked them as good citizens. Such border agricultural settlements in the plan for rural settlement were the only housing solution offered to immigrants, but many refused to settle in these "and be cannon fodder." Instead, they chose to remain in reception camp dwelling conditions rather than accept relocation to border settlements.[61] Even had all the immigrants been enthusiastic about performing their role as pioneers, the pace of border-settlement formation would not have been enough to match the pace of immigration. Ten to fifteen new agricultural settlements were founded monthly, totaling 147 new immigrant *moshav* settlements between January 1949 and May 1952, but they housed only fifty thousand immigrants, a fraction of the approximately seven hundred thousand immigrants who arrived during that time.[62]

Housing Crisis in Immigrant Camps: Violation of the State-Citizen Contract

In the years immediately after independence, the vast influx of immigrants quickly created a severe housing crisis, which escalated with each new immigration wave. The direction of most resources and planning efforts to pioneer settlements in order to curb the perceived Palestinian threat by staking claims to the land came at the expense of providing the masses of new citizens with appropriate housing solutions.[63] It quickly became apparent that Israel's first planning policy was primarily designed to address yesterday's challenges. By comparison, the plan largely ignored the new reality of nation-building: the immense challenge of housing, requiring setting new terms for the state-citizen contract.

The state and the JA subsequently sought to provide immigrants with an interim solution by converting former British army camps into immigrant camps. At the time, responsibility for housing immigrants was divided between the JA and the state. This seemed logical as it utilized the combined advantages of the two bodies. The state's capacity to conduct planning made it responsible for developing permanent housing solutions. It suffered, however, from an acute shortage of foreign currency, leading to a severe austerity regime. And so the JA, funded by world Jewry, assumed responsibility for the immigrants while they remained in the camps. This support was intended to be merely short-term—for the brief period until immigrants were permanently housed in agricultural settlements where they would be able to provide for themselves.

By the end of 1949, some ninety thousand immigrants lived in seven camps throughout the country. With all former British army camps filled, new camps were formed rapidly, with no appropriate infrastructure and in locations far from sources of employment.[64] The camps provided a very cheap answer to the immediate housing problem: each large barrack hall could accommodate fifty immigrants. Here an immigrant's living space was limited to his or her bed, with no division by family, age, or gender. The food provided was also poor, as were the sanitation facilities. Camp barracks housed hundreds of thousands for several months in conditions that were those suitable for an overnight shelter. Disconnected from the rest of the country, unemployed immigrants frequently became frustrated and depressed. Years later immigrants would remember the miserable, aimless living conditions at the reception camps and continue to recount the extreme cold, the muddy, unpaved paths, the soup kitchens, and the crowding (fig. 6.6).[65]

Dr. Giora Yoseftal, head of the JA absorption department, described camp conditions as explosive, embodying a continuing threat of civil unrest.[66] Pinhas Lavon, head of the Histadrut Workers Union, described the situation as putting the young state at risk of a counterrevolution.[67] In addition, Mordechai Bentov, minister of labor and construction, warned that nonstate institutions catering to the immigrants were challenging state sovereignty,[68] and as the immigrant reception camp crisis deepened, Israeli leaders started to identify world Jewry as a threat to its independence and sovereignty. This development was shocking, as until then the JA and JNF had been considered part and parcel of the drive for Israeli sovereignty. Levi Eshkol articulated the threat as follows: "Damned is this system of immigrant camps! I want to kill this system of [JA] clerical administration. . . . Someone invented this system to destroy us."[69]

JA's threat to Israel's sovereignty deepened with the JNF initiative of a new housing and settlement form on JNF lands in response to the immigrant camp crisis: the "work village." Work villages, as the name suggests, were premised on supplying immigrants with work rather than charity. Border locations and detached housing units granted immigrants the status and ethos of Israeli pioneer citizens—outside the framework of

Figure 6.6. Immigrants in one of the barracks at Sha'ar Aliya reception camp, 1949. Photograph by Zoltan Kluger. National Photo Collection.

Israeli sovereignty. The formation of work villages began in the summer of 1949. During late 1949 and the early months of 1950, thirty-seven work villages of 120 families each were established by the JNF: fifteen in the frontier area of the Jerusalem corridor, twelve in the Arab-populated Galilee, and the rest in Mount Gilboa, Mount Carmel, and the Menashe Heights.[70] Housing in the villages consisted of tents and wooden shacks. But unlike the state-sanctioned immigrant-pioneer settlements, housing in JNF work camps was declared a temporary solution and, therefore, did not come with land for subsistence cultivation. Land in them was to be cultivated collectively in the framework of paid public works.[71]

State leaders regarded the work village as a blunt violation of Israeli sovereignty, an act of a state within a state that bypassed the authority of the Israeli government and rendered it irrelevant. It was further evident to state leaders that the consequences of civil unrest could take down the elected government; they could not, however, touch the unelected organizations of world Jewry. Camps and work villages provided material evidence that the state had relegated the vast majority of immigrants to prolonged interim care by the JA, which violated the protracted promise, inherent in immigration, of proper Israeli citizenship. It was not until the JA actively attempted to assume the state's role and house immigrants on JNF lands that the state initiated its own new housing policy. As a result, by 1950, Israel's housing policy was forced to divert itself from addressing the Arab-Palestinian threat to addressing world Jewry's involvement in immigrant housing and citizen-subject formation.[72]

Second State-Citizen Contract: Home in the Homeland

The state housing regime responded to the challenge by initiating a new policy that would replace both immigrant camps and work villages: the *ma'abara* (Hebrew for "transitory"; plural *ma'abarot*). The goal of the *ma'abarott* was to remove immigrants from the domain of world Jewry in interim camps and work villages to the domain of the state by offering them single-family detached housing, albeit temporary, on state land.[73] The first *ma'abara* opened in Ksalon in the Jerusalem Mountains in May 1950. It was founded on the lands of the vacated Arab village of Kasla, which was associated with the biblical town of Ksalon. On May 23, 1950, the newspaper *Davar* reported that the temporary settlement housed 120 families, whose breadwinners were employed in forestry and paid daily wages.[74] While the *ma'abara* was proclaimed to be a new housing and settlement form, it was, in effect, a work village. Indeed, there were many similarities between the two programs. The main difference, of course, involved state land ownership.

Between the years 1949 and 1951, 44,309 *ma'abara* temporary dwelling units were erected—among them wooden shacks, tents, and tin huts—which came to house some two hundred fifty thousand people, 25 percent of Israel's population by 1952.[75] The *ma'abarot*'s building block was the individual dwelling space, which broke down the masses of immigrants into family units, in the interest of the immigrants and the state alike.

Ksalon can be recognized as an experiment in temporary dwellings. As can be seen in an image from 1950 (see fig. 6.7), it included a variety of structures scattered on the landscape: family-size tents, small tin-and-asbestos shacks, and several wooden shacks on poles. In comparison, little attention was given to planning the *ma'abara* as settlement; while space was by no means an issue, dwellings were frequently erected close together, generating acute problems of density in addition to poor housing conditions.

Figure 6.7. Ksalon *Ma'abara*, December 1950. Photograph by Werner Brown. JNF Archive, Jerusalem.

Temporary *ma'abara* dwellings required a state financial investment in housing twice that of the previous housing of immigrants in barracks until permanent rural resettlement. As all researchers in the field have pointed out, the *ma'abara* represented a revolutionary turning point in the state's attitude toward the challenge of absorbing masses of new immigrants. This housing policy, which was intended to give immigrants proper shelter, albeit temporarily, signified a transformation in the terms of the Israeli state-citizen contract from access to land to access to housing. This transformation cemented "housing the persecuted Jewish people" and the Zionist subject formation as the twin raisons d'être of Israeli sovereignty. As a result, the state became a housing regime.

Temporary Dwellings: Second Violation of the State-Citizen Contract

As might have been expected, the very temporariness of *ma'abara* dwellings rapidly led to the deterioration of such constructed environments, developing into a humanitarian crisis during the rough winter of 1950–51. Cheaply constructed dwellings leaked, were blown over by wind, flooded, and filled with mud. Sanitary facilities were also disgraceful and degrading, and health services were insufficient. Indeed, the harsh winter placed more than sixty-five thousand *ma'abara* residents in dire conditions and resulted in the evacuation of ten thousand of them to nearby settlements. There, immigrant children first encountered "a shower with warm running water, a white private toilet right next to the housing, and electricity."[76] In addition to inadequate facilities, *ma'abara* dwellers experienced constant food shortages, because they could not evade the government's austerity measures by producing their own food as residents of kibbutz and *moshav* settlements or of subsistence-farm housing around Ramla did.

Despite recognition of these conditions and continual promises to improve them, a year later, the state housing authorities had done nothing to ensure that the winter of 1951 would be any different. As a result, *ma'abarot* settlements across the country fermented with unrest. Eventually, an alleged theft of food from kibbutz fields by a resident of the Emek Hefer *ma'abara* led to a civil rebellion in November 1952 against the police, which quickly spread across the country.[77] Protesters from dozens of *ma'abarot* took this as their cue to demand that the government attend to their needs, primarily for better housing and an adequate level of services.

At the time, immigrants could not help but notice the stark difference between their *ma'abara* housing and veteran kibbutz or *moshav* housing. They could not care less that, as pioneers, those veteran citizens had once also endured harsh conditions; in fact, they did not associate their harsh living conditions with the "sacrifice of pioneer life." Immigrants did not read the divide between them and the veterans, which was made explicit in housing, as one they would eventually be able to bridge. Rather, as Mizrahi Jews, many immigrants viewed their housing conditions as representing deep racial discrimination, relegating them forever to the status of second-class citizens.[78] Of course, the immigrants' perceptions had solid grounds; strong racial sentiments did exist within the veteran public against the predominantly Mizrahi immigrants, as Jews of European origin were typically the first to be offered permanent housing, since they were "used to proper conditions" (fig. 6.8).[79]

The *ma'abarot* embodied an important dwelling solution in Israel's housing history. First, they pointed to the state's realization that its legitimization lay in its citizenry and that failure to care for them might lead to a loss of sovereignty. Second, they signified a realization that housing is a basic demand placed on the state by its immigrant citizens. Third, the temporary nature and poor dwelling conditions of *ma'abarot*, housing newcomers

Figure 6.8. Woman in Beit-Lit Ma'abara, 1950. Photograph by Teddy Brauner. National Photo Collection.

rather than "founders," established housing as a facet of social class. The *ma'abara* pointed to housing as the arena in which social phenomena were manifest and, in some cases, formed by making visible the political and ethnic divide in Israel two decades before it emerged explicitly in the political arena.

Third State-Citizen Contract: Population Dispersal in Permanent Self-Help Housing

The civil unrest unleashed in the *ma'abarot* marked them as a failure in the state's attempt to form the immigrants into pioneers willing to endure hardship for the goal of access to the homeland. Social unrest also brought state attention to a deep transformation in the citizenry's perception of the state-citizen contract: from one based on access to the homeland to one based on having proper housing. Indeed, mass demand for proper housing cemented housing as a civil right for each and every citizen and as a state responsibility. A new housing solution had to be formulated to address the crisis, the third in four years.

This time, the state housing regime aimed to formulate more than a temporary plan, one that would provide immigrants with the permanent, good-quality housing that they demanded. The attempt to transform immigrants into pioneers was no longer part of the effort. Instead, this new, third policy would become known primarily for producing a national master plan, known as the Sharon plan after its head planner, architect Arieh Sharon.[80]

Much has been written about the Sharon master plan as a form of population dispersal and the formation of "development towns" in Israel's periphery.[81] Here, I focus on the housing proposed by the Sharon plan, which reflected a political program that posed housing as the foundational mechanism for the design of national space. The Sharon team defined its challenge as follows: "1,000 immigrants arrive each day—one dwelling unit has to be erected every two minutes. Should the new houses be built in the existing, already densely populated cities—or should housing and development be directed into new towns?"[82] This question made no reference to architecture or the nature of the dwelling units themselves. Nor did it propose a new housing type for immigrants. Its focus, as scholars have noted, was on the *location* of housing—that is, on planning for population dispersal. Allocation of free public housing enabled the state housing regime to design state territory and the identity and social construction of its citizens, yet it allocated little concern to housing type and design.

With no new housing type or form proposed by the Sharon plan, it relied instead on the available model for permanent housing, constructed until then for the use of veteran citizens (fig. 6.9). As Efrat points out, new towns' planning, as reflected in the Sharon plan, essentially proposed replicating the kibbutz and *moshav* agricultural framework in town planning.[83] This can be seen in Beersheba Neighborhood A, a pivotal case of development town planning, constructed between 1951 and 1953 north of Beersheba's old town. As a reflection of this agricultural model, it featured a curvilinear layout, a central open area designated for public buildings, "green wedges," and small, simple houses on large parcels of land.[84] The Sharon plan and Beersheba Neighborhood A attest to the fact that "development town" housing was actually a replication of proper pioneer core housing. The housing type included in the Sharon plan was core housing designed for self-help improvement, based on the blockon house type discussed above. Each building was composed of two stories, with each containing two one-bedroom apartments of 26–32 square meters. The houses were further allocated large parcels of land in anticipation of their future expansion by residents, explicitly on the model of self-help (fig. 6.10).[85] The actuality contrasts strongly with the usual association of the Sharon plan in Israeli historiography with the anonymous typology of mass-housing blocks.

The Sharon plan took time to develop and is therefore hard to date. It is clear, however, that the process began parallel to, rather than after, the two previous policies of agricultural border settlements and the *ma'abara*. The plan's main principle, population dispersal, was indeed embedded in both border agricultural settlements and *ma'abarot*, which were formed adjacent to existing settlements across the country. The plan was first presented to the public in February 1950 in the framework of a public exhibition at the Tel Aviv Museum of Art and aimed to make the public more planning-minded. The exhibition included a series of posters outlining, in a popular way, the challenges identified by the planners and describing their operational principles. The plan was eventually published in Hebrew in 1951 under the title *Physical Planning in Israel, 1948–1953*.[86] In this document, Sharon stated that his team had "tried very hard to gain the support of public opinion for our national planning" and that the effort was "fully backed" by the powerful prime minister, Ben-Gurion. Sharon's important statement

משרד העבודה

מפעל השיכון העממי

ג. טיפוס הדירות וטיבן

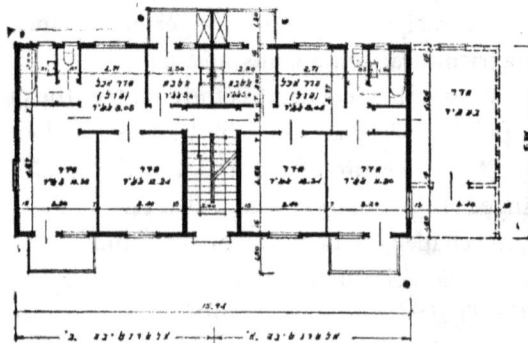

ב"ת ארבע משפחות שני קומות.

Figure 6.9. "Popular housing project" for veteran citizens, Ministry of Labour. Israel State Archive, Jerusalem. Popular Housing file.

Figure 6.10a and b. Beersheva neighborhood. Source: A. Sharon, 1951.

expressed the perception that the public was a sovereign force that should be convinced to approve the plan.

Third Violation of the State-Citizen Contract: Mass Anonymous Housing Blocks

The Sharon master plan initially included permanent immigrant housing identical to housing built for veteran citizens at the time; in the mid-1950s, a different typology began to dominate immigrant housing, primarily in Beersheba and the Negev area. The distinct architecture of mass-housing blocks was directly inspired by Le Corbusier's *Unité d'habitation*, termed *shikun* in Hebrew. Literally meaning "housing," the term *shikun* has been used liberally to denote immigrant and veteran houses up to the late 1950s—later referring exclusively to the housing blocks that characterize immigrant development towns and immigrant neighborhoods around major cities. The *shikun*'s brutalist blocks, designed as repetitive units stacked upon one another and stretching a quarter kilometer, served as a material manifestation of the state's benevolence toward its new citizens. The pace of change in housing type and architecture, as seen here, led to the association of the Sharon plan with mass-housing block dwellings in popular discourse, as well as in scholarship.

Brutalist architecture, therefore, marked a sense of consolidated state sovereignty, no longer as fragile as it perceived itself to be during its first five years. The new discourse identified immigrants as raw material, along with concrete and mortar, for the construction of the new national space. Open discussion of Holocaust survivors and Mizrahim as victims and Levantines, not yet capable of sustaining the nation-state as pioneers, suggested that their main asset, from the standpoint of the state, was their sheer numbers, used to populate vacant, desolate state territory by development towns and massive housing blocks.[87] *Shikun* mass-housing blocks no longer included the self-help principle characteristic of the former housing policy and design, thus sharply departing from the principle of dwellers as self-supporting sovereign citizens.

Yacobi's discussion of the "Mizrahi dwelling machine" has shown that many of these mass-housing blocks have been appropriated through small-scale interventions by their users, although it is difficult to make alterations in them because of the construction technologies used and inflexible planning. The interventions primarily consist of closing off balconies and making minor façade alterations. Residents' alterations, which include re-designing a building's formal language by adding quasi-oriental elements like arches and replacing the brutalist gray with warm color schemes, typically involve the block's look and aesthetic rather than everyday domestic use. Yet, as Yacobi shows, even these cultural appropriations have been made via the state, employing the post-1977 neighborhood rehabilitation program rather than relying on a self-help mechanism.[88]

Efrat has characterized the development town as a paradoxical combination of kibbutz rural planning and mass-housing blocks. Because the towns were located in Israel's desert periphery and offered few employment and mobility options, the people living there were subject to great governmental intervention in every aspect of their lives. The towns were soon identified with a desolate and weak populace, a breeding ground for social unrest.[89] The state apparatus, no longer feeling fragile, also no longer saw the need to provide equal housing and returned to the model of differentiated housing for differentiated citizens.[90]

Apartment house dwellings imposed substantial intervention in the immigrant family's everyday life, with the proclaimed goal of using the dwelling unit as an educational tool for proper family life and adjustment to "accepted residential standards . . . as some habits cannot be accepted and the dweller must be educated to give them up."[91] Apartment houses, which included compact apartments subdivided into rooms with specific functions, were meant to educate immigrants in the modern way of life, including such attributes as the separation of private and public and of "clean" and "dirty" functions. *Shikun* apartments did not allow any means for improvement and adaptability through labor toward construction or upkeep. That is, they did not enable residents to make decisions about their dwelling environment and carry out changes themselves, despite planners' claims that that was one of the advantages of this housing type. Mass anonymous *shikun* housing in peripheral development towns demarcated immigrants as separate from veterans, defining them as second-class citizens and provoking great frustration and a sense of discrimination and degradation among immigrants (fig. 6.11). Rather than core housing enabling citizens to shape their domestic space within the national home, mass anonymous apartment blocks marked the masses of immigrants as improper citizens, whose dwellings were designed to shape and domesticate them in the nation. As in the case of the *ma'abarot* a decade earlier, housing, the emblem of the state-citizen contract, was a clear marker of social difference and exclusion years

Figure 6.11. Quarter-kilometer block, Beersheva. Engineering and Architecture, *Journal of the Bureau of Engineers and Architects in Israel*, 1962, p. 9–10.

before they came to the surface in 1977, when a dramatic change took place in the Israeli political regime.

Conclusion

State sovereignty opened the way for Israel to conduct national planning. But citizens' discontent with top-down planning and with the housing solutions they were initially offered led to dramatic changes in housing policies during Israel's first five years, in a process of ongoing negotiation between state and citizenry. New citizens' involvement in formulating the state-citizen contract, and thus in the nation-building enterprise, was therefore far greater than has previously been suggested. Social unrest and negotiations over Israel's state-citizen contract continued to revolve around housing in the ensuing years. Noted struggles include the Black Panthers' protest, which eventually led to the 1977 regime change and new "build your own house" and "neighborhood rehabilitation" housing programs; protests for civilian settlement of the occupied West Bank in 1974, which led to Israel's settlement enterprise; and recently the massive 2011 housing social movement. In comparison with the social struggle over public space in Turkey and across nations during the Arab Spring, over mobility and transportation in Brazil, and over access to basic resources across South America, Israel's social movements have repeatedly formed around access to housing and have marked housing as the most basic social good for its society.[92]

In the Israeli context, fighting over housing is fighting over citizenship as a substantive and political right, pointing to the significance of Israel's first five years in cementing the state-citizen contract as housing-based. While not yet materialized in real-politics, the struggle over housing as citizenship is continuing in a number of civil initiatives, such as the Social Congress for Housing and a plethora of governmental programs attempting to "lower housing costs" and pacify social unrest.[93] Further research is needed to understand the present unfolding of negotiations between state and citizenry over Israeli citizen housing as materialization of citizens' substantive and political rights.

Notes

1. Mass demonstration in Tel Aviv, July 23, 2011. The author took an active part in the protest movement, both as a citizen and as a scholar of housing.

2. Rachel Kallus and Hubert Law-Yone, "National Home / Personal Home: Public Housing and the Shaping of National Space in Israel," *European Planning Studies* 10, no. 6 (2002): 765–79; Haim Yacobi, *Constructing a Sense of Place: Architecture and the Zionist Discourse* (Aldershot, UK: Ashgate, 2004); Naomi Carmon, "Three Generations of Urban Renewal Policies: Analysis and Policy Implications," *Geoforum* 30, no. 2 (1999): 145–58; Hadas Shadar, "Cultural Issues in Public Housing," *Horizons in Geography*, no. 67 (2006): 18–30; Zvi Efrat, *The Israeli Project: Building and Architecture, 1948–1973* (Tel Aviv: Tel Aviv Museum of Art, 2004); Erez Tzfadia and Haim Yacobi, *Rethinking Israeli Space: Periphery and Identity* (London: Routledge, 2011); Shlomo Svirsky, *Not Retrograde but Retrograded—Mizrahi and Ashkenazi in Israel: Sociological Analysis and Conversations with Activists* (Tel Aviv: Books for Research and Criticism, 1981); Hadas Shadar, "Between East and West: Immigrants, Critical Regionalism and Public Housing," *Journal of Architecture* 9, no. 1 (2004): 727–64.

3. Peter Marcuse, "Housing Policy and the Myth of the Benevolent State," *Social Policy* 8, no. 4 (1978): 21–26.

4. Greg Castillo, *Cold War on the Home Front: The Soft Power of Midcentury Design* (Minneapolis: University of Minnesota Press, 2010); John Archer, *Architecture and Suburbia: From English Villa to American Dream House, 1690–2000* (Minneapolis: University of Minnesota Press, 2005).

5. A distinct building type, housing is nonetheless rarely viewed as an institution as are other building types studied by Foucault and his followers, such as the prison, the clinic, and the hospital. Patricia A. Morton, *Hybrid Modernities: Architecture and Representation at the 1931 Colonial Exposition, Paris* (Cambridge, MA: MIT Press, 2003); Sibel Bozdoğan, *Modernism and Nation Building: Turkish Architectural Culture in the Early Republic* (Seattle: University of Washington Press, 2002); Aihwa Ong, *Flexible Citizenship: The Cultural Logics of Transnationality* (Durham, NC: Duke University Press, 1999); Lawrence J. Vale, *Architecture, Power, and National Identity* (New Haven, CT: Yale University Press, 1992).

6. Étienne Balibar and Immanuel M. Wallerstein, *Race, Nation, Class: Ambiguous Identities* (New York: Verso, 1991).

7. The American dream house was framed as a goal of federal policy in a series of acts since the 1920s, the most noted of which is the GI Bill, which introduced working-class families to homeownership, asserting the nation-citizen contract against Cold War fears of

proletarian revolution. Gail Radford, *Modern Housing for America: Policy Struggles in the New Deal Era* (Chicago: University of Chicago Press, 1996); Kenneth T. Jackson, *Crabgrass Frontier: The Suburbanization of the United States* (Oxford: Oxford University Press, 1985); Archer, *Architecture*; Becky M. Nicolaides, *My Blue Heaven: Life and Politics in the Working-Class Suburbs of Los Angeles, 1920–1965* (Chicago: University of Chicago Press, 2002); Dianne Harris, *Little White Houses: How the Postwar Home Constructed Race in America* (Minneapolis: University of Minnesota Press, 2012); Andrew M. Shanken, *194X: Architecture, Planning, and Consumer Culture on the American Home Front* (Minneapolis: University of Minnesota Press, 2009); Hilde Heynen and Gülsüm Baydar, *Negotiating Domesticity: Spatial Productions of Gender in Modern Architecture* (London: Routledge, 2005); Margaret Crawford, "Alternative Shelter: Counterculture Architecture in Northern California," in *Reading California: Art, Image, and Identity, 1900–2000*, ed. Stephanie Barron, Sheri Bernstein, and Ilene Susan Fort (Berkeley: University of California Press, 2000).

8. Nezar AlSayyad and Ananya Roy, *Urban Informality: Transnational Perspectives from the Middle East, Latin America, and South Asia* (Lanham, MD: Lexington, 2004); Mark Swenarton, Tom Avermaete, and Dirk van den Heuvel, *Architecture and the Welfare State* (London: Routledge, 2014).

9. Kallus and Law-Yone, "National Home."

10. Benny Morris, *The Birth of the Palestinian Refugee Problem, 1947–1949* (New York: Cambridge University Press, 1987).

11. Jewish immigration to Mandate Palestine was severely restricted by Britain in order to maintain the existing population balance between Jews and Arabs. The Jewish *yishuv* found this policy unacceptable because it hindered its ability to form a Jewish national home, and as World War II progressed, they also criticized it as forsaking the need for Jews to escape the Nazis. See Dalia Ofer, *Escaping the Holocaust: Illegal Immigration to the Land of Israel, 1939–1944* (New York: Oxford University Press, 1990).

12. Haim Darin-Drabkin, *Housing in Israel: Economic and Sociological Aspects* (Tel Aviv: Gadish, 1957).

13. Anat Kidron, "The Israeli Navy, Founding Years" (MA thesis, Haifa University, 2000).

14. Moshe Lissak, ed., *Studies in Israel's Social History* (Jerusalem: Bialik Institute, 2009).

15. The Right of Return Law was enacted in July 1950. The Land Entry Law was enacted in August 1952.

16. Efrat, *Israeli Project*; Yacobi, *Constructing a Sense of Place.*

17. Hillel Cohen, *Good Arabs: The Israeli Security Agencies and the Israeli Arabs, 1948–1967* (Berkeley: University of California Press, 2010); Rassem Khamaisi, "Villages under Siege," in *City of Collision*, ed. Philipp Misselwitz and Tim Rienits (Basel, Switz.: Birkhäuser Architecture, 2006).

18. Avital Avni, "Planners, Politicians, Bureaucrats: The Israeli Experience of Physical Planning in Early Years of Statehood" (MS thesis, Technion, 1990).

19. Kallus and Law-Yone, "National Home."

20. The department was later broken down into three departments: the National Planning Department, which operated under the Office of the Prime Minister; the General Planning Department, which operated under the Ministry of the Interior; and the Housing Department, which operated under the Ministry of Labor. Hadas Shadar, "The History of the Public Housing in the State of Israel 1948–1999: The Influence of the Ministry of Housing on the Urban Development of Beer-Sheva" (PhD diss., Technion, 2001).

21. James Scott, *Seeing like a State: How Well-Intentioned Efforts to Improve the Human Condition Have Failed* (New Haven, CT: Yale University Press, 1998).

22. Shadar, "Between East and West"; Efrat, *Israeli Project*; Yacobi, *Constructing a Sense of Place*; Haim Yacobi, "Architecture, Orientalism, and Identity: The Politics of Israeli Built Environment," *Israel Studies* 13, no. 1 (2008): 94–118; Irit Amit and Shalom Reichman, *Experiments in Space: Chapters in Settlement Geography of Eretz Israel* (Tel Aviv: Open University of Israel, 1996); Tzfadia and Yacobi, *Rethinking Israeli Space: Periphery and Identity*.

23. Shadar, "Between East and West"; Oren Yiftachel, *Ethnocracy: Land and Identity Politics in Israel/Palestine* (Philadelphia: University of Pennsylvania Press, 2006); Yacobi, "Architecture, Orientalism, and Identity: The Politics of Israeli Built Environment."

24. Mordechai Naor, ed., *Immigrants and Ma'abarot, 1948–1952* (Jerusalem: Yad Ben Zvi, 1988); Michael Koon, *Man Builds His Home: Freedom and Enforcement in Shikun* (Tel Aviv: HaKibutz HaMeuchad, 1989).

25. Ella Shohat, "Sephardim in Israel: Zionism from the Standpoint of Its Jewish Victims," *Social Text*, nos. 19–20 (1988): 1–35; Edward W. Said, "Zionism from the Standpoint of Its Victims," *Social Text*, no. 1 (1979): 7–58; Tzfadia and Yacobi, *Rethinking Israeli Space: Periphery and Identity*; Shlomo Svirsky, *Not Retrograde but Retrograded*; Yiftachel, *Ethnocracy*.

26. Yosef Jabareen, "'The Right to the City' Revisited: Assessing Urban Rights—the Case of Arab Cities in Israel," *Habitat International* 41 (2014): 135–41; Rassem Khamaisi, "Urbanization without Cities: The Urban Phenomena among the Arabs in Israel," *Horizons in Geography*, nos. 60–61 (2004); Yiftachel, *Ethnocracy*.

27. Haim Yacobi, "The Mizrahi Dwelling Machine," in *Living Forms*, ed. Tula Amir and Shelli Cohen (Tel Aviv: Hargol, 2007). James Holston, *The Modernist City: An Anthropological Critique of Brasilia* (Chicago: University of Chicago Press, 1989).

28. Levi Eshkol, *The Hardships of Settlement* (Tel Aviv: Am Oved, 1959). Eshkol wrote, "We should make a serious attempt to address the new immigrants now located in immigrant reception camps and find options for designing and educating them as settlers" (204–5).

29. Iris Greicer and Ofer Gonen, "Design of the State's Early Settlement Map," in *Studies in Israel's Social History*, ed. Moshe Lissak (Jerusalem: Bialik Institute, 2009); Ilan Troen, "The Transformation of Zionist Planning Policy: From Rural Settlements to an Urban Network," *Planning Perspectives* 3, no. 1 (1988): 3–23.

30. Amit and Reichman, *Experiments in Space*.

31. Walid Khalidi, *All That Remains: The Palestinian Villages Occupied and Depopulated by Israel in 1948* (Washington, DC: Institute for Palestine Studies, 1992).

32. Ilan Pappé, *The Forgotten Palestinians: A History of the Palestinians in Israel* (New Haven, CT: Yale University Press, 2011).

33. Benny Morris, *1948: A History of the First Arab-Israeli War* (New Haven, CT: Yale University Press, 2008); Anita Shapira, ed., *Alyia Bet: A Collection for the History of the Rescue, Escape, Alyiabbet and the Surviving Remnant* (Tel Aviv: Tel Aviv University Press, 1990).

34. Shadar, "History of Public Housing"; Lissak, *Studies*; Efrat, *Israeli Project*; Yacobi, *Constructing a Sense of Place*.

35. Darin-Drabkin, *Housing in Israel*, 224–52.

36. Yossi Goldstein, *Eshkol—Biography* (Tel Aviv: Keter, 2003).

37. Lissak, *Studies*.

38. Ariela Azulai, *Civil Imagination* (Tel Aviv: Resling, 2010). Daniel Monteresku, "The Symbolic History of the Hyphen: Urban Alterity before Jaffa and Tel Aviv," *Zmanim* 106 (2009): 76–93.

39. Naor, *Immigrants*.

40. Madi Benado, Archive of Oral Histories, the Association of Bulgarian Immigrants, Jaffa, Israel.

41. Betty Leon, Archive of Oral Histories, the Association of Bulgarian Immigrants, Jaffa, Israel.

42. Some twenty thousand Palestinians managed to return during the first five years after the Nakba (Palestinian exodus) and were eventually granted Israeli citizenship. The Arab-Palestinian population in Israel thus grew by 15 percent. Hillel Cohen, "The Internal Refugees in the State of Israel: Israeli Citizens, Palestinian Refugees," *Israel-Palestine Journal* 9, no. 2 (2002): n.p.

43. Hana Farah, "Twenty Years I Have Dreamed to Host My Friends in My House, My Father's House, My Grandfather's House," in *Living Forms*, ed. Shelli Cohen and Tula Amir (Tel Aviv: Hargol, 2007).

44. Dan Giladi, "From Austerity to Economic Growth," in *Israel's First Decade*, ed. Ralph Benjamin Noberger (Ra'anana, Israel: Open University, 2002).

45. Author's interviews with former residents Jacob Ninio, August 2011, and Rachel Aruetti, September 2011.

46. Guy Haskell, *From Sofia to Jaffa: The Jews of Bulgaria and Israel* (Detroit: Wayne State University Press, 1994); Azulai, *Civil Imagination*; Cohen, *Good Arabs*. Contemporary studies have stressed the inequalities and indignities of the Arab-Palestinian population in shared cities: Elie Rekhess, ed., *Together but Apart: Mixed Cities in Israel* (Tel Aviv: Tel Aviv University, 2007).

47. Lissak, *Studies*; Goldstein, *Eshkol—Biography*. Directing immigrants to *moshavim* rather than *kibbutzim* was also a political statement on the part of Ben-Gurion. *Kibbutzim* were supporters of the Mapam Party rather than Ben-Gurion's Mapai Party, hence his act to allocate land, resources, and population to *moshavim* rather than *kibbutzim* had significant implications for retaining political power.

48. Yehuda Koren, *The Gathering of Israel in Its Settlement: The History of Immigrant Moshavim in Israel* (Tel Aviv: Am Oved, 1964).

49. David Ben-Gurion, letter to Dr. Grinbaum of the Department of Economic Research in the Ministry of the Interior, August 4, 1949 (Israeli State Archive). Ben-Gurion asks Grinbaum to make sure the plan for agricultural settlement is fulfilled.

50. Guidelines for Government Policy, March 1949, in Government Yearbook 1950, 38; and Eshkol, *Hardships of Settlement*.

51. The Department of Public Health complained it was not invited to examine the house. See State Archive, Blockon file.

52. David Zaslewski, *Immigrant Housing in Israel—Construction, Planning and Development* (Tel Aviv: Am Oved, 1954).

53. Letter from Arieh Sharon, head of the Housing Department, to the Technical Department of the Jewish Agency, September 29, 1949. State Archive, Blockon file.

54. Letter from Solel Boneh Construction Company to Sharon, May 29, 1949. State Archive, Blockon file.

55. Yosef Sleifer, "Urban Settlement, 1948–1963," in *Construction of the Land*, ed. Miriam Tuvia and Michael Bone (Tel Aviv: Hakibbutz Hameuchad, 1999).

56. See Sharon's definition of the blockon above. While the state housing regime did not explicitly term the blockon "self-help," its housing logic fits well in the scope of self-help housing.

57. Letter from Arieh Sharon, head of the Housing Department, to the Technical Department of the Jewish Agency, September 29, 1949. State Archive, Blockon file.

58. Uri Davis and Walter Lehn, "And the Fund Still Lives: The Role of Jewish National Fund in the Determination of Israel's Land Policies," *Journal of Palestine Studies* 7, no. 4 (1978): 3–33.

59. Israel Land Administration, Tirat Yehuda file.

60. "Infiltrators Attacked a Moshav near Lydda," *Davar*, June 10, 1953.

61. Naama Meishar, "Leaving the Castle," in *Living Forms: Architecture and Society in Israel*, ed. Tula Amir and Shelli Cohen (Tel Aviv: Hargol, 2007).

62. Adriana Kamp, "The Face of the Border Like the Face of Janus," *Theory and Criticism* 16 (2000): 13–43.

63. Greicer and Gonen, "Design."

64. Mordechai Naor, ed., *The Second Alyia: 1903–1914* (Jerusalem: Yad Ben Zvi, 1988).

65. "The Ma'abarot," in Naor, *Immigrants*.

66. Jewish Agency Meishar, "Leaving the Castle," board meeting protocols, March 29, 1949, Central Zionist Archive, Jerusalem.

67. Lavon Institute Archive, protocols of the Mapai Party meeting of April 22, 1949, file 1-49/24.

68. Mordechai Bentov, *Public Housing in Israel: Lecture at the University of California, Berkeley* (Jerusalem: Ministry of Housing, 1969).

69. Eshkol, quoted in Sleifer, "Urban Settlement."

70. Lissak, *Studies*; Naor, "Ma'abarot."

71. Israel State Archive, Work Village file. Very little scholarly work on the work village exists; it has largely been forgotten as a housing and settlement form.

72. Greicer and Gonen, "Design."

73. Ibid.

74. "The First Ma'abara for Immigrants Employed in Forestry Was Established," *Davar*, May 23, 1950.

75. David Hacohen, "The Direct Absorption Program for Mass Immigration in the 1950s and Its Consequences," *Reviews of Israel's Independence* 1 (1991): 359–78.

76. Shay Fogelman, "In the Emek Hefer Maabara in 1952 Occurred the First Civil Rebellion in Israel, Buried in the Pages of History," *Haaretz*, January 22, 2010; Svirsky, *Not Retrograde but Retrograded*.

77. "105 Ma'abara Dwellers Arrested," *Ma'ariv*, October 27, 1952.

78. Shohat, "Sephardim in Israel."

79. Efrat, *Israeli Project*.

80. Arieh Sharon, *Kibbutz + Bauhaus* (Stuttgart, Ger.: Kramer, 1976); Kallus and Law-Yone, "National Home."

81. Yacobi, ""Mizrahi Dwelling Machine.""

82. Arieh Sharon, *Physical Planning in Israel, 1948–1953* (Jerusalem: Government Printer, 1951).

83. Efrat, *Israeli Project*.

84. Shadar, "History of Public Housing"; Sharon, *Physical Planning*; Kallus and Law-Yone, "National Home."

85. Zaslewski, *Immigrant Housing*.

86. Sharon, *Physical Planning*.

87. Kallus and Law-Yone, "National Home; Shadar, "Between East and West."

88. Yacobi, "Mizrahi Dwelling Machine."

89. Robert Oxman, "The Revision of Modernism," in *Structuralism in Architecture: Selected Works by Al Mansfeld and His Team*, exhibition catalog (Haifa: Technion Faculty of Architecture and Urban Planning, 1987).

90. Yael Allweil, *Homeland: Zionism as Housing Regime, 1860–2011*, Planning, History and Environment (London: Routledge, 2017).

91. Darin-Drabkin, *Housing in Israel*, 80; Michael Koon, *Man Builds His Home*.

92. Yael Allweil, "Surprising Alliances for Dwelling and Citizenship: Palestinian-Israeli Participation in the Mass Housing Protests of Summer 2011," *International Journal of Islamic Architecture* 2, no. 1 (2013): 41–57; Nathan Marom, "Activising Space: The Spatial Politics of the 2011 Protest Movement in Israel," *Urban Studies* (2013): 2826–41; James Holston, "Insurgent Cities and Urban Citizenship, 2009–2014," in *Citizenship and Place*, Crestin M. Lyon and Allison Goebel (London: Rowman and Littlefield, forthcoming). See also a special issue of *International Journal of Islamic Architecture* dedicated to urban protest in the context of the Arab Spring: *International Journal of Islamic Architecture* 2, no. 1 (2013).

93. The Social Congress on Housing is an association of civil society organizations proposing to rethink solutions to the housing crisis. See https://www.facebook.com/social congress/, accessed September 13, 2018.

For governmental plans for housing cost reduction and redistribution, see the Ministry of Housing, https://www.gov.il/he/Departments/Topics/buy_apartment, accessed September 13, 2018.

Bibliography

Allweil, Yael. *Homeland: Zionism as Housing Regime, 1860–2011*. Planning, History and Environment. London: Routledge, 2017.

———. "Surprising Alliances for Dwelling and Citizenship: Palestinian-Israeli Participation in the Mass Housing Protests of Summer 2011." *International Journal of Islamic Architecture* 2, no. 1 (2013): 41–75.

AlSayyad, Nezar, and Ananya Roy. *Urban Informality: Transnational Perspectives from the Middle East, Latin America, and South Asia*. Lanham, MD: Lexington, 2004.

Amit, Irit, and Shalom Reichman. *Experiments in Space: Chapters in Settlement Geography of Eretz Israel*. Tel Aviv: Open University of Israel, 1996.

Archer, John. *Architecture and Suburbia: From English Villa to American Dream House, 1690–2000*. Minneapolis: University of Minnesota Press, 2005.

Avni, Avital. "Planners, Politicians, Bureaucrats: The Israeli Experience of Physical Planning in Early Years of Statehood." MS thesis, Technion, 1990.

Azulai, Ariela. *Civil Imagination*. Tel Aviv: Resling, 2010.

Balibar, Étienne, and Immanuel M. Wallerstein. *Race, Nation, Class: Ambiguous Identities*. New York: Verso Books, 1991.

Bentov, Mordechai. *Public Housing in Israel: Lecture at the University of California, Berkeley*. Jerusalem: Ministry of Housing, 1969.

Bozdoğan, Sibel. *Modernism and Nation Building: Turkish Architectural Culture in the Early Republic*. Seattle: University of Washington Press, 2002.

Carmon, Naomi. "Three Generations of Urban Renewal Policies: Analysis and Policy Implications." *Geoforum* 30, no. 2 (1999): 145–58.

Castillo, Greg. *Cold War on the Home Front: The Soft Power of Midcentury Design*. Minneapolis: University of Minnesota Press, 2010.

Cohen, Hillel. *Good Arabs: The Israeli Security Agencies and the Israeli Arabs, 1948–1967*. Berkeley: University of California Press, 2010.

———. "The Internal Refugees in the State of Israel: Israeli Citizens, Palestinian Refugees." *Israel-Palestine Journal* 9, no. 2 (2002).

Crawford, Margaret. "Alternative Shelter: Counterculture Architecture in Northern California." In *Reading California: Art, Image, and Identity, 1900–2000*, edited by Stephanie Barron, Sheri Bernstein, and Ilene Susan Fort, 249–70. Berkeley: University of California Press, 2000.

Darin-Drabkin, Haim. *Housing in Israel: Economic and Sociological Aspects*. Tel Aviv: Gadish Books, 1957.

Davar. "The First Ma'abara for Immigrants Employed in Forestry Was Established." May 23, 1950.

Davar. "Infiltrators Attacked a Moshav Near Lydda." June 10, 1953.

Davis, Uri, and Walter Lehn. "And the Fund Still Lives: The Role of Jewish National Fund in the Determination of Israel's Land Policies." *Journal of Palestine Studies* 7, no. 4 (1978): 3–33.

Efrat, Zvi. *The Israeli Project: Building and Architecture, 1948–1973*. Tel Aviv: Tel Aviv Museum of Art, 2004.

Eshkol, Levi. *The Hardships of Settlement*. Tel Aviv: Am Oved, 1959.

Farah, Hana. "Twenty Years I Have Dreamed to Host My Friends in My House, My Father's House, My Grandfather's House." In *Living Forms*, edited by Shelli Cohen and Tula Amir, 167–75. Tel Aviv: Hargol, 2007.

Fogelman, Shay. "In the Emek Hefer Maabara in 1952 Occurred the First Civil Rebellion in Israel, Buried in the Pages of History." *Ha'Aretz*, January 22, 2010.

Giladi, Dan. "From Austerity to Economic Growth." In *Israel's First Decade*, edited by Ralph Benjamin Noberger. Ra'anana, Israel: Open University, 2002.

Goldstein, Yossi. *Eshkol—Biography*. Tel Aviv: Keter, 2003.

Greicer, Iris, and Ofer Gonen. "Design of the State's Early Settlement Map." In *Studies in Israel's Social History*, edited by Moshe Lissak. Jerusalem: Bialik Institute, 2009.

Hacohen, David. "The Direct Absorption Program for Mass Immigration in the 1950s and Its Consequences." *Reviews of Israel's Independence* 1 (1991): 359–78.

Harris, Dianne. *Little White Houses: How the Postwar Home Constructed Race in America*. Minneapolis: University of Minnesota Press, 2012.

Haskell, Guy. *From Sofia to Jaffa: The Jews of Bulgaria and Israel*. Detroit: Wayne State University Press, 1994.

Heynen, Hilde, and Gülsüm Baydar. *Negotiating Domesticity: Spatial Productions of Gender in Modern Architecture*. London: Routledge, 2005.

Holston, James. "Insurgent Cities and Urban Citizenship, 2009–2014." In *Citizenship and Place*, edited by Crestin M. Lyon and Allison Goebel. London: Rowman and Littlefield, forthcoming.

Holston, James. *The Modernist City: An Anthropological Critique of Brasilia*. Chicago: University of Chicago Press, 1989.

Jabareen, Yosef. "'The Right to the City' Revisited: Assessing Urban Rights—the Case of Arab Cities in Israel." *Habitat International* 41 (2014): 135–41.

Jackson, Kenneth T. *Crabgrass Frontier: The Suburbanization of the United States*. Oxford: Oxford University Press, 1985.

Kallus, Rachel, and Hubert Law-Yone. "National Home / Personal Home: Public Housing and the Shaping of National Space in Israel." *European Planning Studies* 10, no. 6 (2002): 765–79.

Kamp, Adriana. "The Face of the Border Like the Face of Janus." *Theory and Criticism* 16 (2000): 13–43.

Khalidi, Walid. *All That Remains: The Palestinian Villages Occupied and Depopulated by Israel in 1948.* Washington, DC: Institute for Palestine Studies, 1992.

Khamaisi, Rassem. "Urbanization without Cities: The Urban Phenomena among the Arabs in Israel." *Horizons in Geography*, nos. 60–61 (2004): 41–50.

———. "Villages under Siege." In *City of Collision*, edited by Philipp Misselwitz and Tim Rienits, 121–29. Basel, Switz.: Birkhäuser Architecture, 2006.

Kidron, Anat. "The Israeli Navy, Founding Years." MA thesis, Haifa University, 2000.

Koon, Michael. *Man Builds His Home: Freedom and Enforcement in Shikun.* Tel Aviv: HaKibutz HaMeuchad, 1989.

Koren, Yehuda. *The Gathering of Israel in Its Settlement: The History of Immigrant Moshavim in Israel.* Tel Aviv: Am Oved, 1964.

Lissak, Moshe, ed. *Studies in Israel's Social History.* Jerusalem: Bialik Institute, 2009.

Ma'ariv. "105 Ma'abara Dwellers Arrested." October 27, 1952.

Marcuse, Peter. "Housing Policy and the Myth of the Benevolent State." *Social Policy* 8, no. 4 (1978): 21–26.

Marom, Nathan. "Activising Space: The Spatial Politics of the 2011 Protest Movement in Israel." *Urban Studies* (2013): 2826–41.

Meishar, Naama. "Leaving the Castle." In *Living Forms: Architecture and Society in Israel*, edited by Tula Amir and Shelli Cohen, 194–211. Tel Aviv: Hargol, 2007.

Monteresku, Daniel. "The Symbolic History of the Hyphen: Urban Alterity before Jaffa and Tel Aviv." *Zmanim* 106 (2009): 76–93.

Morris, Benny. *The Birth of the Palestinian Refugee Problem, 1947–1949.* New York: Cambridge University Press, 1987.

———. *1948: A History of the First Arab-Israeli War.* New Haven, CT: Yale University Press, 2008.

Morton, Patricia A. *Hybrid Modernities: Architecture and Representation at the 1931 Colonial Exposition, Paris.* Cambridge, MA: MIT Press, 2003.

Naor, Mordechai, ed. *Immigrants and Ma'abarot, 1948–1952.* Jerusalem: Yad Ben Zvi, 1988.

———. "The Ma'abarot." In Naor, *Immigrants and Ma'abarot.*

———, ed. *The Second Alyia: 1903–1914.* Jerusalem: Yad Ben Zvi, 1988.

Nicolaides, Becky M. *My Blue Heaven: Life and Politics in the Working-Class Suburbs of Los Angeles, 1920–1965.* Chicago: University of Chicago Press, 2002.

Ofer, Dalia. *Escaping the Holocaust: Illegal Immigration to the Land of Israel, 1939–1944.* New York: Oxford University Press, 1990.

Ong, Aihwa. *Flexible Citizenship: The Cultural Logics of Transnationality.* Durham, NC: Duke University Press, 1999.

Oxman, Robert. "The Revision of Modernism." In *Structuralism in Architecture: Selected Works by Al Mansfeld and His Team*, exhibition catalogue. Haifa: Technion Faculty of Architecture and Urban Planning, 1987.

Pappé, Ilan. *The Forgotten Palestinians: A History of the Palestinians in Israel.* New Haven, CT: Yale University Press, 2011.

Radford, Gail. *Modern Housing for America: Policy Struggles in the New Deal Era.* Chicago: University of Chicago Press, 1996.

Rekhess, Elie, ed. *Together but Apart: Mixed Cities in Israel.* Tel Aviv: Tel Aviv University, 2007.

Said, Edward W. "Zionism from the Standpoint of Its Victims." *Social Text*, no. 1 (1979): 7–58.

Scott, James. *Seeing Like a State: How Well-Intentioned Efforts to Improve the Human Condition Have Failed.* New Haven, CT: Yale University Press, 1998.

Shadar, Hadas. "Between East and West: Immigrants, Critical Regionalism, and Public Housing." *Journal of Architecture* 9, no. 1 (2004): 23–48.

———. "Cultural Issues in Public Housing." *Horizons in Geography*, no. 67 (2006): 18–30.

———. "The History of the Public Housing in the State of Israel 1948–1999: The Influence of the Ministry of Housing on the Urban Development of Beer-Sheva." PhD diss., Technion, 2001.

Shanken, Andrew M. *194X: Architecture, Planning, and Consumer Culture on the American Home Front.* Minneapolis: University of Minnesota Press, 2009.

Shapira, Anita, ed. *Alyia Bet: A Collection for the History of the Rescue, Escape, Alyiabbet and the Surviving Remnant.* Tel Aviv: Tel Aviv University, 1990.

Sharon, Arieh. *Kibbutz + Bauhaus.* Stuttgart, Ger.: Kramer Verlag, 1976.

———. *Physical Planning in Israel 1948–1953.* Jerusalem: Government Printer, 1951.

Shohat, Ella. "Sephardim in Israel: Zionism from the Standpoint of Its Jewish Victims." *Social Text*, no. 19/20 (1988): 1–35.

Sleifer, Yosef. "Urban Settlement, 1948–1963." In *Construction of the Land*, edited by Miriam Tuvia and Michael Bone. Tel Aviv: Hakibbutz Hameuchad, 1999.

Svirsky, Shlomo. *Not Retrograde but Retrograded—Mizrahi and Ashkenazi in Israel: Sociological Analysis and Conversations with Activists.* Tel Aviv: Books for Research and Criticism, 1981.

Swenarton, Mark, Tom Avermaete, and Dirk van den Heuvel. *Architecture and the Welfare State.* London: Routledge, 2014.

Troen, Ilan. "The Transformation of Zionist Planning Policy: From Rural Settlements to an Urban Network." *Planning Perspectives* 3, no. 1 (1988): 3–23.

Tzfadia, Erez, and Haim Yacobi. *Rethinking Israeli Space: Periphery and Identity.* London: Taylor and Francis, 2011.

Vale, Lawrence J. *Architecture, Power, and National Identity.* New Haven, CT: Yale University Press, 1992.

Yacobi, Haim. "Architecture, Orientalism, and Identity: The Politics of Israeli Built Environment." *Israel Studies* 13, no. 1 (2008): 94–118.

———. *Constructing a Sense of Place: Architecture and the Zionist Discourse.* Aldershot, UK: Ashgate, 2004.

———. "The Mizrahi Dwelling Machine." In *Living Forms*, edited by Tula Amir and Shelli Cohen. Tel Aviv: Hargol, 2007.

Yiftachel, Oren. *Ethnocracy: Land and Identity Politics in Israel/Palestine.* Philadelphia: University of Pennsylvania Press, 2006.

Zaslewski, David. *Immigrant Housing in Israel—Construction, Planning and Development.* Tel Aviv: Am Oved, 1954.

YAEL ALLWEIL is Assistant Professor in the Faculty of Architecture and Town Planning at the Technion, Israel and Chair of the Technion Housing Research Group. She completed her PhD in architecture history at UC Berkeley exploring nationalism in Israel-Palestine as a regime of housing. Her research agenda explores the history of housing in Israel and Palestine and the history of struggles over urban public spaces, emphasizing the spatialities of political struggles. Allweil's publications include the monograph *Homeland: Zionism as Housing Regime 1860–2011* (Routledge, 2017) and a number of journal articles in *Urban Studies, City, Footprint, Architecture beyond Europe, International Journal of Islamic Architecture,* and *Traditional Dwellings and Settlements Review.*

7

SOCIAL HOUSING IN COLONIAL CYPRUS: CONTESTATIONS ON URBANITY AND DOMESTICITY

Michalis Sioulas and Panayiota Pyla

S OCIAL HOUSING MADE ITS FIRST APPEARANCE IN CYPRUS during the last two decades of British colonial rule on the island (1878–1960), to respond to the pressures of housing shortages in urban centers. Having previously been under the rule of the Ottomans (1571–1878), the Venetians (1489–1571), and the Franks (1192–1489), Cyprus had a dominantly rural agricultural economy well into the period of British rule. The emphasis on agriculture declined gradually in the twentieth century until World War II, when a rapid increase in urban occupations brought mass migration of peasants into towns and a much faster transition to a commercial economy.[1] Urbanization was further intensified after Britain's forced withdrawal from Arab countries in the 1950s, which turned Cyprus into Britain's most important military base in the eastern Mediterranean.[2] Between 1950 and 1956, British military spending in Cyprus increased fourteenfold. Rapid urban growth in Cyprus was accompanied by the effects of the wartime shortage of building materials, which was manifested both in the unprecedented increases in house prices and in the emergence of urban slums.[3] This serious housing shortage was only exacerbated further after World War II, as the continuing urban growth was coupled with inflation in land prices.[4]

Much as they did in other colonies, the British began to seek solutions to the dire housing shortage in Cyprus through larger efforts to revive town and country planning after the war.[5] Their goals were to stop the creation of slums in and around towns and to prevent labor troubles and social unrest, especially because communism was perceived to hover around the region. This chapter focuses on the initial efforts of the British to house landless urban residents. Analyzing a series of social housing schemes that began as a result of a great strike of government laborers in March 1944, the chapter uncovers the complex historical context that shaped social housing debates in Cyprus. This context was constituted by the reformist drive of metropolitan Britain and the colonial government's postwar attempts to advance urban development and social welfare in Cyprus in the context of larger Cold War anxieties. The historical context of social housing debates was also shaped by a larger disciplinary rethinking of modern architecture and planning in the colonial world, especially in terms of the social role of private homes and gardens. This historical context was also shaped by the diversity of social and spatial aspirations among municipal authorities and local architects, who expressed competing views on appropriate urban density, hygiene, efficiency, economy, social development, and modern lifestyles, even as they had to contend with practical questions of the availability of materials and technologies, the shortage of funds, or even the particularities of the agendas of individual protagonists.

Through a close comparison between the visions expressed by colonial government protagonists, local builders, and other individual actors, the following pages shed light on how social housing in Cyprus was a product of multifaceted influences that cannot be explained simply in terms of colonial agendas of power and control; or in terms of stylistic variations of a "modern vernacular." Rather, social housing was intertwined with the competing aspirations of modern urbanity and domesticity that were advanced by colonial and local protagonists. Such nuances of individual agency are also considered along with the influences of larger, international urban architectural debates. Notions of order (formal and social) and efficiency, or questions of density and control, or debates on the role of open spaces and local spatial practices: all these were crucial for shaping the aesthetic and social agendas of modern architecture at the time, and they certainly exerted influence on local housing practices as well. Further, these architectural disciplinary debates on social housing and urban strategies are considered against the regional sociopolitical instabilities of the 1940s and 1950s that formed the multiple dynamics of Cyprus's colonial social landscape.

The First Debate: Flats or Cottages?

The twenty-three-day-long labor strike in March 1944 was a landmark in the history of the labor movement in Cyprus, not only for instituting wage increases and other benefits for the labor force, but also for prompting colonial government officials to initiate a dialogue for other social provisions. The countless riots and unprecedented social upheaval had underlined the problems of the dire housing shortage and the proliferating slums in urban centers and made social housing programs an emergency.[6] The only similar mode of housing that existed on the island up to that point was some workers' housing for miners in work camps and mining towns early in the twentieth century. The new vision of the colonial government would bring such housing into towns for the first time. And unlike the miners' housing, which had been created by European and US companies with a much more pronounced paternalistic desire to control their workers, the colonial vision was wrapped in the logic of the postwar British welfare state and the desire to socially transform urban space.[7] The Colonial Office in London had already asked all colonies to improve their housing conditions the year before;[8] and the Colonial Development and Welfare Act of 1940 had already provided an (underutilized) opportunity by promising grants to the colonies, underlining the potential for housing to stabilize workers.[9] Up to that point, there was no comprehensive town-planning legislation, and so the need for social housing was also perceived as an opportunity to reform the structure of major urban centers, which faced a housing crisis.[10] Among them were the capital, Nicosia, at the center of the island, which had the highest population at fifty-three thousand; Limassol, a large commercial center and the largest port in the south; and the coastal towns of Famagusta and Larnaca, that were also ports and commercial centers in the east and south, respectively.

Although there was adequate agreement about these four towns as the main sites for social housing, there was not much agreement on the particularities of urban strategies. A key point of contention was whether housing schemes should be on the outskirts of the towns, in the form of individual, cottagelike houses; or whether they should be flats in multistory buildings in the town centers. The former option, which followed the logic of low-density housing development according to Garden City principles, had been widely tested already in the United Kingdom and in the colonies since the interwar period.[11] The latter option—namely, flats designed to minimum dimensions—had already been seen in the industrial cities in the Western world from the nineteenth century onward, and later in colonial towns like New Delhi.[12] Multistory buildings offered the opportunity to also take the form of "hostels"—a building type that had been used in the colonies to house single men who left their families behind in rural and one that was widely encouraged so as to prevent the permanent migration of entire families from the country to the cities.[13]

The Public Works Department (PWD) of the colonial government opposed the cottage idea, and their staff—both local and British architects and engineers, many of whom had already operated in other colonies—suggested that working people in Cyprus, in contrast to the British, wanted to live "in proximity to each other."[14] The PWD was in charge of implementing these housing schemes and had great power in matters of spatial development in the absence of a town planning or housing authority in the colonial structure. The chief architect of the PWD, R. H. Macartney, went as far as arguing that "if [Cypriots] like gardens, they certainly do not show it, judging by the general standard of upkeep and cultivation," and he attacked a housing area in the outskirts of the urban capital, Nicosia, for its "small uncared for plots of land, strewn with rusty petrol tins, each plot bearing its miserable bungalow."[15] What accompanied this Orientalist depiction of natives' indifference to their environment was architect Macartney's preference for creating a "compact and well built up" town that would have maximum efficiency by keeping workers within the town center.[16] In Macartney's view, the colonial concern with overcrowding would be resolved not with individual houses in the outskirts, but with taller buildings in the city center; and this would not only protect the integrity of "productive gardens and agricultural land" on the peripheries of towns; it would also create "in the derelict center . . . its renaissance" and would bring positive changes not only to the town, but also to the society and local people's customs.[17]

The PWD position was opposed by other government officials, who voiced concerns about large concentration of workers, particularly single males, in the center of towns.[18] This fear was tied to the drastic rise of trade unionism during the early 1940s, which had provoked strikes;[19] and it was intensified by the fact that a large portion of the population (namely, the Greek Cypriots, who made up 82 percent of the total population) had already begun to present demands for unification with Greece and were hinting about an anticolonial struggle—which would eventually materialize in the mid-1950s. The close proximity of so many lower-income men presented the threat of workers' housing turning into an incubator of local insurrection. Echoing these government officials, others based their opposition to the PWD's urban vision on practical matters, arguing that the multiple stories increased dependence on imported materials such as iron beams. And still others, such as the Cypriot mayor of Nicosia, opposed housing projects in general for a different reason: he feared that the provision of housing would encourage too much urbanization.[20]

Despite the opposition, the PWD was able to advance its views through an analysis that showed economies both of construction and of networks (road construction, water systems, drainage, etc.), which, they argued, could certainly compensate for the higher cost of land in the town center. The PWD ultimately succeeded in securing a commission to design the first pilot emergency scheme to partially alleviate the housing crisis in Nicosia.[21] The pilot scheme included three housing complexes: a complex of flats for families and two hostels for single males. All schemes were to house both Greek and Turkish Cypriots, who, up to that point, had resided in distinct neighborhoods both in towns and in rural settlements. This innovation was apparently part of the colonial government's effort to strengthen the interaction of the two communities, as a way to counterbalance the competing national aspirations surfacing among Greek and Turkish Cypriots (which in the late 1950s would lead to radical spatial separation of the two communities).

The PWD proposed three sites for the three complexes, all of which within the Venetian walls that enclosed the very center of Nicosia. They were composed of three-story blocks with communal lavatories and laundries, large atriums, and external circulation corridors. The hostels also had communal kitchen facilities and canteens. The complex of flats for families (seventy-eight one-bedroom units) formed three parallel curved wings, each of which consisted of two blocks (fig. 7.1).[22] The first hostel for single males (consisting of 210 rooms) was also organized in three curved arms, but unlike the block of flats, it was connected with a transverse wing through their middle (fig. 7.2). The second hostel (of 189 rooms) had a similar organizational logic but in rectilinear form: it had four parallel rectilinear wings connected with three shorter transverse wings.[23] Echoing the principles of interwar modernist urbanism, which favored taller buildings and large open spaces on the ground to secure access to light and air and a more hygienic environment, all three of the PWD complexes covered just about 30 percent of the area of each site, allowing generous distances among

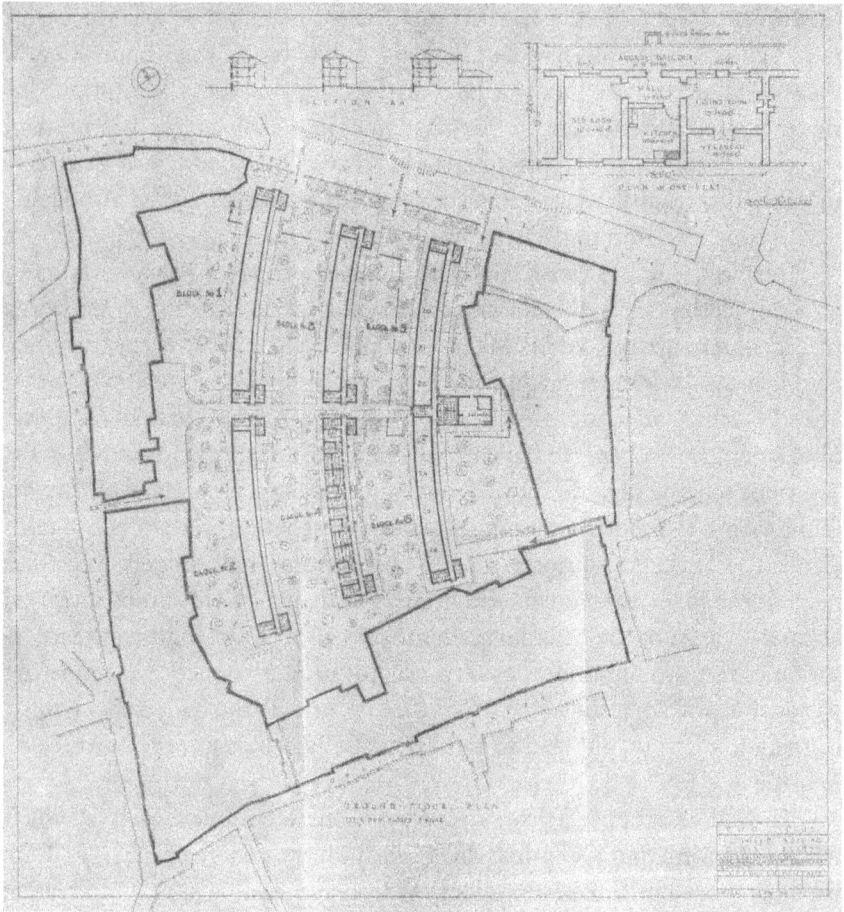

Figure 7.1. Ground-floor plan and section of proposed working-class flats, Nicosia, 1944. State Archives, Cyprus, SA1 705/1944.

wings.[24] The scale and form of these new blocks, which maintained substantial distances from roads and adjacent plots, were introducing an altogether new aesthetic and a mode of living different from the mode that characterized the introspective character of local houses and the labyrinthine urban fabric of town centers (fig. 7.3). Even if population densities remained similar, the sparsity of the new buildings could claim to avoid overcrowding as much as improve sanitation.[25]

Because of both their favorable economic indicators and their promise of reforming the primitive character of indigenous housing in unplanned

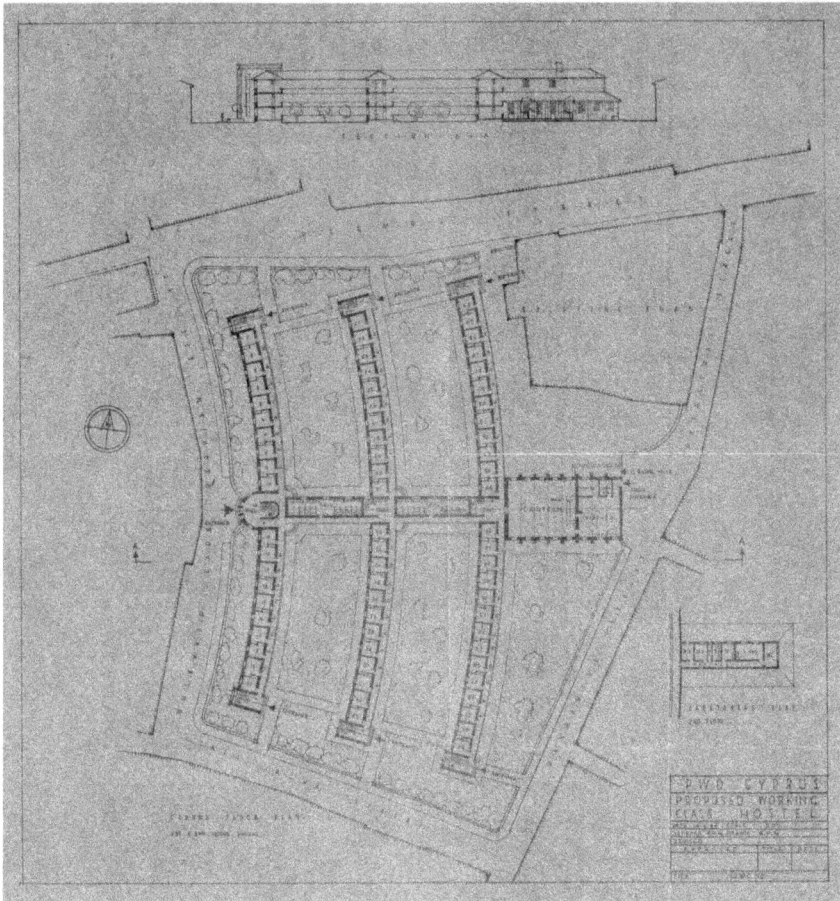

Figure 7.2. Ground-floor plan and section of proposed working-class hostel, Nicosia, 1944. State Archives, Cyprus, SA1 705/1944.

neighborhoods and towns, these schemes were embraced by the government. The regular, geometric design of the schemes appeared to offer order, efficiency, and healthy living, promising to lead workers into modernity. As the governor himself stated, these schemes would provide "a standard of accommodation, convenience, sanitation and appearance, considerably in advance of existing working-class housing in the colony."[26]

Despite the positive reactions to the schemes, however, the colonial government decided to abandon the project, albeit "with reluctance,"[27] for several reasons. The large and tall building masses proved much more

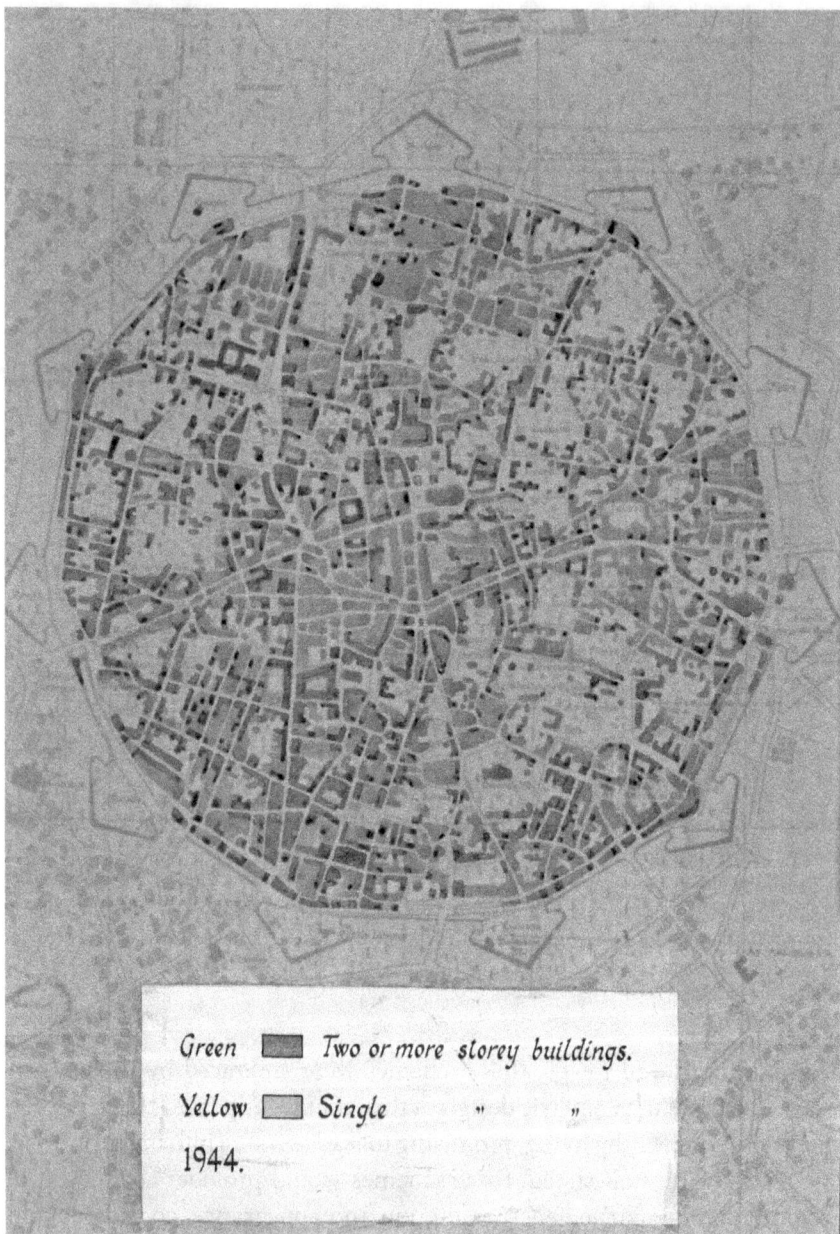

Green ▓ Two or more storey buildings.

Yellow ☐ Single   "   "

1944.

Figure 7.3. Nicosia's center, 1944, indicating the number of building's stories in buildings, Nicosia. State Archives, Cyprus, SA1 705/1944.

costly than initially estimated by the PWD because they necessitated the importation of large quantities of materials, which were in very low supply because of the war. Furthermore, construction required a long time frame, which conflicted with the urgency of delivery. In addition, in order to absorb the cost of construction, rent prices were estimated to be prohibitively high for the workers; and there was no possibility of subsidizing the project from the municipality of Nicosia, as the mayor was clearly opposed to the scheme.

In Search of a "Standard" Typology of Housing for Cyprus

In face of the difficulties faced by multistory developments, the colonial government in the end turned to the design of low-rise houses in the suburbs, as it was convinced that smaller structures would avoid dependence on expensive imported materials and could be completed with the know-how of local builders. This alternative approach, which moved away from the models of large blocks in favor of "cottages on a garden plot,"[28] was more aligned with the logic of the British-based office on colonial development and welfare, which generally followed the practices of postwar reconstruction being promoted in Britain.[29]

This alternative housing type would also save time, in the sense that groups of houses could be assigned variously to several private contractors. The involvement of the private sector would bypass the government's shortage of funds and would have the added benefit of addressing unemployment.[30] Embracing this alternative, the government proposed the immediate creation of 250 units with two separate modes of financing. The first mode, which would finance 100 units, would commission private contractors to immediately construct housing on land that the government could obtain in the periphery of Nicosia.[31] The units would be rented to low-income Greek and Turkish Cypriot families nominated by the government at a low, fixed rate for three years, and contractors would receive a substantial government subsidy on imported materials and would have sole ownership of the property after three years.[32] The second mode of financing the project involved more risk for the contractors, as they had to buy their own property in urban peripheries without any subsidies other than those for imported materials. In this latter mode, contractors could either use the government's (PWD's) design proposals or create their own according to the same specifications.[33] The hidden agenda in this latter

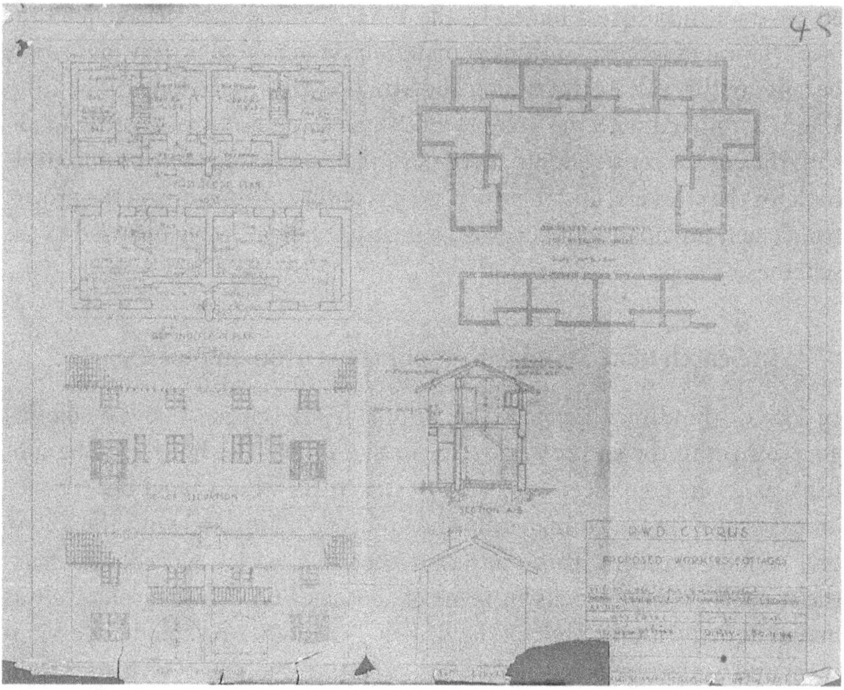

Figure 7.4. The standard design for proposed workers' cottages, Nicosia, 1944. State Archives, Cyprus, SA1 849/1944/1N.

mode was to extend the use of PWD's standardized designs to housing projects by private initiatives, well beyond the projects the government itself could fund.

The government was able to pursue only the first mode—the second mode was rejected by the private contractors—and assigned the PWD a single housing design, which would come to be known by its future residents as "the standard."[34] The PWD design had two floors and a simple rectangular footprint of 25 a 17 feet and could be constructed as a semidetached or attached house in a row (terraced house), or in an L or U formation (fig. 7.4). The standard working-class home had a semiopen space at the entrance; living room, kitchen, and sanitation services in the ground floor; two bedrooms on the first floor, and a small verandah, allowing 48 square feet for each member of a five-person family. This space was considered close enough to the minimum acceptable area of 55 square feet per person set by the 1935 Housing Act in England.[35] Offering cross-ventilation and effective insulation in the bedrooms and living room, along with good sanitation services, the standard design projected ideas of modern and healthy living, even if it offered no electricity (which was generally difficult and expensive to provide in the outskirts of towns).[36]

The very spatial organization of the house was advancing a new mode of family interaction and privacy. Contrary to the multipurpose rooms of vernacular houses in Cyprus, which usually aimed to accommodate large families, the house floor plans of the standard designated specific and separated uses for every single room and was based on the model of a small European nuclear family. The only element in the standard that alluded to local spatial preferences and family life was perhaps the semiopen space at the entrance, in the sense that it was reminiscent of the *iliakos*, a semiopen space typically located on the south façade of vernacular houses. The *iliakos* accommodated utilitarian household tasks and was the heart of the social space of the house in the warm days of the year. It had a rectangular plan, enclosed on three sides by walls, with an open side constructed either with wooden posts or with arches, as in the standard house designed by the PWD. In the case of the standard, however, the semiopen space was proportionally much smaller than a typical *iliakos* and could not replace its important spatial and social role. In general, the standard house type was much more introverted and was not associated with open spaces as much as vernacular Cypriot housing was.

Because the problem of sourcing materials was even more serious than that of funding construction projects, the standard advanced strategies for economizing on imported materials.[37] This was in tune with Downing Street's directive to the colonies to promote their own local construction techniques and experiment more with indigenous materials.[38] Local stone was used for external walls, and mud and straw were used for insulating the roof. In order to reduce the amount of structural timber to a minimum (overcutting of forests for military use during World War II made Cypriot timber practically nonexistent),[39] door and window frames were constructed of arched stone lintels, and the entrance porch was created by an archway, a typical practice on the island.

The PWD developed a master plan for this project in an area northeast of the capital, outside the Venetian walls that defined the urban center of Nicosia. The plot was deemed ideal because it was inexpensive and located in an essentially industrial area where a great number of workers were employed. There was the added benefit of being in proximity to the

Figure 7.5. Omorphita workers' housing scheme model, Nicosia, 1945. State Archives, Cyprus, SA1 849/1944/2N.

town center as well as the public services in the nearby village community of Omorphita, which gave the housing project its name.[40]

The master plan for the Omorphita housing project incorporated a school, two shops, a soccer pitch, and a coffee shop, following the modernist principle of self-sufficient neighborhood units (fig. 7.5).[41] Buildings such as health centers and the schoolmasters' dwellings were designed with the same principle of savings on materials, while also incorporating historical references; the shops, for instance, were designed along the lines of an Ottoman kiosk.[42] Similarly, the coffee shop, which was incorporated within public space, allegedly to enhance social interaction among male inhabitants, consciously made reference to the island's Ottoman past. These gestures were in tune with modernist practice in inserting local character into a standardized master plan, but in the case of Cyprus, the reference to Ottoman (or in other cases Byzantine or Gothic) stylistic traits was also a colonial strategy for managing the competing national aspirations of the ethnically mixed population on the island.[43]

As to residences, the master plan subdivided the land into urban blocks defined by wide streets and sidewalks. The 106 housing units were grouped in complexes of two to six units each, to allow for phasing of construction.

The units were set a substantial distance from the road; one garden was created on the street side and an even larger one at the back, following British suburban development principles that trace back to Garden Cities and anticipate the British New Towns. The PWD opinion that Cypriots were incapable of handling gardens was now being tempered. For British officials, the provision of gardens in projects like Omorphita could decisively initiate changes in local mind-sets that would bring urban society closer to British habits. And indeed, unlike the introverted courtyards of local vernacular houses, the gardens created a relationship between dwelling and the street that was more antiurban and less efficient in terms of shading and heat gain.[44] It is interesting that this type of spatial organization would gradually become typical in Cypriot towns, because it was advanced by planning regulations and the more comprehensive planning legislation that would be adopted one year later.[45]

Through its implementation in the Omorphita Housing Project, the standard housing type underwent some alterations by the PWD when the medical officer instructed that sanitation facilities be located outside the building for reasons of hygiene. This resulted in the creation of an outbuilding for bathing and laundry attached to the rear façade and the transfer of the toilet to a separate ancillary building at the rear boundary of the site, where a small chicken house was also added.[46] Ironically, these ancillary buildings for toilets and animals reintroduced past local practices that had begun to be abandoned.[47]

The project, when finally completed in 1946 (fig. 7.6), introduced the first governmental workers' settlement in a Cypriot town. Residents for Omorphita were chosen by a government-appointed committee that included a government official, an employee of the Nicosia municipality, and two members of local trade unions, one Greek and one Turkish Cypriot. Apart from the prerequisite that the tenant be a worker, other selection criteria took into account wages, family size, and current residential status. The 515 applications showed that the average family had seven members, instead of the five for which the project was designed.[48] The large number of inhabitants in each unit, the limited space, and inhabitants' habits led to several alterations. For example, living rooms were partly transformed into sleeping areas, or the gardens were largely transformed into spaces for domestic labor tasks with the introduction of light roof structures. Once again, colonial aspirations for a particular spatial organization and social reform were confronted by competing local interrelations.

Figure 7.6. A row of houses just after their implementation in Omorphita workers' neighborhood, Nicosia, 1946. State Archives, Cyprus, SA1 849/1944/2N.

Gardens versus Public Spaces

The Omorphita project may have resolved several of the difficulties that the initial multistory project faced, but it did not alleviate the housing crisis much, as it accommodated only a relative handful of families. There was still a need to subsidize 500–650 residences in towns. In response, the government decided to subsidize 290 additional homes as its immediate priority between 1946 and 1948 and 110 homes in 1948 and 1949.[49] These were the limits of the government's available funding for housing, and the schemes were incorporated into a broader ten-year development plan to create prosperity and stability on the island.[50]

For the new housing schemes, the colonial government decided to collaborate with town municipalities. Such collaborations had been avoided before so as to avoid delays; at this point, however, they were considered important for easing public scrutiny and ensuring long-term success, especially because the Omorphita project had been harshly criticized by locals and their elected municipal councils for serving the interests of contractors.[51] Just like the earlier involvement of the private sector, the collaboration with municipalities was a practice already followed in social housing practices followed in the United Kingdom.[52] The housing would be constructed by municipal corporations, which would then own the houses. Once again, the workers would have to pay rent, the cost of which would be determined by the municipalities, which would be responsible for the design as well as the allocation of the units. The government, in turn, would offer a subsidy (which was smaller than in the Omorphita case), and any additional funds required would be provided in the form of a loan. These conditions were notably less beneficial to the municipalities than what Omorphita offered to contractors. Even though the municipalities criticized the government's plan for both the level of funding and the insufficient number of workers' dwellings, they accepted it, under pressure from public opinion and trade unions such as the newly established and left-leaning Pancyprian Labour Federation.[53]

The municipality of Nicosia, which had been allocated the greatest amount of worker housing, decided to follow the government's suggestions to erect the workers' houses in an area on the southern boundary of Omorphita, in order to save on the provision of public amenities. To render the new project an extension of the previous one, the municipality used the standard house type for the construction of 134 dwellings, and the siting of the units followed the pattern of the previous project (fig. 7.7). Nonetheless, the municipality of Nicosia appeared eager to highlight its modernist aesthetics: it eliminated the entrance porch, which had an arch that was widely associated with local formal vocabularies, and it favored plaster over exposed stone for a similar reason.[54]

The municipality of Limassol, the second-largest Cypriot town, on the southern coast of the island, which was to construct a housing complex in the industrial zone on the western periphery of the town, embraced the Omorphita design principle of two-story structures but made significant modifications. Expressing a strong preference for reducing construction cost and rent prices (which was in line with the leftist leanings of the majority of the municipal council), municipal engineer Nicos Rousos reconfigured each floor into a smaller self-sufficient unit in the form of a flat, which would better respond to the smallness of the site (fig. 7.7).[55] Each unit had its own private entrance and an entirely private yard: the ground-floor unit had a yard on the street front, and the upper-level unit had a yard at the rear of the plot, which would be accessed by a balcony staircase. By allocating a yard for each unit, and by omitting internal staircases and corridors within each unit, this dwelling was closer to local vernacular typologies, even if

Figure 7.7. Nicosia's municipal workers' neighborhood (indicated with solid line) and Omorphita's first workers' housing (indicated with dotted line), Nicosia, 1963. Aerial photo. Department of Land and Surveys, Cyprus, 72_19_029, October 1963.

the idea of separate flats stacked in two-story structures was a novelty for local culture. Rousos contended that his proposals were in tune with the "mentality and habits of the locals,"[56] even as they succeeded in providing cost-effective shelter. Still, however, the stacked units in Limassol were limited to meeting the needs of five-member families, as was the case in Omorphita. (See fig. 7.8.)

In the Limassol version of the standard, the bathroom was reinstated within the unit, as the locals opposed the medical officer's view that placed these facilities outside in Omorphita. Local materials were again used, stone being the main building component. In contrast to Omorphita, the first-floor slab was replaced with reinforced concrete, which was considered more economical than structural timber; the small quantity of material required would be imported. The stacked flats in free-standing complexes had a much higher density than in Omorphita, even if the free-standing

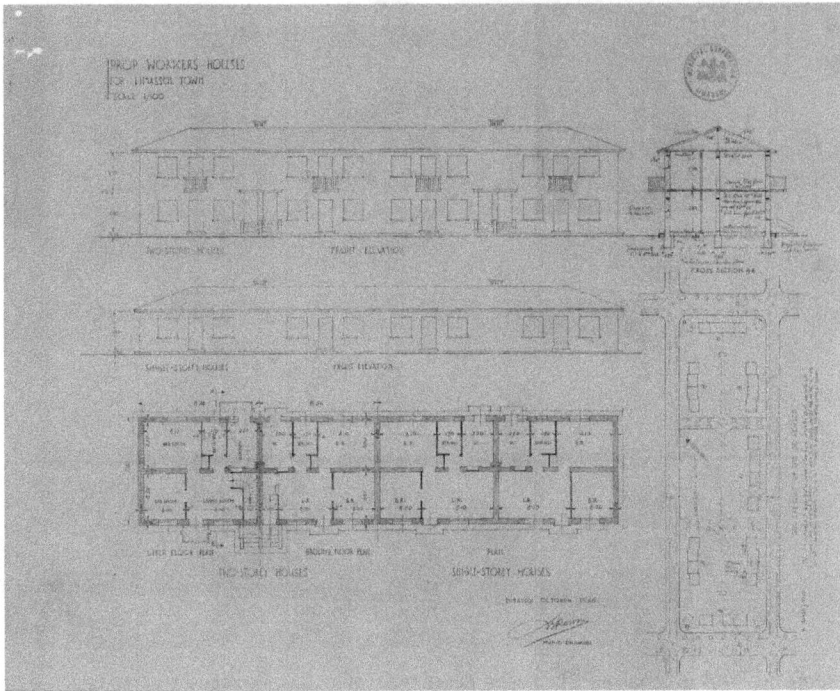

Figure 7.8. Plans of proposed workers' houses for Limassol Town, Limassol, 1945. Municipality of Limassol Archives, ΔΛ1/616.

buildings they formed still echoed Garden City principles. The master plan also included pedestrian paths and plants along with a municipal playground.

The PWD was not positive about the changes advanced by the municipality of Limassol, not only because of the modifications in the standard house design but also because of the master plan's configuration of open spaces. The PWD expressed numerous concerns about the many open spaces, the pedestrian walkways, and other public spaces between the housing complexes, which it criticized for being disproportionately large in comparison with the small private yards in individual houses. The PWD framed its concern in terms of practicality, stating that the "maintenance of public spaces in small housing estates is problematic."[57] But it quickly tied its argument to its strategies for social control: "encouraging gardening, growing vegetables, etc." within a unit's yard, they argued, has a good moral influence on the tenants";[58] and more important, "it keeps [men] away from

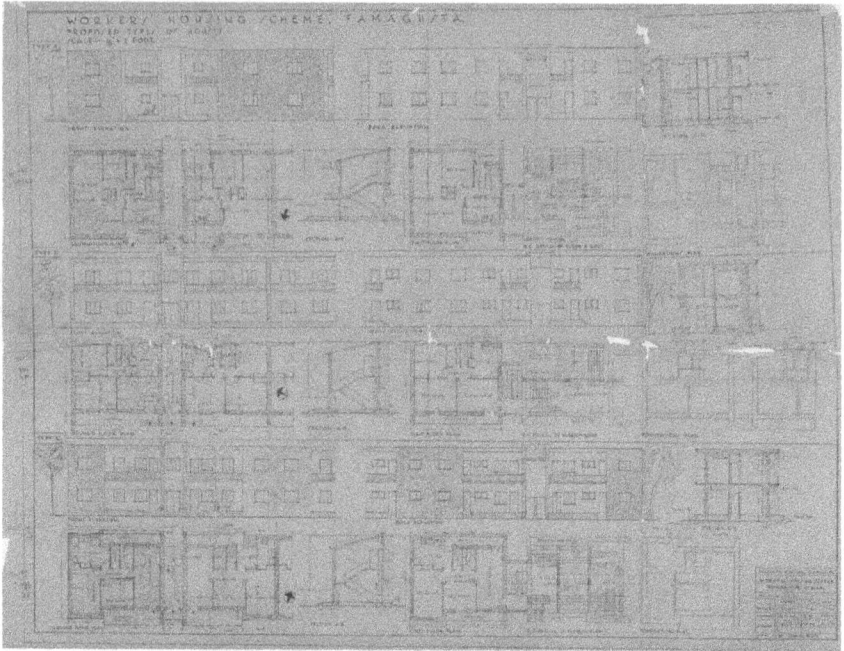

Figure 7.9. Workers' housing scheme, proposed types of houses, Famagusta, 1947. State Archives, Cyprus, SA1 580/1945.

the coffeehouse—that source of most of our troubles."[59] In other words: the debate on private yards versus public spaces was not merely a practical matter of maintenance, nor a mere question of how to facilitate family life and make "living at home interesting."[60] It came down to colonial anxieties of handling local aspirations and implementing social control.

Municipal engineer Stavros Economou also followed the concept of units as self-contained flats for the municipality of Famagusta using reasoning similar to the reasoning in Limassol. The flats were similarly arranged in small, free-standing two-story complexes. In this case, however, Economou designed three variations of the unit so as to optimize sunlight (fig. 7.9).[61] As was the case in Limassol, the layout secured a private yard for each unit. The difference was that all yards were designed on the inner side of the plot, with the fronts given over for public use. The use of local materials was once again the driving force in the construction, especially because by 1947, when the project began, the cost of construction on the Omorphita standard model had risen by 20 percent. Because concrete and steel could

by this point be easily supplied from the Middle East, a flat slab of reinforced concrete replaced the pitched roofs of the other housing projects.

The municipality of Famagusta developed a master plan for 150 residences rather than the 50 that the government had allocated to Famagusta
and based them on the aforementioned typologies, on the outskirts of
the town center.[62] The master plan included shops, a community center, a
sports ground, and parks. The government flatly refused to view the master
plan, pointing out that such a scheme would create "an undesirable heavy
density of population for an outer zone." As in the case of Limassol, the
PWD recommended houses instead of flats and favored private yards over
public spaces.[63]

The municipal housing projects of the three largest towns were finally
completed in 1950. The difficult economic circumstances of the period
and the huge delays in approvals and discussions caused by the triangu-
lar cooperation between the municipalities, the local government, and the
United Kingdom resulted in the abandonment of other housing projects.
Nevertheless, the logic of social housing had spread across the island,
leaving this new type of housing as the sole responsibility of elected municipal councils, under the supervision and partial funding of the British
government.

Conclusion

The worker houses that were created in the aftermath of World War II only
scratched the surface of the 1940s housing crisis in Cyprus, but they created
a catalyst for advancing visions of social reform. These visions were tied to
British efforts to advance ideas of the welfare state while stabilizing workers, in the context of larger colonial anxieties relating to the rise of trade
unionism and worker riots; ethnic tensions and the beginnings of local ethnic groups' demands for self-determination; and larger regional fears of a
communist threat. The colonial agendas on housing were unveiled along
with those of local municipalities, whose aspirations to modernize urban
territories expressed the same, or sometimes even greater, zeal to embrace
modernist social and aesthetic agendas pertaining to notions of hygiene,
standardization, rationalism, and orderliness—even if they did not share
similar conceptions of family life and social order, and even if they certainly
had very different aspirations to modernity, as the anticolonial struggle of
1955–59 would soon make evident.

The British policies on social housing in Cyprus, in combination with the rapid urban development of the 1940s and 1950s, shaped the physical landscape of Cyprus to a great extent. The logic of low-density suburban development and the demand for open spaces on the perimeter of buildings were never challenged in the years after colonialism. As a result, towns continue to develop according to the principle of free-standing structures even to this date—and even if the alternative of higher densities would be more in tune with the historical centers of (medieval) towns and would shape a more cohesive urban tissue.

Notes

1. According to Demetrios Christodoulou, agriculture was 70 percent of GDP in 1881 and gradually dropped to less than 50 percent by the end of World War II. See Demetrios Christodoulou, *Inside the Cyprus Miracle: The Labours of an Embattled Mini-economy* (Minneapolis: University of Minnesota Press, 1992), xxviii.

2. Between 1931 and 1946, the urban population rose by 53.6 percent. By the time the British left Cyprus in 1960, it rose by another 78.1 percent (Cyprus Census of Population and Agriculture 1946, 3; Cyprus Census of Population and Agriculture 1960, vol. 1, 6). For the socioeconomic and political forces that created the various urbanization waves from the interwar period until the end of colonialism, see Michael Attalides, *Social Change and Urbanization in Cyprus: A Study of Nicosia* (Nicosia: Social Research Center, 1981), 49–97; and Simoni Angelides, "The Cyprus Economy under British Rule (1878–1960)," in *The Development of the Cypriot Economy, from the Prehistoric Period to the Present Day*, ed. Vasos Karageorghis and Demetrios Michaelides (Nicosia: University of Cyprus and Bank of Cyprus, 1996), 209–23.

3. Acting governor to the secretary of state for the colonies, October 24, 1944, Cyprus State Archives, SA1 849/1944/1/N, 36.

4. Extract from commissioner of Nicosia's August report, September 16, 1946, Cyprus State Archives, SA1 849/1944/2/N, 234; extract from commissioner of Limassol's confidential monthly report (for September 1946), October 7, 1946, Cyprus State Archives, SA1 849/1944/2/N, 242; Pancyprian Federation of Labour, an interview with the attorney general, October 3, 1952, Cyprus State Archives, SA1 1656/1952/1, 16–23; and Report of a Subcommittee of the Committee Appointed to Review the Housing Problem in Cyprus, Cyprus State Archives, SA1 1656/1952/1, 128–38.

5. For other British postwar activities in the colonies, see, for example, Ambe J. Njoh, *Planning Power: Town Planning and Social Control in Colonial Africa* (New York: UCL Press, 2007), 60; Robert K. Home, "From Barrack Compounds to the Single-Family House: Planning Worker Housing in Colonial Natal and Northern Rhodesia," *Planning Perspectives* 15 (2000): 341–44; Viviana d'Auria, "In the Laboratory and in the Field: Hybrid Housing Design for the African City in Late-Colonial and Decolonising Ghana (1945–57)," *Journal of Architecture* 19, no. 3 (2014): 329–56; Andrew Byerley, "Displacements in the Name of (Re) Development: The Contested Rise and Contested Demise of Colonial 'African' Housing

Estates in Kampala and Jinja," *Planning Perspectives* 28, no. 4 (2013): 553–56; Richard Harris, "Making Leeway in the Leewards, 1929–51: The Negotiation of Colonial Development," *Journal of Imperial and Commonwealth History* 33, no. 3 (2005): 410–12; Richard Harris, "From Trusteeship to Development: How Class and Gender Complicated Kenya's Housing Policy, 1939–1963," *Journal of Historical Geography* 34 (2008): 311–37; Gavin Ure, *Governors, Politics and the Colonial Office: Public Policy in Hong Kong, 1918–58*, Royal Asiatic Society Hong Kong Studies Series (Hong Kong: Hong Kong University Press, 2012), 135–61; and Richard Harris and Alison Hay, "New Plans for Housing in Urban Kenya, 1939–63," *Planning Perspectives* 22 (April 2007): 195–223.

6. The first workers' housing schemes in Cyprus came from recommendations submitted by the Wages Commission, appointed as a result of this strike. Controller of supplies to MESCO, June 5, 1944, Cyprus State Archives, SA1 705/1944, 22–24. Another key colonial gesture after the strike focused on technical education. For an analysis of the architectural history of colonial technical education in Cyprus, see Michalis Sioulas and Panayiota Pyla, "Technical Schools for Inter-Communal Crisis Management in Mid-20th Century Cyprus," in the proceedings of the conference Entangled Histories, Multiple Geographies, organized jointly by the University of Belgrade and the European Architectural History Network (Belgrade: University of Belgrade, Faculty of Architecture, 2017), 310–16.

7. For workers' housing in mining communities in Cyprus, see Michael Given, "Mining Landscapes and Colonial Rule in Early Twentieth Century Cyprus," *Historical Archaeology* 39, no. 3 (2005): 49–60.

8. General Aspects of the Housing Problem in the Colonial Empire, Papers on Colonial Affairs, December 1943, Cyprus State Archives, SA1 613/1943, 18–22.

9. Under the Colonial Development and Welfare Act of 1940, Britain subsidized development projects in the colonies, across the colonial empire. See, for example, Njoh, *Planning Power*, 60.

10. The lack of comprehensive town planning legislation and of planning schemes related to the fact that not many British nationals resided in Cyprus, and native urban areas of local population usually did not attract much attention; in addition, up to World War II, the island was perceived as one of the less valuable colonies. Regarding town planning in Cyprus, see Costas Georghiou, *British Colonial Architecture in Cyprus* (Nicosia: En Tipis, 2013), 42–47.

11. During the interwar period, council houses on cottage estates were the dominant type of housing in the United Kingdom. Over 1 million such houses were constructed, and council flats numbered about one hundred thousand units, developed mainly in London. In the 1940s, too, this type of development continued on suburban estates, and a relatively small number of blocks of flats were built, mainly on bomb sites. See Matthew Taunton, *Fictions of the City: Class, Culture and Mass Housing in London and Paris* (London: Palgrave Macmillan, 2009), 141; and Patrick Dunleavy, *The Politics of Mass Housing in Britain, 1945–1975: A Study of Corporate Power and Professional Influence in the Welfare State* (New York: Oxford University Press, 1981), 35.

12. In New Delhi, such housing was provided for lower-ranking workers and clerical staff. See Jyoti Hosagrahar, *Indigenous Modernities: Negotiating Architecture and Urbanism* (New York: Routledge, 2005), 147.

13. Especially in East and Central Africa, until World War II this kind of housing was well established, as the British preferred African men "to retain ties to the land." This type of housing was also provided for the armed forces, mining operations, and plantations. See

Harris and Hay, "New Plans for Housing," 195–202; and Home, "From Barrack Compounds," 330–36.

14. R. H. Macartney, the Office of the Architect, PWD, to the director of PWD, March 31, 1944, Cyprus State Archives, SA1 705/1944, 1–3.

15. Ibid. Macartney, a young architect who had been working in Cyprus since 1939, was responsible for a variety of housing projects for government officials. See Kenneth W. Schaar, Michael Given, and George Theocharous, *Under the Clock: Colonial Architecture and History in Cyprus, 1878–1960* (Nicosia: Bank of Cyprus, 1995), 82–86.

16. R. H. Macartney, the Office of the Architect, PWD, to the director of PWD, March 31, 1944.

17. Ibid.

18. Commissioner of Nicosia and Kyrenia to colonial secretary, July 31, 1944, Cyprus State Archives, SA1 705/1944, 41–42.

19. Regarding the rise of trade unions in Cyprus, see Attalides, *Social Change*, 58.

20. Commissioner of Nicosia and Kyrenia to colonial secretary, July 31, 1944, Cyprus State Archives, SA1 705/1944, 41–42; Themistoklis Dervis, mayor of Municipal Corporation Nicosia, to the commissioner of Nicosia, September 5, 1945, Cyprus State Archives, SA1 849/1944/2/N, 76.

21. Governor of Cyprus to the secretary of state for the colonies, July 24, 1944, Cyprus State Archives, SA1 705/1944, 38–39.

22. R. H. Macartney, the Office of the Architect, PWD, to the director of PWD, May 4, 1944, Cyprus State Archives, SA1 705/1944, 15–16.

23. R. H. Macartney, the Office of the Architect, PWD, to the director of PWD, April 16, 1944, Cyprus State Archives, SA1 705/1944, 5–6; and director of public works to colonial secretary, April 21, 1944, Cyprus State Archives, SA1 705/1944, 12.

24. Regarding the complexes' accommodation to the environment, the PWD stated, "The Hostel has been planned so that all the bedrooms face approximately to the West. It is considered that on the whole this aspect is the most pleasant for use all the year around. It neither gets the cold winds in the winter, nor the worst of the summer heat, it also gets the cool night wind in the hot weather. . . . The distance between arms is about 60 feet, resulting in an angle of light from the roof of one arm to the ground floor window sill of the adjacent arm of approximately 24 degrees, which is very generous." See R. H. Macartney, the Office of the Architect, PWD, to the director of PWD, April 16, 1944, Cyprus State Archives, SA1 705/1944, 5.

25. According to 1946 statistics, the population density in the old town of Nicosia within ramparts was 66.8 persons per acre, and the proposed plans show that this was more or less maintained by the projects. See Cyprus Census of Population and Agriculture 1946, 2.

26. Acting governor to secretary of state for the colonies, October 24, 1944, Cyprus State Archives, SA1 849/1944/1/N, 33–37.

27. Ibid.

28. See, for example, Home, "From Barrack Compounds," 330, 339–40.

29. Ibid., 340.

30. The assistance for unemployment was "a secondary but not a less important justification for launching" the housing scheme. See acting governor to the secretary of state for the colonies, October 24, 1944.

31. Record of meeting held at the colonial secretary's office, September 8, 1944, Cyprus State Archives, SA1 849/1944/1/N, 12–23.

32. The subsidies would reach one-third of the value of the houses, including the cost of land. See Workers' Housing Scheme for Nicosia, Cyprus State Archives, SA1 849/1944/1/N, 66.

33. Housing in the Towns, Government Proposals for Assisting Private Enterprise, Cyprus State Archives, SA1 849/1944/1/N, 46–47, 51.

34. Schaar, Given, and Theocharous, *Under the Clock*, 90.

35. See Blueprint of Proposed Workers Cottages, PWD Cyprus, November 30, 1944, Cyprus State Archives, SA1 849/1944/1N, 48; Specifications of Materials for the Approved "Standard" Working-Class Home, Cyprus State Archives, SA1 849/1944/1/N, 48A; Hosagrahar, *Indigenous Modernities*, 165.

36. At that time, only 41.9 percent of households had access to electricity in towns, and only 10 percent in the country as a whole.

37. Similar experiments were performed in countries such as neighboring Egypt and Ghana, which built dwellings for low-income households using local materials and methods of construction. See, for example, Panayiota Pyla, "The Many Lives of New Gourna: Alternative Histories of a Model Community and Their Current Significance," *Journal of Architecture* 14, no. 6 (2009): 715–30; and d'Auria, "In the Laboratory."

38. General Aspects of the Housing Problem in the Colonial Empire, Papers on Colonial Affairs, December 1943; and Circular Letter from Oliver Stanley, secretary of state for the colonies to colonial governments, December 16, 1943, Cyprus State Archives, SA1 613/1943, 17–17a.

39. Resuscitation of the Building Trade, colonial secretary to all commissioners, April 10, 1944, Cyprus State Archives, SA1 613/1943, 23–25.

40. Workers' Housing Scheme for Nicosia, January 12, 1945, SA1 849/1944/1/N, 58, 66.

41. The Omorphita Project is briefly discussed in Schaar, Given, and Theocharous, *Under the Clock*, 88–90; some further discussion appears in Georghiou, *British Colonial Architecture*, 230–33.

42. The use of an amalgam of styles, local and imported, was well established in other colonies too, such as in India and Southeast Asia. See Jan Morris, Charles Allen, Gillian Tindall, Colin Amery, and Gavin Stamp, *Architecture of the British Empire* (London: Weidenfeld and Nicolson, 1986), 44.

43. See Michael Given, "Architectural Styles and Ethnic Identity in Medieval to Modern Cyprus," in *Archaeological Perspectives on the Transmission and Transformation of Culture in the Eastern Mediterranean*, ed. Joanne Clarke (Oxford: Oxbow, 2005), 207–13; and Michael Given, "Star of the Parthenon, Cypriot Mélange: Education and Representation in Colonial Cyprus," *Journal of Mediterranean Studies* 7, no. 1 (1997): 59–82.

44. Giorgos Papacharalambous, *H Kypriaki Oikia* [The Cypriot dwelling] (Nicosia: Cyprus Research Center, 2001); and Stefanos Sinos, *Anadromi sti Laiki Arxitektoniki stin Kipro* [Review of vernacular architecture in Cyprus] (Athens: NTUA, 1975), 152–57.

45. For the way these regulations affected the Cypriot towns, see Socratis Stratis, "Sxeseis metaksi dimosiou kai idiotikou, kai o rolos tis topografias: H Paragogi tou Kypriakou Domimenou Topiou" [Relations between public and private and the role of topography: The production of the Cyprus built landscape], *Arxitektonika Themata* [Architectural issues] 41 (2007): 66–71.

46. The Office of the Director of L. R. & Surveys to colonial secretary, May 21, 1945, Cyprus State Archives, SA1 849/1944/2/N, 133.

47. For the influence of the question of hygiene in British architecture, see, for example, Paul Overy, *Light, Air and Openness: Modern Architecture between the Wars* (London: Thames and Hudson, 2008).

48. For information about the tenants and the criteria for their selection, see Press Communiqué, Applications from Prospective Tenants under the Nicosia Workers' Housing Scheme, Cyprus State Archives, SA1 849/1944/2/N, 178; governor of Cyprus to the secretary of state for the colonies, May 9, 1946, Cyprus State Archives, SA1 849/1944/3, 30; and Extract from Part II of the Development Report, Housing, SA1 849/1944/3, 22–26.

49. Extract from Part II of the Development Report, Housing, February 12, 1946, SA1 849/1944/3, 22–26.

50. A Ten-Year Programme of Development for Cyprus, 1946.

51. Housing Schemes, February 12, 1946, Cyprus State Archives, SA1 819/1944/3, 9–11. Severe criticism of the projects led the led the government to issue a written statement in their defense. See Workers' Housing Scheme Defended, Cyprus State Archives, SA1849/1944/1/N, 86–88.

52. Miles Glendinning, "A Modernist Vernacular? The Hidden Diversity of Post-war Council Housing," in *Built from Below: British Architecture and the Vernacular*, ed. Peter Guillery (New York: Routledge, 2011), 174.

53. Governor to the secretary of state for the colonies, July 11, 1946, Cyprus State Archives, SA1 849/1944/3, 42–44.

54. Nicosia Housing Scheme, Cyprus State Archives, SA1 1111/1945/2, 32.

55. Workers' Housing, Report by Municipal Engineer Nikos Rousos, October 16, 1945, Municipality of Limassol Archives, ΔΛ1/616, 3–9.

56. Ibid.

57. Ibid.

58. Ibid.

59. Ibid.

60. Ibid.

61. Georghiou, *British Colonial Architecture*, 239–40; Workers' Housing Schemes at Larnaca and Famagusta, July 12, 1948, Cyprus State Archives 580/1945, 92–94.

62. Famagusta Municipal Housing Scheme, Cyprus State Archives, SA1580/1945, 50.

63. Ibid.

Bibliography

Attalides, Michael. *Social Change and Urbanization in Cyprus: A Study of Nicosia*. Nicosia: Social Research Center, 1981.

Angelides, Simoni. "The Cyprus Economy under British Rule (1878–1960)." In *The Development of the Cypriot Economy, from the Prehistoric Period to the Present Day*, edited by Vasos Karageorghis and Demetrios Michaelides, 209–23. Nicosia: University of Cyprus and Bank of Cyprus, 1996.

Buckley, Cheryl. "Modernity, Tradition, and the Design of the 'Industrial Village' of Dormstown, 1917–1923." *Journal of Design History* 23, no. 1 (2010): 21–41.

Byerley, Andrew. "Displacements in the Name of (Re)Development: The Contested Rise and Contested Demise of Colonial 'African' Housing Estates in Kampala and Jinja." *Planning Perspectives* 28, no. 4 (2013): 547–70.

Christodoulou, Demetrios. *Inside the Cyprus Miracle: The Labours of an Embattled Mini-economy*. Minneapolis: University of Minnesota Press, 1992.

D'Auria, Viviana. "In the Laboratory and in The Field: Hybrid Housing Design for the African City in Late-Colonial and Decolonising Ghana (1945–57)." *Journal of Architecture* 19, no. 3 (2014): 329–56.

Dunleavy, Patrick. *The Politics of Mass Housing in Britain, 1945–75: Study of Corporate Power and Professional Influence in the Welfare State.* Oxford: Oxford University Press, 1981.

Georghiou, Costas. *British Colonial Architecture in Cyprus.* Nicosia: En Tipis, 2013.

Given, Michael. "Architectural Styles and Ethnic Identity in Medieval to Modern Cyprus." In *Archaeological Perspectives on the Transmission and Transformation of Culture in the Eastern Mediterranean*, edited by Joanne Clarke, 207–13. Oxford: Oxbow Books, 2005.

———. "Mining Landscapes and Colonial Rule in Early Twentieth Century Cyprus." *Historical Archaeology* 39, no. 3 (2005): 49–60.

———. "Star of the Parthenon, Cypriot Mélange: Education and Representation in Colonial Cyprus." *Journal of Mediterranean Studies* 7, no. 1 (1997): 59–82.

Glendinning, Miles. "A Modernist Vernacular? The Hidden Diversity of Post-War Council Housing." In *Built from Below: British Architecture and the Vernacular*, edited by Peter Guillery, 169–72. New York: Routledge, 2011.

Harris, Richard. "Making Leeway in the Leewards, 1929–51: The Negotiation of Colonial Development." *Journal of Imperial and Commonwealth History* 33, no. 3 (2005): 393–418.

———. "From Trusteeship to Development: How Class and Gender Complicated Kenya's Housing Policy, 1939–1963." *Journal of Historical Geography* 34 (2008): 311–37.

Harris, Richard, and Alison Hay. "New Plans for Housing in Urban Kenya, 1939–63," *Planning Perspectives* 22 (April 2007): 195–223.

Home, Robert K. "From Barrack Compounds to the Single-Family House: Planning Worker Housing in Colonial Natal and Northern Rhodesia." *Planning Perspectives* 15 (2000): 327–47.

Hosagrahar, Jyoti. *Indigenous Modernities: Negotiating Architecture and Urbanism.* New York: Routledge, 2005.

Morris, Jan, Charles Allen, Gillian Tindall, Colin Amery, and Gavin Stamp. *Architecture of the British Empire.* London: Weidenfeld and Nicolson, 1986.

Njoh, Ambe. *Planning Power: Town Planning and Social Control in Colonial Africa.* New York: UCL Press, 2007.

Overy, Paul. *Light, Air and Openness: Modern Architecture between the Wars.* London: Thames and Hudson, 2008.

Papacharalambous, Giorgos. *H Kypriaki Oikia* [The Cypriot dwelling]. Nicosia: Cyprus Research Centre, 2001.

Pyla, Panayiota, ed. *Landscapes of Development: the Impact of Modernization Discourses on the Physical Environment of the Eastern Mediterranean.* Cambridge, MA: Harvard University Press, 2013.

———. "The Many Lives of New Gourna: Alternative Histories of a Model Community and Their Current Significance." *Journal of Architecture* 14, no. 6 (2009): 715–30.

Schaar, Kenneth, Michael Given, and Giorgios Theocharous. *Under the Clock: Colonial Architecture and History in Cyprus, 1878–1960.* Nicosia: Bank of Cyprus, 1995.

Sinos, Stefanos. *Anadromi sti Laiki Arxitektoniki stin Kipro* [Review of vernacular architecture in Cyprus]. Athens: NTUA, 1975.

Sioulas, Michalis, and Panayiota Pyla, "Technical Schools for Inter-Communal Crisis Management in Mid-20th Century Cyprus." In the proceedings of the conference

Entangled Histories, Multiple Geographies, organized jointly by the University of Belgrade and the European Architectural History Network. Belgrade: University of Belgrade, Faculty of Architecture, 2017, 310–16.

Stratis, Socratis. "Sxeseis metaksi dimosiou kai idiotikou, kai o rolos tis topografias: H Paragogi tou Kypriakou Domimenou Topiou" [Relations between public and private and the role of topography: The production of the Cyprus built landscape]. *Arxitektonika Themata* [Architectural issues] 41 (2007): 66–71.

Taunton, Matthew. *Fictions of the City: Class, Culture and Mass Housing in London and Paris.* London: Palgrave Macmillan, 2009.

Ure, Gavin. *Governors, Politics and the Colonial Office: Public Policy in Hong Kong, 1918–58.* Royal Asiatic Society Hong Kong Studies Series. Hong Kong: Hong Kong University Press, 2012.

MICHALIS SIOULAS is Lecturer in Architecture at Neapolis University, Pafos and researcher at the Mesarch Lab, a research laboratory focusing on the history and theory of modern architecture in the eastern Mediterranean, at the University of Cyprus. Between 2011 and 2013 he was Adjunct Lecturer at the University of Nicosia. He holds a MS in conservation and rehabilitation of historic buildings and sites from the National Technical University of Athens (2009), where he is a PhD candidate. His research focuses on the architecture of Cyprus in the colonial and early postcolonial periods and the industrial heritage of the island.

PANAYIOTA PYLA is Associate Professor of Architecture at the University of Cyprus and previously served on the architecture faculty of the University of Illinois at Urbana-Champaign. She holds a PhD in the history-theory of architecture from the Massachusetts Institute of Technology. Among her works are the coauthored chapter "An Island of Dams: Ethnic Conflict and Supra-national Claims in Cyprus" (with Petros Phokaides) in *Water, Technology and the Nation-State* (Routledge, 2018); the *Journal of Architectural Education* article "Crisis Spins" (2015); the edited volume, *Landscapes of Development: The Impact of Modernization Discourses on the Physical Environment of the Eastern Mediterranean* (Harvard University Aga Khan Program, 2013); and the guest editing of the special issue "Sustainability's Prehistories" of *Design and Culture* (2012).

8

CONSTRUCTED MARGINALITY: WOMEN, PUBLIC HOUSING, AND NATIONAL IDENTITY IN KUWAIT

Mae al-Ansari

PUBLIC PROTEST IN 2006 OVER THE DILAPIDATION OF women's public housing in Sabah al-Salem, Kuwait, caused many to call for the government's repossession of the property.[1] While some blamed the problem on maintenance, others claimed that establishing a homeowners association would resolve challenges and help to implement and regulate security measures. While minimal action has been taken since that time, the concurrent discourse nevertheless highlighted the role of the built environment in intensifying the adverse social conditions of Kuwaiti female-headed households in public housing. In the mid-1980s, the National Housing Authority (NHA) decided to house Kuwaiti widows and divorcees in the Sabah al-Salem Housing Project (SSHP) only after Kuwaiti families declined to live in the apartments. The widows' and divorcees' marginal position as women without male guardians exacerbated their spatial marginalization. The urban displacement (distance) of the apartment housing project from the city center—partly the result of a failed attempt to create a second city center close to Sabah al-Salem neighborhood—as well as SSHP's spatial, programmatic, and stylistic characteristics, seem to further isolate the residents whose social status already alienated them from the neighborhood. Archival records, however, show that SSHP's original urban and architectural conditions were in fact independent of the subsequent gendering of the housing project, and that the architecture's debilitation seems to be mainly correlated to the socioeconomic and political contexts of gendered national identity in Kuwait. Upon close examination, one realizes that SSHP is situated within the vast complexities of nationalism, the intentions of government authorities to appropriate "tradition" and build the nation, the growing demands of urbanization, and the socioeconomic and political implications of gender in Kuwait. These conditions, in the act of nation-building, enabled the normalization of patriarchal relations and the disproportionate access of women to state resources such as public housing, thereby gendering national identities and creating inequality. As a result, the residents' female bodies and the architectural body of SSHP both appear to be encapsulated in adversities that are reflected in the architecture's dilapidation.

SSHP was conceived as part of Kuwait's public-housing program, initiated in the early 1950s with the influx of oil wealth, the institution of a modern welfare state, and rapid urban development in the Old Town. The new "cradle-to-grave" state welfare initiative aimed to offer Kuwaitis modern, single-family detached housing that resembled the affluent villas of the upper class. In the late 1970s, however, the NHA began to develop modern apartment schemes for middle-income families to meet increasing demands for housing. Consequently, SSHP was commissioned as an apartment housing project for low- or limited-income Kuwaiti families in the suburban neighborhood of Sabah al-Salem.[2] But the NHA soon realized that male-headed Kuwaiti families were reluctant to live in apartments, at which time they were offered to nontraditional Kuwaiti families with "different lifestyles and preferences," including divorcees, widows, and Kuwaiti women married to non-Kuwaitis.[3] Over the past three decades, SSHP has undergone variations of appropriation strategies, mainly by its residents, that were meant to tackle growing family demands, poor maintenance on the project grounds, and overcrowding. These appropriations have come to represent residents' marginal positions with regard to gendered nationalism.

Women, National Identity, and Apartment Schemes within Kuwait's Public Housing Initiative

This essay situates the design intentions of SSHP in their original political, economic, social, religious, and historical contexts. The examination of these forces aims to uncover the relationships between state authorities, single mothers (divorcees and widows), and society at large. In its attempt to examine architecture as a text that engages in and reflects on contemporary Middle Eastern societies like Kuwait, particularly during this time of social and political upheaval in the Arab world, the essay helps to improve understanding of the conditions of those community members whom the larger society wishes to make less visible—or hide away—and the complicity of state authorities in creating architectural spaces, on the pretext of providing social housing, in order to fulfill hidden agendas that seem to marginalize women. Kuwait's position as a modern welfare state with a Muslim patriarchal society that is embedded in a longstanding tribal social structure where women have traditionally played the role of unequal participants makes the undertaking of this case study all the more significant.

To that end, the inquiry examines the cultural trends that affected the project's design in late 1970s Kuwait, the distance of SSHP from the city center, and the design decisions taken by the architects and clients. The aim is to understand how marginality and gendered national identities were perhaps intentionally or unintentionally constructed for the project's female residents and how cultural identity might relate to the architectural and social dilapidation witnessed at SSHP. In this pursuit, three themes are examined— systems of center-periphery (distancing and urban dislocation), exclusion (enclosure), and negotiations of the traditional-modern in Kuwaiti nationalist discourse and architectural style. The underlying premise is that, in Kuwait's 1970s and 1980s public-housing discourse, identity is construed within the politics of location (as a physical position and socioeconomic condition).

By examining texts on women and architecture, the essay reveals how gender and nationality have been translated politically and spatially so that certain individuals are granted access to state services whereas others are denied them. In identity discourse, political scientists V. Spike Peterson and Anne Sisson Runyan's notion of "gendered nationalism" articulates the ways in which the manipulation of gender produces inequitable power relations that build and preserve national unity.[4] Likewise, feminist scholar Deniz Kandiyoti illustrates how women's disenfranchised citizenry in nationalist projects creates difference in cultural identity.[5] Moreover, within feminist geography, Tamar Mayer finds that nationalism, nation-building, and the construction of national identity are, ironically, gendered processes that often produce gender divisions between men, who control access to national resources, and women, who carry the burdens of building the nation and maintaining national identity.[6] Notably, ethnic, religious, racial, and class hierarchies, as well as strategies of inclusion and exclusion, have been shown to be crucial to the establishment and renegotiation of gendered national identities.[7] Linda McDowell suggests that spatial scales of embodiment (e.g., body, home, community, city, and nation) also produce gendered divisions that construct identities.[8] These texts reveal the ways in which national identities are constructed and gendered. They also establish that national unity relies on the disparate distribution of resources and privileges among nationals, as well as the paternalistic manipulation of gender. As architecture represents a significant segment of national resources and the symbols of material culture, it becomes an instrument for the state to create and maintain national unity. The analysis of SSHP can therefore be positioned within the complexities of gender and nationality in Kuwait.

SSHP was commissioned as a low-income apartment housing scheme, part of the state's cradle-to-grave welfare mission to supply "every Kuwaiti [with] a modern roof over his head."[9] This government policy stipulated that housing was "available to all Kuwaiti citizens, provided they do not own property and that they form a 'family' (which means a married couple, with or without children)."[10] The goal was to "provide adequate houses in a healthy environment to all [Kuwaiti] citizens who are not able financially to build their own houses."[11] Although the public-housing initiative mostly produced detached and semidetached single-family houses (apartments were generally identified with lower-class, non-Kuwaiti labor housing), Kuwait's NHA ventured into modern high-rise apartment schemes for middle-income families in the late 1970s as a way to reconcile rising land costs, growth in housing demands, a low availability of land, and the obligation to provide efficient, centralized public services.[12]

Between 1976 and 1978, three apartment complexes were commissioned and designed, chronologically, at Sawaber in central Kuwait City (524 units built), East Sulaibikhat, sixteen kilometers southwest of Kuwait City (2,000 units proposed), and Sabah al-Salem, a suburb about nineteen kilometers southeast of Kuwait City (564 units built) (fig. 8.1). By 1983, however, after several housing surveys concluded that apartments were unpopular for middle-income Kuwaiti families, who refused to move into them, the NHA halted plans to design new apartment blocks.[13] At the time, construction in Sabah al-Salem and Sawaber had begun, the East Sulaibikhat project was permanently put on hold, and plans for another complex in northeast Sawaber were canceled because demand for apartments was lacking.[14] SSHP was completed in 1984, but by 1985 it became apparent to the NHA that Kuwaiti families remained reluctant to accept the newly

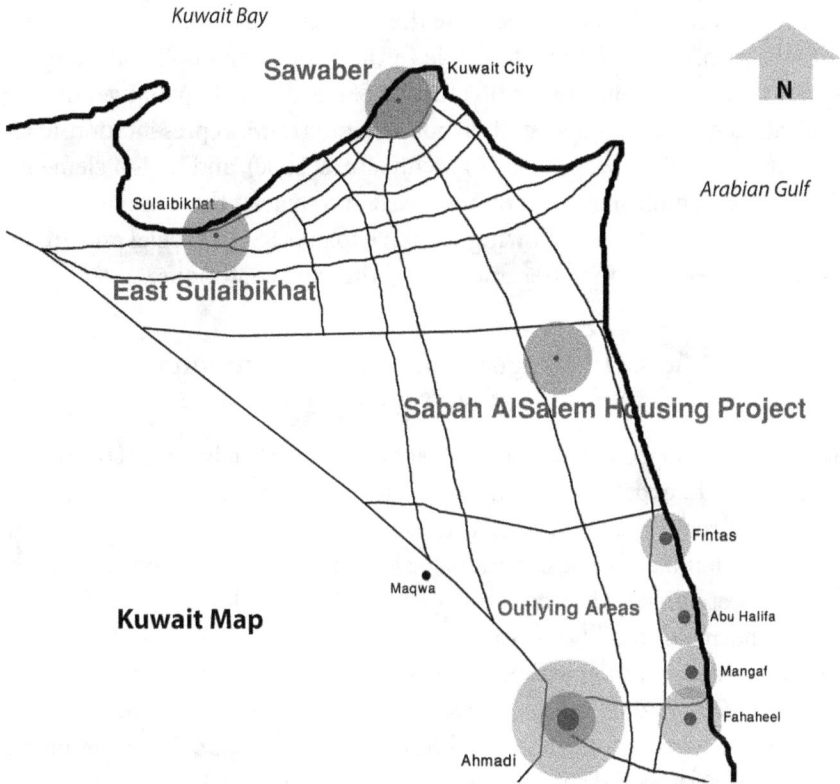

Figure 8.1. Locations of apartment housing projects as well as general locations of Kuwait City, Ahmadi, Fintas, and Fahaheel. Shankland Cox Partnership with Salem al-Marzouk and Sabah Abi Hanna, *Master Plan for Kuwait: First Review 1977 Final Report*, vol. 3, *Supporting Studies* (Kuwait: Municipality of Kuwait, 1977), 61. Extra graphics and text by the author.

completed apartment units. The housing project was then offered to Kuwaiti widows and divorcees either for leasing or purchase according to the socioeconomic means of each woman.[15] The women, who made up a large portion of the low-income group, did not hesitate to occupy the project.[16]

Over the years, the women at SSHP customized their spaces by building additional rooms, incorporating open spaces as storage, and enclosing roof terraces to create extra bedrooms, without government approval. These changes, compounded by overcrowding, subletting, the lack of regular building maintenance, and the absence of a homeowners' organization, have been associated with the project's deterioration and social degeneration. The women's spatial appropriations may not be completely to blame for the project's debilitation, because their positions as vulnerable "women without men" play an important role in their social and political marginalization. In addition, the architecture of SSHP displays spatial gendering (e.g., a male-dominated spatial layout and program), representation (e.g., the government's appropriation of architectural style), and design elements that isolate its buildings from their context and weaken them as constituent parts of the project. The following section explores SSHP's social and architectural dimensions to better understand the site's conditions.

The SSHP Design Competition, Architectural Composition, and Program Components

SSHP was developed as a design competition undertaken by the NHA in November 1977 to experiment with two relatively new housing schemes: apartments and rowhouses. The design brief, which required the provision of a maximum number of housing units for low-income Kuwaiti families, called for a project "designed to conform with the basic traditions of Arabic and Islamic norms of life."[17] The Industrial and Engineering Consulting Office (INCO), in collaboration with Shiber Consultants, was announced as the winner of the competition in February 1978. The project designers were Krzysztof Wisniowski, Wojciech Jarzabek, and Andrzej Bohdanowicz, Polish architects from Wrocław who had been invited by Victor Shiber, principal of Shiber Consultants and younger brother of renowned Arab planner Saba George Shiber, to participate in the competition.[18] While Bohdanowicz had designed the rowhouse scheme, which won third prize, Wisniowski's master plan study and apartment scheme won first prize in the overall competition.[19] After the winning scheme was announced, the architects worked together to develop SSHP's design as affiliates of INCO.[20] In March 1979, INCO reported that design services—including contract documents and services, final working drawings, specifications, preliminary and infrastructure design, and required government approvals —were complete.[21] Although construction was completed in 1984, some buildings were altered between 1985 and 1987. (For the façade circa 1985, see fig. 8.2.) Once the NHA designated SSHP for Kuwaiti widows and divorcees, elevators had to be installed in each stairwell of the project.[22]

SSHP, originally intended to house small Kuwaiti families, comprises 564 apartment units of 160 to 210 square meters distributed on a sixteen-hectare plot in 188 buildings. Each building is essentially a three-story walk-up with a split-level unit of two to four bedrooms per floor.[23] Conceptually,

Figure 8.2. Photograph taken from SSHP's parking lot showing façades along the pedestrian walkway, Sabah al-Salem, Kuwait, ca. 1985. The image shows the vertical circulation core of the three-story apartment structures, the core's connection to each apartment, the recessed bedroom windows with flowerbeds and shading devices, and the sequences of arches on the pedestrian level. Photograph by Krzysztof Wisniowski.

the traditional Kuwaiti house with its linked courtyards and small gardens was the inspiration for the design. Wisniowski wanted to create a pedestrian axis linking each three-story structure to the next in an organic additive approach. The design was intended to foster a sense of community (fig. 8.3).[24] The architect underlined the importance of pedestrian walkways, landscaping, separate circulation routes for automobiles, and an independent master

Figure 8.3. Site model of SSHP showing the project's overall design scheme, building heights, and spatial relationships, ca. 1978. INCO Archive, Kuwait.

plan, which he called a "self-sufficient plan" that included schools, kindergartens, and a mosque. He noted that the commercial facilities presently on the site were part of the original scheme and that the purpose of the walkway axis was to introduce a pedestrian avenue that could connect the apartments. It is interesting to note that visitor parking as well as the traditional male-only *diwaniya* spaces received special attention in SSHP's design.[25] Their convenient locations within the site (with facilitated pedestrian and vehicular access), as well as the *diwaniya*'s lower-ground-level position and separation from the main housing levels, illustrate their programmatic and cultural significance.

By reading SSHP's program features as representations of political agendas and state ideology, one can recognize the intentions of the NHA for Kuwaitis of low income. For the state, the stable family unit is important, and therefore the government fosters the family unit through its housing policy. In this context, income level is clearly related to family size and the nature of activities accommodated in the project. For example, the allocation of four bedrooms in most apartments (276) implies the encouragement of large families that have at least three children.[26] Moreover, while literature on public housing in Kuwait claims that the low-income residents were generally allotted three bedrooms and residents of middle-income were allotted *at least* three bedrooms, SSHP encompasses a greater variety of bedroom configurations that blur the distinctions of income level.[27] Before 1977, middle-income groups could apply for a "land and loan" option to build their homes. In 1984, however, the middle- and low-income classifications were merged into a unified government housing category after complaints about discrimination based on income level were received.[28]

The insistence on continuing the *diwaniya* as a program component that links back to the traditional Kuwaiti courtyard house underscores the patriarchal nature of Kuwaiti society. It also can be read as the state's cognizance of the importance of maintaining "tradition" (i.e., in the form of the males' *diwaniya*—a traditionally gendered space), as well as its acquiescence to public opinion even if it excludes the opposite sex.[29] In addition, the provision of visitor parking suggests the furtherance of social interaction and networking, which are important exchanges in Kuwaiti society and would most probably serve to promote *diwaniya* activity. Alternatively, one might claim that the presence of internal courtyards at SSHP, symbolizing the traditional female harem, creates a balance of gendered spaces.[30] But courtyard spaces were introduced to the design scheme by the architect and were not required as an original program component. Therefore, it may be observed that the architect's—not the state's—introduction of courtyards into the design infuses it with a more gender-balanced program. In all, SSHP's program is a testament to the state's promotion of a patriarchal social structure founded upon the male-headed family unit, or the basic component of Kuwaiti identity.

Social Displacements: A Community Marginalized

Several of the social aspects found at SSHP—for example, property ownership, citizenship, and nationality, as well as the fostered sense of community—participate in the gendering of public housing, the creation of social conflict among residents, and the construction of marginality. These forces—through the imperatives of preserving tradition and building the nation—become tools for the normalization of patriarchal relations and the asymmetrical distribution of rights to certain citizens.

Namely, the overwhelming presence of female-headed households at SSHP, popularly known as the "widows and divorcees complex," seems to have gendered apartment living within Kuwait's public-housing schemes as a women's accommodation.[31] Moreover, SSHP's conflicts over owner-ship and upkeep stem partly from a structural problem involving the way the units are distributed by governing bodies.[32] For example, project oc-cupancy is made up of a large mix of owners and tenants. The breakdown of apartment owners to renters, according to a 2006 press release, follows: 70 to 75 units owned with titles; 144 permanent apartments without titles; 208 rental apartments without titles; and 129 short-term lease apartments being transitioned into rental apartments.[33] This mix of owners and renters has discouraged the formation of a close-knit community by causing social problems. For one, an owner may live in her apartment, sell it, or lease it to anyone of her choice without prior notice to any governing body (e.g., a housing board or government authority). Additionally, renters approved by the government often sublet their units and move in with relatives to gen-erate a monthly income (around 300KD).[34] This has led to criminalization and conflict among residents.

Furthermore, the presence of government offices on the premises at SSHP functions as state surveillance of residents.[35] In addition, the Min-istry of Social Affairs and Labor conducts unannounced house visits to inspect the women's conditions, and the visits are occasions of embarrass-ment, especially in front of neighbors.[36] These practices with residents of public housing can easily eliminate residents' sense of freedom and au-thority over their lives and foster a sense of powerlessness in their dwelling units.[37] Through the paternalistic governmental gaze, the resident becomes self-aware and powerless to her compromised position socially and spa-tially. Social marginalization and stigmatization are further intensified by such visits.[38]

Over time, SSHP underwent major alterations to its original structures as residents attempted to accommodate their domiciles and face the dev-astating consequences of a lack of regular maintenance and the absence of homeowners' regulations. As a result, unsanitary and dangerous condi-tions have become everyday experiences for residents: overcrowded park-ing, water damage, hazardous trash compilation and storage in odd places, the overflow of sewage lines, bricks detaching and falling off of façades, the illegal addition of accessibility ramps and concrete steps at ground level, the enclosure of roof terraces and balconies without approval, and the un-hygienic raising of chickens.[39] This situation has caused the destruction of original architectural features like arched windows and air-conditioning containers custom-designed to serve as shading devices. Furthermore, building additions and alterations have required that independent contractors replace original building materials (sand-lime bricks locally produced by the National Industries Company) with different and aesthetically incompatible materials (e.g., corrugated aluminum and exposed concrete blocks). These issues, in addition to problems of investment subletting and overcrowding, have created conflicts between residents that led to police intervention. While the changes to SSHP's structures may not specifically reflect a gendering component, they nevertheless shed light on the neglect of the housing project by the NHA, as well as the resident women's plight in coping with the consequences. These conditions have prompted many women to speak out in the media.

Spatial Displacements: Urban Dislocations and Alienating Enclosures

SSHP's urban and architectural characteristics provide further examples of the project's gendering and spatial displacement through its urban dislocation, alienating enclosure, and regionalist architectural style. For instance, the distant siting of the project bespeaks its urban dislocation, while its enclosed structure creates an interiorized environment that isolates itself from its neighborhood. Also, the attempt to reproduce a regionalist architectural style by implementing traditional motifs and spatial elements at SSHP has created an environment of inauthenticity and superficiality. Although SSHP is not the only regionalist project with traditional motifs in Kuwait, its superficially regional style, when juxtaposed with the project's function as housing for divorcees and widows, brings into question the legitimacy and honor of its female residents.

First, the suburban location of SSHP outside of the city center results in spatial dislocation and social displacement for its resident divorcees and widows. With distance created between the city center and the site of the project, physical access and spatial mobility become limited. In turn, this constrains the residents' opportunities for economic gain, which is in fact a prerequisite to qualify for this type of housing.[40] In order to qualify for low-income housing, Kuwaiti women must be divorced or widowed, unemployed, and on social welfare, and they must have at least one child. Childless divorcees and widows do not qualify for housing and are expected to reside with relatives, especially if they are of desirable marriage age (under forty). Physical distancing also dissociates these women from other family members, who often live in the inner neighborhood units closer to the city center, thereby severing social ties that form crucial links of financial and emotional support for them. Urban exclusion and social displacement result, space is reorganized according to marital and economic status, and the social group inhabiting these quarters is reconstituted as powerless and underprivileged.

As noted, the government's original intention was not the urban distancing of SSHP or the housing of women in the project. In reality, the project's siting occurred in line with the government's urban development scheme along Kuwait's southern coastline, and the allocation of SSHP to women seems to have come about as a last-minute resort in order to occupy the project. Urban expansion schemes established in the 1960s planned an outward growth of urbanization from Kuwait City along the southern coast.[41] By the 1950s, many isolated villages had already emerged near Fahaheel, and so it seemed natural that urbanization would progress toward these areas. Moreover, the 1971 National Master Plan designed by Colin Buchanan and Partners, who had been involved in Kuwait's urbanization since its initial planning stages, proposed to decentralize the Central Business District and relieve transportation pressures by establishing the nearby Fintas neighborhood as the "second major urban centre in the State of Kuwait."[42] This secondary center would also support areas where industrial labor housing was set up near Ahmadi and Fahaheel (see fig. 8.1). By 1980, architect Arthur Erickson had proposed designs for the Fintas Town Center, but plans were halted and the project was not built. This suggests that, had plans to create another urban center so close to Sabah al-Salem neighborhood become a reality, perhaps SSHP would not be regarded in the same way today—at least from the perspective of urban displacement.

Consequently, plans to disperse the population were not completely carried out. This might be attributed to political and economic factors that may have diminished the rights and privileges of those in the center. Employment and real-estate values remained anchored at the city center even though commercial centers, schools, housing, and public services became suburbanized and spatially detached from the center. There remains social gravitation toward the city center as a cultural node and site of Old Kuwait; the historical hub of commercial, social, religious, and political activities that has come to symbolize what many consider to be authentic Kuwaiti culture and heritage.[43] The closer to the center one lives, the greater the prestige, power, and privilege one is presumed to have. Complex

Figure 8.4. View over SSHP taken ca. 1990 shows the extent to which the project became an isolated "city within a city," Sabah al-Salem, Kuwait. National Housing Authority, *Annual Report 1990 [al-kitab al-sanawi 1990]* (Kuwait: n.p., n.d.), 89.

power relations play a role in how urban spaces and built environments are produced and socially valued. In this case, proximity to the center is a measure of patriotism, ethnic authenticity, and nationality. As a result, real-estate values increase remarkably moving toward the city center. And even though, for various reasons, the Sawaber Housing project failed to entice Kuwaitis of means to live there, its centrally located and prestigious siting remains a mark of privilege for the Kuwaiti family.[44]

Architecturally, both Sawaber Housing and SSHP attempted to re-create the prominent detached villa of the Kuwaiti family.[45] But the SSHP scheme's inability to produce a social or spatial condition comparable to that of the villa renders it a work of mimicry, wherein it is "almost a villa but not quite," creating a sense of "almost Kuwaiti but not quite."[46] A double articulation of sameness and difference is produced here through repetition and distancing that reveals the appropriation of an "other" through discipline and reform, the repercussions of which are felt most distinctly by the residents of SSHP, who are alienated and stigmatized within their society. The apartment, as a result, is not a legitimate space for living; it loses value, authenticity, and honorability. The irony here is that, in the noble act of housing low-income single mothers, an identity of disenfranchisement develops, and the suffering they endure is normalized and controlled.

In terms of site layout, SSHP's original concept proposed open green space near the adjacent neighborhood center and internal courtyards that symbolized the single-family social unit. The original scheme incorporated significant landscaping in the courtyards (e.g., water features, seating areas, trees), but the ideas were discarded by the NHA.[47] Large green areas were suggested to envelope the project and create aesthetically pleasing spaces, but they also were turned down. Consequently, the leftover open spaces bordering SSHP became a buffer zone or no-man's-land that distances and separates the project from neighboring homes and public facilities. Within the project's interior, the courtyard sequencing produces axes that visually pull the buildings in toward the large open central space, further highlighting the external and isolating empty spaces. As a result, the project forms a city-within-a-city model that segregates the project grounds from the neighborhood context (fig. 8.4).

Appropriating and Remaking Arab-Islamic Regionalism

The design's adoption of stylistic motifs such as the arch, courtyard, and "traditional Arab-Islamic city" as elements of regionalism to bridge modern and traditional design further complicates and intensifies the condition of isolation at SSHP. The pursuit risks the conjuring of memory and nostalgia, which romanticize regionalism and give way to kitsch and pastiche.[48] In the process of appropriating traditional motifs in modern spaces, a separation from the authentic center occurs that isolates the new (peripheral) regional identity. Moreover, since regionalism aims to represent architectural and cultural authenticity, then "any claim to regionalism is bound to remain a mimetic and reductive exercise."[49]

On the other hand, regionalism, which emphasizes the opposition between geographical distance and globalization, has been used in Western inquiry to establish and frame cultural difference with the East. Within that process, Eastern culture and architecture are construed as irrational, romantic, and backward.[50] This position, which draws from Edward Said's *Orientalism*, is also prevalent in postcolonial feminist discourse, which claims that the Orientalized East has been constructed as feminine in opposition to a masculine West.[51] At SSHP, the appropriation of elements such as courtyards, arches, and enclosures recalls regionalist (Arab-Islamic) architectural identity. The action also conjures up concerns about postcolonial

Figure 8.5. Arab-Islamic architectural elements are incorporated into the design of SSHP: "blank walls, little openings, single entrances," Sabah al-Salem, Kuwait, 2014. Photograph by Mae al-Ansari.

spaces and their feminization. One might question here whether the architect's use of traditional motifs to produce "regionalist" architecture limits his design to an essentialism of Eastern cultural signifiers.

For the project's foreign architect (Wisniowski), SSHP was an exercise in incorporating his extensive knowledge of Arab-Islamic architecture into Kuwait's built environment. It is unsurprising that he seems to incorporate Western conceptions of what Arab architecture looks like (or should look like), which he describes as "blank walls, little openings, single entrances" (fig. 8.5).[52] Nevertheless, the architect pays close attention to privacy, introducing private spaces and discerning them from the public in elements like split-level floors and entry thresholds. He also provides garden decks, balconies, and patios that overlook the internal courts in order to frame views and create spatial variety. The innovative split-level approach adopted at SSHP can be linked to social housing trends in late 1970s Polish architecture publications such as Association of Polish Architects' *Architektura*, which presented competition entries and case studies that incorporated split-level rowhouses as part of a postmodern and regionalist (and government-contested) design approach.[53]

For the commissioning client (the NHA), adopting regionalism seems to have been interpreted as a sign of loyalty to Islam, the Arab community, and the Kuwaiti nation. For example, the competition design brief for SSHP explicitly requires the design of housing fit for "Arab and Islamic norms of life" of the Kuwaiti family.[54] By choosing INCO's design for SSHP, the NHA clearly enforced their loyalties and revealed partiality for formalistic representations of Arab-Islamic culture.[55] Thus, the selection of an architectural design close in formal composition to what was locally recognized as regionalist and Arab-Islamic announced the state's political alliances and ideological agenda. It also provided a physical manifestation of the prevalent Arab-Islamic movement, which took over the Middle East and filled powerful government positions in the late 1970s. Ghazi Sultan, Kuwaiti architect and partner at Kuwait Engineering Corporation, attested to this powerful trend in the state's public housing at the April 1978 "Architectural Transformations in the Islamic World" seminars (organized as a precursor to the first Agha Khan Award for Architecture):

> The only way you can evaluate [religion] is the way it is interpreted and used by the people in power, the people who make decisions. . . . The Ministry of Housing was taken over by very devout Muslims about three years ago. It started at the top and went all the way through. We were asked to come and do a project for them, a quite large one, about six hundred or seven hundred houses for three thousand to four thousand families. . . .
>
> We were asked to develop ten alternative housing plans, each one for different types of people from medium income to very poor for different social status and different types of families. These ranged from courtyard houses to the duplex system to the individual house. . . . [The client] said, "This is contradictory to all values of Islam, this is an Islamic country. You have produced houses for American families. They are not for Arabs, the people of Islam. . . . You have to put four walls on each and every room, and you must be absolutely sure that the woman of the house can walk from one part of the house to the other and be totally sure that no strangers will see her." . . .
>
> The rest of the designs were thrown out, and only the houses which had this division were accepted. . . .

> This is not one client. These people handle the equivalent of twenty thousand housing units a year.[56]

Sultan's remarks provide a glimpse into the decision-making processes and power dynamics at play in the Ministry of Housing and NHA that shaped housing as an instrument of public policy and an architectural type in late 1970s Kuwait. His comments are pertinent, especially because Sultan was former director of Kuwait's Master Planning Department and was accustomed to the routines of government projects.[57] What he encountered in 1978 at the Ministry of Housing was evidently not considered normal before 1975. This prompts questions about the apparent Islamicization of regionalism in Kuwait at this time.[58] The Islamic style—by the end of the 1970s and well into the 1980s—was synonymous with the national Kuwaiti style, such that the categories "region" and "nation" were apparently collapsed into the "Islamic."

One element that symbolizes the Arab-Islamic architectural heritage at SSHP is the arch. But the use of arches in series or sequences here creates a filter or veiling mechanism that obscures visual exposure to the site (fig. 8.6). This element has allowed for the introduction of contemporary spaces of secrecy within the project, which is deemed taboo for women in modern society. Thereby, the arches that are meant to offer privacy and protect the honor of women in traditional Arab-Islamic architecture have been transformed into modern elements that harbor deviance, shame, and criminalization for the women at SSHP. In addition, the veiling arches become a perversion of the honorable, traditional Arab-Islamic motif. This further emphasizes the project's feminization, and when compared with the design approach adopted by Erickson at Sawaber Housing—characterized by a modernist absence of stylistic motifs and occupied by honorable legitimate Kuwaiti families—difference and otherness are clearly articulated.

SSHP's courtyards are other indicators of Arab-Islamic architectural identity. Wisniowski sought complexity by repeating and sequencing courtyards at SSHP, his very first building project. Later, for the Shuwaikh Port Complex (1992), he duplicated four small courtyards and plotted them in four corners within a larger square court to centralize the building. At the Ministry of Interior headquarters (2011), he adopted a courtyard-within-a-courtyard concept to produce a centralized office building.[59] But through the processes of repetition and duplication, which resemble operations of

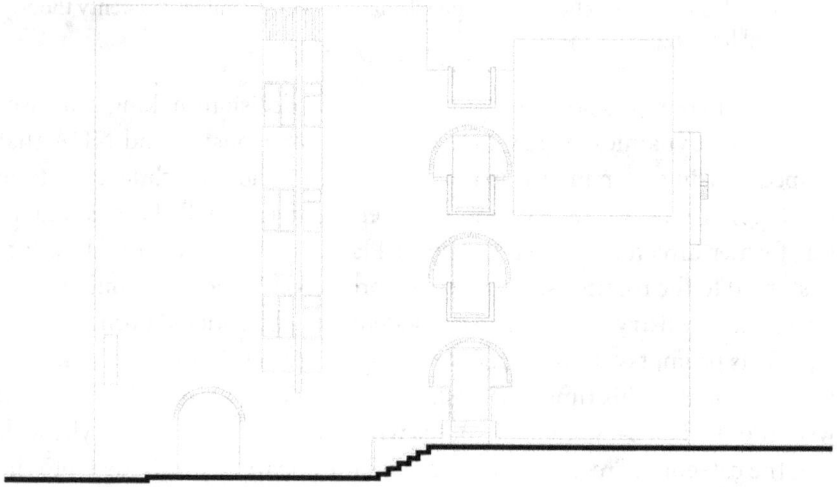

Figure 8.6. The "veiling" arches at SSHP. PAHW Archives, Kuwait.

mass production, the decontextualization, depoliticization, and degendering of the traditional courtyard motif occurs. The courtyard has been reconfigured in contemporary terms mimicking modern forms for modern functions.

Consequently, the courtyards at SSHP have become abandoned.[60] Empty signifiers remain, with spatial and formal relationships of proximity to nearby apartment blocks, landscaped areas, and axes resulting from the alignment of the courtyards, which regulate and discipline program components and create order and spatial hierarchy within the project (fig. 8.7). The architect's intention was to organize the site by applying an organic approach and to use repetitions of courtyards and arches to produce a hybrid architectural identity and meet program requirements of the client.[61] For residents, however, views, activities, and movement are also conditioned by these relationships. When the courtyard loses its social, cultural, and historical significance without being attached to new or pertinent meanings (e.g., if the courtyards were to lead somewhere), it becomes an artificial component. This artificiality would perhaps partly explain the forms of aggression the project grounds have witnessed (e.g., graffiti and defacement) since SSHP's completion (fig. 8.8).

Connotations of the "Arab city" are also present in SSHP's design, and they further complicate the project. Art historian Udo Kultermann, author

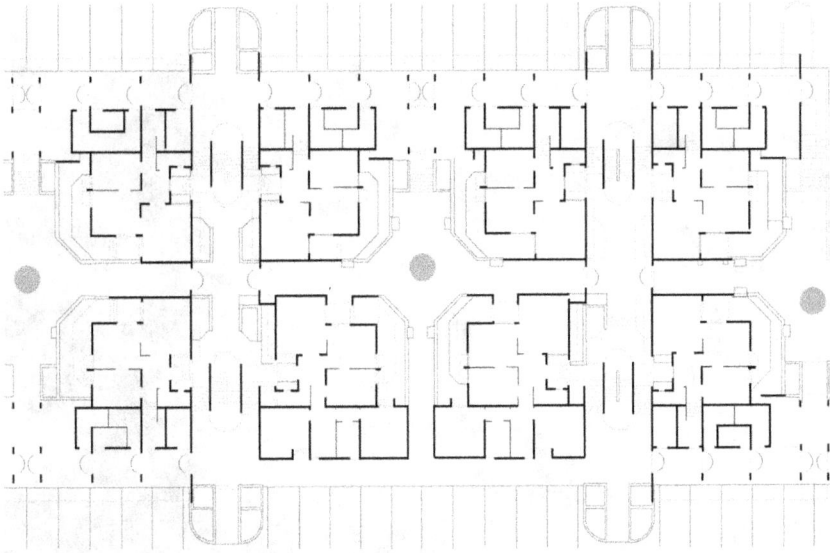

Figure 8.7. Wisniowski's 1977 courtyard scheme for SSHP reincorporated the traditional courtyard to forge a new and hybrid architectural identity. INCO Archive, Kuwait.

of *Contemporary Architecture in the Arab States*, describes the "Arab city" model as a "continuous architecture" that is the most important link between city and building in contemporary Arab architecture.[62] In Kultermann's words, the Arab city model is a "meaningful neighborhood organization of the urban community" that is characterized by a fluidity within the physical, spiritual, and commercial amenities uniting building, street, and plaza and eliminating borders.[63] Ironically, at SSHP a romanticized model of the Arab city exists that creates an isolated complex that is socially and spatially set apart from the community. Considering the project's physical separation from the rest of the neighborhood, the apparent discontinuity of what Kultermann might call "continuous architecture" further isolates the site. Solid walls, left blank in homage to Kuwaiti courtyard houses and the fortified gates of traditional Arab cities, have in contemporary times become signs of internalization and spatial exclusion (figs. 8.4 and 8.8). Moreover, the empty center that connects the project with the neighboring commercial center implies a self-centering that distances the site from its surroundings. The result is spatial stigmatization of the already socially stigmatized divorcees and widows that reflects their disenfranchisement in a neglected and isolated housing complex.

Figure 8.8. Evidence of graffiti and defacement at SSHP, Sabah al-Salem, Kuwait, 2014. Photograph by Mae al-Ansari.

Notably, cultural theorists and architectural historians have considered the connection between architecture, the female body, and the construction of identity.[64] For example, art historian Helen Hills explores the concept of architecture-as-body when examining convents in early modern Italy and suggests that confinement inside the convent constructs a social identity particular to nuns living within that private space dedicated to personal sacrifice and religious worship. Architectural devices like layers of curtains, screens, grilles, bars, and choirs deter the female gaze, which threatens to ruin a nun's chastity. But at the same time, as a metaphor for the nun's body, the convent is made publicly invisible through architecture.[65] Similarly, SSHP, as an architectural "body" with low visibility (e.g., in its solid walls and veiling arches), reflects the particularly marginalized social identities of its "invisible" resident women.

Constructing Marginality

At SSHP, the construction of marginality has not only been demonstrated in the project's spatial and social displacements, but the appropriation of architectural style brings to the forefront the intentions of nationhood.[66] Architectural historian Gwendolyn Wright claims that "Seeking to preserve a supposed purity or superiority in race, religion, nationhood, or cultural preferences, people often turn against other groups and alternative points of view."[67] Similarly, political scientist Mary Ann Tetreault and sociologist Haya al-Mughni forewarn that nationalist policies that continuously subordinate women have not succeeded in Kuwait, where the family unit is politicized and employed to sustain national unity, and women living outside this norm receive disparate access to resources like public housing in Sabah al-Salem.[68]

In the scope of public housing in Kuwait, women have occupied a space in between. In consequence, this example illustrates and problematizes the dire need to integrate excluded and less-visible groups. But SSHP is not an isolated precedent of marginalization in the Arab world. Recently, scholars have documented the divisiveness of residential and social segregation in Arab cities such as Abu Dhabi, Cairo, Dubai, Manama, and Riyadh on the basis of categories like ethnicity and income level.[69] Considered within the regional context of more recent political shifts in the aftermath of the Arab Spring as well as worldwide calls for greater social sustainability and urban inclusiveness, it is imperative to address issues encompassing women's housing.[70] These issues include improving public-housing-allocation policies, increasing the affordability of homeownership, promoting mass transit and zero-commute living, implementing residential zoning reform for extended families, encouraging collective housing types (e.g., residential conversions and accessory apartments), and designing flexible architectural spaces that accommodate growth and changes such as these.[71]

Conclusion

The 2006 protests at SSHP helped to bring attention to the site's social and architectural devastation resulting from multiple processes involving nation-building, urbanization, gender, the appropriation of architecture, and the construction of national identities. Accordingly, this essay has proposed that SSHP demonstrates an architectural narration of being "almost Kuwaiti but not quite" by suggesting that gendered nationalism is operating through the disparate distribution of public housing units (as a Kuwaiti entitlement). Moreover, the project's architectural and urban characteristics had been determined before SSHP was gendered as a housing project for divorcees and widows. Despite the state's objectionable interventions (e.g., the NHA's disproportionate distribution of apartments rather than villas to these women and the Ministry of Social Affairs and Labor's stigmatizing visits), a direct architectural intention to create marginality for residents of SSHP does not seem to exist. Rather, the architecture's dilapidation has worked as a correlational circumstance that signifies the socioeconomic devastation present on site. Nevertheless, it is important to recognize that the design decisions that were made at SSHP have increased the alienation, segregation, and isolation of its resident widows and divorcees, a condition that intensifies the social marginalization these women already face because they lack male guardianship. The analysis prompts further questions like these: How might the female body and architecture be connected in the contexts of Kuwait, the Arab world, and the Middle East? How might Arab-Islamic regionalism, as an apparently Orientalized or inferior architectural style, have become gendered or marginalized through the search for national identity? What is the state's role in this process? The inquiry necessitates an increase in the visibility of feminized spaces like SSHP in addition to their consideration as architectural settings reflective of past and present socioeconomic and political conditions locally, regionally, and globally.

Unfortunately, the Kuwaiti government's recent decision to tear down Sawaber Housing portends a similar fate that may await SSHP.[72] It is unclear at this point, however, how demolition might affect SSHP's female residents, especially since the Public Authority for Housing Welfare has proclaimed apartment living the primary Kuwaiti public-housing type for the future.[73] While this might lead to more equal or selective allocation of housing for these women (e.g., special accommodations near family members), it might also cause further marginalization and public outcry as the sense of entitlement and competition for state resources (e.g., land and financial capability) rises among citizens.[74]

Acknowledgments

This essay is based on the author's PhD dissertation (2016), and portions of the text have been adapted from the dissertation manuscript. Earlier versions of this text have been presented at Taft Research Center's "humanitiesNOW" graduate conference (University of Cincinnati, March 4–6, 2015) and DAKAM's ArchTheo'15 conference (Istanbul, Turkey, November 5–6, 2015). I would like to gratefully thank Mr. Mohammed al-Sinan (INCO) for providing archival data, drawings, and images that were crucial to this study. I would also like to thank Mr. Krzysztof Wisniowski for the interviews, drawings, images, and personal information he graciously shared about working in both Poland and Kuwait. Finally, I would like to recognize the efforts of those without whom this body of work would not be complete: my PhD advisors at the University of Cincinnati and the architects, planners, engineers, and archivists at the Master Planning Department of Kuwait Municipality, the Public Authority for Housing Welfare (Kuwait), and the National Library of Kuwait.

Notes

1. Fahad al-Hajri, "Ladies of the Sabah al-Salem Complex: 'Protestors at the National Assembly Don't Represent Us'" [Sayyedaat mujama' sabah alsalem: allawati tajama'na amam majles alomma la yomathelnana], *al-Qabas*, March 14, 2006, http://www.alqabas.com.kw /node/141634.

2. Industrial and Engineering Consulting Office (INCO), "Sabah al-Salem Housing Project," project documents, INCO Archives, Kuwait. The terms "low-income" and "limited-income" here are interchangeable as an effect of translation in government documents and academic literature. The original term is in Arabic (*thawi aldakhl almahdood*), and different authors have translated it to English as either low- or limited-income. In this case, mentioning both translations recognizes the variety of terms present in the literature.

3. Rula Muhammad Sadik, "Nation-Building and Housing Policy: A Comparative Analysis of Urban Housing Development in Kuwait, Jordan, and Lebanon" (PhD diss., University of California, Berkeley, 1996), 257–58.

4. V. Spike Peterson and Anne Sisson Runyan, *Global Gender Issues*, 2nd ed., Dilemmas in World Politics (Boulder, CO: Westview, 1999), 192.

5. Deniz Kandiyoti, "Identity and Its Discontents: Women and the Nation," *Millennium* 20 (1991): 431, 440.

6. Tamar Mayer, *Gender Ironies of Nationalism: Sexing the Nation* (London: Routledge, 2002).

7. Ida Blom, Karen Hagemann, and Catherine Hall, eds., *Gendered Nations: Nationalisms and Gender Order in the Long Nineteenth Century* (New York: Berg, 2000).

8. Linda McDowell, *Gender, Identity, and Place: Understanding Feminist Geographies* (Minneapolis: University of Minnesota Press, 1999).

9. Jane Carroll, "Housing: A Roof over Every Head," *MEED Special Report* (1980): 38.

10. Ibid.

11. Abdulhadi M. Alawadi, "Low- and Middle-Income Housing in Kuwait," *Habitat International* 4 (1979): 340.

12. Bader al-Eisa, "A Qualitative Study: The Low and Middle-Income Housing Problem in the State of Kuwait" (PhD diss., University of Minnesota, 1985), 83. There is some misunderstanding about whether apartment schemes in Kuwait were for middle- or low-income groups. Most literature on Kuwait's public-housing history states that apartments were specifically designated for middle-income families. Project documents, however, refer to SSHP as a LIG project.

13. Abdulkarim al-Dekhayel, "The Role of the State in Housing," in *Kuwait: Oil, State and Political Legitimation* (Reading, UK: Ithaca, 2000), 144.

14. "Kuwait: Infrastructure and Services; High-Rise Debate Stalls Housing Effort," *MEED Special Report* (1983): 67–68.

15. To qualify for the government-subsidized welfare-housing program, female public-housing recipients must be Kuwaiti, without income or property, and previously married with children. Kuwaiti divorcees and widows with Kuwaiti children are offered ownership contracts with the possibility of receiving a title once subsidized payment is complete, and those with non-Kuwaiti children are given rental leases because only citizens can own property in the state. Once the mothers of non-Kuwaitis pass away, the government takes possession of the property. See Sadik, "Nation-Building," 287; Mary Ann Tetreault and Haya al-Mughni, "Modernization and Its Discontents: State and Gender in Kuwait," *Middle East Journal* 49 (1995): 403–17; Mary Ann Tetreault and Haya al-Mughni, "Gender, Citizenship and Nationalism in Kuwait," *British Journal of Middle Eastern Studies* 22 (1995): 64–80.

16. The qualifying monthly income is designated as 250 Kuwaiti dinars (around US$825) and below.

17. INCO, "Sabah al-Salem."

18. The Wrocław architects were able to work in Kuwait through labor contracts with Polservice, the central agency in socialist Poland, which mediated the exchange of professional, technical, and labor services with other countries. See Lukasz Stanek, "Mobilities of Architecture in the Global Cold War: From Socialist Poland to Kuwait and Back," *International Journal of Islamic Architecture* 4 (2015): 369.

19. Krzysztof Wisniowski, personal interview by author, Kuwait City, January 11, 2015. During the interview, Wisniowski clarified that SSHP had not been designed exclusively for women. The decision to house women at SSHP was made after INCO had completed design services and the project was built. In addition, a preliminary search seemed to suggest that none of the designing parties had worked specifically with gender issues in their architectural practice or writing.

20. For the purposes of this chapter and because SSHP was developed according to Wisniowski's original scheme, reference is made to Wisniowski as the project's architect or designer. The author acknowledges that contributions by Bohdanowicz and Jarząbek were made in the project's design development and that credit for the project belongs to INCO.

21. INCO, "Sabah al-Salem." For details on the circumstances of SSHP's design, see Mae al-Ansari, "Masked in the Protective Act: Women, Public Housing, and the Construction of 'Modern/National' Identities in Kuwait" (PhD diss., University of Cincinnati, 2016), 136–41.

22. For more on low-income housing in Kuwait, see Shankland Cox Partnership and Salem AlMarzouk and Sabah Abi Hanna, *Master Plan for Kuwait: First Review 1977 Final Report*, vol. 3, *Supporting Studies* (Kuwait: Municipality of Kuwait, 1977), 50–51.

23. National Housing Authority, "Sabah al-Salem Block 9 Apartments," in *Annual Report 1990 [Al-kitab al-sanawi 1990]* (Kuwait: National Housing Authority, 1990), 105.

24. Wisniowski interview.

25. The *diwaniya* is a male-only social space particular to Kuwaiti culture. Within the traditionally gender-segregated Kuwaiti courtyard house, the *diwaniya* served as a space for the male head of the household to host male visitors and conduct business with other men. It has been carried over into contemporary architectural spaces as a cultural preserver reserved exclusively for Kuwaiti males, and it functions as an important site for the proliferation of local economic, religious, social, and political discourse. For more on the *diwaniya* in traditional Kuwaiti architecture, see Saleh A. al-Mutawa, *History of Architecture in Old Kuwait City and the Influence of Its Elements on the Architect* (Kuwait: AlKhat, 1994), 18–19; Ronald Lewcock, *Traditional Architecture in Kuwait and the Northern Gulf* (London: Art and Archaeology Research Papers, 1978), 2–10.

26. The occupancy ratio for Kuwaitis in 1975 averaged 1.8 persons per room. With that in mind, the four-bedroom unit at SSHP might comfortably house eight family members. See al-Eisa, "Qualitative Study," 63.

27. Alawadi, "Low- and Middle-Income," 342; al-Eisa, "Qualitative Study," 83. The middle-income group is also referred to as the average income group in academic literature and government documents. To note, the NHA began offering housing to middle-income families as early as 1977, at which time the design competition for SSHP was just beginning. See Omar Khattab and Adil al-Mumin, "The Evolution of Public Housing Policies in Kuwait from 1960s to 1990s," *International Journal for Housing Science and Its Applications* 24 (2000): 355; al-Eisa, "Qualitative Study," 51.

28. Al-Eisa, "Qualitative Study," 84; al-Dekhayel, "Role of the State," 144.

29. The decision to maintain tradition through the preservation of the *diwaniya* is a complicated topic that prompts further examination in relation to gender in Kuwait. See, for example, Mohammad al-Jassar, "Constancy and Change in Contemporary Kuwait City: The Socio-Cultural Dimensions of the Kuwaiti Courtyard and *Diwaniyya*" (PhD diss., University of Wisconsin–Milwaukee, 2009), 192–216; Mohammed al-Ajmi, "History of Architecture in Kuwait: The Evolution of Traditional Kuwaiti Architecture Prior to the Discovery of Oil" (PhD diss., University of Nebraska, 2009), 144–54.

30. The Kuwaiti house traditionally employed courtyards as private outdoor spaces within the family home. These acted as integral spatial joints and catered to household needs through gender segregation. For example, an affluent Kuwaiti house would have (in order of importance) a business courtyard, a men's courtyard, a family (women's) courtyard, a kitchen courtyard, and an animal courtyard. In the family and kitchen courtyards, the women would spend their days carrying out household chores. Hence researchers often refer to the polarity between the "male" *diwaniya* and the "female" courtyard. See Lewcock, *Traditional Architecture*, 2–10; al-Jassar, "Constancy," 166–73; al-Ajmi, "History," 144–54; Mae al-Ansari, "Irreducible Essence: Tectonics and Cultural Expression in Traditional Forms of Kuwaiti Dwelling" (master's thesis, University of Cincinnati, 2011), 57–60.

31. Tarek al-Aidan, "Citizens Unaccounted for by the Government" [Muwatenoon saqatoo men hesaabaat alhokooma], *al-Qabas*, February 9, 2009, https://alqabas.com/old/?ajax=1&article=463994&highlight=جالت20%القبس.

32. Ibid. This is a complicated and often confusing partnership between the Ministry of Housing, the Ministry of Social Affairs and Labor, and other government agencies.

33. "Sabah al-Salem Residential Complex Renovation Team Redistributes Eight Apartments to Kuwaiti Women" [Fareeq 'amal tatweer mujama' sabah alsalem alsakani yuwazze' thamani shiqaq li muwatenat kuwaitiyat], Kuwait News Agency (KUNA), May 31, 2006, http://www.kuna.net.kw/ArticleDetails.aspx?id=1614142&language=ar.

34. Kuwaiti dinars; roughly equal to US$1,000.

35. "Hammad: Sabah al-Salem Housing Residents Complain of Security Checkpoint That Restricts Their Freedom" [Hammad: qatenat mujama' sabah alsalem yashtakeen men nuqta amniya toqayyed horriyyatihin], *al-Rai*, February 2, 2010, 9; Abdullah al-Ramli, "Sabah al-Salem Divorcee Housing Is Only Missing Ghosts" [Sakan mutallaqat sabah alsalem tanqus'ho alashbah], *Annahar* no. 884 (March 7, 2010), 24. Al-Ramli documents the presence of police forces and government representatives at SSHP around the clock. The project has an on-call government-appointed guard for maintenance requests and security issues. Police routinely set up random checkpoints at the points of vehicular entry and egress. Also, some government agencies have been provided with apartments that operate as temporary offices during business hours at SSHP.

36. Lubna Ahmed al-Kazi, "Divorce: A Structural Problem Not Just a Personal Crisis," *Journal of Comparative Family Studies* 39 (2008): 247. To qualify for financial assistance and subsidized public housing, the women must not have any pension or income. If they qualify for assistance, the Ministry of Social Affairs and Labor makes unannounced house visits to ensure that the women remain without income.

37. Al-Eisa, "Qualitative Study," 94–95.

38. A major factor that plays a role in public housing for divorcees and widows is their children's nationality. A mother of non-Kuwaiti children is issued temporary rental housing at SSHP, which reverts to government possession upon her death, while a mother of Kuwaiti children is offered ownership. Here, nationality becomes a defining factor that distinguishes renters from owners. Kuwaiti mothers are not able to give their children Kuwaiti citizenship because nationality is inherited through the male line, and some of the women at SSHP were formerly married to non-Kuwaitis. As a result, non-Kuwaiti children of single Kuwaiti mothers are given second-class status with few to no prospects of property ownership, employment, or permanent residency.

39. Al-Ramli, "Sabah al-Salem"; al-Aidan, "Citizens"; Abdullah al-Shemari, "225 Building Infractions at Sabah al-Salem Housing Complex" [Rasd alta'adiyat: 225 mokhalafa fee mujama' sabah alsalem], *al-Watan*, June 16, 2013; Naser al-Farhan, "Danger Knocks on Sabah al-Salem's Doors" [Alkhatar yaduq abwab sabah alsalem], *al-Rai* (no. 11359), August 7, 2010, 4; Dania Shoman, "Sabah al-Salem Complex for Widows and Divorcees: 'PAHW Threatens Us with Eviction'" [Aramil wa mutallaqat mujama' sabah alsalem: alsakaniya tohaddedna bisahb alsheqaq], *al-Anba*, June 14, 2013, http://www.alanba.com.kw/ar/kuwait-news /388796/14-06-2013; Alaa Khalifa, "*al-Anba* Examines the Sabah al-Salem Housing Complex" [Alanba to'ayen mujama' sabah alsalem alsakani], *al-Anba*, July 15, 2015, http://www.alanba .com.kw/ar/kuwait-news/572195/15-07-2015.

40. Sociologist Daphne Spain claims that restraining access to public space decreases social status by reducing opportunities to acquire socially valued knowledge. Daphne Spain, *Gendered Spaces* (Chapel Hill: University of North Carolina Press, 1992).

41. Saba G. Shiber, *The Kuwait Urbanization: Documentation, Analysis, Critique* (Kuwait: Kuwait Ministry of Guidance and Information, 1964), 251–71.

42. Arthur Erickson, "Fintas Town Centre," https://www.arthurerickson.com/unbuilt -projects/fintas-town-center/1/caption, accessed March 1, 2015.

43. See, for example, Ahmad M. Abu-Hakima, *The Modern History of Kuwait: 1750–1965* (London: Luzac, 1983), 93–159; Shiber, *The Kuwait Urbanization*; al-Ajmi, "History."

44. Asseel al-Ragam, "The Destruction of Modernist Heritage: The Myth of al-Sawaber," *Journal of Architectural Education* 67 (2013): 243–52.

45. Arthur Erickson, "Sawaber Housing Development," in *The Architecture of Arthur Erickson* (New York: Harper and Row, 1988), 152–53. Erickson designed the Sawaber Housing units as "stacked villas."

46. See Homi Bhabha, "Of Mimicry and Man: The Ambivalence of Colonial Discourse," in *The Location of Culture* (New York: Routledge, 1994), 85–86. Mimicry, as a colonial condition, is a complex strategy of reform and discipline that appropriates the other in a power relation. The colonized mimics the colonizer, and the colonizer imagines another being that can be *"almost the same, but not quite"* (86).

47. Wisniowski interview.

48. Alexander Tzonis and Liane Lefaivre, "Critical Regionalism," in *The Critical Landscape*, ed. Michael Speaks and Jasper de Haan (Rotterdam: 010, 1996), 130–34. Architects Tzonis and Lefaivre discuss regionalism in architecture as a vehicle for realizing new identity by using memory, nostalgia, and familiarization through the implementation of regional folkloristic motifs. They argue that "romantic regionalism" manifests a "double awareness" of belonging to a group that is simultaneously separate and peripheral to a foreign center.

49. Gülsüm B. Nalbantoğlu and Wong Chong Thai, "Introduction," in *Postcolonial Space(s)*, ed. Gülsüm B. Nalbantoğlu and Wong Chong Thai (New York: Princeton Architectural Press, 1997), 9.

50. Alan Colquhoun, "The Concept of Regionalism," in Nalbantoğlu and Thai, *Postcolonial Space(s)*, 13–23.

51. Edward Said's work focuses on the West's literary representation of an orientalized Eastern culture that is rigid, backward, and inferior and hence in need of development. See Edward W. Said, *Orientalism* (New York: Vintage, 1979). The feminization of the East, constructed through claims of its romanticism, irrationality, inferiority, and backwardness, thus necessitates and justifies the construction of the West as masculine, rational, superior, and progressive. For more on the feminization of the East, see, for example, Meyda Yegenoğlu, "Veiled Fantasies: Cultural and Sexual Difference in the Discourse of Orientalism," in *Colonial Fantasies: Towards a Feminist Reading of Orientalism* (Cambridge: Cambridge University Press, 1998), 39–67; Chandra Talpade Mohanty, "Under Western Eyes: Feminist Scholarship and Colonial Discourses," in *Third World Women and the Politics of Feminism*, ed. Chandra Talpade Mohanty, Ann Russo, and Lourdes Torres (Bloomington: Indiana University Press, 1991), 51–80.

52. Wisniowski interview. In Poland, Wisniowski was assistant professor at Wrocław University of Technology specializing in the history of urban planning and design. For more on the discussion of architectural style at SSHP, see al-Ansari, "Masked in the Protective Act," 351–80.

53. *Architektura* is the official publication of the Association of Polish Architects (SARP). For examples of the split-level design approach adopted in Polish social housing, see, for example, *Architektura* 7–8 (1978).

54. INCO, "Sabah al-Salem."

55. For Kuwait, the late 1970s and early 1980s were a time of economic prosperity as well as a reaction to nationalist modernization schemes that had taken place up to the early 1970s, which had alienated people from traditional society and "true" Islam. In reaction, Islamist social movements emerged, and large-scale Islamization schemes were put into place. The proliferation of architectural representations of Arab-Islamic identity became integral to the implementation of these ideas.

56. Ghazi Sultan, "Designing for New Needs in Kuwait," in *Toward an Architecture in the Spirit of Islam*, ed. Renata Holod (Philadelphia: Aga Khan Award for Architecture, 1978), 94.

57. See Ghazi Sultan, "Planning: Kuwait," *Architects' Journal* 159, no. 21 (1974): 792.

58. Sultan, "Designing for New Needs in Kuwait," 94; Jim Antoniou, "The Challenge of Islamic Architecture," *Middle East Construction* 10 (1979): 16–17; Lynda Relph-Knight, "Sunshine and the Rule of Law," *Building Design* 501 (1980): 24–25; INCO, "Sabah al-Salem."

59. Wisniowski's architectural practice in Kuwait has mostly been carried out under INCO. Since 2005, he has been managing and designing projects as director at Soor Engineering, Kuwait. He retired and moved back to Poland in 2015.

60. Al-Ansari, "Masked in the Protective Act," 478–81. Recent images of SSHP's courtyards reveal abandonment and encroachment by residents who have built additions into the open spaces. See Stanek, "Mobilities," 377.

61. Wisniowski interview.

62. Udo Kultermann, *Contemporary Architecture in the Arab States: Renaissance of a Region* (New York: McGraw-Hill, 1999), 14.

63. Ibid., 11–14.

64. See, for example, Spain, *Gendered Spaces*; Leslie K. Weisman, *Discrimination by Design: A Feminist Critique of the Man-Made Environment* (Urbana: University of Illinois Press, 1994); Beatriz Colomina, "The Split Wall: Domestic Voyeurism," in *Sexuality and Space*, ed. Beatriz Colomina (New York: Princeton Architectural Press, 1996), 73–128; Elizabeth Grosz, "Bodies-Cities," in Colomina, *Sexuality and Space*, 241–53.

65. Helen Hills, "Architecture as Metaphor for the Body: The Case of Female Aristocratic Convents in Early Modern Italy," in *Gender and Architecture: History, Interpretation, Practice*, ed. Louise Durning and Richard Wrigley (New York: John Wiley, 2000), 67–112.

66. For further discussion of the construction of marginality at SSHP, see al-Ansari, "Masked in the Protective Act," 249–57, 488–505. Nationhood here is based on Benedict Anderson's concept of the nation as an imagined community. See Benedict Anderson, *Imagined Communities: Reflections on the Origin and Spread of Nationalism*, rev. ed. (London: Verso, 1991).

67. Gwendolyn Wright, "Global Ambition and Local Knowledge," in *Modernism and the Middle East: Architecture and Politics in the Twentieth Century*, ed. Sandy Isenstadt and Kishwar Rizvi (Seattle: University of Washington Press, 2008), 243.

68. Tetreault and al-Mughni, "Modernization," 403.

69. Yasser Elsheshtawy, ed., *The Evolving Arab City: Tradition, Modernity and Urban Development* (New York: Routledge, 2008).

70. Nezar AlSayyad, "From Modernism to Globalization: The Middle East in Context," in Isenstadt and Rizvi, *Modernism and the Middle East*, 263.

71. Weisman, *Discrimination by Design*, 114–59; Thomas Dolan, *Zero-Commute Housing* (Hoboken, NJ: Wiley, 2012).

72. Mohamed Anwar, "Sawaber Complex Nears Its Demise" [Mujama' alsawaber ila alzawal qareeban], *al-Rai*, April 4, 2016, 5.

73. Yousef al-Mutairi and Mohamed al-Mosleh, "Jaber al-Ahmed Housing Complex: 400m² Floors per Family Provide Privacy" [Mujama' jaber alahmed lil benaa al'amoodi: dor 400m² likul osra.. tamattu' bilkhusoosiya], *al-Qabas*, May 6, 2014, 1, 14–15. PAHW was established in 1993 as a merger between the Ministry of Housing and the NHA.

74. Nawara Fattahova, "Sawaber Tenants Disappointed by Lack of Services at New Homes," *Kuwait Times*, January 17, 2016, 2.

Bibliography

al-Aidan, Tarek. "Citizens Unaccounted for by the Government" [Muwatenoon saqatoo men hesaabaat alhokooma]. *al-Qabas*, February 9, 2009, https://alqabas.com/old/?ajax=1&a rticle=463994&highlight=جالت%20القبس

Abu-Hakima, Ahmad M. *The Modern History of Kuwait: 1750–1965*. London: Luzac, 1983.

Al-Ajmi, Mohammed. "History of Architecture in Kuwait: The Evolution of Traditional Kuwaiti Architecture Prior to the Discovery of Oil." PhD diss., University of Nebraska, 2009.

Al-Ansari, Mae. "Irreducible Essence: Tectonics and Cultural Expression in Traditional Forms of Kuwaiti Dwelling." Master's thesis, University of Cincinnati, 2011.

——. "Masked in the Protective Act: Women, Public Housing, and the Construction of 'Modern/National' Identities in Kuwait." PhD diss., University of Cincinnati, 2016.

Al-Dekhayel, Abdulkarim. "The Role of the State in Housing." In *Kuwait: Oil, State and Political Legitimation*, 135–56. Reading, UK: Ithaca, 2000.

Al-Eisa, Bader. "A Qualitative Study: The Low and Middle-Income Housing Problem in the State of Kuwait." PhD diss., University of Minnesota, 1985.

Al-Farhan, Naser. "Danger Knocks on Sabah al-Salem's Doors" [Alkhatar yaduq abwab sabah alsalem]. *al-Rai* (no. 11359), August 7, 2010, 4.

Al-Hajri, Fahad. "Ladies of the Sabah al-Salem Complex: 'Protestors at the National Assembly Don't Represent Us'" [Sayyedaat mujama' sabah alsalem: allawati tajama'na amam majles alomma la yomathelnana]. *al-Qabas*, March 14, 2006.

Al-Jassar, Mohammad. "Constancy and Change in Contemporary Kuwait City: The Socio-Cultural Dimensions of the Kuwaiti Courtyard and *Diwaniyya*." PhD diss., University of Wisconsin–Milwaukee, 2009.

Al-Kazi, Lubna Ahmed. "Divorce: A Structural Problem Not Just a Personal Crisis." *Journal of Comparative Family Studies* 39 (2008): 241–57.

Al-Mutairi, Yousef, and Mohamed al-Mosleh. "Jaber al-Ahmed Housing Complex: 400m² Floors per Family Provide Privacy" [Mujama' jaber alahmed lil benaa al'amoodi: dor 400m² likul osra.. tamattu' bilkhusoosiya]. *al-Qabas*, May 6, 2014, 1, 14–15.

Al-Mutawa, Saleh A. *History of Architecture in Old Kuwait City and the Influence of Its Elements on the Architect*. Kuwait: AlKhat, 1994.

Al-Ragam, Asseel. "The Destruction of Modernist Heritage: The Myth of Al-Sawaber." *Journal of Architectural Education* 67 (2013): 243–52.

Al-Ramli, Abdullah. "Sabah al-Salem Divorcee Housing Is Only Missing Ghosts" [Sakan mutallaqat sabah alsalem tanqus'ho alashbah]. *Annahar* no. 884 (March 7, 2010), 24.

Al-Shemari, Abdullah. "225 Building Infractions at Sabah al-Salem Housing Complex" [Rasd alta'adiyat: 225 mokhalafa fee mujama' sabah alsalem]. *al-Watan*, June 16, 2013.

Alawadi, Abdulhadi M. "Low- and Middle-Income Housing in Kuwait." *Habitat International* 4 (1979): 339–44.

AlSayyad, Nezar. "From Modernism to Globalization: The Middle East in Context." In *Modernism and the Middle East: Architecture and Politics in the Twentieth Century*, edited by Sandy Isenstadt and Kishwar Rizvi, 255–66. Seattle: University of Washington Press, 2008.

Anderson, Benedict. *Imagined Communities: Reflections on the Origin and Spread of Nationalism*. Rev. ed. London: Verso, 1991.

Antoniou, Jim. "The Challenge of Islamic Architecture." *Middle East Construction* 10 (1979): 16–17.

Anwar, Mohamed. "Sawaber Complex Nears Its Demise" [Mujama' alsawaber ila alzawal qareeban]. *al-Rai*, April 4, 2016, 5.

Architektura 7–8 (1978).

Bhabha, Homi. "Of Mimicry and Man: The Ambivalence of Colonial Discourse." In *The Location of Culture*, 85–92. New York: Routledge, 1994.

Blom, Ida, Karen Hagemann, and Catherine Hall, eds. *Gendered Nations: Nationalisms and Gender Order in the Long Nineteenth Century.* New York: Berg, 2000.

Carroll, Jane. "Housing: A Roof over Every Head." *MEED Special Report* (1980): 38–39.

Colomina, Beatriz. "The Split Wall: Domestic Voyeurism." In *Sexuality and Space*, edited by Beatriz Colomina, 73–128. New York: Princeton Architectural Press, 1996.

Colquhoun, Alan. "The Concept of Regionalism." In *Postcolonial Space(s)*, edited by Gulsum B. Nalbantoglu and Wong Chong Thai, 13–23. New York: Princeton Architectural Press, 1997.

Dolan, Thomas. *Zero-Commute Housing.* Hoboken, NJ: Wiley, 2012.

Elsheshtawy, Yasser, ed. *The Evolving Arab City: Tradition, Modernity and Urban Development.* New York: Routledge, 2008.

Erickson, Arthur. "Fintas Town Center." http://www.arthurerickson.com/master-planning /fintas-town-center/4. Accessed March 1, 2015.

———. "Sawaber Housing Development." In *The Architecture of Arthur Erickson*, 152–53. New York: Harper and Row, 1988.

Fattahova, Nawara. "Sawaber Tenants Disappointed by Lack of Services at New Homes." *Kuwait Times*, January 17, 2016, 2.

Grosz, Elizabeth. "Bodies-Cities." In *Sexuality and Space*, edited by Beatriz Colomina, 241–53. New York: Princeton Architectural Press, 1996.

"Hammad: Sabah al-Salem Housing Residents Complain of Security Checkpoint That Restricts Their Freedom" [Hammad: qatenat mujama' sabah alsalem yashtakeen men nuqta amniya toqayyed horriyyatihin]. *al-Rai*, February 2, 2010, 9

Hills, Helen. "Architecture as Metaphor for the Body: The Case of Female Aristocratic Convents in Early Modern Italy." In *Gender and Architecture: History, Interpretation, Practice*, edited by Louise Durning and Richard Wrigley, 67–112. New York: John Wiley, 2000.

Industrial and Engineering Consulting Office (INCO). "Sabah al-Salem Housing Project." Project documents, INCO Archives, Kuwait.

Kandiyoti, Deniz. "Identity and Its Discontents: Women and the Nation." *Millennium* 20 (1991): 429–43.

Khalifa, Alaa. "*al-Anba* Examines the Sabah al-Salem Housing Complex" [Alanba to'ayen mujama' sabah alsalem alsakani]. *al-Anba*, July 15, 2015, http://www.alanba.com.kw/ar /kuwait-news/572195/15-07-2015.

Khattab, Omar, and Adil al-Mumin. "The Evolution of Public Housing Policies in Kuwait from 1960s to 1990s." *International Journal for Housing Science and Its Applications* 24 (2000): 353–60.

Kultermann, Udo. *Contemporary Architecture in the Arab States: Renaissance of a Region.* New York: McGraw-Hill, 1999.

"Kuwait: Infrastructure and Services; High-Rise Debate Stalls Housing Effort." *MEED Special Report* (1983): 67–68.

Lewcock, Ronald. *Traditional Architecture in Kuwait and the Northern Gulf.* London: Art and Archaeology Research Papers, 1978.

Mayer, Tamar. *Gender Ironies of Nationalism: Sexing the Nation.* London: Routledge, 2002.

McDowell, Linda. *Gender, Identity, and Place: Understanding Feminist Geographies.* Minneapolis: University of Minnesota Press, 1999.

Mohanty, Chandra Talpade. "Under Western Eyes: Feminist Scholarship and Colonial Discourses." In *Third World Women and the Politics of Feminism*, edited by Chandra Talpade Mohanty, Ann Russo, and Lourdes Torres, 51–80. Bloomington: Indiana University Press, 1991.

Nalbantoğlu, Gülsüm B., and Wong Chong Thai. "Introduction." In *Postcolonial Space(s)*, edited by Gulsum B. Nalbantoglu and Wong Chong Thai, 7–12. New York: Princeton Architectural Press, 1997.

National Housing Authority. "Sabah al-Salem Block 9 Apartments." In *Annual Report 1990* [*Al-kitab al-sanawi 1990*]. Kuwait: National Housing Authority, 1990.

Peterson, V. Spike, and Anne Sisson Runyan. *Global Gender Issues.* 2nd ed. Dilemmas in World Politics. Boulder, CO: Westview, 1999.

Relph-Knight, Lynda. "Sunshine and the Rule of Law." *Building Design* 501 (1980): 24–25.

"Sabah al-Salem Residential Complex Renovation Team Redistributes Eight Apartments to Kuwaiti Women" [Fareeq 'amal tatweer mujama' sabah alsalem alsakani yuwazze' thamani shiqaq li muwatenat kuwaitiyat]. Kuwait News Agency (KUNA), May 31, 2006, http://www.kuna.net.kw/ArticleDetails.aspx?id=1614142&language=ar

Sadik, Rula Muhammad. "Nation-Building and Housing Policy: A Comparative Analysis of Urban Housing Development in Kuwait, Jordan, and Lebanon." PhD diss., University of California, Berkeley, 1996.

Said, Edward W. *Orientalism.* New York: Vintage, 1979.

Shankland Cox Partnership (SCP) and Salem AlMarzouk and Sabah Abi Hanna (SSH). *Master Plan for Kuwait: First Review 1977 Final Report.* Vol. 3, *Supporting Studies.* Kuwait: Municipality of Kuwait, 1977.

Shiber, Saba G. *The Kuwait Urbanization: Documentation, Analysis, Critique.* Kuwait: Kuwait Ministry of Guidance and Information, 1964.

Shoman, Dania. "Sabah al-Salem Complex for Widows and Divorcees: 'PAHW Threatens Us with Eviction'" [Aramil wa mutallaqat mujama' sabah alsalem: alsakaniya tohaddedna bisahb alsheqaq]. *al-Anba*, June 14, 2013, http://www.alanba.com.kw/ar/kuwait-news/388796/14-06-2013.

Spain, Daphne. *Gendered Spaces.* Chapel Hill: University of North Carolina Press, 1992.

Stanek, Lukasz. "Mobilities of Architecture in the Global Cold War: From Socialist Poland to Kuwait and Back." *International Journal of Islamic Architecture* 4 (2015): 365–98.

Sultan, Ghazi. "Designing for New Needs in Kuwait." In *Toward an Architecture in the Spirit of Islam*, edited by Renata Holod, 94. Philadelphia: Aga Khan Award for Architecture, 1978.

——. "Planning: Kuwait." *Architects' Journal* 159, no. 21 (1974): 792–94.

Tetreault, Mary Ann, and Haya al-Mughni. "Gender, Citizenship and Nationalism in Kuwait." *British Journal of Middle Eastern Studies* 22 (1995): 64–80.

——. "Modernization and Its Discontents: State and Gender in Kuwait." *Middle East Journal* 49 (1995): 403–17.

Tzonis, Alexander, and Liane Lefaivre. "Critical Regionalism." In *The Critical Landscape*, edited by Michael Speaks and Jasper de Haan, 126–48. Rotterdam: 010, 1996.

Weisman, Leslie K. *Discrimination by Design: A Feminist Critique of the Man-Made Environment.* Urbana: University of Illinois Press, 1994.

Wright, Gwendolyn. "Global Ambition and Local Knowledge." In *Modernism and the Middle East: Architecture and Politics in the Twentieth Century,* edited by Sandy Isenstadt and Kishwar Rizvi, 221–54. Seattle: University of Washington Press, 2008.

Yegenoğlu, Meyda. "Veiled Fantasies: Cultural and Sexual Difference in the Discourse of Orientalism." In *Colonial Fantasies: Towards a Feminist Reading of Orientalism,* 39–67. Cambridge: Cambridge University Press, 1998.

MAE AL-ANSARI is Assistant Professor in the College of Architecture at Kuwait University, specializing in architecture history, theory, and criticism. Al-Ansari received her BArch from Kuwait University in 2006 with honors. She was Project Architect in the Design Department at the Ministry of Public Works (Kuwait), after which she earned a full scholarship to pursue graduate studies in the United States. Al-Ansari received both her MSc and PhD in architecture (2016) from the University of Cincinnati, Ohio, where she also earned a graduate certificate in women's studies. Her PhD dissertation focuses on public housing, women, and identity construction in Kuwait. She is interested in intersections of architecture, gender, power, tectonics, and materiality.

PART III

DESIGN AND CONSTRUCTION: TRANSNATIONAL SYSTEMS AND LOCALIZED PRACTICES

9

RABBIS, ARCHITECTS, AND THE DESIGN OF ULTRA-ORTHODOX CITY-SETTLEMENTS

Noam Shoked

A T THE BEGINNING OF JUNE 1967, THE STATE of Israel, which had come into existence some twenty years earlier, was drawn into a war against the neighboring states of Egypt, Syria, and Jordan. That war left Israel in control of the Sinai Peninsula, the Gaza Strip, the Golan Heights, and the West Bank. Almost immediately after the conquest of the West Bank, which previously had been under Jordanian rule, civilian settlements began to be built on its bare hilltops. Today, five decades after that war, there are more than two hundred such settlements scattered across the West Bank, housing some four hundred thousand Jewish settlers.[1]

In the first two decades after the war, most settlements took the shape of small and medium-sized suburban neighborhoods, built for communities of either secular or national-religious Jews. With their single-family houses, lush lawns, and pitched red-tile roofs dotting the hilltops of the West Bank, they became emblematic of the Israeli occupation of the West Bank. But, by the early 1990s, the construction of settlements began to change as a different kind of Jewish community moved into the West Bank. A push on the political right inside Israel proper to increase the number of Jewish settlers in the West Bank, combined with a housing crisis experienced by the ultra-Orthodox community, had resulted in an influx of ultra-Orthodox families whose religious beliefs and practices made a new kind of demand on the construction of settlements. In response to these demands, a new kind of settlement emerged: the ultra-Orthodox city-settlement. Among the ultra-Orthodox community these new cities—mainly composed of state-funded large, multistory apartment buildings designed for lower-income families—were called, not without both irony and pathos, "the Projects." Today, with half the construction in settlements in the West Bank taking place in these cities, they have come to form one-third of the total population of Jewish settlers.[2]

The design of city-settlements for the ultra-Orthodox community posed a number of challenges to local architects. Faced with the task of planning the first modern cities ever designed exclusively for ultra-Orthodox Israelis, architects sought an aesthetic language that would relate to the customs of the ultra-Orthodox community.[3] Seeing ultra-Orthodox Jews as resistant to modernity and adhering to traditional Jewish laws, many architects experimented with forms they associated with quaint or sentimental notions of tradition and antiquity. This experimentation went in unexpected directions, such as sourcing architectural elements from native Palestinian building practices and urban forms from Catholic Europe.[4] In addition, when many in the ultra-Orthodox community had come to resent the Projects, and it was unclear whether young ultra-Orthodox couples would settle in the West Bank, architects began to study and accommodate the unique needs of the ultra-Orthodox community. Although these needs proved to be more complex than the architects had imagined, and most of their attempts failed, these architects provoked a peculiar dialogue between professional planning and the ultra-Orthodox community.

This chapter examines the short history of these city-settlements and the design debates that accompanied their development. Focusing on the settlement of Beitar Illit and its predecessor, Immanuel, it shows how negotiations between the planners and the residents resulted in paradoxical outcomes that problematize the received narrative of the history of settlement design as the outcome of decisions made by individual politicians. Instead, these negotiations and their outcomes point to the intricate relations between top-down and bottom-up design processes in engendering the urban formation around which the Israeli occupation is built. In turn, they also complicate intellectual frameworks that foreground the emancipatory nature of bottom-up design processes and force us to question whether the much-lauded triumph of the user is always a good thing.

Unlikely Settlers

Until the 1980s, the ultra-Orthodox community was an unlikely candidate to take part in the settlement project. Because they believed the state of

Israel would be reconstituted only after the coming of the Messiah, leaders of the ultra-Orthodox community deemed the founding of modern Israel and, later, the occupation of the West Bank religiously flawed. In fact, they prohibited their followers from moving to the occupied territories. Not only were they uninterested in taking part in such a nationalist project, but, considering other countries' opposition to the settlement project, they perceived the construction of settlements as "teasing the *goyim* [Gentiles]"—a strict religious prohibition.[5]

The lifestyle and customs of ultra-Orthodox Israelis were also at odds with the commuter-based suburban pattern of most settlements. Insisting on traditional forms of life that had developed in Eastern Europe in the eighteenth and nineteenth centuries, most ultra-Orthodox people lacked modern professional skills.[6] Combined with their high fertility rates, standing at an average of seven children per family,[7] and the fact that most men dedicated their time to the study of rabbinic literature, they consistently suffered from high poverty rates.[8] In keeping with their lifestyle, many ultra-Orthodox families did not own a car, and life in a remote settlement, poorly connected to an urban center with commercial, religious, and educational facilities, would have doomed them to impractical isolation.

Therefore, even though ultra-Orthodox people approached secular urban culture with suspicion and usually resided in segregated neighborhoods, they preferred living in mixed cities, where they could take advantage of various public services.[9] Until the 1960s, they centered in two main urban areas: the northern neighborhoods of Jerusalem and the city of Bnei Brak at the outskirts of Tel Aviv. But by the mid-1960s, these areas became too small for the rapidly growing community, and many young couples were forced to move out. At first, some moved to neighborhoods in existing medium-sized cities and remote towns known as development towns.[10] But these locales were either too expensive or too small, and, more often than not, their secular residents expressed hostility toward the new ultra-Orthodox tenants. By the early 1980s, as more and more ultra-Orthodox couples were trapped in small apartments with rocketing rent prices, a more comprehensive solution was needed.[11]

Traditional Landscape for Tradition-Abiding Residents

The first serious attempt to solve the ultra-Orthodox housing crisis came from a rather unexpected source. After a series of government decisions from 1979 to 1982 that aimed at opening the settlement project to private developers, ultra-Orthodox developers decided to erect an ultra-Orthodox city-settlement in the heart of the West Bank.[12] The first of its kind, both in the occupied territories and in Israel proper, it was planned for some two hundred thousand residents and named after one of the characters from the book of Isaiah: Immanuel.[13] By the end of 1982, the developers had obtained all required approvals and construction was in full swing.[14]

To overcome influential rabbis' opposition to the idea of erecting an ultra-Orthodox city in the occupied territories, and to downplay its remote location, the developers embarked on an unprecedented marketing campaign. The campaign included free flight tickets from across the world for potential home buyers, guided tours, lectures, and a Hassidic music festival on the bare hilltop, attended by some ten thousand potential home buyers.[15] The city, as the campaign promoted it in these events, was to bring the newest technologies from abroad and adopt them to suit traditional Jewish customs. For example, describing his plans for the city, one of the developers explained, "I have seen this in the US: a computer in each house. You press a button and you order a cottage cheese . . . you want to order a baby sitter—you press a button; you have a question about Halakha [traditional Jewish law]—you press the button and the Halakhic computer replies. . . . I even plan a video recording studio that will broadcast Gamara and Judaism classes."[16]

Visual references to history and tradition also played an important role in both the promotion and the planning of Immanuel. In advertisements, graphic designers underlined Immanuel's resemblance to the Old City of Jerusalem. In the renderings they crafted, domed buildings and large arches dominated Immanuel's skyline (fig. 9.1). The architects involved in the planning of Immanuel were also keen on weaving historical building forms into their design. Not only were their clients known for their hostility toward modernity, but also, like many Israeli-born architects of that generation, they themselves were overwhelmed by the Oriental landscapes of the Palestinians.[17] As Yossi Sivan, one of the architects involved in the project, explained, "We felt like the local [architectural] language there [in the West Bank] was very important, and there was a lot to draw upon there."[18]

Like Sivan, Thomas Leitersdorff, a graduate of the Architectural Association and lead designer of Immanuel's master plan, was fascinated by the architecture of the Arab village. Romanticizing many of the Palestinian villages he saw on his way to the bare hilltop, he imagined they were places

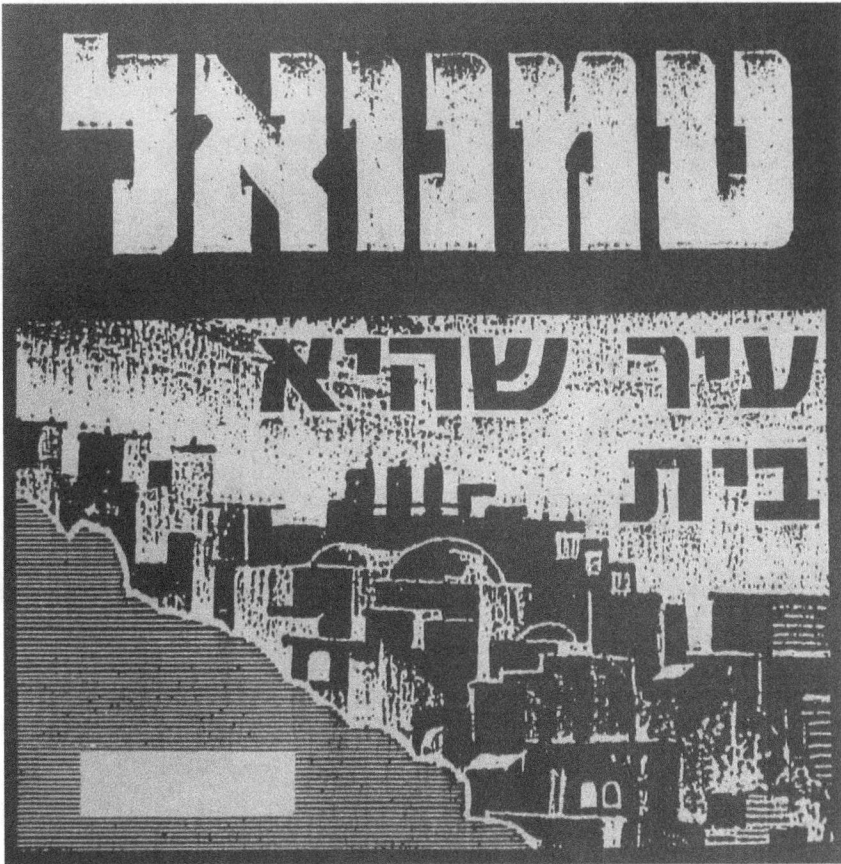

Figure 9.1. "Immanuel: A City That Is a Home." Drawing of Immanuel inspired by representations of the Old City of Jerusalem, 1982. City Planning Division in Immanuel.

where time stood still. Their unpaved, curvilinear pathways and the lack of division lines between the plots represented purity for him, something architects "could only ruin."[19] Accordingly, when he approached the drafting table, he attempted to echo the unplanned road network of the Arab village, designed a few curvilinear walking paths, and proposed to break up monolithic building masses into smaller units, layering them one atop the other in a staggered pattern (fig. 9.2).[20]

Sharing Leitersorff's vision, other architects responsible for designing buildings in Immanuel also drew their inspiration from the Arab house. Most notably, designs for houses in the neighborhoods of Shevo and

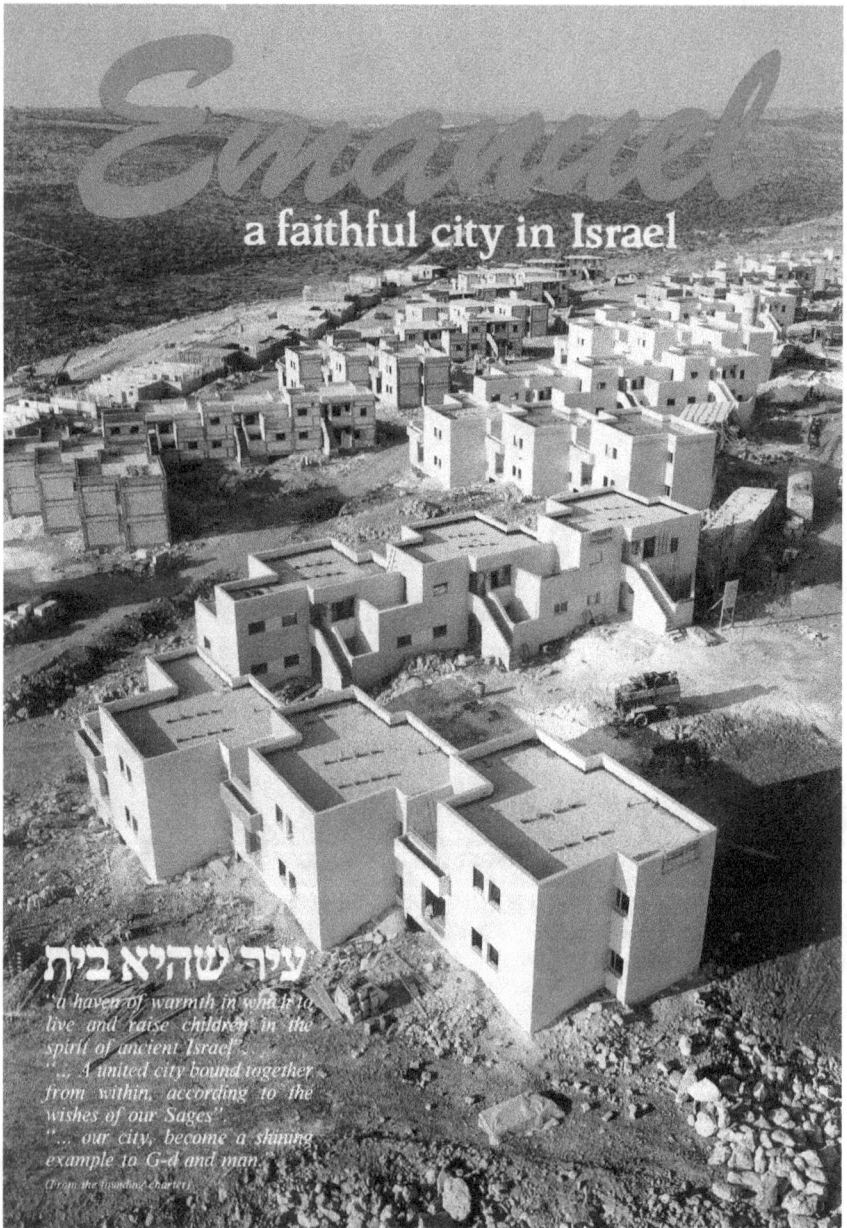

Figure 9.2. Ad for Immanuel (spelled as Emanuel) showing residential units arranged in a staggered pattern, ca. 1982. Star of Samaria offices in Immanuel.

Figure 9.3. Examples of residential units partially inspired by Palestinian architecture: (a) two-story house in the neighborhood of Shevo, unknown architect, 1983; (b) housing complex in the neighborhood of Leshem designed by Yaski-Gil-Sivan Architects, 1983. City Planning Division in Immanuel.

Leshem, located in the western part of the city, incorporated various allusions to Palestinian building elements (fig. 9.3). For example, the multistory apartment buildings in Leshem neighborhood were dotted with prefabricated concrete arches and covered with a thin layer of stone, referencing the local *tubsa* stone. Below them, woven into the natural topography, seventy-two cottages, also decorated with concrete arches, were staggered one on top of the other, enclosing multiple inner courtyards in ways that resonated with the traditional patio house.

It is hard to tell whether these allusions to an Arab vernacular were going to satisfy the aesthetic preferences of the ultra-Orthodox community. Soon after the plans were finalized, the developers encountered financial difficulties and pressured the architects to work under an extremely tight budget. Under the new constraints, most of the houses in Leshem and Shevo neighborhoods were never executed. Instead, the few buildings that were actually built in Immanuel were extremely rudimentary. Significantly, they showed no consideration of vernacular aesthetics or of the special needs of the ultra-Orthodox community.[21]

In order to accommodate the strict modesty rules and religious customs of ultra-Orthodox people, the living space must incorporate several design features. Among these, the most basic features include a balcony large enough to serve as a *sukkah* on the *Sukkot* holiday, as well as the spatial division of the house into areas accommodating the wife and children and those serving the husband and his male friends (fig. 9.4a). Perplexed by the original challenge of designing the first modern ultra-Orthodox city-settlement and the increasing budget cuts, some of the architects failed to account for these special needs. For example, the units in one building that was replicated in large numbers in Immanuel were too small and had no partition between the entrance door and the living room, resulting in unwanted interactions between men and women (fig. 9.4b). Another multistory house, built already after the first stage of construction, had rounded balconies that rendered them too small for a *sukkah*, and had no partitions dividing the living room from the kitchen or the parents' bedroom (fig. 9.4d). Adding to this, the apartments had in-between spaces, such as small family corners, that were considered wasted and unusable space. Furthermore, the placement of the bathroom door in the parents' bedroom made it impossible to lay out two twin beds, leaving ultra-Orthodox couples unable to follow strict gender-segregation rules requiring them to sleep in separate beds. As a result, many of these apartments remained unoccupied.

Things got even worse when the developers went into bankruptcy, causing construction to stop in 1985. At that point, many home buyers found themselves paying mortgages for apartments they would never own, and those who had already moved in were isolated in the middle of the West Bank, with almost no public facilities, and, at times, not even paved roads

a

b

c

d

Figure 9.4. Apartment layouts in Immanuel: (a) a three-bedroom unit, showing partition walls that separate the living room from the entrance space, the kitchen, and the bedrooms. Original plan by Leitersdorf Goldenberg Planning and Architecture, ca. 1982; (b and c) units lacking partitions between the entrance door and the living room planned by architect David Nofar (b) and architect Israel Levitt (c), c. 1983; (d) unit with no partitions dividing the private from the public spaces of the house, but with a balcony too small to serve as a sukkah, a family corner, and a master bedroom that cannot accommodate two twin beds. Schematic plans drawn by the author. Author's drawings based on original plans available at the City Planning Division and Star of Samaria offices in Immanuel.

leading to their houses.[22] If all this was not enough, the outbreak of the Palestinian uprising, a grassroots resistance to the Israeli occupation that included occasional stone-throwing at Jewish settlers and lasted from 1987 to 1993, dealt a final blow to Immanuel. Within just a few years, those who could afford it moved out, leaving behind them a poor community that, still today, barely makes up 2 percent of the city's projected population.

Siena on the Hills of Judea

After the fall of Immanuel, few imagined that the ultra-Orthodox community could be recruited again to the settlement project. But by the late
1980s, the housing crisis facing the ultra-Orthodox community had grown
worse, finally reaching a tipping point.[23] At the same time, Teddy Kollek,
the then-mayor of Jerusalem, saw the ultra-Orthodox community as an
economic burden and wanted to reduce their number in the city.[24] Furthermore, as the Palestinian uprising continued, the growing number of attacks
against Jewish settlers in the West Bank made it difficult to attract Israelis seeking a tranquil suburban life to the occupied territories. In order to
continue Israel's unofficial policy of making facts on the ground, someone,
preferably with a high fertility rate, had to ensure the gradual growth of
Jewish presence in the occupied territories.

It was under these conditions that when a special governmental committee in charge of new settlements heard about the availability of three
hilltops, just a few hundred meters away from the Israeli border, it quickly
made a decision: an ultra-Orthodox city-settlement, to be called Beitar Illit,
would be erected on the site, with the first move-in date scheduled for May
1990.[25] Since, unlike Immanuel, the hills of Beitar Illit were close to Jerusalem,
state officials imagined it would attract many in the ultra-Orthodox
community. To ensure the city's appeal, the Ministry of Housing founded
a special steering committee of rabbis and community leaders in charge of
promoting the city among young ultra-Orthodox couples (fig. 9.5).

In order to attenuate the nationalist nature of the project, the Ministry
of Housing's involvement was limited to funding and supervision, while
construction and promotion were allocated to a private company.[26] Hoping
to avoid the planning mistakes that contributed to the fall of Immanuel, the
company hired Yaacov and Ora Yaar, a pair of well-known Tel Aviv–based
architects who had designed numerous housing projects across the country
and taken part in the redevelopment and preservation of Old Jerusalem.[27]

Uncertain about the future prospects of the settlement, the Yaars and
their team of architects began planning the first hilltop of Beitar Illit, designed for some seven thousand ultra-Orthodox young families. When
approaching the drafting table, the architects did not consider the Arab village as a source of inspiration, as their counterparts in Immanuel had a few
years prior; after all, it proved to be a failure in Immanuel, and with the outbreak of the Palestinian uprising, many Israelis, especially those residing

Figure 9.5. Beitar Illit's special steering committee with Ministry of Housing officials by the entrance to the city, 1989. *Hadshot Beitar Journal* 1 (October 1989): 5.

in the West Bank, had expressed a clear dislike of Palestinian building elements.[28] Instead, influenced by works of the New Urbanism group, the architects looked to the Italian town of Siena for inspiration. Accordingly, they designed all houses with pitched red-tile roofs and created mixed-use streets with commercial spaces on the ground floor (fig. 9.6).[29]

To study the specific needs of ultra-Orthodox people, the Yaars made a trip to the ultra-Orthodox neighborhoods of Jerusalem with David, a civil engineer assigned to the project who happened to be ultra-Orthodox. Together, they walked around the crowded streets of Jerusalem and discussed the residents' lifestyles and building elements that are unique to the ultra-Orthodox apartment. Satisfied with the information they collected, the architects returned to their office and adjusted the plan drawings. They enlarged the balconies, added small sinks outside the restrooms for hand-washing rituals, and paid careful attention to the gendered division of the house. Most notably, the living room was closed off from the rest of the house whenever possible, so it could function as a study room for the husband (fig. 9.7).[30] Proud of this design process, Yaacov Yaar later concluded, "Planning a

Figure 9.6. Mixed-use street in Beitar Illit with commerce on the ground floor, behind the arched colonnade on the left, 1991. Photograph by Moshe Leibovitz.

Figure 9.7. Typical residential unit with a living room closed off from the rest of the house. Beitar Illit, Hill A, Yaar Architects, ca. 1989. Schematic plan drawn by author. Author's drawing based on original plan available at the City Planning Division of Beitar Illit.

city for ultra-Orthodox people is, first and foremost, an original challenge. When approaching it, planners have to carefully study the needs and customs of the people. . . . And, indeed, we did it, both in the design of the residential units and the planning of public spaces."[31]

Yet, when residents started moving into the first neighborhood, Yaar's self-congratulatory statement proved to be too hasty, and Moshe Leibovitz, the first mayor of Beitar Illit, found himself struggling to somehow keep the city from falling apart. As he explained, "The architects got everything wrong. Whatever planners shouldn't do when planning for the ultra-Orthodox community—they did."[32] Most significantly, he complained, they gathered all public facilities—the central synagogue, school, community center, and park—in one large land plot. In doing so, they failed to account for the numerous sects that constitute the ultra-Orthodox community.[33] Each sect conducts its own ceremonies, daily prayers, and educational system and refers to different textual traditions. Mixing between sects is unacceptable. In fact, it is so unacceptable that in 1990, when Raphael Dankner, the former manager of the City Planning Division, tried to convince a resident to send his three-year-old daughter to a kindergarten that catered to children of another sect, the man was appalled and asked, "You think their girls are like mine?"[34] Not surprisingly, then, almost all of the spacious public buildings the architects designed remained empty.

The architects' assumptions about the buying behavior and labor capacity of the ultra-Orthodox community were also flawed. Considering the scarce funds available to most ultra-Orthodox families, very few were able to afford renting the spacious ground-floor commercial spaces the Yaars borrowed from Siena, and many remained empty.[35] In addition, the architects placed the only industrial area at a small site with harsh topographical conditions that precluded much-needed employment opportunities, damaging the city's economic prospects.[36]

As for the residential units, even though the Yaars and their team tried to accommodate some of the elementary needs of ultra-Orthodox families, they never really consulted with the future residents, and most units were inadequate. Most notably, as Tamar, a draftsperson of ultra-Orthodox faith, explained, the architects failed to account for the exceptionally large ultra-Orthodox family size—nine members, on average.[37] Planned for standard families, the units in the first neighborhood were too small and allowed little space for future expansions. Moreover, the Yaars' insistence on designing the living room as a secluded study space for the husband worked against the main purpose of the ultra-Orthodox living room: accommodating Shabbat dinners for the extended family. As Avishai Meiron, manager of the City Planning Division in Beitar Illit, observed, such dinners require an elongated space leaving enough room for an exceptionally long dining table and easy access to the kitchen.[38] With overcrowded apartments and dysfunctional public spaces, many worried that Beitar Illit, which quickly came to be known as the Projects, was doomed to end up like its older sister, Immanuel.

From Public Participation to Self-Governance

Frustrated with secular planners and the conventional housing programs they drew upon, the leaders of the local ultra-Orthodox community decided to take things into their own hands. Since only the first neighborhood was completed, they focused their efforts on the other ones. With little time at hand, Mayor Moshe Leibowitz scheduled a meeting with Prime Minister Yitzhak Rabin. Before heading to the meeting, he took the master plan of the city and painted it in black, leaving only public and green spaces in white. The plan, as Leibovitz recounted, was almost entirely black. With this plan at hand, Leibovitz approached Rabin and explained, "I am not going to be part of this mistake the state is about to make. Look at how it all looks here? All looks black! You will place blacks [colloquial name for ultra-Orthodox people in Israel] in black areas, and you will mark the state with black. . . . Where do you think kids could play here? Would you send your grandkids to live here?" When he saw the prime minister laughing, Leibovitz insisted, "Don't laugh, Mr. Prime Minister, they may be Ba'aley Teshuva ['born again Jews'] and live in Beitar."[39] It is hard to imagine Rabin was convinced by the latter argument, but by the end of that meeting the two had agreed that the design must be changed.

Overseeing all design decisions in the following months, Leibovitz and his team of community representatives transformed the Projects. Under their direction, the architects added public buildings and green spaces, subdivided existing ones into smaller plots, and distributed them across the city.[40] In addition, they drew clusters of buildings that enclosed small public courtyards, allowing vehicle-free playgrounds for the disproportionately large number of children residing in the city. Furthermore, they supervised the redesign of the residential units. Apartments in the circumference of these playgrounds were designed with their kitchens facing the courtyard, allowing the mothers to watch over their children playing downstairs while they cooked and breastfed. Accommodating the needs of large families, Leibovitz and his team also insisted that, in order to get building permits, architects include plan drawings outlining future additions of at least two rooms for each new unit.[41] To strengthen the city's connection to Jerusalem, they even initiated a low-rate, gender-segregated bus system.

The residents, in turn, also helped transform the city. Instead of the commercial spaces the architects crafted for them on the ground floor, they opened small stores in private apartments, usually in one of the bedrooms or other, more informal spaces like the building's staircase and corridors. In the same fashion, subcommunities opened small separate synagogues and other public facilities in portable structures and private apartments. Moreover, in order to adjust the overcrowded apartments built in the first neighborhood, a number of ultra-Orthodox wives, usually with a two-year diploma in architectural engineering, had overseen the expansion of almost all units (fig. 9.8).[42] The experience they gained in the first years encouraged many others to acquire professional skills, and today some are involved in the design of a new industrial zone, intended to create new employment opportunities.

Over time, these spatial tactics have evolved into new forms of self-governance and management. Suspicious of secular planners working at the Ministry of Housing, Beitar's residents founded a number of community organizations that took over many of the ministry's responsibilities. Most notably, shortly after the first residents moved in, they founded an informal populating committee. The committee, composed of rabbis and community representatives, was mainly in charge of securing the religious nature of the settlement. Among its various activities, it enforced new property laws, requiring all potential home buyers and renters to submit an application specifying their religious affiliation and family status. In addition, the committee initiated an unofficial call center for residents' complaints about "spiritual hazards" and a plethora of community-based charity funds.[43]

The Tyranny of the Users

Within just a few years, the populating committee and other informal groups had gained a significant amount of power, yet some of their activities transformed the city in unexpected ways. For instance, the populating committee has been accused of applying discriminatory practices, favoring

Figure 9.8. Building additions planned by ultra-Orthodox draftspersons in Beitar Illit. Additions highlighted in white. Photographs by Noam Shoked, 2015.

applicants from certain rabbinic dynasties or ethnic backgrounds over others. In addition, after gaining control over the city's building laws and real-estate market, the committee gave unofficial, disproportionately generous building permits to several individuals. Their decisions were based on an arbitrary logic, and more often than not these permits were given at the expense of open public spaces or other individuals. Making things all the more complex, the identities of populating committee members are kept secret and remain unknown to residents. Equally unexpected was the establishment of an informal police force, run by another residents' group, that had been patrolling the city and penalizing residents who did not follow the city's unofficial laws. Among these were women caught wearing jeans or other clothing items that did not adhere to a strict dress code, men who associated with unmarried women, and those who used the wrong entrance to the bus (men at the front; women at the back).[44]

It didn't take long before these residents' organizations had extended their reach and enforced rules that applied to the private sphere. For instance, a special committee took it on itself to make sure residents did not have television sets or Internet connections in their homes. Since enforcing this rule required access to all units in Beitar Illit, a task beyond the committee members' reach, they circulated leaflets that encouraged residents to report any suspicious satellite dishes their neighbors might have installed, or unwarranted television sets they had noticed.[45] Residents who felt uncomfortable with these laws developed tactics that afforded them some freedom. For example, a few have hosted martial arts classes, which were prohibited in public space, in their private apartments.[46] But these are rare, and those found violating such city laws are likely to be deprived of elementary public services and become the object of public condemnation. Therefore, while many residents have found these committees favorable, allowing them to adhere to Jewish laws in their strictest form, some view them as oppressive and exclusionary.

Neither the residents who found themselves disempowered by these groups nor officials at the Ministry of Housing have been able to counterbalance the committees' increasing influence. For example, in 2007, after several resident complaints, the Ministry of Housing attempted to end the committees' unlawful activities. After all, not only did the committee members apply discriminatory measures in allocating apartments to certain groups, but some of these apartments were the property of the Ministry of Housing. Since committee members' identities were unknown and direct contact with them was impossible, Ministry of Housing officials decided to circulate a warning message, underlining the illegality of the committee and its land laws. Residents and local newspapers refused to collaborate, however, and did not publish the message, and it remained unnoticed. When asked for his assistance, the former mayor of Beitar Illit admitted he had no control over the populating committee.[47] In fact, when his deputy submitted an application for a new apartment to the populating committee, it was rejected.[48]

Furthermore, while those who did not obey the city laws of Beitar Illit or did not belong to the right rabbinic court were unwelcome, the Palestinian residents of neighboring villages were subjected to greater offenses. Even though many residents of Beitar Illit do not identify with the settlement movement, it is hard to ignore the fact that Beitar sits on lands that were confiscated and declared state lands[49] despite the protests of native

Palestinians.[50] It is also hard to ignore the numerous military watchtowers and checkpoints erected in its vicinity. Built in order to secure the uninterrupted daily activities of the residents of Beitar Illit, they have severely limited the mobility of the Palestinians and subjected them to occasional security checks.[51] Although military officials and politicians ordered these measures, it was the residents of Beitar Illit who pressured for them and, later, oversaw their execution.

In fact, the benign attitude of the residents of Beitar Illit toward their Palestinian neighbors changed over time. Initially, as anti-Zionist residents of the West Bank, the settlers of Beitar Illit had signed multiple peace agreements with the residents of the neighboring Palestinian villages. "We the sons of Abraham" were the words that opened most of these agreements, which aimed at suppressing stone-throwing attacks on passing cars and, in some cases, ordered the channeling of electricity and water from Beitar Illit to its neighbors.[52] But as political tensions grew, these agreements were increasingly cast aside and forgotten. Life in the West Bank seems to have hardened the views of the ultra-Orthodox community, and in recent years they have become more directly involved in actions common in other settlements. For example, at times of political tension in 2015, the residents of Beitar Illit decided to expel all the Palestinian day laborers working at the city's numerous construction sites.

Conclusion

Such activities on the part of the residents make it hard to assess Beitar Illit. On the one hand, they attest to a success story, a story of a weak and stigmatized public that, against all odds, managed to transform a poorly planned public housing project and adapt it to its unique needs. And indeed, in surveys, the majority of the residents have expressed their unambiguous satisfaction with Beitar Illit.[53] In fact, the city proved to be so successful that it came to form a model, an urban type that was replicated elsewhere, both in the West Bank and in Israel. But, on the other hand, it is hard to ignore the darker side of the techniques the residents of Beitar Illit employed in order to appropriate the Projects, techniques that proved to be oppressive toward others.

The double-sided nature of these practices complicates recent accounts that prioritize bottom-up design processes. Following Michel de Certeau's notion of "tactics" and the ideas developed by Henri Lefebvre in *The Pro-duction of Space*, many works in the fields of architectural history and ur-ban studies have highlighted the ways in which the user, through ephemeral everyday practices or permanent design interventions "from below," is able to coauthor the built environment.[54] Astutely, these accounts show how, in places like São Paulo, Los Angeles, or Stockholm, the practices of the user facilitate the fight of subaltern groups over their right to the city, which, in turn, endows them with a sense of active citizenship. Common to almost all these accounts is the understanding that these practices make space more inclusive. In Beitar Illit, however, the everyday practices of the users pro-moted the creation of spaces of exclusion. The right to transform the city afforded an imaginary of autonomous space where basic social contracts between people are ignored. In that way, the case of Beitar Illit reminds us that the user can also be an active participant in the engendering of spatial domination in ways that may counter his disadvantaged position.

In the context of the Israeli occupation, the emergence of the tyranny of the users in Beitar Illit also highlights the gap between *intention* and *practice* in the design of West Bank settlements. It points toward a chain of mistakes, a process unforeseen by its founders that resulted in para-doxical outcomes: anti-Zionist settlers, architects crafting a Palestinian vil-lage look-alike city-settlement or modeling one after a medieval town for ultra-Orthodox users, and a public housing project over which the govern-ment lost control. These contradictions preclude oversimplified readings of settlements as good or bad. In turn, they also make it difficult to interpret settlement design as the outcome of a clear political ideology, as war ma-chinery, or panoptic mechanisms, as suggested by other scholars, like Eyal Weizman.[55] For, as Michel Foucault explains, architecture can serve such ends only if the intentions of the architects coincide with the practices of the users.[56] Instead, then, these negotiations between the inhabitants of the Projects and their secular planners reveal a history that may not be entirely evil-intentioned, but rather a series of contradictory, circumstantial events that defy simple interpretations.

Acknowledgments

The author would like to thank Margaret Crawford, Greg Castillo, and Paul Rabinow for their invaluable comments on earlier drafts of this text.

Notes

1. Among these are both settlements authorized by the state of Israel, *hitnachaluyot* in Hebrew, as well as unauthorized ones, commonly referred to as *ma'achazim* in Israel. According to the Israel Central Bureau of Statistics, by December 2014 there were 370,700 Israeli citizens residing in the West Bank. Unofficial surveys, however, reveal that the settler population has increased since then, reaching 400,000 by 2015. In both accounts, settlements in East Jerusalem, housing some 375,000 Jewish Israelis, are not included. See Israel Central Bureau of Statistics, Statistical Abstract of Israel, Population by District, Sub-District (Jerusalem: CBS, September 10, 2015), 2.15; Yaakov Katz, "407,118: This Is the Up to Date Number of Jewish Residents in Judea and Samaria as of 31/12/2015," *Besheva*, January 7, 2016, http://www.inn .co.il/Articles/Article.aspx/14370; and Peace Now, "Settlements and Outposts Numbers and Data," Peace Now Settlements Watch Reports, Tel Aviv, June 2009.

2. Lea Cahaner and Yossef Shilhav, "Ultra-Orthodox Settlements in Judea and Samaria," *Social Issues in Israel* 16 (2013): 41. Exact numbers of ultra-Orthodox settlers residing in the West Bank, as recorded in 2009, are available in the reports of Peace Now's Settlements Watch. See Peace Now, "Settlements and Outposts," 2009.

3. On the design of an ultra-Orthodox neighborhood in the town of Hatzor HaGlilit that preceded ultra-Orthodox city-settlements, see Oryan Shachar, Alona Nitzan-Shiftan, and Rachel Sebba, "Gvulot Veptahim Shel Kdusha: HaKirya HaHasidit Behatzor Haglilit," in *Living Forms: Architecture and Society in Israel*, ed. Shelly Cohen and Ṭulah Amir (Tel Aviv: Xargol Books and Am Oved Publishers, 2007), 65–91.

4. This was not the first time Israeli architects had referred to Palestinian architecture. On the special interest Israeli architects had taken in Palestinian vernacular and the Arab village since the late 1950s, see Alona Nitzan Shiftan, *Seizing Jerusalem: The Architectures of Unilateral Unification* (Minneapolis: University of Minnesota Press, 2017), especially 45–78.

5. Yossef Shilhav, *Ultra-Orthodoxy in Urban Governance in Israel*, trans. Lisa Perlman (Jerusalem: Floersheimer Institute for Policy Studies, 1998), 43; Cahaner and Shilhav, "Ultra-Orthodox Settlements," 42–43. In addition, moving to the West Bank involved transgressing another religious commandment—"Shomer Nafsho, Irhak"—that prohibits ultra-Orthodox Jews from residing in a hostile environment, away from large Jewish concentrations, where there is a danger to their lives. See Aviva Luri, "Immanuel Doesn't Spread," *Mussaf Haaretz*, November 13, 1998, 32–38.

6. Shilhav, *Ultra-Orthodoxy*, 1, 7.

7. Cahaner and Shilhav, "Ultra-Orthodox Settlements," 45.

8. Shilhav, *Ultra-Orthodoxy*, 128. In a study from 2009, it was found that 59 percent of those self-identifying as ultra-Orthodox in Israel were living below the poverty line. See the National Economic Council at the Prime Minister's Office, *The Haredi Sector: Empowerment through Employment* (Jerusalem: Prime Minister's Office, 2009), 10.

9. Shilhav, *Ultra-Orthodoxy*, 3.

10. Cahaner and Shilhav, "Ultra-Orthodox Settlements," 50; Shilhav, *Ultra-Orthodoxy*, 3–6. Development towns, initially referred to as new towns, are modernist towns the Israeli government built in the country's periphery in order to absorb the masses of immigrants that flocked to the country after independence. For studies of development towns, see Miriam Tuvia and Michael Boneh, eds., *Building the Land: Public Housing in the 1950s* (Tel Aviv: Hakibbutz Hameuchad, 1999); Rachel Kalush and Hubert Lu-Yon, "The National House and

the Personal House: The Role of Public Housing in the Shaping of Space," in *Space, Land, Home*, ed. Yehuda Shenhav (Tel Aviv: Hakibbutz Hameuchad, 2003), 166–93.

11. Haim Nachum Freeman, "Beitar—A City That Brings Pride and Honor," interview by Y. Ben Moshe, *Hamodia*, September 29, 1989; Shilhav, conversation with author, June 30, 2015; Cahaner and Shilhav, "Ultra-Orthodox Settlements," 51.

12. This process had begun after the rise of the Likud Party in 1977. See Shlomo Gazit, *Trapped Fools: Thirty Years of Israeli Policy in the Territories* (Tel Aviv: Zmora Beitan, 1999), 244–45. Pertinent to the founding of Immanuel, in 1979 government officials agreed to open Ministry of Housing bids to a larger number of private construction firms. Firms that wanted to be included in these bids, however, had to show proof of extensive experience with large-scale construction projects. The developers of Immanuel were granted the right to oversee the construction, even though they failed to satisfy some of the preliminary requirements as outlined in the government's decision. See Bathia Avlin (legal consultant to the Ministry of Housing) to the state comptroller of Israel, June 10, 1985, folder 14616/12-בג, Israel State Archives. Only later, in April 1982, was a more conclusive decision allowing private developers to erect settlements in the West Bank made. See Meeting of the Committee for State Critique, February 12, 1985, folder כ-1423/26, transcript 31, Israel State Archive.

13. Star of Samaria/Gal. Beit-El, "Emmanuel—The Big City," Star of Samaria Offices, Immanuel. According to other publications, Immanuel's master plan was designed to accommodate only 10,000 units. See, for example, Amiram Harlap, ed., "Emmanuel—A New Town in Samaria," in *Israel Builds 1988* (Jerusalem: Ministry of Housing, 1988), 147.

14. Bathia Avlin to the state comptroller of Israel, June 10, 1985, folder 14616/12-בג, Israel State Archives.

15. Pinhas Arnreich and Yaacov Kaufman (Star of Samaria managers) to Minister of Housing and Vice Prime Minister David Levi, November 2, 1982, folder 14615/9-בג, Israel State Archives.

16. Pinhas Arnreich, "Forgotten City," interview by Yedidiya Meir, *Haaretz*, December 16, 2001, B3.

17. For an excellent account of Israeli architects of that generation and the special interest they took in Palestinian vernacular, see Nitzan-Shiftan, *Seizing Jerusalem*.

18. Yossi Sivan, interview by author, December 10, 2015.

19. Thomas Leitersdorff, "Starting a City from Scratch," interview by Eran Tamir Tawil, 2002, http://readingmachine.co.il/home/books/book_1_85984_549_5/1193036487.

20. Ibid.

21. David Nofar, telephone interview by author, December 3, 2015.

22. Elihu Merav (head of Immanuel's local council) to Asher Winner (manager of the Ministry of Housing), March 12, 1985; Baruh Ovitz (resident of Immanuel) to Asher Winner, July 7, 1985, בג-14616/12, Israel State Archives. For interviews with residents, see Luri, "Immanuel Doesn't Spread," 32–38.

23. Y. Ben Moshe, "A Glamorous City: Conversation with the Manager of Mishkenot Shaananim," *Hamodia*, September 29, 1989. See also Meir Rabinovich, "With the Blessing of Rabbi Shah," *Nekuda Journal*, no. 145 (November 1990): 13, 39.

24. Moshe Leibovitz (first mayor of Beitar Illit), interview by author, May 11, 2015.

25. An earlier attempt to settle the three hilltops took place a few years before, in 1982, when Joseph Rosenberg, an immigrant from South Africa, was given the right to build "Hadar Beitar"—a suburban settlement planned for national-religious Jews. For some reason,

Rosenberg failed to attract potential settlers. After he died, the settlement was reconceptual-ized as an ultra-Orthodox city-settlement. Initial meetings with architects Yaacov and Ora Yaar had taken place already in 1985. On March 25, 1987, a cornerstone-laying ceremony attended by Minister of Housing David Levi was held on the site. See Shilhav, *Ultra-Ortho-doxy*, 18–19; Uri Bar On (assistant to the minister of security) to Yehuda Nahari (commis-sioner of government property), November 2, 1982; Israel Dekel (vice minister of security) to Yehuda Nahari, November 7, 1982 Nahari to Yeshuv Beitar Ltd., March 27, 1983; Bar On to Nahari, September 2, 1984, folder 46701-בג, Israel State Archives; Ministry of Housing, Jerusalem District, "Beitar Illit," September 8, 1985, Yaar Collection, 77 Beitar, Built Heritage Research Center, the Technion; Ministry of Housing, "Invitation for Cornerstone Laying for the City of Beitar," March 1987, Yaar collection, 77 Beitar, Built Heritage Research Center, the Technion.

26. Meir Rabinowich, "The Report Is on the Table, the Outcomes Are on the Ground," *Nekuda Journal*, no. 145 (November 1990): 14.

27. On the Yaars and their work in Jerusalem, see Nitzan-Shiftan, *Seizing Jerusalem*, 48–54 and 63–67.

28. Adina (archivist of the settlement of Alfei Menashe), interview by author, July 8, 2015. Also, these aesthetic preferences become clear when examining settlers' publications from the late 1980s. In these publications, Palestinian towns were presented as places of decay and cultural backwardness, and Palestinian construction workers were condemned as unprofes-sional. For examples, see Hanan Sever, "Curfew on All Settlements," *Nekuda Journal*, no. 115 (November 1987), 22–25, 48, and Yehuda Etzion, "The Occupation Destroys: Hebrew Labor," *Nekuda Journal*, no. 111 (May 1987), 18–21. On the influence of the Palestinian uprising and other political events on architectural preferences and discourse in Israel, see Alona Nitzan-Shiftan, "On Concrete and Stone: Shifts and Conflicts in Israeli Architecture," *Traditional Dwellings and Settlements Review* 21, no. 1 (2009): 51–65.

29. Yaacov and Aviv Yaar, interview by author, April 20, 2015. The Yaars took a relatively similar approach in Pisgat Ze'ev in Jerusalem, where they copied elements from what they referred to as "traditional cities." See Amiram Harlap, ed., "General and Detailed Town Plan, Pisgat Zeev," *Israel Builds 1988* (Jerusalem: Ministry of Housing, 1988), 95. See Yaacov Yaar's discussion of postmodern urbanism in Yaacov Yaar, *Life and Architecture* (Haifa, Israel: Architectural and Landscape Heritage Research Center, the Technion, 2016), 123–27.

30. Yaacov and Aviv Yaar, interview by author.

31. Yaacov Yaar, "Beitar Will Be a Beautiful City with a High Quality of Life and Maxi-mum Adjustment for the Ultra-Orthodox Public: Interview with Architect Yaacov Yaar," *Hadshot Beitar Journal* 2 (December 1989): 8–9.

32. Moshe Leibovitz, interview by author.

33. For comparison, today in the city of Immanuel there is a synagogue for every thirty to thirty-five families.

34. Raphael Dankner (first manager of Beitar Illit's City Planning Division), interview by author, July 22, 2015.

35. For correspondences on Beitar Illit's commercial spaces, see Z. Gluzmann to Yaacov Yaar and Z. Ovadiya, January 8, 1991, Yaar collection, 77 Beitar, Built Heritage Research Center, the Technion; Adi Shrist (project manager), "Beitar Project—Discussion Number P-B-355," October 27, 1991, Yaar collection, Beitar Binder 1, Built Heritage Research Center, the Technion.

36. Moshe Leibovitz, interview by author.

37. Tamar, interview by author, June 26, 2015.

38. Avishai Meiron (manager of the City Planning Division in Beitar Illit), interview by author, June 6, 2015.

39. Moshe Leibovitz, interview by author.

40. For debates on these changes, see, for examples, Yaacov Yaar to Adi Shrist (project manager), "Beitar A1—Changes to Master Plan," May 27, 1991, Yaar collection, Beitar Binder 1, Built Heritage Research Center, the Technion; Yaacov Yaar to David Ovadiya, "Beitar— Supervision Offices," April 17, 1991, Yaar collection, Beitar Binder 1, Built Heritage Research Center, the Technion.

41. Leibovitz, interview by author. For sketches of building clusters, see Yaacov Yaar to Yair Eshel, September 3, 1993, Yaar collection, Beitar Binder 1, Built Heritage Research Center, the Technion.

42. Reizi (a young ultra-Orthodox female designer working in Beitar Illit), interview by author, June 18, 2015. Also Tamar, interview by author.

43. Avishai Ben-Haim, "Haredi to Their City," *Ma'ariv*, July 9, 2007, 16.

44. Akiva Peled, "This Is How the Modesty Patrol Worked," *Kooker*, May 22, 2013, http://www.kooker.co.il/רובינשטי-מאיר-של-הצניעות-משמרת-פעלה-כך/, and Yossef Pe'er, "Police Statement: Investigation of Rubinstein and the Modesty Patrols Will Continue," *Kikar HaShabat*, February 18, 2013, http://www.kikar.co.il/תימש-רובינשטיין-חקירת-המשטרה.html; "To the Cautious, and the One Warning," *Kore BeBeitar Journal* 1 (2008): 6.

45. Ben-Haim, "Haredi," 16.

46. Israel (resident of Modi'in Illit, second ultra-Orthodox city-settlement built after Beitar Illit), interview by author, June 21, 2015.

47. Ben-Haim, "Haredi."

48. Tamar Rotem, "You Shall Not Live Here," *Haaretz*, February 8, 2008, Hashavua.

49. Taking advantage of Ottoman land laws that were never revoked in the West Bank, the Israeli government gained the right to confiscate for public use lands that had not been cultivated for the previous three years. These lands are officially designated state lands. According to Talia Sasson, former head of the State Prosecution Criminal Department, since 1979 the practice of declaring uncultivated lands state lands in the West Bank has become an unfair mechanism that facilitates the construction of new settlements and the expansion of existing ones. She argues that the mapping of these lands and their allocation to certain groups were ill-conceived and suffered from severe inaccuracies. For example, she recalls hearing the head of the civil administration admitting that about 30 percent of all state lands in the West Bank were mistakenly registered as such. In addition, she recalls, by 2013, while 37 percent of these state lands were allocated to settlers, only 0.7 percent were given to Palestinians. See Talia Sasson, *At the Edge of the Abyss* (Jerusalem: Keter, 2015), 113–25.

50. In June 1983, the Palestinian residents of Hussan submitted an appeal against the commissioner of government property, arguing some of the lands allocated to the future settlement were privately owned. According to their appeal, about four thousand *dunams* (more than one and a half square miles) were confiscated from the residents of Hussan, Nahalin, and Wadi Fukin. After deliberation by the court, however, the appeal was dismissed on January 9, 1985. A few years later, when work on Beitar Illit was in full swing, it was reported that Palestinians from the nearby villages and towns were uprooting trees planted at the outskirts of the city, blocking roads leading to the construction site, and throwing stones at workers for the Jewish National Fund. See Mahmud Hayun, *Ali Shvahin et al. v. Commissioner of Government Property*, 23/83-עתר (VA, 1985); Joe Rosenberg, "Beitar—an Urban Settlement in Etzion

Block," January 21, 1985, folder 46701-בג, Israel State Archives; Nathan Sass to Shlomo Ariav, June 14, 1987, and Sass to Mordechei Roh, March 2, 1989, folder KKL5/64425, Central Zionist Archives.

51. For example, journalist Amira Hass describes how, in December 1999, a new military checkpoint was erected next to Hussan, limiting the access of Palestinians to the local commercial center. According to Hass, some of the residents of Beitar were encouraging the soldiers and construction workers while the checkpoint was being erected. Amira Hass, "All of a Sudden, the Green Line Got Closer to Hussan," *Haaretz*, February 19, 2000, B3.

52. Offer Petersburg, "Yalla Beitar Yalla," *Ma'ariv*, August 30, 1994, Business, 10; Koby Blich, "The Tales of Moshe in the Big City," *Ma'ariv Hayom*, May 23, 1995, 16; Avirama Golan, "They Will Bring a Sheep, We Will Bring a Butcher," *Haaretz*, November 13, 1994, B2.

53. For example, in a survey conducted by the Geo-Cartography Institute, 79 percent of the residents of Beitar Illit expressed satisfaction with their housing conditions and the municipal services available in the city. See "Most Residents Are Happy with the Housing, Urban Services and Municipality," *Zo Irenu*, July 14, 2005, 1. In addition, in 2003 the city won "five stars" in a national competition organized by the Council for a Beautiful Israel, which also crowned it "The Prettiest Ultra-Orthodox City." See Beitar Illit Won Five Stars and Enjoys the Title: The Prettiest Ultra-Orthodox City," *Zo Irenu*, December 11, 2003, 3.

54. For examples, see John Chase, Margaret Crawford, and John Kaliski, eds., *Everyday Urbanism* (New York: Monacelli, 1999); James Holston, *Insurgent Citizenship* (Princeton, NJ: Princeton University Press, 2009); Teresa P. R. Caldeira, *City of Walls: Crime, Segregation, and Citizenship in São Paulo* (Berkeley: University of California Press, 2001); and Jennifer Mack, "New Swedes in the New Town," in *Use Matters: An Alternative History of Architecture*, ed. Kenny Cupers (London: Routledge, 2013). On the limitations of everyday practices in Jerusalem, see Rachel Kallus, "The Political Role of the Everyday," *City* 8, no. 3 (December 2004): 341–61.

55. See Eyal Weizman, *Hollow Land: The Architecture of the Israeli Occupation* (London: Verso, 2007).

56. Michel Foucault, "Space, Knowledge, and Power," interview by Paul Rabinow, in *Architecture Theory since 1968*, ed. K. Michael Hays (Cambridge, MA: MIT Press, 2000), 433–34.

Bibliography

Ben-Haim, Avishai. "Haredi to Their City." *Ma'ariv*, July 9, 2007.

Blich, Koby. "The Tales of Moshe in the Big City." *Ma'ariv Hayom*, May 23, 1995.

Caldeira, Teresa P. R. *City of Walls: Crime, Segregation, and Citizenship in São Paulo.* Berkeley: University of California Press, 2001.

Chase, John, Margaret Crawford, and John Kaliski, eds. *Everyday Urbanism*. New York: Monacelli, 1999.

Cahaner, Lea, and Yossef Shilhav. "Ultra-Orthodox Settlements in Judea and Samaria." *Social Issues in Israel* 16 (2013): 41–62.

Cupers, Kenny, ed. *Use Matters: An Alternative History of Architecture*. London: Routledge, 2013.

Etzion, Yehuda. "The Occupation Destroys: Hebrew Labor." *Nekuda Journal*, no. 111 (May 1987): 18–21.

Foucault, Michel. "Space, Knowledge, and Power." Interview by Paul Rabinow. *In Architecture Theory since 1968*, edited by Michael K. Hays, 433–34. Cambridge, MA: MIT Press, 2000. Originally published in *Skyline*, March 1982.

Freeman, Haim Nachum. "Beitar—A City That Brings Pride and Honor." Interview by Y. Ben Moshe. *Hamodia*, September 29, 1989.

Gazit, Shlomo. *Trapped Fools: Thirty Years of Israeli Policy in the Territories*. Tel Aviv: Zmora Beitan, 1999.

Golan, Avirama. "They Will Bring a Sheep, We Will Bring a Butcher." *Haaretz*, November 13, 1994.

Hadshot Beitar Journal. "Beitar Will Be a Beautiful City with a High Quality of Life and Maximum Adjustment for the Ultra-Orthodox Public: Interview with Architect Yaacov Ya'ar." *Hadshot Beitar Journal* 2 (1989): 8–9.

Harlap, Amiram, ed. "Emmanuel—A New Town in Samaria." In *Israel Builds 1988*, 147. Jerusalem: Ministry of Housing, 1988.

Hass, Amira. "All of a Sudden, the Green Line Got Closer to Hussan." *Haaretz*, February 19, 2000.

Holston, James. *Insurgent Citizenship*. Princeton, NJ: Princeton University Press, 2009.

Israel Central Bureau of Statistics. Statistical Abstract of Israel, Population by District, Sub-District. Jerusalem: CBS, September 10, 2015.

Kallus, Rachel. "The Political Role of the Everyday." *City* 8, no. 3 (December 2004): 341–61.

Kalush, Rachel, and Hubert Lu-Yon. "The National House and the Personal House: The Role of Public Housing in the Shaping of Space." In *Space, Land, Home*, edited by Yehuda Shenhav, 166–93. Tel Aviv: Hakibbutz Hameuchad, 2003.

Katz, Yaakov. "407,118: This Is the Up to Date Number of Jewish Residents in Judea and Samaria as of 31/12/2015," *Besheva*, January 7, 2016. http://www.inn.co.il/Articles /Article.aspx/14370.

Luri, Aviva. "Immanuel Doesn't Spread." *Mussaf Haaretz*, November 13, 1998.

Mack, Jennifer. "New Swedes in the New Town." In *Use Matters: An Alternative History of Architecture*, ed. Kenny Cupers. London: Routledge, 2013.

Meir, Yedidiya. "Forgotten City." *Haaretz*, December 16, 2001.

Moshe, Y. Ben. "A Glamorous City: Conversation with the Manager of Mishkenot Shaananim." *Hamodia*, September 29, 1989.

National Economic Council at the Prime Minister's Office. *The Haredi Sector: Empowerment through Employment*. Jerusalem: Prime Minister's Office, 2009.

Peace Now. "Settlements and Outposts Numbers and Data." Peace Now Settlements Watch Reports, Tel Aviv, June 2009.

Pe'er, Yossef. "Police Statement: Investigation of Rubinstein and the Modesty Patrols Will Continue." *Kikar HaShabat*, February 18, 2013. http://www.kikar.co.il /המשטרה-חקירת-רובינשטיין-תימשך.html. Accessed May 1, 2016.

Peled, Akiva. "This Is How the Modesty Patrol Worked." *Kooker*, May 22, 2013. http://www .kooker.co.il/כך-פעלה-משמרת-הצניעות-של-מאיר-רובינשטי/. Accessed May 1, 2016.

Petersburg, Offer. "Yalla Beitar Yalla." *Ma'ariv*, August 30, 1994.

Rabinowich, Meir. "The Report Is on the Table, the Outcomes Are on the Ground." *Nekuda Journal*, no. 145 (November 1990): 14.

———. "With the Blessing of Rabbi Shah." *Nekuda Journal*, no. 145 (November 1990): 13, 39.

Sasson, Talia. *At the Edge of the Abyss*. Jerusalem: Keter, 2015.

Shachar, Oryan, Alona Nitzan-Shiftan, and Rachel Sebba, "Gvulot Veptahim Shel Kdusha: HaKirya HaHasidit Behatzor Haglilit." In *Living Forms: Architecture and Society in Israel*, edited by Shelly Cohen and Tulah Amir, 65–91. Tel Aviv: Xargol Books and Am Oved Publishers, 2007.

Sever, Hanan. "Curfew on All Settlements." *Nekuda Journal*, no. 115 (November 1987): 22–25, 48.

Shiftan, Alona Nitzan. *Seizing Jerusalem: The Architectures of Unilateral Unification.* Minneapolis: University of Minnesota Press, 2017.

———. "On Concrete and Stone: Shifts and Conflicts in Israeli Architecture." *Traditional Dwellings and Settlements Review* 21, no. 1 (2009): 51–65.

Shilhav, Yossef. *Ultra-Orthodoxy in Urban Governance in Israel.* Translated by Lisa Perlman. Jerusalem: Floersheimer Institute for Policy Studies, 1998.

Tuvia, Miriam, and Michael Boneh, eds., *Building the Land: Public Housing in the 1950s.* Tel Aviv: Hakibbutz Hameuchad, 1999.

Weizman, Eyal. *Hollow Land: The Architecture of the Israeli Occupation.* London: Verso, 2007.

Yaar, Yaacov. *Life and Architecture.* Haifa, Israel: Architectural and Landscape Heritage Research Center, Technion, 2016.

NOAM SHOKED is a Princeton-Mellon Postdoctoral Fellow at Princeton University. He received his PhD from the University of California, Berkeley and taught architecture at the California College of the Arts. Shoked studies the history and theory of the built environment, with a focus on the relationship between architecture and politics in Israel and the West Bank.

10

NOTIONS OF CLASS AND CULTURE IN HOUSING PROJECTS IN TEHRAN, 1945–60

Jaleh Jalili and Farshid Emami

IN FEBRUARY 1946, A FLOOD DESTROYED PARTS OF a poor area in the southern periphery of Tehran. Some seventy-five families were left without housing, and many more had to live in dire conditions. The flood was the last in a series of disasters at the end of a harsh winter, during which an unprecedented accumulation of snow crippled the city for weeks, resulting in the demolition of feeble houses in the rapidly growing squatter areas of south Tehran. The *Ettela'at* daily reported that after the massive snow, an architect from the municipality visited the affected neighborhoods, pledging to those who had lost property to build new houses with more stable materials and better conditions.[1] Chaharsad-Dastgah, a social housing project built in eastern Tehran, was intended, in part, for the slum dwellers left homeless by the flood.

This incident hints at two novel transformations that affected the discourse and practice of urban planning in Iran: the expansion of blighted urban areas and the emergence of the architect as an expert in public housing. Both transformations had their roots in the social and urban modernization programs of the 1930s. During this period, under the autocratic state of Reza Shah Pahlavi (r. 1925–41), Tehran was subjected to radical interventions: the city gates and walls were dismantled, broad avenues were cut through urban fabric, and imposing governmental buildings were erected at the city core.[2] The emerging city structure not only embodied and represented the modernized state of Reza Shah but was also central to the rise of a new bourgeois class, of which the architect was a representative member.[3] Nevertheless, as elsewhere in the "developing world" of the twentieth century, rapid top-down modernization of Tehran—the utopian vision of a straightforward leap into modernity—remained fragmented, ambiguous, and contested: behind the façades of the new avenues, the dense urban fabric of the old city (and its concomitant social structures) prevailed, and informal settlements expanded in vacant lands opened up by the destruction of the city's ramparts.[4] Demolitions had created a blank slate only partially inscribed with the projected plan of tree-lined boulevards and austere modernist structures. While marginal to the extensive modernization programs of the 1930s, "housing" (*maskan*) appeared as a public topic in the post–World War II period. Housing deficiency began to symbolize a plethora of social ills. Primarily intended for the poor and lower middle classes, not only were the housing projects instrumental in shaping new discourses and forms of professional practice in the entangled domains of politics and architecture, they also affected the course of physical and social development in Tehran.

This chapter analyzes the ways in which professionalization, shifting political contexts, and ideas of class and culture were intertwined with the conception and design of Tehran's lower- and middle-income housing projects. Concentrating on the two decades that followed the end of World War II, the chapter shows how the specific sociopolitical context of Iran meshed with models and conceptions of housing adapted from international discourses. The projects, which include social housing for low-income groups as well as neighborhood designs for the middle classes, are examined not as self-contained entities in the city's peripheries, but rather as components of a broader urban system, informed by top-down modernization and various unplanned developments and reactions. This study particularly concentrates on aspects of design and production of the housing projects, as manifested in the writings and drawings of the architects.

Spanning the period between 1945 and 1965, the projects are examined in three chronological sections. The first part considers the entangled stories of the rise of a professional class of architects and the construction of the first known housing project in Tehran, Chaharsad-Dastgah. The second part examines the development of financial and bureaucratic institutions in relation to two housing projects conceived and completed in the 1950s, the neighborhoods of Narmak and Nazi-abad. The chapter concludes with a brief discussion of two representative projects of the period after the coup d'état of 1953—Aban social housing and an unrealized plan for the Oudla-jan neighborhood—analyzing the shifts in planning and design of housing projects in the 1960s.

The *Architecte* as Social Reformer: Chaharsad-Dastgah

In February 1945, a group of eight foreign-educated Iranian architects established the Society of Iranian Diplomate Architects (SIDA), the first professional association of its kind in the country.[5] Soon after, the "diploma-holding" architects residing in Tehran joined the association and elected the board of directors. The public image of the SIDA was bolstered by the publication of the *Architecte*, a bimonthly magazine entirely dedicated to architecture and urbanism. As noted, the emergence of architecture as an independent profession had its roots in the modernization programs of the preceding decades: architecture was among the technical fields in which scores of Iranian students were educated in Europe through a state-sponsored program.[6] To distinguish themselves from local masons, members of the new professional class used the French term *architecte* rather than the traditional term *me'mar*.[7] The new appellation was deliberately chosen to convey a message on both local and international scenes: the emerging Iranian architect belonged to an international class of professionals, distinct from traditional local builders.

The establishment of an independent civil institution was made possible by the political context of the postwar era, during which a democratic parliamentary system replaced the authoritarian state of Reza Shah. With young Mohammad Reza Shah (r. 1941–79) ruling as constitutional monarch, members of bourgeoisie and old aristocracy administered the country until the 1953 coup d'état, which toppled the government of the premier, Mohammad Mosaddeq (in office 1951–53), and reinstalled the shah as an autocratic ruler.[8] It was in this context of relative political freedom that architects, who had primarily acted as state agents, began to claim more autonomy for their profession, expanding its purview to urban and social matters.[9] In fact, concerns for social housing and expertise in urbanism were central to the fashioning of the self-image of the *architecte*. Collaboration with the municipality and other state institutions in urban projects was one of the stated goals of the SIDA.[10] Indeed, in addition to identifying themselves with the label *architecte*, most members of the SIDA also self-identified as *urbaniste* or *shahrsaz* (literally, "city builder").[11] On the pages of the *Architecte*, articles on city planning and social housing appeared alongside drawings and photographs of ultramodern villas designed for bourgeois clients. The articles discussed inadequate housing as a national problem and expounded examples in western Europe and north America as models for dealing with housing deficiency.[12]

The ascending status of architects as experts in mass housing and urbanism is manifest in the conception, design, and implementation of Chaharsad-Dastgah (literally, "four hundred units"). Constructed between 1946 and 1949, the project was managed by the municipality and financed by the National Bank (Bank-e Melli) and by the Mortgage Bank (Bank-e Rahni), which specialized in investments in construction projects, housing loans, and mortgages.[13] The complex was designed by four Iranian architects, Ali Sadeq, Manuchehr Khorsand, Abbas Azhdari, and Hosayn Sadeq, who were all SIDA members and frequent contributors to the *Architecte*. Sadeq, who also served as the CEO of the Mortgage Bank, appears to have played a leading role in the design and implementation of the project.

By the mid-1940s, when Chaharsad-Dastgah was being conceived and implemented, the problem of housing in Tehran had become more and more pressing. Migrants from villages and provincial towns were arriving in larger numbers, and squatter areas were rapidly proliferating. By 1946, the population of Tehran exceeded eight hundred thousand, having doubled in the span of a decade.[14] The roots and causes of the rapid rise of Tehran's population were numerous. Chief among them was the concentration of industries, which attracted a working-class population to the capital.[15] Also accelerating migration to Tehran was the 1943 lifting of a law requiring a permit to settle in a new city.[16] The relative security and safety of the capital had turned it into an appealing magnet for those seeking employment, education, or a safe haven in a war-torn country.[17] The overpopulation of the city and insufficient housing had led to a highly expensive market, both inside and outside the city's official boundaries.[18] Initially, new neighborhoods were created through subdivision of vacant lands and distribution of plots among salaried government employees (*karmandan*) and army officials in the areas to the north of the old town.[19] While high-ranking civil servants and well-to-do migrants were able to build private houses in the northern outskirts of the city, the poor settled in slums outside the city's official borders. Further exacerbating the situation was the rise of a real-estate

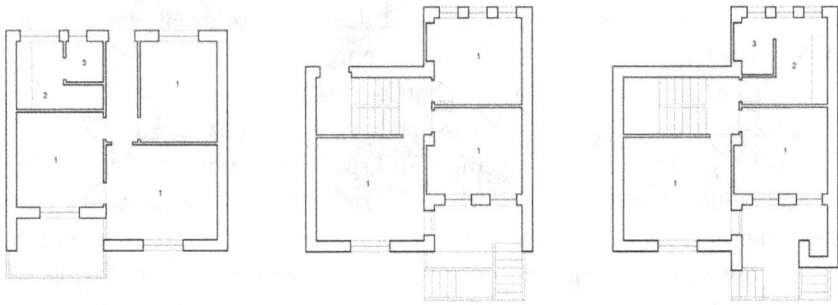

Figure 10.1. Unit plans—Chaharsad Dastgah: (left) plan of typical one-story unit; (center) lower level of two-story unit; (right) upper level of a two-story unit. Legend: 1. room; 2. kitchen; 3. storage. Reproduced by the authors based on the plans published in *Architecte* 4 (1325 [1947]): 128.

market in the vacant lands surrounding Tehran. It was in this context that social housing emerged as a solution for the problem of accommodating the lower classes.[20]

Occupying an area of 12.5 hectares, Chaharsad-Dastgah was constructed on an irregularly bounded plot of land on the eastern border of the city.[21] The units were arranged in orthogonal blocks, subdivided into rectangular plots oriented north-south. The public facilities were laid along an east-west axis leading from the mosque to the local municipal building (*shahrdari-ye barzan*). Lined with a row of arcaded shops, the axis expanded in front of the municipality to form a rectangular plaza, to be dominated by an unrealized clock tower. The model of the original design suggests that the mosque was to feature a dome and two minarets, which together with the clock tower would have given a clearer visual definition to the central axis of the complex.

The housing blocks consisted of three principal types of single-family units (fig. 10.1). The first type was one-story with three rooms; the second had five rooms in two stories; a third two-story type, with shops on the first floor, was specifically designed for the blocks facing the central spine. The floor plans were fairly simple, consisting of a tiny foyer with doors opening to three or four "rooms." All units were to feature a private yard with a small pool (*hozche*). While a kitchen and storage (*anbar*) were included in the main building, the toilets were situated at the opposite end of the yard, presumably to accommodate the living habits of the intended inhabitants. Except for the kitchen, the rooms were almost of the same size and with no assigned function, a layout deemed appropriate for the life-style of the large households who were supposed to occupy the units.[22]

While the unadorned blocks of houses in Chaharsad-Dastgah are more in tune with the functionalist aesthetics of the Bauhaus and the International Style, the axial arrangement and space definition of the complex's central spine are reminiscent of Beaux-Arts compositional principles. Indeed, elements such as a clock tower and the semicircular form of the plaza are suggestive of a traditional European model for the quarter. This is not surprising considering the fact that the architects of the project had been trained in France and Belgium, where a similar amalgam of Beaux-Arts principles and industrial modes of production was prevalent.[23] Ultimately, in terms of design genealogy, the roots of the layout and program of the project can be traced back to utopian urban plans of the early twentieth century, particularly the garden city movement, as initially formulated in 1898 by the British social activist and urban planner Ebenezer Howard (1850–1928) and his followers, as well as the *cité industrielle*, an ideal city proposed in 1917 by the French architect and urban planner Tony Garnier (1869–1948).[24]

In addition to such selective borrowings from European models, the design of Chaharsad-Dastgah also exhibited a deliberate attempt to adjust to the context. The contextual features are manifest in the choice of private houses over apartment buildings, in the provision of private yards with a pool and toilet, and in the multifunctionality of interior spaces. These modifications were justified in terms of "local customs and climatic conditions," concepts that were formulated within the discourse of modernism. (Arguably, even the most radical modernist projects of the twentieth century were not devoid of such considerations of climatic or cultural conditions.) Sensitivity to cultural and geographical differences was considered an essential part of the design process; as one of the project's designers wrote, "it is the duty of architects and other professionals to understand these differences and design accordingly."[25]

What is striking about the incorporation of these local customs in the scheme of Chaharsad-Dastgah is that they do not appear in private luxurious residences designed by the very same architects. Indeed, unlike the housing project units, interior spaces of the bourgeois villas of the same period were designated as dining rooms, living rooms, and so on. As Pamela Karimi notes in her study of domesticity and interior spaces in contemporary Iran, while resonating with older aristocratic mansions, such divisions were largely novel in Iranian houses.[26] This contrast between the functional division of the bourgeois domestic spaces and the multifunctionality of the housing project units suggests that perhaps the underlying dichotomy lies less in an opposition between modernity and tradition and more between the lower and upper classes; what were understood as local customs were in effect the habits of the lower classes and not shared by their supposedly acculturated upper-class compatriots. As Khorsand, one of the architects of the complex, notes, "since those who were to occupy the units had a lower standard of hygiene, toilets were built outside the living areas and in the courtyards."[27] Such statements clearly signify how a combination of income and cultural distinction shaped the image that the architects held of the intended occupants of the project.

The design of the complex was also informed by the discourses of hygiene and public health. A fairly large program of public facilities was envisioned for the complex, including a primary school, a hospital, a public bath, and a laundry. The project was claimed to be the first in the city provided with sanitary water and electricity, a remarkable feat at a time when the city itself lacked a sanitary water system.[28] Such facilities allowed the project to be represented as a model of progress and modernization for the poor. Up to this point, ordinary people had experienced urban modernization in the form of destruction of properties, construction of boulevards and squares, and massive governmental buildings. In Chaharsad-Dastgah, the lower classes became subject to the fundamental discourses of modernization—with its emphasis on technology, rationality, and sanitation—in their very living spaces.

Still, despite these modern amenities, the writings of the designers of the project suggest that it failed to meet their vision of a truly modern housing complex. For instance, Azhdari notes, "in foreign countries, low-cost housing is mostly in the form of multistory apartments. Clearly, the cost of such structures is lower than single-family houses, but it was not so fitting for Tehran's climate and local customs. Thus it was decided to build houses with private yards."[29] Rather than a smooth negotiation of the local and international, the design process is indicative of a tension between idealized images of modern housing and a presumed set of local customs.

Institutions, Professionals, and Banks: Narmak and Nazi-abad

Chaharsad-Dastgah was the precursor of scores of housing projects built in Tehran in the 1950s and 1960s, a period marked by the development of the legal and institutional framework for housing projects. The most prominent of these new institutions was the Plan Organization (Sazman-e Barnameh va Budjeh), which was set up in 1948 to coordinate the preparation of development plans for the country. In 1949, the organization commissioned the New York–based firm Overseas Consultants to prepare the country's first seven-year development plan, in which a substantial section was devoted to town improvement and housing.[30] Dismissing the undertakings of local architects in urbanism, the report highlighted "the lack of technical staff in town planning" and advised the Plan Organization to set up a town planning bureau and employ "foreign experts."[31] Instead of formal features and aesthetics, urban planning and housing were now to be understood in terms of "statistics and data," areas that required their own experts. The report attributed the housing shortage to the effects of war, higher construction prices, rural migration, destruction of properties through "road improvements," and low maintenance, and it highlighted the problem of "unsuitable houses": "In the southern areas of Tehran, where approximately half the population is accommodated, most of the houses can be described as slum buildings."[32] The labeling of half of the city as slum, under the rubric of technical assessment, paved the way for the ensuing urban interventions.

New legislation in 1952 on the registration of unused lands (*zaminha-ye mavat*, i.e., lands without known owners) provided the legal basis for subsequent housing projects, according to which the government became the proprietor of vacant lands surrounding the city.[33] In 1955, the newly established Construction Bank (Bank-e Sakhtemani) acquired these lands and was entrusted with the task of planning and constructing housing projects.[34] The major projects of the Construction Bank were two neighborhoods: one near Narmak, in the northeastern part of Tehran and the other in Nazi-abad, in the southern part of the city. These projects not only introduced a new conception of housing but also altered the course of the city's development for the years to come.

Intended for twenty thousand inhabitants, the Narmak project was unprecedented in terms of scale and urban layout. Occupying an area of 5.5 square kilometers, the urban scheme was based on a rectangular grid, with cross-axial boulevards functioning as main access roads (fig. 10.2). Carved at the center of the neighborhood, along the main north-south boulevard, was a vast square bordered by commercial and office buildings. The residential areas were disposed in more than one hundred rectilinear blocks, each consisting of a small square of greenery with four dead ends

Figure 10.2. View of the model of Narmak. From *Bank-e Sakhtemani* 1 (1335 [1956]), cover.

branching off from its corners. By creating semiprivate open spaces detached from the passing traffic, these introverted blocks were clearly meant to foster a sense of community. Each part of the neighborhood had its own bathhouse, school, and shopping area. Industrial functions were located in the far north, at a distance from residential areas, and a large park and athletic facilities were provided in the eastern part of the neighborhood.[35] Ranging in area from two hundred to six hundred square meters, the plots were oriented north-south to allow optimal use of natural light and air circulation.

A similar organizational scheme was employed in the design of Nazi-abad, a smaller neighborhood in the south of the city, close to a railroad station (fig. 10.3). It consisted of one thousand housing units for low-income residents.[36] Oriented north-south, the units were forty-square-meter one-story houses built on eighty-square-meter lots, consisting of two rooms, a kitchen, and a toilet. Compared to Narmak, the units were less elaborate, which was deemed more fitting for the intended lower-income residents.[37] In a sense, Narmak and Nazi-abad were both built according to the same architectural and urban planning principles, but for two different types of users. While in both neighborhoods there was an overarching design scheme, only the infrastructure was developed and built by the banks and professional architects who designed the neighborhoods, leaving the building of the units to individual local builders for lack of funding and because of changes in organizational priorities.[38]

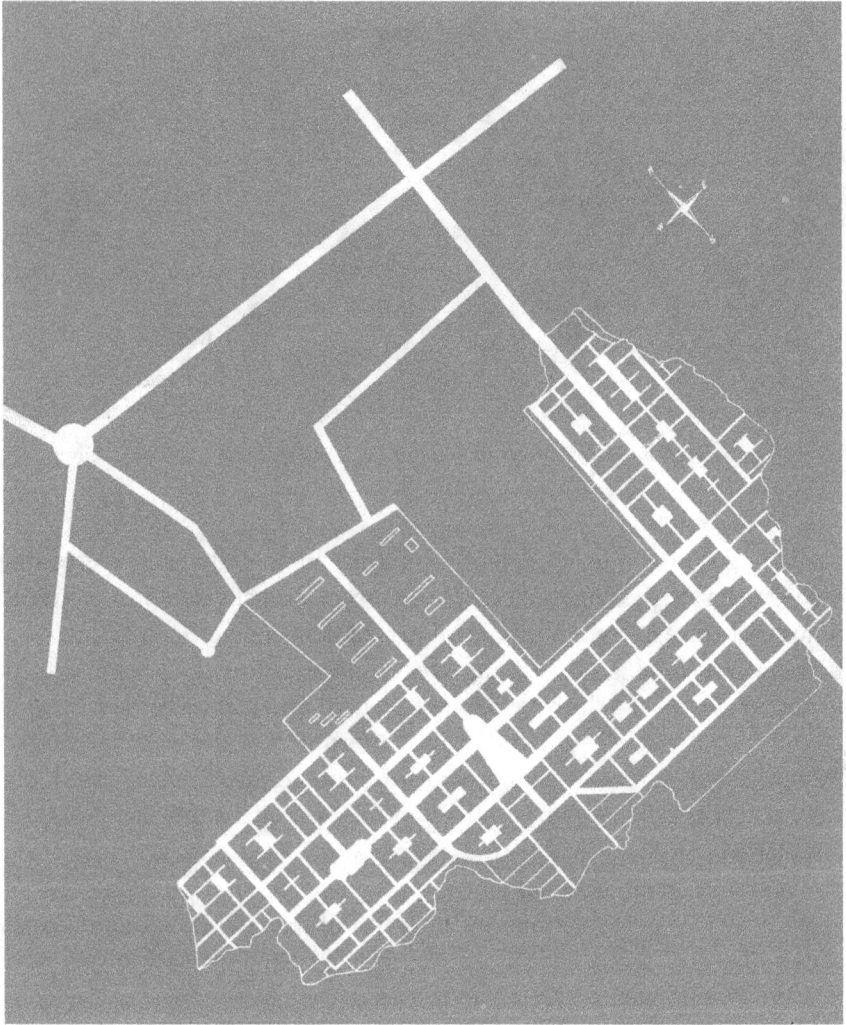

Figure 10.3. Schematic plan of Nazi-abad. From *Bank-e Sakhtemani* 1 (1335 [1956]), cover.

Because of the size of the neighborhood and the diversity of the units (with one, two, and three bedrooms), Narmak provided a unique opportunity for architects to design and implement an ideal modern neighborhood on a large scale. Separation of vehicular circulation from residential blocks and functional zoning point to a closer adherence to the principles and images of modernist urban planning. Rather than a clock tower, for instance, the most salient structures of the neighborhood were to be cubical office towers. Moreover, unlike the multifunctional units of Chaharsad-Dastgah, in which all rooms were of equal size with no designated function, the units of Narmak had assigned functions designed for a modern nuclear family, with bedrooms on one side of the service area (including kitchen and toilets) and the living room on the other, representing a clear separation of public and private areas within residential units. The toilets were no longer designed away from the residential area either.

At the same time, an attempt at harmonizing the project with aspects of local culture is evident in the size of the apartments, as well as the choice of single-family units with private yards. In fact, if these aspects are considered as part of the schema of a larger design in which residential blocks enjoy intimate semipublic spaces and each part of the neighborhood has its own schools and other local services (such as bathhouses and shops), then the influences of other neighborhood design models, particularly those developed by the US planners Clarence Perry (1872–1944) and Clarence Stein (1882–1975), become evident.[39] Thus, the design of the neighborhood can be interpreted as an active interaction between ideals in modern urban planning and neighborhood designs, on the one hand, and consideration of local conditions, on the other. In Narmak, however, while the neighborhood was designed as a single project and the infrastructure was implemented by the bank, not all the units were built as planned. With the exception of a small part of the neighborhood for which the bank used a newly imported prefabrication technology, most of the units were constructed by local master builders or *me'mars*—anathema to the *architecte*—without necessarily adhering to the original master plan.[40] It is not surprising that the professional architects were not satisfied with the final results, as reflected in the articles published in the journal of the Construction Bank.[41]

In a way, the greatest significance of the Narmak and Nazi-abad projects—and the activities of the Construction Bank in general—lies in the patterns of development that they established for Tehran. Indeed, in addition to direct involvement in the construction of these housing projects, in the course of seven years in the 1950s, the Construction Bank allocated more than seventeen thousand plots to government employees.[42] Consequently, by the early 1960s, orthogonal streets and rectangular plots had turned into the primary model of urban development in both public and private sectors. Covering expansive areas around the city, the grid pattern gave a sense of order to the new developments, although the city as a whole lacked an overarching master plan. In 1963, after a decade of experimentation in housing projects, the Construction Bank was replaced by two new organizations, another sign of a shift toward a more centralized and bureaucratic approach to housing.[43]

Cleansing the Old City, Expelling the Squatters

The housing projects of the 1950s and 1960s—as exemplified by Narmak, Nazi-abad, and Chaharsad-Dastgah—were marked by an effort to adapt imported models of development to local realities. They exude a fairly egalitarian vision of urban society, showing an attempt—or at least a gesture—to ameliorate the living conditions of the middle and lower classes through application of modern technology and rational methods of design. From the late 1950s onward, however, the notion embodied in these early plans gave way to more radical solutions. The shifts in planning strategies were propelled by transformations in both internal politics and international urban planning paradigms. On the political scene, having regained his throne through the coup d'état of 1953, Mohammad Reza Shah gradually developed the apparatuses of authoritarian rule and, in 1963, embarked on an extensive modernization program, called the White Revolution.[44] Meanwhile, modernism turned into the dominant paradigm of urban and housing development around the globe. From this period onward, spatial strategies and state policies guiding the social housing projects became more and more authoritarian and exclusive.[45] The two projects discussed below—an unrealized proposal for the Oudlajan neighborhood and the Aban low-cost housing project—reflect these transformations in professional and political contexts.

Located in the east of the former citadel (*arg*), Oudlajan was one of the original five neighborhoods of old Tehran. Despite the massive destructions of the 1930s, vestiges of the old city had survived in the bazaar and neighborhoods such as Oudlajan. With a dense fabric of narrow, winding alleyways and courtyard houses, the spatial structure of these quarters stood in sharp contrast to the streetscape of the broad, straight avenues that surrounded them. As islands trapped amid a network of avenues and squares, these areas continued to function not only as centers of social life but also as bastions of the conservative classes, and particularly the bazaar merchants.

In 1959, the Mortgage Bank prepared a proposal for the redevelopment of Oudlajan: the entire neighborhood was to be razed to the ground and replaced with modernist towers (fig. 10.4). Espousing such a radical plan is all

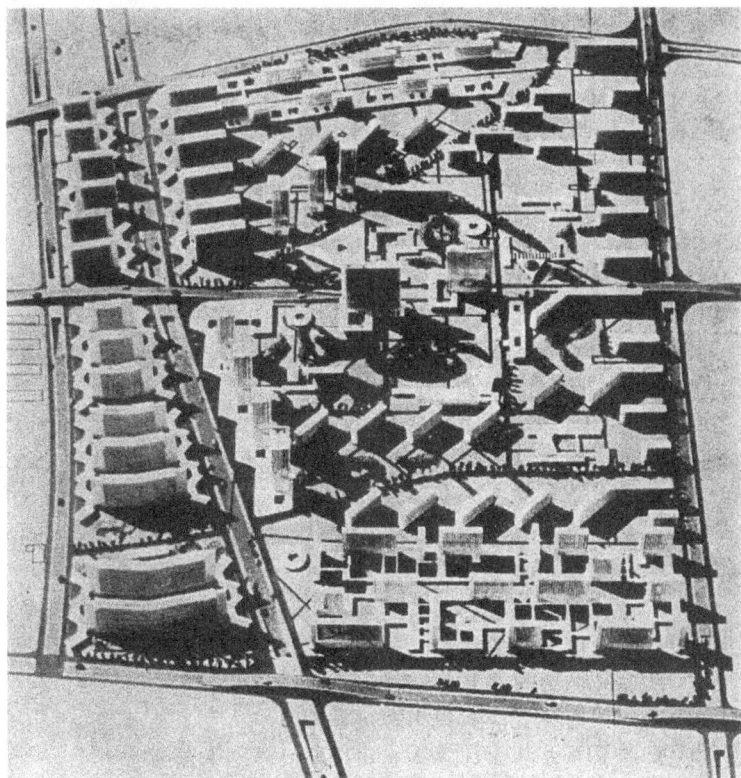

Figure 10.4. Views of the model for development of Oudlajan. From Bank-e Rahni, *Mokhtasari az tarikhche-ye khadamat-e bist saleh* (1338 [1959]), 49.

the more striking in light of the fact that the plan was designed and advocated by Ali Sadeq and Abbas Azhdari, founding members of the SIDA and the architects of Chaharsad-Dastgah. A departure from the design ideals of Chaharsad-Dastgah is evident not only in formal aspects of the project but also in its proposed location at the city core. As Sadeq remarks, "Tehran has developed in a disorganized manner, while at the heart of the city old quarters remain as they were a century ago. This is the best situation for modern urbanism. With these neighborhoods within the city, building in deserts is a mistake."[46] In a similar vein, Azhdari laments the absence of a legal framework that would allow the wholesale redevelopment of existing neighborhoods.[47] The very same architects who had boasted of considering local conditions—and had to compromise their ideals to meet what they saw as climatic and cultural exigencies of the context—now advocated a radical urban scheme. It seems as if the contrast between modern suburbs of the city and its centuries-old urban core—the incomplete status of the tabula rasa—had become a source of anxiety for modernist architects.

The surviving photographs of the model prepared for the Oudlajan development (fig. 10.4) show the degree to which its architects had embraced the urbanistic tenets of modernism, as formulated by the Congrès International d'Architecture Moderne and the Swiss-French architect Le Corbusier (1885–1965). Freestanding slab blocks are disposed in a lush setting, ordered in abstract geometric patterns. Although, in a report on the project, Azhdari claims that the existing mosques and other religious establishments (*tekiyehs*) were preserved in the proposal, the model exhibits no trace of the old urban fabric of the neighborhood or any of its components.[48] By the late 1950s, the urbanistic principles of modernism were no longer mere designs on paper but had materialized in cities across the globe. It is indeed no coincidence that this ultramodern design was proposed for an existing neighborhood rather than vacant land. After all, top-down interventions and negation of the past through destruction of old urban fabrics were integral to the ideology propagated by Le Corbusier and other modernist urban designers.

If the unrealized proposal for Oudlajan aimed to eradicate the residues of the old urban fabric, the Aban project was meant to vacate the city of its unwelcome inhabitants: the squatters. Specifically intended for the slum dwellers, the Aban social housing project was conceived and implemented by the Ministry of Housing (Vezarat-e Maskan) and the Housing Organization (Sazman-e Maskan), which had replaced the Construction Bank and

Figure 10.5. View of the Aban project. From Bahrambeygui, *Tehran*, 122.

Mortgage Bank as the primary sponsors of housing projects.[49] Constructed between 1965 and 1967, the Aban project consisted of twenty-two one-bedroom units and was provided with sanitary water, electricity, and urban facilities such as markets and elementary and high schools. The neighborhood consisted of orderly blocks of one-story houses, each with a tiny private yard (fig. 10.5). An east-west main street, lined with stores and public services such as a post office, police station, and local municipal building on both sides, functioned as the neighborhood center. Farther north and close to the mosque, a daily bazaar was to provide a venue for social interaction. According to Khadijeh Kiakajuri, who prepared a report on the neighborhood in 1972, despite the poor condition of the housing units, the public spaces functioned well and were used by the residents: "Children tend to play in the streets near their houses rather than the park, and women do many of their daily chores together in front of their houses."[50] According to the same report, the design of the interiors did not allow sufficient sunlight or ventilation, and being directly built on the ground caused issues, including flooding, whenever there was precipitation.

But the construction of the project was not merely a benevolent act by the state for the sake of the squatters. Rather, the project was part of a broader vision of what Tehran was supposed to be and represent. By the 1960s, a strict social polarity had formed in Tehran: unlike lower- and middle-class projects such as Narmak and Chaharsad-Dastgah, Aban was not even in the proximity of the city. A strict hierarchy was now to determine the place of people in the city: the north was to be the exclusive domain of the rich, totally devoid of the stain of the lower classes. In his reminiscences about the project, Mohammad Hadi Javadi relates that the day after the project's inauguration, army vehicles went to Behjat-abad, a squatter area in what was then north of Tehran, forcefully removed all the slum dwellers and their belongings, and relocated them to Aban, where "each family was given a unit. Soon after, all slum buildings of Behjat-abad were razed to the ground so that no one could return."[51] Not surprisingly, those who were forced to settle in the projects were very dissatisfied at first, as the new neighborhood lay at a distance from the city, where they worked as servants and maids at the houses of the affluent families of north Tehran. According to Javadi, the men complained that back in Behjat-abad, "their wives worked in the nearby houses of the wealthy and earned an income, and that the wealthy often threw big parties and gave the remainder of the food to them."[52]

While the majority of the projects planned and built between 1945 and 1960 were aimed at the middle classes, the lower middle classes, and the poor, beginning in the 1960s, more housing projects were designed and constructed for the upper classes. Notable among them are the housing complex of Sahebgharaniye, built in the early 1960s as a luxurious complex for the wealthy,[53] and the Shahrara residential buildings in the west of Tehran, also built in the 1960s, which were aimed at the upper middle classes.[54] By the mid-1970s, housing projects shifted from neighborhoods with low-rise buildings to ultramodern high-rise apartments intended for the middle and upper classes. In 1971, one such complex of high-rise apartment towers was inaugurated in Behjat-abad, which had been emptied of its squatters a few years earlier. On the eve of the 1979 Revolution, both the public and private sectors had scores of apartment buildings under construction in north Tehran, and designing and building low-cost housing as a central focus of Tehran's urban development was already a thing of the past.

Conclusion

The earliest housing projects in Tehran were conceived in the period of rapid urbanization and relative political opening that came with the end of World War II. Designed and promoted by local professionals and funded by newly established state institutions, the projects reflected this altered political context while responding to the urban and social forces set in motion in the preceding decades. Intended for the lower strata of the new urban dwellers (middle- and lower-income government employees and squatters), the projects followed prevalent international models, but, as in other contemporary contexts, this entailed more than a straightforward transfer of ideas. In this early period, adaptations were made in terms of "climatic conditions" and "local customs." But as this chapter shows, the housing projects also demonstrate a constant negotiation of class positions and cultural assumptions.

Later accounts of the projects reveal some of the paradoxes of these notions of class and culture. In her report, for instance, Kiakajuri draws a somewhat disappointing picture of the status of Chaharsad-Dastgah in 1972, twenty-five year after its construction. In her judgment, the units were "not designed in accordance with Tehran's climate, with no attention to sunlight and air ventilation."[55] In fact, most of the original ideas—consideration of local climate, provision of public spaces, and sensitivity to cultural habits (such as private yards and separation of toilets from living areas)—seemed not to work as they were intended: "the stores are closed and no public life happens on the main street. The only green space in the neighborhood, the park, is closed to the public and children have no place to play."[56] While financial limitations were to blame for some of these shortcomings, other observations raise questions about the validity of the initial cultural assumptions: "most units have built toilets within the living areas to avoid the inconvenience of passing through the yard to use them."[57] The traits assumed to be fixed cultural habits were either inaccurate from the outset or were ultimately subject to change in a short period of time.

Similarly, another report on the Aban project, published in 1976, suggests a failure in achieving some of the socioeconomic goals of the project. Based on extensive survey data, the report indicates that less than ten years after its construction, more than 70 percent of the initial owners had sold their units and left the neighborhood (excluding those who had rented out the apartments). The survey data further suggest that the initial squatter population was soon replaced by a somewhat higher social class of workers and government employees with higher levels of income and status.[58] The physical layout of the units was transformed, too, to respond to the needs of the new occupants.

Once new experiences in urban planning and design, located in the outskirts of the city and catering to specific social groups, the housing projects discussed in this chapter are now part of an expanding metropolis with a much higher density and a fairly different social construct. In the rapidly developing urban context and housing market, little remains of the housing units that once constituted these complexes. Such transformation has taken different forms, from completely replacing old units with new multistory buildings in Narmak and Chaharsad-Dastgah to dividing units and adding half stories to adapt the old units for a new generation in Aban.[59] In fact, in most cases all that remains is the grid pattern and some public spaces that remind older residents of a past that no longer exists.

Notes

1. *Ettela'at* (21 Bahman 1324 [February 11, 1946]).

2. For a study of the urban transformation of Tehran during the reign of Reza Shah, see Kamran Safamanesh and Behruz Monadi-zadeh, "Tahavvolat-e me'mari va shahrsazi 1299–1320 Sh" [Transformations in architecture and urbanism, 1920–41], in *Majmu'eh maqalat-e dovvomin kongere-ye me'mari va shahrsazi-ye Iran* [Proceedings of the second congress of history of Iranian architecture and urbanism], ed. Baqer Ayatollahzadeh Shirazi, 5 vols. (Tehran: Sazman-e miras-e farhangi-ye keshvar, 1378 [1999]), 2: 247–73. Also see Eckart Ehlers and Willem Floor, "Urban Change in Iran, 1920–41," *Iranian Studies* 26, nos. 3–4 (1993): 251–76; Amir Bani-Mas'ud, *Me'mari-ye mo'aser-e Iran* [Contemporary Iranian architecture] (Tehran: Honar-e me'mari-ye qarn, 1390 [2011]).

3. For a study of the social associations of architects in this period, see Talinn Grigor, "The King's White Walls: Modernism and Bourgeois Architecture," in *Culture and Cultural Politics under Reza Shah*, ed. Bianca Devos and Christoph Werner (London: Routledge, 2013), 95–118. For a more comprehensive study, see Talinn Grigor, *Building Iran: Modernism, Architecture, and National Heritage under the Pahlavi Monarchs* (New York: Periscope, 2009).

4. On the structure and urban transformations of Tehran under the Pahlavi dynasty, also see S. M. Habibi, *Az shar ta shahr* [De la cité à la ville: Analyse historique de la conception urbaine et son aspect physique] (Tehran: University of Tehran Press, 1999), 149–90.

5. For a study of professionalization of architecture in Iran and the Anjoman-e Architectha-ye Irani-ye Diplome [Society of Iranian Diplomate Architects], see Shawhin Roudbari, "Instituting Architecture: A History of Transnationalism in Iran's Architecture Profession, 1945–1995," in *The Historiography of Persian Architecture*, ed. Mohammad Gharipour (New York: Routledge, 2016), 173–200.

6. On state programs for sending students abroad, see Rudi Matthee, "Transforming Dangerous Nomads into Useful Artisans, Technicians, Agriculturalists: Education in the Reza Shah Period," in *The Making of Modern Iran: State and Society under Riza Shah, 1921–1941*, ed. Stephanie Cronin (New York: Routledge, 2003), 138–40.

7. As Manuchehr Khorsand, one of the founding members of the society, writes, "since the term *me'mar* has become 'banal' (*mobtazal*) due to overuse, and void of its meaning, the

SIDA has decided to use the term *architecte*, which has an international connotation." See Manuchehr Khorsand, "Anjoman-e architectha-ye Irani-ye diplomeh" [Society of Iranian Diplomate Architects], *Architecte* 1 (1325 [1946]): 3.

8. For a discussion of the ruling elements in postwar Iran, see Ervand Abrahamian, *Iran between Two Revolutions* (Princeton, NJ: Princeton University Press, 1982), 169–76.

9. It is important to note that although SIDA members claimed autonomy through the establishment of a professional association, many of them already held, or went on to hold, a leading role in the management of governmental institutions that sponsored housing projects. For instance, Ali Sadeq and Abbas Azhdari served in the municipality, in the Mortgage Bank, and later in the Construction Bank. Likewise, Naser Badiʿ was employed by the Construction Bank. A close relationship with the state is also evident in the inclusion of prominent political figures as honorary members of the SIDA. See *Architecte* 1 (1325 [1946]): 39.

10. Iraj Moshiri, "Hadaf-e ma" [Our goal], *Architecte* 1 (1325 [1946]): 1–2.

11. *Architecte* 1 (1325 [1946]): 2–3.

12. For examples, see *Architecte* 1 (1325 [1946]) and *Architecte* 4 (1326 [1947]).

13. Mortgage Bank (Bank-e Rahni) was established in 1939 as the first specialized bank for housing and construction. Hiring architects and engineers, the bank directly engaged in building housing projects from 1946 onwards.

14. Ali Madanipour, *Tehran: The Making of a Metropolis* (New York: John Wiley and Sons, 1998), 16. Also see Abrahamian, *Iran between Two Revolutions*, 147–48.

15. According to Nikki Keddie, by 1940, 58.5 percent of domestic capital investment was centered in Tehran. See Nikki Keddie, *Modern Iran: Roots and Results of Revolution* (New Haven, CT: Yale University Press, 2003), 95.

16. Mohammad Hadi Javadi, "Gozashteh cheraq-e rah-e ayandeh ast: tajrobeh-ha-ye dolat dar khaneh-ha-ye arzan" [The past is the light to the future: state experiments with low-cost social housing], in *Majmuʿeh maqalat-e dovvomin kongere-ye meʿmari va shahrsazi-ye Iran* [Proceedings of the second congress of history of Iranian architecture and urbanism], ed. Baqer Ayatollahzadeh Shirazi, 5 vols. (Tehran: Sazman-e miras-e farhangi-ye keshvar, 1378 [1999]), 1:109–27, at 110. Also see Abbas Azhdari, "Masʾale-ye tahiyye-ye maskan dar Tehran va shahrestanha" [The problem of housing in Tehran and other cities], *Architecte* 1 (1325 [1946]): 15.

17. Madanipour, *Tehran*, 16.

18. Azhdari, "Masʾale-ye tahiyye-ye maskan."

19. The lands of Yusef Abad and Abbas Abad, for instance, had been distributed among government employees and army personnel, respectively, although most were unable to build and ended up selling their allocated lots. See Naser Badiʿ, "ʿElal-e peydayesh-e kuyha-ye tazeh: Yusef-abad, Narmak, Nazi-abad" [Reasons for construction of new neighborhoods: Yusef-abad, Narmak, Nazi-abad], in *Barresi-ye masaʾel-e ejtemaʿi-ye shahr-e Tehran* [Study of social problems of Tehran] (Tehran: University of Tehran, 1343 [1964]): 210–14; and Javadi, "Gozashteh cheraq-e rah-e ayandeh ast," 111.

20. For a study of urban development in Tehran in this period, see H. Bahrambeygui, *Tehran: An Urban Analysis* (Tehran: Sahab, 1977).

21. Abbas Azhdari, "Sakhteman-e khaneha-ye arzan dar Iran" [Building low-cost housing in Iran], *Architecte* 4 (1326 [1947]): 125. For another study of Chaharsad-Dastgah, see Hamed Khosravi, "Politics of Urban Form: Architecture of Tehran (1921–1953)," in *Cities to Be Tamed? Spatial Investigations across the Urban South*, ed. Francesco Chiodelli, Beatrice De Carli, Maddalena Falletti, and Lina Scavuzzo (Newcastle upon Tyne, UK: Cambridge Scholars, 2013), 237–61.

22. It seems that even though the primary motivation for instigating the project was to accommodate the slum dwellers who had lost housing as a result of the flood, the units were given to the lower echelons of government employees. Indeed, the two main criteria set for allocating the apartments were that buyers have low incomes and large families.

23. Khorsand and Azhdari had studied at an architectural school in Paris. Sadeq received his training in Belgium.

24. See Ebenezer Howard, *Garden Cities of Tomorrow* (London: Swan Sonnenschein, 1902); Tony Garnier, *Une cité industrielle: Étude pour la construction des villes* (New York: Princeton Architectural Press, 1989). For a critical study of these paradigms, see Peter Hall, *Cities of Tomorrow: An Intellectual History of Urban Planning and Design in the Twentieth Century* (Chichester, UK: Wiley Blackwell, 2014).

25. Azhdari, "Mas'ale-ye tahiyyeh-ye maskan," 52.

26. See Z. Pamela Karimi, *Domesticity and Consumer Culture in Iran: Interior Revolutions of the Modern Era* (New York: Routledge, 2013), 72–79.

27. Manuchehr Khorsand, "Tozih-e digar darbare-ye khaneha-ye arzan-e kuy-e chahar-sad khane" [Another explanation of the low-cost houses of the four-hundred-unit neighborhood], *Architecte* 4 (1326 [1947]): 135.

28. Khadijeh Kiakajuri, "Motale'eh darbareh-ye kuy-ha va masaken dar noh mahaleh-ye shahr-e Tehran" [A study of nine residential districts in Tehran], study conducted under the supervision of the Ministry of Housing and Development, Building Research and Code Division (Tehran: Vezarat-e maskan va abadani, 1351 [1972]), 37–40.

29. Azhdari, "Sakhteman-e khaneha-ye arzan dar Iran," 129.

30. Overseas Consultants, *Report on Seven Year Development Plan for the Plan Organization of the Imperial Government of Iran*, 5 vols. (1949). Especially see vol. 3, 221–74.

31. Ibid., 3:231.

32. Ibid., 3:239.

33. Tabataba'i, "Arazi-ye mavat va moqarrarat-e marbut beh an" [Unused lands and their regulations], in *Barresi-ye masa'el-e ejtema'i-e shahr-e Tehran* (Tehran: University of Tehran, 1343 [1964]), 63–70.

34. Badi', "Elal-e paydayesh-e kuyha-ye tazeh," 214–16; Javadi, "Gozashteh cheraq-e rah-e ayandeh ast," 112.

35. Javadi, "Gozashteh cheraq-e rah-e ayandeh ast," 112–13.

36. Ibid., 113.

37. Kiakajuri, "Motale'eh," 27–29.

38. See Javadi, "Gozashteh cheraq-e rah-e ayandeh ast."

39. For a detailed explanation of the design ideals, see Clarence S. Stein, *Toward New Towns for America*, 2nd ed., rev. (New York: Reinhold, 1957).

40. For a more detailed study of Narmak and the influences of local builders and me'mars on the future of the neighborhood, see Rana Habibi and Bruno De Meulder, "Architects and 'Architecture without Architects': Modernization of Iranian Housing and the Birth of a New Urban Form Narmak," *Cities* 45 (2015): 29–40.

41. Abbas Azhdari, "Nokati darbare-ye kuy-ha-ye Narmak va Nazi-Abad" [Issues in Narmak and Nazi-abad proposal], *Bank-e Sakhtemani* 4 (1335 [1956]): 21–22.

42. Tabataba'i, "Arazi-ye mavat va moqarrarat-e marbut beh an," 68.

43. The two organizations were the Housing Organization (Sazman-e Maskan) and Ministry of Housing and Urban Planning (Vezarat-e Maskan va Shahrsazi).

44. On the White Revolution, see Ervand Abrahamian, *A History of Modern Iran* (Cambridge: Cambridge University Press, 2008), 123–54.

45. For a study of a representative urban project of this period, see Farshid Emami, "Urbanism of Grandiosity: Planning a New Urban Centre for Tehran (1973–76)," *International Journal of Islamic Architecture* 3, no. 1 (2014): 69–102.

46. Bank-e Rahni, *Mokhtasari az tarikhche-ye khadamat-e bist saleh* [A brief overview of twenty years of service] (Tehran: Bank-e Rahni, 1338 [1959]), 49. Archived at the library of the central branch of Bank-e Maskan, Tehran, Iran.

47. Despite the support of the shah, the project was never realized. Advocating the idea of razing all old neighborhoods in Tehran to build modern residential, commercial, and office buildings, Azhdari regrets the lack of funding and political will for building the project proposed by the Mortgage Bank for Oudlajan. According to Azhdari, relocating the whole population of the neighborhood and its huge associated costs and practical difficulties prevented the municipality and the government from implementing the "perfect design of a whole neighborhood." See Abbas Azhdari, "Porozheh-ye shahrsazi-ye yek bakhsh-e qadimi-ye Oudlajan" [Urban project for an old part of Oudlajan], in *Barresi-ye masa'el-e ejtema'i-e shahr-e Tehran*, 198–201.

48. Ibid., 199.

49. The project was inaugurated in October 1965 (9 Aban 1344, in the solar hijri calendar), on the birthday of the crown prince and thus became known as the Nohom-e Aban (literally, Aban 9) neighborhood.

50. Kiakajuri, "Motale'eh," 33–35.

51. Javadi, "Gozashteh cheraq-e rah-e ayandeh ast," 126.

52. Ibid.

53. Ibid., 123.

54. Kiakajuri, "Motale'eh," 9–13.

55. Ibid., 38.

56. Ibid.

57. Ibid., 39.

58. See Sohrab Mashhudi, "Negareshi bar karkardha va naresa'i-ha-ye kuy-e nohom-e Aban" [An overview of the functions and shortcomings in Nohom-e Aban neighborhood] *Nashriye tahqiqat-e estandard-ha-ye fanni* (1355 [1976]).

59. For a study of the current state of the Aban neighborhood, see Homa Maddah, "Barresi-ye ensanshenakhti-e ta'sirat-e porozheh-ha-ye tose'eh-i bar zendegi-ye zanan (motale'eh moredi mahaleh kuy-e Sizdah-e Aban)" [Anthropological assessment of development projects' effects on women's lives (A case study of thirteen Aban district of Tehran)] (master's thesis, University of Tehran, 2010). Maddah shows that although, in the first ten years after the inauguration of the project, a shift in the occupants of the neighborhood happened, most of the current residents have been living in the neighborhood since then. According to her observations, because of legal limitations, lack of interest on the part of the investors, and residents' limited financial means, most of the original units still exist, but they have been adapted to satisfy current needs. Also, as the new generation takes over their parents' houses, new legal and physical arrangements shape the neighborhood. For instance, in many cases the units are divided into two to house more than one family, or half stories are built to accommodate new family members.

Bibliography

Abrahamian, Ervand. *A History of Modern Iran.* Cambridge: Cambridge University Press, 2008.

———. *Iran between Two Revolutions.* Princeton, NJ: Princeton University Press, 1982.

Azhdari, Abbas. "Mas'ale-ye tahiyye-ye maskan dar Tehran va shahrestanha" [The problem of housing in Tehran and other cities]. *Architecte* 1 (1946 [1325]):15.

———. "Nokati darbare-ye kuy-ha-ye Narmak va Nazi-Abad" [Issues in Narmak and Nazi-abad proposal]. *Bank-e Sakhtemani* 4 (1956 [1335]): 21–22.

———. "Porozheh-ye shahrsazi-ye yek bakhsh-e qadimi-ye Oudlajan" [Urban project for an old part of Oudlajan]. In *Barresi-ye masa'el-e ejtema'i-ye shahr-e Tehran* [Study of social problems of Tehran], 198–201. Tehran: University of Tehran, 1343 [1964].

———. "Sakhteman-e khaneha-ye arzan dar Iran" [Building low-cost housing in Iran]. *Architecte* 4 (1947 [1326]): 125–33.

Badi', Naser. "'Elal-e peydayesh-e kuy-ha-ye tazeh: Yusef-abad, Narmak, Nazi-abad." In *Barresi-ye masa'el-e ejtema'i-e shahr-e Tehran* [Social problems of Tehran], 210–14. Tehran: University of Tehran, 1343 [1964].

Bahrambeygui, H. *Tehran: An Urban Analysis.* Tehran: Sahab, 1977.

Bani-Mas'ud, Amir. *Me'mari-ye mo'aser-e Iran* [Contemporary Iranian architecture]. Tehran: Honar-e me'mari-ye qarn, 1390 [2011].

Bank-e Rahni. *Mokhtasari az tarikhche-ye kahdamat-e bist saleh* [A brief overview of twenty years of service]. Tehran: Bank-e Rahni, 1338 [1959]).

Barresi-ye masa'el-e ejtema'i-e shahr-e Tehran [Social problems of Tehran]. Tehran: University of Tehran, 1343 (1964).

Ehlers, Eckart, and Willem Floor. "Urban Change in Iran, 1920–41." *Iranian Studies* 26, nos. 3–4 (1993): 251–76.

Emami, Farshid. "Urbanism of Grandiosity: Planning a New Urban Centre for Tehran (1973–76)." *International Journal of Islamic Architecture* 3, no. 1 (2014): 69–102.

Garnier, Tony. *Une cité industrielle: Étude pour la construction des villes.* New York: Princeton Architectural Press, 1989.

Grigor, Talinn. *Building Iran: Modernism, Architecture, and National Heritage under the Pahlavi Monarchs.* New York: Periscope, 2009.

———. "The King's White Walls: Modernism and Bourgeois Architecture." In *Culture and Cultural Politics under Reza Shah*, edited by Bianca Devos and Christoph Werner, 95–118. London: Routledge, 2013.

Habibi, S. M. *Az shar ta shahr* [De la cité à la ville: Analyse historique de la conception urbaine et son aspect physique]. Tehran: University of Tehran Press, 1999.

Habibi, Rana, and Bruno De Meulder. "Architects and 'Architecture without Architects': Modernization of Iranian Housing and the Birth of a New Urban Form Narmak." *Cities* 45 (2015): 29–40.

Hall, Peter. *Cities of Tomorrow: An Intellectual History of Urban Planning and Design in the Twentieth Century.* Chichester, UK: Wiley Blackwell, 2014.

Howard, Ebenezer. *Garden Cities of Tomorrow.* London: Swan Sonnenschein, 1902.

Javadi, Mohammad Hadi. "Gozashte cheraq-e rah-e ayandeh ast: tajrobeh-ha-ye dolat dar khaneh-ha-ye arzan" [The past is the light to the future: state experiments with low-cost housing]. In *Majmu'eh maqalat-e dovvomin kongere-ye me'mari va shahrsazi-ye Iran* [Proceedings of the second congress of history of Iranian architecture and urbanism], ed. Baqer Ayatollahzadeh Shirazi, 5 vols. (Tehran: Sazman-e miras-e farhangi-ye keshvar, 1378 [1999]), 1:109–127. Tehran: Sazman-e Miras Farhangi-e Keshvar, 1378 [1999].

Karimi, Z. Pamela. *Domesticity and Consumer Culture in Iran: Interior Revolutions of the Modern Era.* New York: Routledge, 2013.

Keddie, Nikki. *Modern Iran: Roots and Results of Revolution*. New Haven, CT: Yale University Press, 2003.

Khorsand, Manuchehr. "Anjoman-e architectha-ye Irani-e diplomeh" [Society of Iranian Diplomate Architects]. *Architecte* 1 (1946 [1325]): 3.

———. "Tozih-e digar darbareh khaneh-ha-ye arzan-e kuy-e 400 khaneh" [Another explanation for the low-cost houses of the four-hundred-unit neighborhood]. *Architecte* 4 (1947 [1326]): 134–35.

Khosravi, Hamed. "Politics of Urban Form: Architecture of Tehran (1921–1953)." In *Cities to Be Tamed? Spatial Investigations across the Urban South*, edited by Francesco Chiodelli, Beatrice De Carli, Maddalena Falletti, and Lina Scavuzzo. Newcastle upon Tyne, UK: Cambridge Scholars, 2013.

Kiakajuri, Khadijeh. "Motale'eh darbareh kuy-ha va masakendar noh mahaleh shahr-e Tehran" [A study of nine residential districts in Tehran]. Study conducted under the supervision of the Ministry of Housing and Development, Building Research and Code Division, Tehran: Vezarat-e maskan va abadani, 1972 [1351].

Madanipour, Ali. *Tehran: The Making of a Metropolis*. New York: John Wiley and Sons, 1998.

Maddah, Homa. "Barresi-e ensanshenakhti-e ta'sirat-e porozheh-ha-ye tose'eh-i bar zendegi-ye zanan (motale'eh moredi mahaleh kuy-e Sizdah-e Aban)" [Anthropological assessment of development projects' effects on women's lives (A case study of thirteen Aban district of Tehran)]. Master's thesis, University of Tehran, 2010.

Mashhudi, Sohrab. "Negareshi bar karkardha va naresa'i-ha-ye kuy-e nohom-e Aban" [An overview of the functions and shortcomings in Nohom-e Aban neighborhood]. *Nashriye Tahqiqat-e Estandard-ha-ye Fanni* (1355 [1976]).

Matthee, Rudi. "Transforming Dangerous Nomads into Useful Artisans, Technicians, Agriculturalists: Education in the Reza Shah Period." In *The Making of Modern Iran: State and Society under Reza Shah, 1921–1941*, edited by Stephanie Cronin, 123–45. New York: Routledge, 2003.

Moshiri, Iraj. "Hadaf-e ma" [Our goal]. *Architecte* 1 (1946 [1325]): 1–2.

Overseas Consultants. *Report on Seven Year Development Plan for the Plan Organization of the Imperial Government of Iran*, 5 vols. 1949.

Rahni, Bank-e. *Mokhtasari az tarikhche-ye kahdamat-e bist saleh* [A brief overview of twenty years of service]. Tehran: Bank-e Rahni,1338 [1959].

Roudbari, Shawhin. "Instituting Architecture: A History of Transnationalism in Iran's Architecture Profession, 1945–1995." In *The Historiography of Persian Architecture*, edited by Mohammad Gharipour, 173–200. New York: Routledge: 2016.

Safamanesh, Kamran, and Behruz Monadi-zadeh. "Tahavvolat-e me'mari va shahrsazi 1299–1320 Sh" [Transformations in architecture and urbanism, 1920–41]. In *Majmu'eh maqalat-e dovvomin kongere-ye me'mari va shahrsazi-ye Iran* [Proceedings of the second congress of history of Iranian architecture and urbanism], ed. Baqer Ayatollahzadeh Shirazi, 5 vols. (Tehran: Sazman-e miras-e farhangi-ye keshvar, 1378 [1999]).

Stein, Clarence S. *Toward New Towns for America*. 2nd ed., rev. New York: Reinhold, 1957.

JALEH JALILI is Visiting Assistant Professor of Sociology at Oberlin College. She obtained her PhD in sociology from Brandeis University in May 2018. Her dissertation explores how public spaces in Tehran mediate social relations in a rapidly changing urban environment. Bridging her background in architecture and urban design with sociology, she is interested in social, political, and cultural meanings of space, particularly public spaces in the Middle East. She has presented extensively at conferences, including the American Sociological Association, Society for the Study of Social Problems, and Eastern Sociological Society. She is a recipient of a dissertation fellowship from the Mellon Foundation and a travel award from the Crown Center for Middle East Studies.

FARSHID EMAMI is Assistant Professor of Islamic Art History at Oberlin College. He received his PhD in architectural history from Harvard University in 2017. His primary area of research is art and architecture in early modern Islamicate empires, with a focus on Safavid Iran. He is currently completing a book manuscript that offers a new interpretation of architecture and urbanism in seventeenth-century Isfahan, the Safavid capital, through the analytical lens of city experience. His published and forthcoming articles also address such topics as architecture in the contemporary Middle East and lithography in nineteenth-century Iran.

11

DISCREPANT SPATIAL PRACTICES: CONTEMPORARY SOCIAL HOUSING PROJECTS IN İZMİR

Gülsüm Baydar, Kıvanç Kılınç, and Ahenk Yılmaz

SOCIAL HOUSING HAS BEEN A PRESSING NEED IN İzmir since the mid-twentieth century, and especially from the beginning of the 2000s, mostly as a result of the popularization of urban renewal policies in Turkey. These policies target the central areas of İzmir to build revenue-generating estates for upper-income groups. The residents of these areas who live on meager means are displaced to newly built neighborhoods on the outskirts of the city. Their new environments, which consist of modernist high-rise blocks, are radically different from their previous homes not only in physical but also in social and economic terms.

This chapter emphasizes the daily practices of the inhabitants in two such housing settlements in İzmir, Örnekköy (2005) and Uzundere (2010), as they are affected by planning and administrative decision making and the historical development of social housing. Our analysis is inspired by critical urban theorist Henri Lefebvre's renowned spatial triad.[1] According to Lefebvre, space is not a passive setting, but a creative habitus and facilitator of human interaction.[2] It is "never either simple, or stable,"[3] but is continually acted on and socially (re)produced.[4] Lefebvre argues that, emerging from the dynamism of heterogeneous and multiple spatial experiences, this constant production process involves three interrelated components: spatial practices, spaces of representation, and representational spaces. Spatial practices involve "close association, within perceived space, between daily reality and urban reality"; representations of space include mental representations such as maps, plans, and models conceived by "scientist, planners and urbanists"; and finally, representational spaces or spaces of representation relate to ideals, imaginations, and other forms of discourses that are "directly lived through images and symbols."[5]

Inspired by Lefebvre's spatial triad, this chapter delves into the Örnekköy and Uzundere housing sites at three layers. The first layer focuses on the materiality of the two settlements' architecture, including plans, construction materials, and infrastructure. This layer roughly corresponds to Lefebvre's representations of space, as it focuses on planned aspects of the housing. It also includes research findings on the amendments and interventions made by the residents. The second layer analyzes the social practices of the residents in relation to public facilities, spaces of socialization, and the notion of neighborliness, which directly corresponds to Lefebvre's spatial practices. The final layer, agency, focuses on the relationship between space and subjectivity and is based on the comments made by the users of these two settlements. In that it focuses on the ideals and interpretations of the residents, it relates to Lefebvre's representational spaces.

Lefebvre emphasizes that conceived, perceived, and lived spaces should never be considered autonomous and that this "triad loses all force if it is treated as an abstract 'model.'"[6] Thus, the three layers of analysis in this study are interdependent, congruent at some levels and divergent at others. The outcomes are intended to inform future projects for the planning of livable environments that benefit both their users and the quality of the urban environment at large. We begin with an attempt to recount the historical context of social housing projects both in Turkey and more specifically in Örnekköy and Uzundere, in order to provide a background for this analysis.

Social Housing and Urban Renewal in Turkey

Displacement of the poor to the peripheries of urban centers is a global phenomenon that dominates the neoliberal urban agenda of not only the "developing" countries of the Middle East–North Africa region,[7] but also most of the industrialized states in Europe and North America.[8] Lower-income groups are being moved either to densely populated housing areas built outside city limits or to "mixed-income neighborhoods." Such policies are often concealed behind the mask of social integration but actually serve to render hitherto neglected areas of cities accessible to private entrepreneurs. Inadequate access to basic services such as clean water and sanitation, and the lack of safety, which actually stem from the failure of public housing policies in the first place, are used as a justification for urban renewal projects. Driven by a widespread tendency to support "owner occupation" to prompt construction-based economic growth models,[9] these policies have resulted in the production of cities that are socially and spatially segregated.[10]

Contemporary Turkish cities, where public housing projects are exclusively produced by the Mass Housing Administration (TOKİ), suffer from similar policy deficiencies.[11] Since 2002, the Mass Housing Administration has produced more than six hundred thousand housing units nationwide, predominantly for lower- and middle-income groups.[12] These figures are significantly higher than the number of housing units directly built or subsidized by the government in earlier decades.[13] The administration became the most powerful national authority on mass housing, especially after it was linked to the Office of the Prime Minister in 2004 and restructured in accordance with the ruling party's ambitious policy of building ninety thousand units each year.[14] This goal was realized within two years with only fifty-four staff members, who were responsible for developing projects for not only housing settlements all around the country, but also related public buildings, ranging from primary schools to mosques and shopping centers. The average completion time of each housing settlement was as short as fifteen months.[15]

In the context of İzmir, the Mass Housing Administration's mission is described as follows: "The Mass Housing Administration provides İzmir, which is among the cities where the amount of slums and unauthorized construction has peaked, with a modern appearance."[16] Despite this heroic mission statement, the agency's projects have been subject to incessant criticism for their low quality of construction and dull architecture: tall blocks of concrete that have multiplied in detriment to the urban fabric and natural habitat, designed without regard to the social, ethnic, cultural, and family backgrounds of the people who inhabit them.[17] Örnekköy and Uzundere are the first two social housing settlements built by the Mass Housing Administration in İzmir, where the residents belong to lower-income groups who used to live in unauthorized buildings at the central areas of the city. They are subjects of forced migration whose moving experience has been in stark contrast with the mission statement of the Mass

Housing Administration. As one resident emotively explained, "They threw people in. They did not think that it is human beings who live here—like dogs. Even dogs live in better places."[18]

The two extreme evaluations of the projects in İzmir, in spite of their broad generalizations, reveal a major discrepancy between the perspectives of the planners and those of users of urban residential space. Looking at the image of the city, the first adopts a bird's-eye view, while the second comes from the depths of daily life. A close analysis of Örnekköy and Uzundere provides significant administrative and planning clues about how their residents' quality of everyday life can be improved. In fact, a detailed look into social housing in Turkey and its evolution into the current settlements built by the Mass Housing Administration, brings to the surface a complex history, in which locality plays an important role in both the production and (re)appropriation of modernist architectural forms.

In Turkey, the term "housing crisis" appeared in government documents as early as 1924, only one year after the foundation of the Turkish Republic. But low-cost housing could not be given top priority until the 1940s.[19] Until then, there were not sufficient funds, infrastructure, and industry in Turkey for the realization of such grand schemes.[20] For those reasons, examples of mass housing similar to those in Europe, North America, and the (post)colonial housing programs in the Middle East–North Africa region did not appear in major Turkish cities until the end of World War II. An exception was the major industrial complexes built in the 1930s and 1940s, which included housing for workers and both lower- and middle-income civil servants.[21]

From the beginning of the 1930s, successive governments adopted various methods to deal with the growing shortage of affordable housing in Turkey, including rental allowance and rent control.[22] One of the most preferred methods, direct state intervention, could not produce a sufficient quantity of housing.[23] Another common approach was to encourage home-ownership through minimum public subsidies to workers' cooperatives. As economist Barış Alp Özden pointed out, however, "Housing cooperatives continued to build largely middle class housing during the period, which was far too costly for workers, while unauthorized land appropriations and squatting became the primary mechanism through which the working poor could be incorporated into the urban fabric."[24] For instance, for the mass housing projects developed in İstanbul by Emlak Kredi Bank in the late 1950s, "costs reached levels affordable only by upper-income groups," and most of the units were too large to count as social housing.[25] Furthermore, housing cooperatives in Turkey have been based on individual ownership and have often been liquidated after the buildings were sold to members, leaving no collective decision-making body for their administration.[26]

Notwithstanding the fact that Turkish housing production has had a narrower scope than that of neighboring countries, social housing projects in Turkey were still diverse.[27] Informed by local building practices, many incorporated hybridized forms that varied from the single or twin houses of the 1930s, which echoed the Siedlungen in Weimar Germany, to multi-story buildings of the 1950s, which showed US influence; and from low-cost midsized dwellings built by social democratic municipalities in the 1970s to the larger-scale high-rise developments of the 1980s and 1990s.[28] Furthermore, the variety of social housing in Turkey built from the 1930s to the present is not limited in architectural characteristics or plan types. A brief survey would illustrate a diverse array of methods employed for the production of social housing and forms of ownership, as well as strategies adopted by central and local governments to deal with the growing problem of housing shortages.[29] Contemporary social housing projects built in the country, however, are a clear sign that such experiences did not set a strong precedent for later designs.

Like other large cities of Turkey, İzmir in the first half of the twentieth century showed the symptoms of Turkey's prevailing affordable housing shortage. The first examples of social housing blocks in the city emerged in the early 1950s, as in Istanbul, but they were smaller in scale. One such project, initiated by the municipality of İzmir, was alongside the newly built "United Nations Road," which connected Konak, one of the oldest centers of the city, to the historical Kadifekale district, and a second was in Güzelyalı, a predominantly residential area. Both projects were called "Halk Tipi Apartmanlar" (Public Type Apartment Buildings). The latter had twenty-four flats, which the municipality sold to those who did not own a house (with lowered costs) to be paid in ten yearly instalments. The former had eighteen flats and was never used for its original purpose.[30] Beginning in the 1970s, the pace of construction, types, and number of social housing production in İzmir increased. While some of these projects were built in designated "gecekondu önleme bölgeleri" (squatter settlement prevention zones) on the fringes of the city, others were built in in central urban areas.[31]

By contrast, because of budgetary restrictions, the majority of social housing settlements provided by the Mass Housing Administration in

Figure 11.1. Uzundere Settlement, İzmir, 2016. Photograph by Ezgi Kocabalkanlı.

İzmir are built on municipality-owned lands on the outskirts of cities. In the case of Uzundere and Örnekköy (figs. 11.1 and 11.2, respectively), the housing units were purchased through long-term installments paid to the İzmir Metropolitan Municipality, which commissioned the project from the Mass Housing Administration. Örnekköy and Uzundere are the first two settlements to be completed as part of urban-renewal plans. Örnekköy, which consists of twenty-one apartment blocks, is inhabited mostly by residents who have been dislocated from the Karşıyaka district in order to make room for high-income residences. This dislocation was heavily promoted in local media with headlines such as "Aegean's Pearl Karşıyaka Is Getting Rid of Squatters"[32] and "Örnekköy Will Be a Model [urban renewal project]."[33] Uzundere incorporates fifty-eight apartment blocks, most of whose population came from squatter houses in Kadifekale, a central neighborhood of İzmir. Despite the importance of Kadifekale's close proximity to the historical center of the city, it had long been declared a landslide area. By 2010, the whole neighborhood was evacuated and turned into an "urban forest"—a decision that was positively received by the local media, as it would increase the amount of green space in İzmir.[34]

At first sight, Örnekköy and Uzundere differ from each other in a number of respects. The latter is pushed to the peripheries of urban services, and the former is more accessible to the city center and has more advantages in

Figure 11.2. Örnekköy Settlement, İzmir, 2015. Photograph by Kıvanç Kılınç.

terms of public facilities in its neighborhood. Uzundere has a number of planned open spaces within the settlement, including children's play areas, parks, and public facilities such as a school, a mosque, a social center, and a market. Such facilities are outside the settlement boundaries of Örnekköy. The two settlements differ in terms of building heights as well. Örnekköy consists of eight-story blocks, whereas Uzundere mostly incorporates fifteen-story blocks and is more densely populated. Despite these differences, research reveals that the spatial practices and demands of the residents are surprisingly similar and relatively independent of the differences between the physical planning decisions.

Materiality: Typology, Discontents, and Appropriations

Most of the social housing projects built in Turkey since the 1950s, including those produced by the Mass Housing Administration, are adaptations of a commonly repeated multistory apartment building typology, the so-called 2+1 or 3+1 (i.e., either two or three bedrooms plus a living room). This anonymous layout dominating the cities of contemporary Turkey has gradually evolved from earlier typologies of the so-called cubic homes (modernist detached housing) and rental houses (usually four- or five-story apartment

buildings with a single owner) built in the early years of the Turkish Republic, as well as the mid-rise apartment building typology, which was popu-
larized with the passage of the flat ownership law in 1965.[35] Especially the
projects developed for the lower-ranking civil servants and workers show
the influence of Siedlungen, which were built extensively in Frankfurt and
Berlin during the 1920s and 1930s.[36] The *Siedlung* planning concept was
based on the themes of minimum subsistence and efficiency. In most social
housing settlements built in Europe during the interwar period, although
there was strong emphasis on collective activities outside the home, the
interiors were supposed to augment the well-being of the worker families
and their "sense of privacy and ownership" by means of a clear separation
between the public and private spheres.[37] Common spaces for collectivity
and socialization were atypical of most Turkish situations, but the interior
arrangements reflected European lifestyles.

In Örnekköy and Uzundere, as in many other examples in Turkey, interior spaces in the apartments are clearly divided into public and private
spheres by the sequential order of a living room and bedrooms. The entrance
is small and functions as a barrier to block direct visual access to the living areas. This niche connects to a corridor, which provides access to more
private spaces, such as the bedrooms and the bathroom. An additional toilet
is placed near the entrance, mostly reserved for guests. In this layout, each
flat is a standardized compartment that reproduces the middle-class modern nuclear family ideal, a model extensively promoted nationwide from the
1930s and applied to housing schemes for a broad array of income groups. In
the history of social housing in Turkey, only a few cases deviate from conventional, standardized, modernist layouts by incorporating local building
traditions or responding to user needs and profiles.[38] Thus, the imagined
dwellers in the modernist blocks built by the Mass Housing Administration
still remain within the rigid definition of a modern nuclear family: the plans
of the Örnekköy and Uzundere settlements follow the 2+1 and 3+1 typologies.
The chief architect of the projects, Şeref Ömeroğlu, explained that approximately twenty plan types were created by the design office of the Mass Housing Administration, which were classified into five categories by apartment
size and regional, that is, climatic, properties. Although the use of preplanned
types saved significant design and implementation time, it also disregarded
the particularities of different sites and their prospective inhabitants.

Regardless of size and design differences, all these types are based on
the same modern apartment building model, which fails to accommodate

the needs of larger or extended families. To begin with, the spatial mechanisms employed to designate the private spaces (i.e., bedrooms) against the public (i.e., the living room) in a minimally designed lower-class home inhabited by an extended family would be different from those applied in an upper-class apartment with its more compartmentalized interiors. As the Örnekköy and Uzundere examples demonstrate, these typologies do not serve their intended functions as the floor area shrinks and the number of inhabitants increases. Many of the apartments in Örnekköy and Uzundere are inhabited by extended families, who have to turn the living room into a bedroom during the night. Furthermore, the large number of overnight guests who need to be accommodated during such rituals as weddings and funerals results in the need to stack beds even along the corridors. In other words, what marks the ever-shifting boundaries of public and private spheres inside the home does not solely depend on spatial divisions but on the relationship between the size of spaces and families, everyday customs, and dwelling cultures.[39] The public and private are cultural constructions, and they may acquire new meanings from the spatial setting, time period, and context.[40] Moreover, the meanings attached to public and private spheres change along with the concept of the family. This is where and how inhabitants maneuver to insert their own modalities within any modernist scheme.

As on-site observations reveal, in Örnekköy and Uzundere most of the inhabitants have tinkered not only with the functions but also with the materiality of the spaces that had been provided to them. Most commonly, because the apartments are rather small, the small toilet areas near the entrances turn into storage spaces. In Uzundere, even the emergency staircase landings and shelters are used to store household excesses, which seriously jeopardizes the residents' safety. It seems that a second toilet that is reserved for the guests, which meets the need for the demarcation of public and private spaces for small families, turns out to be ineffective for relatively large households. Especially when living rooms and even corridors need to be converted to bedrooms every night, ample storage space is needed to stack mattresses and bedspreads, let alone such regular household items as toiletries and cleaning supplies.

A common need that is voiced by many residents of both Örnekköy and Uzundere is spacious balconies. These semiprivate spaces enable their users to communicate both verbally and visually with their neighbors and feel part of the community without leaving the privacy of their homes. In the mild climate of İzmir, balconies are heavily used as living and dining spaces, especially during the long summer months. For low-income families who cannot afford vacations, let alone summer residences, balconies provide a space of relief from the cramped interiors. As one Örnekköy resident aptly put it, "İzmir, as you know, has a hot climate. People spend most of their time outside. Here, there are no balconies. You are closed up inside. If you want to go outside, you either go to the market or just walk along the street and come back. There is no other choice."[41] In both settlements, each apartment is provided with a small balcony that is attached to the kitchen and can comfortably seat only two people (fig. 11.3). Furthermore, most residents closed up the area to enlarge the tight kitchen space, to dry laundry or store their goods (fig. 11.4). While the original plans have open kitchens adjoining the living rooms to compensate for the tightness of both areas, many residents added walls to separate the two spaces. Both the smell and the messiness of cooking needed to be kept away from the order of the living room (figs. 11.5 and 11.6). The gradual appropriation of these homes offers insights into the question of whether modernist blocks can be sensitized to locality and culture. When middle-class formulas are translated into low-income housing to produce smaller units, spatial divisions need to be seriously reconsidered.

The aforementioned shortcomings of the interiors in Örnekköy and Uzundere are partially a result of the lack of attention paid to the spatial needs of extended families and partially the result of temporal and constructional limitations. For example, the chief architect admitted that the kitchens could have been two or three square meters larger in both settlements, but this detail had been overlooked by staff under the tight production schedule.[42] He further stated that open kitchens were provided to offer flexibility to the residents, and large balconies were provided for the settlements only in the southern provinces. Yet the specific cultural conditions in Örnekköy and Uzundere bear witness to the limitations of such well-meaning decisions. Ömeroğlu admitted the necessity of having local design offices and some degree of user participation in design, which proved impossible within the required speed of construction. Many times, the design office could not even pay site visits, as they had to prepare construction drawings in three to four days. In terms of construction limitations, the tunnel system, which speeds up the building process, restricts the flexibility of plan types and affects the sizes of rooms and balconies. It also results in excessively large spaces that are less functional, such as the halls between

Figure 11.3. Balcony with a view of the neighborhood, Örnekköy, 2015. Photograph by Sevcan Sönmez.

Figure 11.4. The balcony included into the kitchen, Örnekköy, 2015. Photograph by Sevcan Sönmez.

Figure 11.5. Open kitchen with relocated door, Uzundere, 2015. Photograph by Sevcan Sönmez.

Figure 11.6. Kitchen and living room separated by a wall with a window, Örnekköy, 2015. Photograph by Sevcan Sönmez.

individual apartments. Ömeroğlu explained that they had to construct one floor a day to complete one block in two weeks. Such time constraints did not allow the construction of large cantilevered balconies either, as that would have increased the heating time of the tunnel formwork after pouring the concrete.

The choice of construction materials, the lack of insulation against humidity, smells, and sounds, and the quality of workmanship are also frequent topics of grievance from the users. One weary resident described her frustration as follows: "Whatever I touch falls apart. The water heater of my upstairs neighbors broke down four times. My parquet floors are ruined because of water dripping from the ceiling. These houses are worthless. Nothing works. . . . The moment we moved in, we rebuilt the bathrooms. The moment we moved in, we rebuilt the toilets. . . . We rebuilt the kitchen. We changed the tiles. Not even a single stone is laid properly."[43] Sustainability seems to have been sacrificed to reduce initial costs, to the detriment of residents' comfort. In Uzundere, even the infrastructure, including sewage systems and sidewalks, is reported to be constructed or repaired by the residents (fig. 11.7).

To summarize, research on the materiality of the social housing units in Örnekköy and Uzundere reveals that both their spatial and constructional shortcomings are rooted in the planning process. Decision-making processes were not participatory and were constrained by temporal and financial limitations. These examples clearly demonstrate the waste that is produced by social housing policies that are driven by short-term political interests rather than the consideration of the long-term needs of users.

Sociality: Interactions, Conflicts, and Negotiations

The social housing projects in Turkey that reproduced variations of the *Siedlung* typology overlooked the fact that the latter fashioned a collective lifestyle outside the home by including public services and support mechanisms for the families, such as nurseries, public laundries, kindergartens, and allotments.[44] Except for a few examples built in the factory complexes in the 1930s and 1940s, the scope of social services in Turkey has usually been limited to public schools, mosques, shopping facilities, and recreational parks.[45] In the case of Mass Housing Administration projects, the inclusion of such facilities was based on practical rather than social concerns. Since these projects were located in remote sites, at a considerable

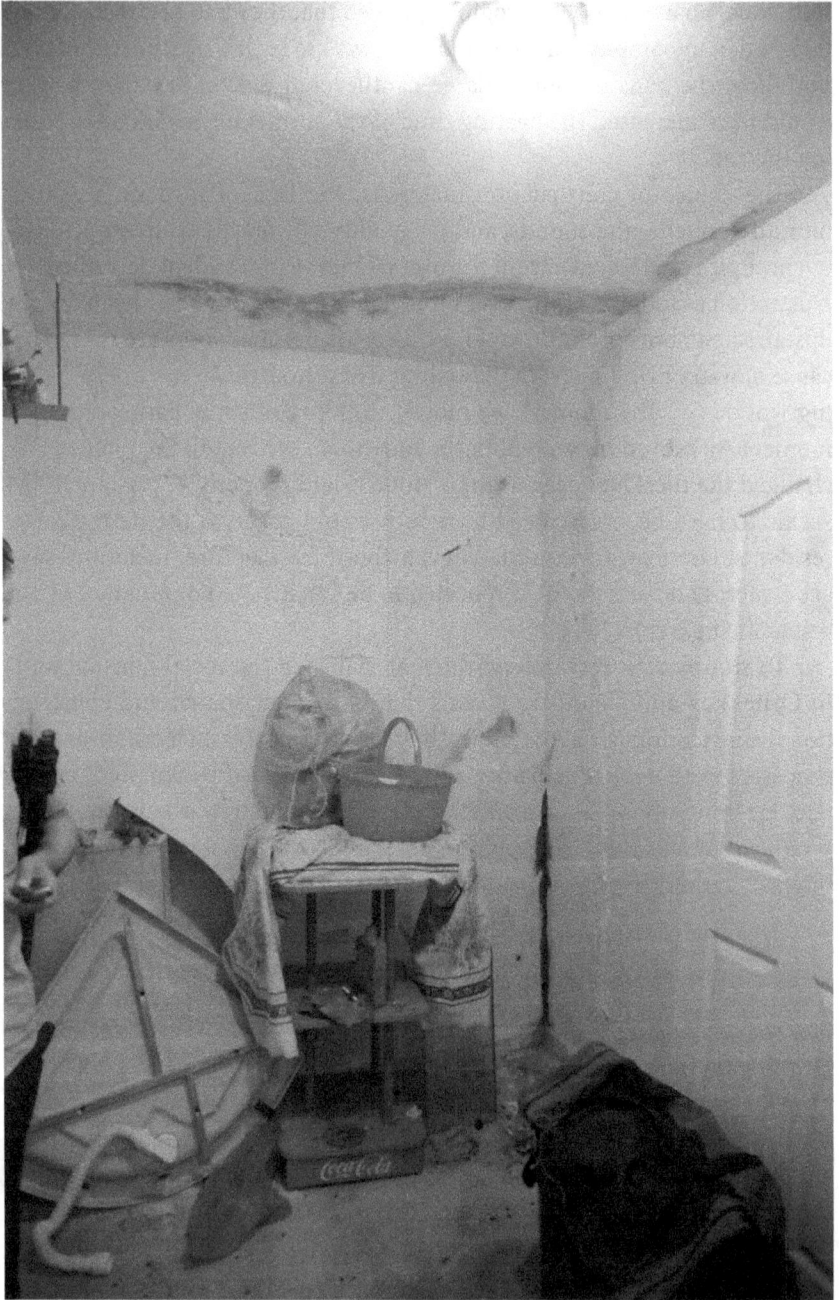

Figure 11.7. Construction and insulation problems, Uzundere, 2015. Photograph by Sevcan Sönmez.

distance from public services and main transportation networks, the design office of the Mass Housing Administration decided to provide a center for each settlement, with a school, a market, and a mosque and subcenters for larger settlements of over five thousand units with similar facilities. In some cases, however, such as Uzundere, topographical conditions did not allow the creation of multiple subcenters, which caused considerable hardship for the residents.

Indeed, the scarcity of public spaces is a recurrent topic of criticism from the residents of Örnekköy and Uzundere. In both settlements, such significant public rituals as weddings and funerals are often held at open areas between the blocks, sometimes complemented by a rented tent. In one instance, the residents in Uzundere have converted the emergency shelters in their basement into prayer halls. The presence of proper spaces for such activities within the settlements becomes particularly critical in the absence of efficient public transportation networks, which would have enabled the residents to meet their needs elsewhere in the city. In Uzundere, which is built on exceptionally steep terrain, even such on-site facilities as the mosque and the market are unreachable, especially for the elderly, who need to resort to neighborly relations (fig. 11.8). As one resident explained in frustration, "Say I am in the midst of preparing a meal and realize that I am out of eggs. There are no markets nearby. To get to the nearest one and return home takes an hour, and there is the risk of missing the occasional bus. So you go to your neighbors and ask if you can borrow from them. Here we are left at the mercy of our neighbors."[46]

Many residents of Örnekköy and Uzundere reported that they were obliged to retire when they moved because public transportation to their workplace was inadequate. Further, those who owned commercial spaces attached to their previous homes were not compensated for their shops. Being deprived of their business affected not only their income but also their social life. Because public spaces are lacking and public transportation is insufficient, women mostly socialize through house visits and men go to coffee shops in the vicinity. When the weather permits, both meet in the open areas between the blocks to sit around on the benches, sharing tea and snacks that they bring from home (fig. 11.9). House visits can also be formalized to take place on a weekly basis, where women get together for a prayer session followed by a meal. In both Örnekköy and Uzundere, some of the residents built pergolas near their blocks, where they plant herbs and vegetables and picnic with their families or neighbors on the weekends (fig. 11.10).

Figure 11.8. Mobile markets, Uzundere, 2015. Photograph by Sevcan Sönmez.

Figure 11.9. Recreational use of open spaces, Uzundere, 2015. Photograph by Sevcan Sönmez.

Figure 11.10. Pergola built by the residents, Örnekköy, 2015. Photograph by Sevcan Sönmez.

While neighborly relations ease the lives of Örnekköy and Uzundere residents to a considerable extent, they may make life more difficult in other ways. First of all, as most of the residents appear to have moved from single-family houses with gardens, they have difficulties in adjusting to the communal obligations that come with apartment life. It is not surprising that financial issues take the forefront in that respect. In both settlements, each apartment has to make an equal contribution to the collective expenditures of the related block. This applies to all units regardless of the differences between the amount of water and electricity consumption, which may differ according to measurable factors like family size, but also unmeasurable ones like the number of family members who stay at home during the day, and their different use patterns. As such differences cause an unfair distribution of administrative bills, they also cause blame and conflict among neighbors, a good number of whom fail to pay their bills on time in any case.

To illustrate the residents' discontent better, a brief explanation of the administrative and maintenance policies of the public housing settlements is in order. While there is no centralized administration for each settlement, each block is assigned a resident block administrator and a janitor. Both are exempted from administrative bills, and the janitor does not pay rent. In the absence of an electoral system, such as during the time of purchase, these positions are assigned randomly. Hence, the residents suffer from incompetent administrative decisions and lack of proper maintenance of not only the individual blocks but also the open spaces. Although some take the initiative to plant trees and flowers in the leftover areas and to maintain public property like pavements and playgrounds, others complain about such unasked-for responsibilities. One Uzundere resident complained that the janitor even tried to prevent her from planting flowers, saying that he would do it himself in a more suitable area.[47] In Örnekköy, the toys on a playground that was erected by the municipality were damaged "by children who have no sense of civility" to such an extent that eventually what remained had to be discarded.[48]

Blame and complaints are often underscored by deeper conflicts, which often bear traces of ethnic hostility. In both settlements, Kurdish and Turkish residents generally refrain from socializing with each other. As the Kurdish population forms the relatively less-privileged income group, their rate of literacy is lower, the number of breadwinners per apartment is fewer, and the family size is larger.[49] Needless to say, ethnicist remarks against the Kurds are fueled by recent political developments that resulted in alarmingly intensifying armed conflict, especially in the eastern regions. One Örnekköy resident was embarrassingly explicit in her lack of sympathy when she said that "our brain structures are incompatible; there are irreconcilable cultural differences between us."[50] Another statement by an Uzundere resident reveals the limits of (in)tolerance: "I do not come from the Citadel, *of course*, but I respect those who do. *They are also human beings*" (emphases added).[51] Such generalized statements are reflected in everyday practices, as Kurds are blamed for speaking in their mother tongue, arranging their own house visits, offering preferential treatment to their kin in administrative matters, theft, and drug use.

Whether they are based on ethnic discrimination or not, adjusting to the social obligations of public housing settlements is an incomplete process for the residents of Örnekköy and Uzundere. Although much of their discontent seems to arise from behavioral conflicts, the underlying factors are more structural than personal. They cover a broad array of administrative, economic, and social issues as varied as unemployment, lack of education, and discriminatory cultural politics.

Agency: Nostalgia, Autonomy, and Volition

The majority of the residents of the Örnekköy and Uzundere settlements used to live in close proximity to central areas of the city as owners of detached houses with gardens. There they were free to make additions to their houses as their families grew, to do gardening and horticulture, and to enjoy easy access to public facilities. These opportunities endowed them with a sense of agency, which they feel deprived of in the social housing settlements. Hence, descriptions of their previous homes are filled with a sense of irrecoverable loss and nostalgia. One of the primary themes in their stories is the way they had built their own spaces. As one Örnekköy resident said, "Our house was spacious. It was very spacious, beautiful and spacious. We made it spacious because we built it ourselves. I worked for five years on that house."[52] *Spaciousness* is a term that repeatedly features in descriptions from previous residents. Their investment of time and labor in the construction, too, seems to be an important component of their identification with their homes. Another resident stated, "Our living room was huge, like village houses, very nice. We made it large because we made it ourselves. It was very pretty. We transported two kilos of iron bars. You should have seen how we built it."[53]

Despite their limited means, there is an unmistakable sense of abundance in the discourses of the interviewees. The following is an extreme example, which conjures paradisiacal images of wealth and sovereignty: "My land was 530 square meters. I built a wall around it. Nobody saw what was inside. There were all kinds of trees and fruits. I had an artesian well for water. I had two houses. I would plant everything for my own consumption. I lived there for thirty years."[54]

These descriptions echo with pride in the labor that had been invested in making one's own space. They contrast with descriptions of their present houses, which abound with such phrases as "they jammed us into apartments,"[55] "they stacked people like sheep and lambs,"[56] and "nobody asked us anything; they crammed people in like they drive animals into stables."[57]

The great majority of the interviewees who had previously lived in detached houses nostalgically stated that those were preferable because they could behave as they wished without being bothered by their neighbors. Many said that neighborly relations had been much smoother because nobody minded what others did in their own territory. The public-private divide seems to have been better defined in their previous settlements, where interaction between neighbors was voluntary rather than obligatory.

Residents did not have to be concerned about such issues as the noise that their neighbors made, the trees and vegetables that they planted, and the amount of water or electricity that they consumed.

Nostalgia points to a sense of loss, which appears to be a longing for a place. But, as critical theorist Svetlana Boym puts it, "it is actually a yearning for a different time—the time of our childhood, the slower rhythms of our dreams."[58] The nostalgic reflections of Örnekköy and Uzundere residents are associated less with a home that they left behind than with a time when they had a sense of agency and autonomy. Uzundere residents tried to overcome this loss through such collective actions as setting up a blog page and organizing a public demonstration both to share and to publicize their agony during their initial settlement process.[59] Despite their discontent with the social housing environment, when asked whether they would rather return to their previous homes, many answered negatively. Residents of both settlements found their new homes more functional, orderly, and safe. They said that they enjoyed the comforts of central heating; the absence of flies and mosquitoes; and even the layout of the rooms, which open to a corridor, giving a sense of orderliness. In Boym's terms, theirs can be read as a form of reflective nostalgia, which "dwells on the ambivalences of human longing and belonging and does not shy away from the contradictions of modernity," rather than restorative nostalgia, which "attempts a transhistorical reconstruction of the lost home."[60]

The discourse of Örnekköy and Uzundere residents reveals their awareness of the ambivalences and contradictions of so-called modern urban life that surfaced in their new environments. Rather than going back to their previous homes, however, they seek to have their own word in their housing arrangements. Their complaints about the inconvenient site conditions, poor quality of building materials, and inadequate maintenance are rooted in decision-making processes that exclude the users. The consideration of long-term use rather than immediate economic benefit in the choice of materials and construction system would definitely improve the living conditions of social housing environments. What is more important is the inclusion of the users in the production of their everyday spaces from the earliest stages of planning. Given a sense of agency, public housing may turn into a desirable rather than detested mode of inhabitation. Clearly, this does not mean it will lead to a happy conclusion that eliminates all conflicts and contradictions. As spatial theorists like Lefebvre have argued, space is the outcome of a continuous production process, which is always already incomplete.[61] What needs to be kept in sight is a democratic conduct of this process that does not deprive the users of active agency.

Conclusion

Current social housing schemes produced by the Mass Housing Administration in İzmir continue to reproduce a cramped and cheaper version of the much-idealized middle-class apartment typology in Turkey, which offers only limited place for sociability. The tunnel system also limits user intervention and modification of living spaces, which has contributed to the discrepancies discussed herein and has increased the discontent of the users. Furthermore, the planning of these settlements neglects the cultural integration of different income and ethnic groups and issues of social welfare. Apparently, the developers of the largest mass and social housing programs in the history of modern Turkey did not feel the urge to take into account any of the recent and more flexible typologies of social housing extant in both the international and the national arena or experiences of Turkey's various institutions.

On the other hand, our analysis of the two social housing projects in İzmir in terms of materiality, sociality, and agency has also revealed that spatial production does not cease when construction ends. The inhabitants from various backgrounds set their own modalities into given modernist housing schemes. As a result, these homes have been both owned and disowned: in theory, apartments were categorically welcome, for they offered modern and comfortable lifestyles. Nevertheless, the actual buildings often fell short of the expectations of their inhabitants. While the inherent promise of an ideal middle-class family life and the possibility of upward mobility have since lingered in the air, the inhabitants have continued to make adjustments not only to their homes but also to the very idea of a much-desired "modern house" in their efforts to make home out of the high-rise modernist blocks. At times when there was little or no space for changing any physical entity, they extended the activity of space making to virtual spaces, such as online forums, discussing the legal, social, and infrastructure problems related to the settlements, and formed civil society organizations to have negotiating power with the local administration.[62] In doing so, the dwellers have continued to play an increasingly significant part in the material, social, and emotional production of their immediate built environments on the outskirts of the city.

More important, as findings from our on-site research have clearly indicated, a more localized housing program informed by prospective residents during the planning phase could well be developed if the Mass Housing Administration chooses to decentralize and hand over the social housing production strategy to provincial administrative offices. Such decentralization would definitely contribute to the production of architectural schemes that are more suitable to various needs and expectations of different users and to the generation of on-site urban renewals that would lead to the formation of socially and economically integrated communities.

Acknowledgments

This chapter is based on a research project titled "Analysis of the Relationship between Space, Design, and Everyday Life in Public Housing Settlements That Are Built in the Context of Urban Renewal Plans in İzmir: The Örnekköy and Uzundere Settlements," funded by the Scientific and Technological Research Council of Turkey (TÜBİTAK Program 1002, Project no. 114K966) and conducted at Yaşar University. The project team consists of Gülsüm Baydar (director); Murat Komesli, Kıvanç Kılınç, Ahenk Yılmaz, Sevcan Sönmez (researchers); Zeynep Akçay, Çiğdem Çetinkaya, Ebru Bengisu, Gizem Özmen, Umut Altıntaş, Yasemin Oksel, Zeynep Oral, Nazlı Yatağan, Özgecan Zafer ve Sevinç Alkan Korkmaz (assistants), Su Taşbaş ve Gözde Karadağ (software developers), and Fatih Duvahan (technical support).

Notes

1. Henri Lefebvre, *The Production of Space*, trans. D. Nicholson-Smith (Oxford: Blackwell, 1984). Data used in this article have been digitalized under a Digital Humanities project, the details of which were published in Gülsüm Baydar, Murat Komesli, Ahenk Yılmaz, and Kıvanç Kılınç, "Digitizing Lefebvre's Spatial Triad," *Digital Scholarship in the Humanities* 33, no. 1 (April 2018): 6–20.

2. Critical theorists such as Doreen Massey have further contributed to Lefebvre's perspective by arguing that space "has a density (substance) of its own" and that it "is the very possibility of the existence of a simultaneous (positive) heterogeneity or multiplicity." See Lawrence Grossberg, "Theorizing Context," in *Spatial Politics: Essays for Doreen Massey*, ed. David Featherstone and Joe Painter (Malden, UK: Wiley-Blackwell, 2013), 34. For Massey's reading of Lefebvre's arguments, see Doreen Massey, "Politics and Space/Time," *New Left Review* 196 (November–December 1992): 65–84. Similarly, referring to Lefebvre, Christian Schmid asserts that "a social space includes not only a concrete materiality but a thought concept and a feeling—an 'experience.'" Christian Schmid, "Henri Lefebvre's Theory of the

Production of Space: Towards a Three-Dimensional Dialectic," in *Space, Difference, Everyday Life: Reading Henri Lefebvre*, ed. K. Goonewardena, S. Kipfer, R. Milgrom, and C. Schmid (New York: Routledge, 2008), 41.

3. Lefebvre, *Production of Space*, 46.

4. Henri Lefebvre, "Reflections on the Politics of Space," *Antipode* 8, no. 2 (1976): 30–37; Grossberg, "Theorizing Context," 34.

5. Lefebvre, *Production of Space*, 38–39, 358.

6. Ibid., 40.

7. Eliana Abu-Hamdi, "The Jordan Gate Towers of Amman: Surrendering Public Space to Build a Neoliberal Ruin," *International Journal of Islamic Architecture* 5, no. 1 (2016): 73–101; Joomi Lee, "Riad Fever: Heritage Tourism, Urban Renewal and the Medina Property Boom in Old Cities of Morocco," *e-Review of Tourism Research* 6, no. 4 (2008): 76.

8. Mindy Thompson Fullilove and Rodrick Wallace, "Serial Forced Displacement in American Cities, 1916–2010," *Journal of Urban Health* 88, no. 3 (2011): 381; Justus Uitermark and Maarten Loopmans, "Urban Renewal without Displacement? Belgium's 'Housing Contract Experiment' and the Risks for Gentrification," *Journal of Housing and the Built Environment* 28, no. 1 (2013): 158.

9. Ya Ping Wang and Alan Murie, "Social and Spatial Implications of Housing Reform in China," *International Journal of Urban and Regional Research* 24, no. 2 (2000): 397.

10. Kathy Arthurson, "From Stigma to Demolition: Australian Debates about Housing and Social Exclusion," *Journal of Housing and the Built Environment* 19 (2004): 257; Lena Magnusson and Bengt Turner, "Municipal Housing Companies in Sweden: Social by Default," *Housing, Theory, Society* 25, no. 4 (2008): 277.

11. For an excellent study on the transformation of self-built neighborhoods (*gecekondu*) to mass housing sites developed by the Mass Housing Administration within the context of neoliberal urbanism and urban renewal, please see Tahire Erman, *Mış Gibi Site: Ankara'da bir TOKİ-Gecekondu Dönüşüm Sitesi* ["As if housing": a TOKI-*Gecekondu* transformation compound in Ankara] (İstanbul: İletişim, 2016).

12. See https://www.toki.gov.tr/; https://www.toki.gov.tr/en/housing-programs.html.

13. For instance, see Aykut Namık Çoban, "Cumhuriyetin İlanından Günümüze Konut Politikası" [Housing policy since the foundation of the Turkish Republic], *Ankara Üniversitesi SBF Dergisi* 67, no. 3 (2012): 75–108; Mehmet Ali Göktaş, *Türkiye'de Konut Sorunları ve Sosyal Konut Politikası* [The housing problem in Turkey and social housing policy] (İzmir: İstiklal Matbaası, 1974).

14. The Mass Housing Administration was previously linked to the Ministry of Public Works and Settlements. This and the following information are based on the authors' interview with Şeref Ömeroğlu, architect in charge of the project division of the office at the time of the construction of the two settlements, on October 6, 2015, at Yaşar University, İzmir. All further references to the architect are based on this interview.

15. Ömeroğlu interview.

16. Headline of Mass Housing Administration newsletter, 2014, http://www.arkitera.com/haber/20263/izmir-in-cehresi-degisiyor, March 13, 2014.

17. Turkish Chamber of Civil Engineers, "TOKİ Değerlendirme Raporu" [TOKİ assessment report], 2008, http://www.imo.org.tr/resimler/dosya_ekler/2d6528de98702ba_ek.pdf?tipi=4&turu=H&sube=0.

18. Authors' interview with SÇ, resident of social housing in Örnekköy, İzmir, May 6, 2015.

19. "Mesken buhranın halli için takibat yapmak üzere Sosyal Yardım Müdürü Doktor Ahmet Fikri başkanlığında bir heyet oluşturulması" [A committee was formed to investigate the housing shortage, chaired by Dr. Ahmet Fikri, director of social assistance], 28/4/1924, File: 1038, No. 30..10.0.0, Location: 124.883..8., Republic of Turkey Prime Ministry, General Directorate of State Archives, the Directorate of Republican Archives in Ankara. Also see, Ali Cengizkan, "Discursive Formations in Turkish Residential Architecture (Türk Konut Mimarlığında Söylemsel Oluşumlar) Ankara, 1948–1962" (PhD diss., METU, 2000), 86; in 1944, the Housing Law (Memur Meskenleri İnşası Hakkında Kanun) was enacted, giving the government the responsibility to build housing for civil servants. This was followed by a cabinet decision to allocate housing built by the state to civil servants who most needed them. Date: 30/11/1945, Cabinet Decision, resolution no. 6/789.

20. İnci Aslanoğlu, Erken Cumhuriyet Dönemi Mimarlığı 1923–1938 [Early republican architecture, 1923–1938] (Ankara: METU Faculty of Architecture Press, 2001), 45.

21. For such examples, please see Ali Cengizkan, ed., Fabrika'da Barınmak: Erken Cumhuriyet Dönemi'nde Türkiye'de İşçi Konutları—Yaşam, Mekân ve Kent [Dwelling in the factory: workers' houses in early republican Turkey—everyday life, space, and the city] (Ankara: Arkadaş Yayınevi, 2009).

22. N. Doğu, "İbrahim Karaahmetoğlu Kira Evleri—Ankara" [İbrahim Karaahmetoğlu rental houses—Ankara], Arkitekt 5, no. 5 (1938): 147, quoted in Aslanoğlu, Erken Cumhuriyet Dönemi Mimarlığı, 87.

23. L. Yıldız Tokman, Konut Politikaları Uygulamalarında Özel Bir Örnek: Yenimahalle [A special example in the implementation of housing policies: Yenimahalle] (Ankara: KentKoop Yayınları, 1985), 4, 16; also see Göktaş, Türkiye'de Konut Sorunları.

24. Barış Alp Özden, "Health, Morality, and Housing: The Politics of Working Class Housing in Turkey, 1945–1960," New Perspectives on Turkey 49 (Fall 2013): 91.

25. "Türkiye'de Konut Sorununa Genel Bir Bakış" [A general overview of the housing problem in Turkey], Report by the Chamber of Architects of Turkey, Mimarlık 115 (1973): 9–11.

26. Ayten Alkan, Türkiye'de 1980'den Sonra Dar Gelirlilerin Konut Sorunu ve Konut Kooperatifleri [The housing problem of the lower-income in Turkey after 1980 and housing cooperatives] (Ankara: İmaj Yayınevı, 1998), 54.

27. The urbanscapes of the twentieth-century Middle East, especially in countries that underwent (post)colonial urban transformations, were marked by large-scale social housing experiments. See, for instance, Zeynep Çelik's seminal work on Algiers, Urban Forms and Colonial Confrontations: Algiers under French Rule (Berkeley: University of California Press, 1997).

28. See Esra Akcan, Architecture in Translation: Germany, Turkey, and the Modern House (Durham, NC: Duke University Press, 2012); Bülent Batuman, "Turkish Urban Professionals and the Politics of Housing, 1960–1980," METU Journal of the Faculty of Architecture 23, no. 1 (2006): 59–81; Yıldız Sey, "To House the New Citizens: Housing Policies and Mass Housing," in Modern Turkish Architecture, ed. Renata Holod and Ahmet Evin (Philadelphia: University of Pennsylvania Press, 1984), 153–77.

29. For the implementation of such methods, see Cevat Geray, "Türkiye'de Kendi Evini Yapana Yardım Yöntemi Uygulaması" [The implementation of the aided self-help housing method in Turkey], Amme İdaresi Dergisi 5, no. 2 (1972): 42–73; Yıldız, "Konut Politikaları Uygulamalarında."

30. In 1958, the municipality decided to hand it over to İzmir Maarif Müdürlüğü (İzmir Directorate of Education), and the building was turned into a dormitory for female students.

For both buildings, see Hülya Koç, *Cumhuriyet Döneminde İzmir'de Sosyal Konut ve Toplu Konut Uygulamaları* [Examples of social housing and mass housing in İzmir during the republican period] (İzmir: DEÜ Mimarlık Fakültesi Yayınları, 2001), 120–21.

31. *İzmir Belediyesi 1975 Çalışmaları* [İzmir Municipality 1975 activities] (İzmir: Karınca Matbaacılık ve Tic. Koll. Şirketi, 1975), 69, 71.

32. "Ege'nin İncisi Karşıyaka Çevresini Saran Gecekondulardan Kurtuluyor," *Yeni Asır* (İzmir), June 22, 2007.

33. "Örnekköy 'Örnek' Olacak," *Yeni Asır* (İzmir), March 6, 2007.

34. "Yeşil Alan Arttı," *Yeni Asır* (İzmir), March 9, 2007.

35. Multifamily apartment buildings became the dominant residential culture of the middle class after the 1950s. Also, during the 1960s, "planned development" and housing cooperatives further extended the perimeter to lower-income groups. See İlhan Tekeli, "Türkiye Kentlerinde Apartmanlaşma Sürecinde İki Aşama" [Two phases in the "apartmentalization" process in Turkish cities] *Çevre* 4 (July–August 1979): 79.

36. Manfredo Tafuri, "The Attempts at Urban Reform in Europe between the Wars," in Manfredo Tafuri and Francesco Dal Co, *Modern Architecture 1* (London: Faber and Faber/Electa, 1986), 153–55.

37. Elizabeth Darling, "'A Citizen as Well as a Housewife': New Spaces of Domesticity in 1930s London," in *Negotiating Domesticity: Spatial Productions of Gender in Modern Architecture*, ed. Hilde Heynen and Gülsüm Baydar (London: Routledge, 2005), 57–58.

38. The Workers' Houses Settlement built for the Turkish State Railroads in Ankara (1939–40) is one example of adapting to users' needs. In this project, the architect reintroduced the idea of the traditional Ottoman-Turkish *sofa* (central hall) into the planning of a minimal layout, otherwise similar to the Siedlungen. Designed by a European-trained Greek architect, Dimitri Petousis, the twin houses in the Workers' Housing Settlement are one-story-high buildings with pitched roofs, built alongside allotments. In his design, while the rooms are still organized according to a basic division between places seen fit for more formal familial activities and places of greater familial intimacy, because of the central location of the hall, which served as a multipurpose room, the border between public and private areas can be much more easily transgressed. The hall's direct connection to all the other rooms inevitably blurred the boundaries between the areas. For an extended discussion of this particular example, please see Kıvanç Kılınç, "Imported but Not Delivered: The Construction of Modern Domesticity and the Spatial Politics of Mass-Housing in 1930s Ankara," *Journal of Architecture* 17, no. 6 (2012): 819–46.

39. Jane Rendell, *The Pursuit of Pleasure: Gender, Space, and Architecture in Regency London* (New Brunswick, NJ: Rutgers University Press, 2002), 20.

40. Rendell, *Pursuit of Pleasure*, 3.

41. Interview with NÇ, Örnekköy, May 6, 2015.

42. Ömeroğlu interview.

43. Interview with HÇ, Örnekköy, May 13, 2015.

44. For major examples of Siedlungen, see Markus Jager, *Housing Estates in the Berlin Modern Style* (Munich: Deutscher Kunstverlag, 2007).

45. See, for instance, Burak Asiliskender, "Anadolu'da Modern Bir Yaşam Kurmak: Sümerbank Kayseri Bez Fabrikası ve Lojmanları," in Cengizkan, *Fabrika'da Barınmak*, 111–29.

46. Interview with EA, Uzundere, June 18, 2015.

47. Interview with YA, Uzundere, June 10, 2015.

48. Interview with NÇ, Örnekköy, May 6, 2015.
49. The majority of the Kurdish population in Turkey come from eastern and southeastern regions. Difficult economic conditions and lack of security that originated in political conflict resulted in unprecedented migration rates in the last decade. On the basis of Turkish Institute of Statistics records, researcher and journalist Mustafa Sönmez states that between 2007 and 2012, 2 million Kurds migrated to western cities. İzmir received 15.2 percent of the migrants in 2007, which increased to 20.3 percent in 2012. Kurds constituted more than 20 percent of İzmir's population in 2013. They mostly live in self-help illegal housing areas and do menial jobs in construction work and mussel hunting. http://mustafasonmez.net/?p=2912 (accessed January 26, 2016).
50. Interview with NE, Örnekköy, April 22, 2015.
51. "Citadel" refers to Kadifekale, a formerly popular region for İzmir's Kurdish population, which has been evacuated for urban renewal.
52. Interview with MS, Örnekköy, May 20, 2015.
53. Interview with MS, Örnekköy, May 20, 2015.
54. Interview with TB, Örnekköy, May 6, 2015.
55. Interview with YA, Uzundere, June 10, 2015.
56. Interview with SÇ, Örnekköy, May 6, 2015.
57. Interview with MS, Örnekköy, May 20, 2015.
58. Svetlana Boym, "Nostalgia and Its Discontents," *Hedgehog Review* 9, no. 2 (2007): 8.
59. They created their own blog page: http://tokiuzundere.blogspot.com, accessed June 3, 2015. Their public demonstration made news in the local media: "Uzundere Sakinleri: Ev var ama hizmetimiz yok," *Yeni Asır* (İzmir), October 12, 2010.
60. Boym, "Nostalgia," 13.
61. Lefebvre, *Production of Space*.
62. In Uzundere, for instance, they formed a civil society organization that negotiated with the municipality for the addition of a "multifunction social facility building" to the project.

Bibliography

Abu-Hamdi, Eliana. "The Jordan Gate Towers of Amman: Surrendering Public Space to Build a Neoliberal Ruin." *International Journal of Islamic Architecture* 5, no. 1 (2016): 73–101.

Akcan, Esra. *Architecture in Translation: Germany, Turkey, and the Modern House*. Durham, NC: Duke University Press, 2012.

Alkan, Ayten. *Türkiye'de 1980'den Sonra Dar Gelirlilerin Konut Sorunu ve Konut Kooperatifleri* [The housing problem of the lower-income in turkey after 1980 and housing cooperatives]. Ankara: İmaj Yayınevi, 1998.

Arthurson, Kathy. "From Stigma to Demolition: Australian Debates about Housing and Social Exclusion." *Journal of Housing and the Built Environment* 19 (2004): 255–70.

Asiliskender, Burak. "Anadolu'da Modern Bir Yaşam Kurmak: Sümerbank Kayseri Bez Fabrikası ve Lojmanları" [Building a modern life in Anatolia: The Sümerbank Kayseri cloth factory and employee houses]. In *Fabrika'da Barınmak: Erken Cumhuriyet Dönemi'nde Türkiye'de İşçi Konutları—Yaşam, Mekân ve Kent*, edited by Ali Cengizkan. Ankara: Arkadaş Yayınevi, 2009.

Aslanoğlu, İnci. *Erken Cumhuriyet Dönemi Mimarlığı 1923–1938* [Early republican architecture, 1923–1938]. Ankara: METU Faculty of Architecture Press, 2001.

Batuman, Bülent. "Turkish Urban Professionals and the Politics of Housing, 1960–1980." *METU Journal of the Faculty of Architecture* 23, no. 1 (2006): 59–81.

Baydar, Gülsüm, Murat Komesli, Ahenk Yılmaz, and Kıvanç Kılınç. "Digitizing Lefebvre's Spatial Triad." *Digital Scholarship in the Humanities* 33, no. 1 (April 2018): 6–20.

Boym, Svetlana. "Nostalgia and Its Discontents." *Hedgehog Review* 9, no. 2 (2007): 7–18.

Cengizkan, Ali, ed. "Discursive Formations in Turkish Residential Architecture (Türk Konut Mimarlığında Söylemsel Oluşumlar) Ankara, 1948–1962." PhD diss., METU, 2000.

———. *Fabrika'da Barınmak: Erken Cumhuriyet Dönemi'nde Türkiye'de İşçi Konutları—Yaşam, Mekân ve Kent* [Dwelling in the factory: workers' houses in early republican Turkey, everyday life, space, and the city]. Ankara: Arkadaş Yayınevi, 2009.

Çelik, Zeynep. *Urban Forms and Colonial Confrontations: Algiers under French Rule.* Berkeley: University of California Press, 1997.

Çoban, Aykut Namık. "Cumhuriyetin İlanından Günümüze Konut Politikası" [Housing policy since the foundation of the Turkish Republic]. *Ankara Üniversitesi SBF Dergisi* 67, no. 3 (2012): 75–108.

Darling, Elizabeth. "'A Citizen as Well as a Housewife': New Spaces of Domesticity in 1930s London." In *Negotiating Domesticity: Spatial Productions of Gender in Modern Architecture*, edited by Hilde Heynen and Gülsüm Baydar, 49–64. London: Routledge, 2005.

Erman, Tahire. *Mış Gibi Site: Ankara'da bir TOKİ-Gecekondu Dönüşüm Sitesi* ["As if housing": A TOKİ-*Gecekondu* transformation compound in Ankara]. İstanbul: İletişim, 2016.

Fullilove, Mindy Thompson, and Rodrick Wallace. "Serial Forced Displacement in American Cities, 1916–2010." *Journal of Urban Health* 88, no. 3 (2011): 381–89.

Geray, Cevat. "Türkiye'de Kendi Evini Yapana Yardım Yöntemi Uygulaması" [The implementation of the aided self-help housing method in Turkey]. *Amme İdaresi Dergisi* 5, no. 2 (1972): 42–73.

Göktaş, Mehmet Ali. *Türkiye'de Konut Sorunları ve Sosyal Konut Politikası* [The housing problem in Turkey and social housing policy]. İzmir: İstiklal Matbaası, 1974.

Grossberg, Lawrence. "Theorizing Context." In *Spatial Politics: Essays for Doreen Massey*, edited by David Featherstone and Joe Painter Malden, 32–43. Malden, UK: Wiley-Blackwell, 2013.

İzmir Belediyesi 1975 Çalışmaları [İzmir Municipality 1975 activities]. İzmir: Karınca Matbaacılık ve Tic. Koll. Şirketi, 1975.

Jager, Markus. *Housing Estates in the Berlin Modern Style.* Munich: Deutscher Kunstverlag, 2007.

Kılınç, Kıvanç. "Imported but Not Delivered: The Construction of Modern Domesticity and the Spatial Politics of Mass-Housing in 1930s Ankara." *Journal of Architecture* 17, no. 6 (2012): 819–46.

Koç, Hülya. *Cumhuriyet Döneminde İzmir'de Sosyal Konut ve Toplu Konut Uygulamaları* [Examples of social housing and mass housing in İzmir during the republican period]. İzmir: DEÜ Mimarlık Fakültesi Yayınları, 2001.

Lee, Joomi. "Riad Fever: Heritage Tourism, Urban Renewal and the Medina Property Boom in Old Cities of Morocco." *e-Review of Tourism Research* 6, no. 4 (2008): 66–78.

Lefebvre, Henri. *The Production of Space.* Translated by D. Nicholson-Smith. Oxford: Blackwell, 1984.

———. "Reflections on the Politics of Space." *Antipode* 8, no. 2 (1976): 30–37.

Magnusson, Lena, and Bengt Turner. "Municipal Housing Companies in Sweden: Social by Default." *Housing, Theory, Society* 25, no. 4 (2008): 275–96.

Massey, Doreen. "Politics and Space/Time." *New Left Review*, no. 196 (1992): 65–84.

Özden, Barış Alp. "Health, Morality, and Housing: The Politics of Working Class Housing in Turkey, 1945–1960." *New Perspectives on Turkey* 49 (Fall 2013): 57–86.

Rendell, Jane. *The Pursuit of Pleasure: Gender, Space, and Architecture in Regency London.* New Brunswick, NJ: Rutgers University Press, 2002.

Sey, Yıldız. "To House the New Citizens: Housing Policies and Mass Housing." In *Modern Turkish Architecture*, edited by Renata Holod and Ahmet Evin, 153–77. Philadelphia: University of Pennsylvania Press, 1984.

Schmid, Christian. "Henri Lefebvre's Theory of the Production of Space: Towards a Three-Dimensional Dialectic." In *Space, Difference, Everyday Life: Reading Henri Lefebvre*, edited by K. Goonewardena, Stefan Kipfer, Richard Milgrom, Christian Schmid, 27–45. New York: Routledge, 2008.

Tafuri, Manfredo, and Francesco Dal Co. *Modern Architecture 1.* London: Faber and Faber/Electa, 1986.

Tekeli, İlhan. "Türkiye Kentlerinde Apartmanlaşma Sürecinde İki Aşama" [Two phases in the "apartmentization" process in Turkish cities]. *Çevre* 4 (July–August 1979): 79.

Tokman, L. Yıldız. *Konut Politikaları Uygulamalarında Özel Bir Örnek: Yenimahalle* [A special example in the implementation of housing policies: Yenimahalle], Ankara: KentKoop Yayınları, 1985.

"Türkiye'de Konut Sorununa Genel Bir Bakış" [A general overview of the housing problem in Turkey]. Report by the Chamber of Architects of Turkey. *Mimarlık* 115 (1973): 9–11.

Uitermark, Justus, and Maarten Loopmans. "Urban Renewal without Displacement? Belgium's 'Housing Contract Experiment' and the Risks for Gentrification." *Journal of Housing and the Built Environment* 28, no. 1 (2013): 157–66.

Wang, Ya Ping, and Alan Murie. "Social and Spatial Implications of Housing Reform in China." *International Journal of Urban and Regional Research* 24, no. 2 (2000): 397–417.

GÜLSÜM BAYDAR teaches at the Architecture Department at Yaşar University, İzmir. She received her PhD in architectural history at UC Berkeley and has taught design, history, and theory courses at universities in the United States, Singapore, Australia and Turkey. Her work explores the intersections between architectural and other discourses, including psychoanalytical, postcolonial, and feminist theories, in order to question the boundaries of the architectural discipline. Her articles have appeared in such journals as *Assemblage, Journal of Architectural Education, Society and Space, Signs*, and *Gender, Place and Culture*. She is coeditor of *Postcolonial Space(s)* (Princeton Architectural Press, 1997) and *Negotiating Domesticity* (Routledge, 2005).

KIVANÇ KILINÇ is Assistant Professor of architecture at Yaşar University in Turkey. He received his PhD (2010) in the History and Theory of Art and Architecture Graduate Program at SUNY Binghamton and his master's degree at the Middle East Technical University (2002). He also serves as managing editor of the *International Journal of Islamic Architecture*. Kılınç has published in such academic journals as *Architectural Histories, History and Memory, Digital Scholarship in the Humanities,* and *The Journal of Architecture*, as well as in edited books. His current research focuses on the transnational connections and their consequences that shaped social housing practices in contemporary Turkey and the Middle East.

AHENK YILMAZ is Associate Professor at the Department of Architecture of Yaşar University in Turkey. Yılmaz received her master's and PhD degrees in architecture from Izmir Institute of Technology. She undertook a collaborative research project at Brighton University in 2011 in the United Kingdom funded by TÜBİTAK and the Paul Mellon Centre for Studies in British Arts. Her research interests lie in the interaction between architectural design and the production of spatial experience, with a special focus on the pivotal concepts of memory and memorialization, on which she has published many articles in edited volumes and refereed national and international journals.

INDEX

Ababsa, Myriam, 13

Aban social housing (Tehran), 18, 269, 278, 280–82, *281*, 284, 287n59

Abdel-Nasser, Gamal, 80, 81, 122

Abdullah I (prince of Transjordan), 39

Abdullah II (king of Jordan), 40, 54, 55, 58

Abulfottuh, Hassan, 80–81

Abu Nuseir (Amman), 15, 37, 42–43, *52*, *53*; construction of, 50–51; politics and aesthetics of, 51–53

agency: of the user, 292, 309–11. *See also* spatial agency

agricultural settlements, 148, 157, 158

Alfar, Ibrahim, 81

Algeria: architecture in, 10–11; social housing in, 12

al-Mughni, Haya, 227

Alnsour, Jamal, 45, 46

anticolonialism, 118, 199

apartment block, 8–9

apartment rents, 71–72, 81–82, 100, 195, 243, 294

apartments: extensions to, 9; in Kuwait, 228, 230n12; modernist high-rise, 291; multi-family, 315n35; in Tehran, 282; typology of, 297; unpopularity of, 210–11

Arab architectonics, 47

"Arab city" model, 224–25

Arab-Islamic movement, 220–27

Arab-Palestinians. *See* Palestinians

Arab Spring, 7, 170

Aravena, Alejandro, 5, 6, 20

Archer, John, 144

arches, 223, *224*, *252*

architect: as member of bourgeois class, 268; as public housing expert, 267, 270; as social reformer, 269–73

Architecte, 269, 270

architecture: in the Age of Turmoil, 12–14; Arabic, 11; Arab-Islamic, 220–26; Arab village, 244–45; Beaux-Arts, 272; as body,

226; brutalist, 168–69; Circassian, 46–47; colonial, 10–11; as independent profession, 269; indigenous, 123; local, 11, 12, 15, 17–18, 244–45, 272, 277, 280, 298; modern, 2, 19; modernist, 15, 19; and neoliberal economics, 5; Ottoman, 11, 192; Palestinian, *247*, 251, 259, 260n4; postcolonial, 10, 12, 15; primitive, 132n6; regionalist, 217–18, 220–26, 233n48; social mission of, 5; spatial and social agency of, 6; traditional, 47, 262n29; in Tunisia, 130; and the ultra-Orthodox community, 242; and the user, 259; vernacular, 15, *49*, 131, 195–96, 203n37, 244–47; and visions for the nation, 144; Western influence in, 47

Arwa Bint al-Hareth School, 47

Atatürk, Kemal, 10

autonomy: of architects, 5, 83, 269, 285n9; national, 119; political, 122; of residents, 310; of the state, 37, 39, 40, 41, 56

Azhdari, Abbas, 270, 280

Bahrain, 9

balconies, 248, 251, 299–300, *301*, 303

Baqa'a refugee camp (Amman), 45–46

Başakşehir (Istanbul), 89, 91–97, *92*, *93*, *94*, *96*, 106

Bauhaus, 272

Bayat, Asef, 90

bayt, 46–50

Beaux-Arts style, 272

Bedouins: in Jordan, 39, 49–50; in Tunisia, 128

Behjat-abad (Iran), 282

Beirut, 12, 13

Beitar Illit settlement (Israel), 242, 250; commercial spaces, 251, *252*, 253, 255; expansion of units, 255, *256*; green spaces, 254; populating committee practices, 255–58; public buildings, 253, 254; residents' organizations, 255–58; steering committee, 251; typical residential unit plan, *252*

9780253039859